ANABAPTISM AND ASCETICISM
A Study in Intellectual Origins

Anabaptism and Asceticism

A Study in Intellectual Origins

BY

KENNETH RONALD DAVIS

Wipf & Stock
PUBLISHERS
Eugene, Oregon

Wipf and Stock Publishers
199 West 8th Avenue, Suite 3
Eugene, Oregon 97401

Anabaptism and Asceticism
A Study in Intellectual Origins
By Davis, Kenneth R.
Copyright©1974 Herald Press
ISBN 978-1-5326-6665-0
Publication date 10/17/1998
Previously published by Herald Press, 1974

TO
MY WIFE
In Affection and Gratitude

INTRODUCTION

This volume may well mark a new era in the study of Anabaptism, not in the recital of events in Zürich, Switzerland, 1523-25, but as a careful study in the spiritual antecedents of Anabaptism in the *Devotio Moderna* tradition, including the strong figure of Erasmus and his influence on many of the founding fathers of the Swiss Brethren, the Moravian Hutterites, the Anabaptists of South Germany, and the Obbenite-Mennists of the Low Countries.

The author sought to carefully research the literature pertaining to the medieval monastic tradition, particularly the type reflected in the *Imitation of Christ* and the *Theologie Deutsch*, and in the entire *Devotio Moderna* tradition as it culminated in Erasmus; also the Anabaptism of the Swiss (Grebel, Manz), Moravian (Hutterites), South German (Hut, Denck, Hubmaier), and Dutch (Obbe, Dirck, Menno) areas. He found amazing antecedents for many of the features of Anabaptism in the older monastic tradition of the *Devotio Moderna* type.

Dr. Davis sees three major kinds of Christianity in the early sixteenth century: (1) the sacramental-sacerdotal emphases, later endorsed at Trent; (2) the Augustinian emphases of the Magisterial Reformers with their inclusivist state churches, their views of human depravity and divine predestination, and their emphasis on forensic justification; and (3) the *Devotio Moderna* emphasis on penitence, personal holiness, and active discipleship to Christ — understood to involve the rejection of a life of affluence, the use of the civil oath, and participation in the military and the magistracy; and positively, a Christlike life of loving service: a total emphasis on a Christian life which our author designates as "ascetic" and "synergistic" — for the Augustinian views on the total bondage of the will and on predestination were rejected.

When the Anabaptists adopted the emphases of this third way in a Protestant context, they were too "Protestant" for Roman Catholics, and too "pietistic" for the Magisterial Reformers. They were therefore denounced as fanatics (*Schwärmer*) and literally driven away from the Magisterial Reformers, and then subjected to the anti-Donatist sanctions of the fourth and fifth centuries as rebaptizing ("Anabaptist") schismatics.

The editors are happy to include this creative study in their series, and anticipate that its support of Ritschl (Anabaptism's similarity to the Franciscan Tertiaries) will evoke lively debate.

> J. C. Wenger
> January 18, 1973

PREFACE

This study, first presented as a doctoral dissertation at the University of Michigan under the title "Evangelical Anabaptism and the Medieval Ascetic Tradition," and written under the guidance of Dr. Thomas Tentler of that university, owes much to his encouragement and scholarly advice. Others who made valuable suggestions on portions of the original manuscript or its revision include the late Dr. Robert Friedmann, and Drs. Albert Hyma, Palmer Throop, Sylvia Thrupp, Claus-Peter Clasen, and John S. Oyer.

I want to thank especially the staff of the Mennonite Historical Library at Goshen, Indiana, for their generosity in granting the use of its archival materials and facilities, and for much technical assistance, especially by its curator, Mr. Nelson Springer. Moreover, I acknowledge with gratitude that this book has been published with the help of a grant from the Humanities Research Council of Canada, using funds provided by the Canada Council. Above all, I appreciate the patience and encouragement of my wife and family.

Kenneth Ronald Davis
University of Waterloo
Waterloo, Ontario
November 20, 1972

CONTENTS

1. INTRODUCTION 19
   Definitions and Delineations 19
   Historiography of the Problem of Origins 26
   Statement of the Problem 31
   Methodology, Sources, and Limitations 32

2. THE CHRISTIAN ASCETIC TRADITION BEFORE THE
   REFORMATION 36
   A General Definition of Christian Asceticism 36
   Its Biblical Foundations 38
   Its Ideological and Institutional Structuring: Pre-Monastic .. 39
   Its Ideological and Institutional Structuring: Monastic 41
     The Desert Fathers 41
     Cenobitism in the West 45
   Its Vitality and Trends: Fifteenth Century 54
     Continuous Decline? 54
     Monastic Reform 55
     Preachers of Repentance 61
     Christian Humanism 62
     Printing and Literature 62
   Summary 63

3. ASCETIC FACTORS IN THE EMERGENCE OF
   ANABAPTISM 65
   In Pre-Anabaptist Dissent 65
   In the Formulation of the Earliest Anabaptists: the Swiss
      Brethren 67
      The Schism in the Zwingli Circle 67
      Zwingli: Reluctant Progenitor of Anabaptism? 83
      Asceticism in the Leaders Outside the Zwingli Circle . . . 92
   In the Expansion and Consolidation of the Swiss Brethren 99
      Balthasar Hubmaier 99
      Ex-monks as Anabaptist Leaders 108
      Martin Weninger 117
   In Anabaptist Preaching 119
   In Anabaptist-Magisterial Polemics 121
      Magisterial Reform 121
      Criticism of the Anabaptists 125
   Summary 127

4. THE DOMINANCE OF ASCETICISM IN THE
   STRUCTURING OF ANABAPTIST THEOLOGY
   Elements Comprising an Ascetic Theology of Holiness 129
   Anabaptism as an Ascetic Theology of Manifest Holiness and
      Relative Perfectionism 135
      The Theological Primacy of the Pursuit of Holiness . . . 135
      The Supporting Principles:
         (1) Renunciation and Separation 144
         (2) Freedom to Choose 145
         (3) Synergism 149
            Conflicts and Contradictions
            Capacity to Respond
            Cooperation in Regeneration
            Cooperation in Sanctification
         (4) Brotherhood 192
         (5) Internality 193
         (6) Necessity 195
   Ascetic Forms in the Practical Expression of Anabaptist
      Theology 196
   Holiness as the Dominant Principle of Interpretation 202
      The Doctrine of God 202
      Soteriology 202

    The Sacraments 203
    Ecclesiology 209
    Eschatology 212
    Hermeneutics 213

5. AGENCIES OF MEDIATION 218
    German Mysticism 219
        Influence on the Swiss Brethren 219
        Influence on the South German Anabaptists 221
        Franciscan Spirituality 232
        Ritschl's Thesis 232
        Ritschl's Thesis Reevaluated 233
    The Devotio Moderna 243
        Implications of Definition 243
        Implications of Cross-Fertilization 245
        Devotio Moderna and Anabaptist Theology Compared . . 247
        Devotio Moderna and Anabaptist Contacts Evaluated . . . 260
    Erasmianism 266
        Historiography of Erasmus and the Devotio Moderna . . 266
        Historiography of Erasmus and the Anabaptists 270
        Erasmus' Contacts with the Anabaptists 273
        Anabaptist Theology in Erasmus' Religious Writings . . 277

6. SUMMARY AND CONCLUSIONS 293
    Reform Expectations 293
    Anabaptists as Protestants 294
    Anabaptism as Distinct from the Magisterial Reformation . . . 294
    Anabaptism as Distinct from Medieval Heresy 295
    Anabaptism and the Ascetic Tradition 296
    Anabaptism and Interpreting the Reformation 297

NOTES 298

BIBLIOGRAPHY 349

ABBREVIATIONS

ARG	*Archiv für Reformationsgeschichte*
CH	*Church History*
CR	*Corpus Reformatorum*
Egli:Akten	Egli, Emil (ed.), *Actensammlung zur Geschichte der Züricher Reformation, 1519-1533*
Epist. Grebel	E. Yoder (ed. & trans.), *Epistolae Grebelianae*
Hutterite Chronicle	Zieglschmid, A. J. F. (ed.), *Die älteste Chronik der Hutterischen Brüder*
LCC:Mysticism	Petry, R. C. (ed.), *Late Medieval Mysticism*
LCC:Reform	Spinka, M. (ed.), *Advocates of Reform*
LCC:SAW	Williams, G. H. (ed.), *Spiritual and Anabaptist Writers*
ME	*The Mennonite Encyclopedia*
MM	Braght, T. J. van (ed.), *Martyrs Mirror*
MQR	*Mennonite Quarterly Review*
QGT	*Quellen zur Geschichte der Täufer* (Täuferakten)

QRG	*Quellen und Forschungen zur Reformationsgeschichte*
TA:Baden	Krebs, M. (ed.), *Baden und Pfalz*, QGT, IV
TA:Bayern, I	Schornbaum, K. (ed.), *Bayern I*, QGT, II
TA:Bayern, II	Schornbaum, K. (ed.), *Bayern II*, QGT, V
TA:Denck	Baring, G. and Fellmann, W. (eds.), *Hans Denck: Schriften*, QGT, VI
TA:Elsass, I	Krebs, M. and Rott, G. (eds.), *Elsass, I: Stadt Strassburg, 1523-1532*, QGT, VII
TA:Elsass, II	Krebs, M. and Rott, G. (eds.), *Elsass, II: Stadt Strassburg, 1533-1535*, QGT, VIII
TA:Hesse	Franz, G. (ed.), *Urkundliche Quellen zur Hessischen Reformationsgeschichte*, IV, *Wiedertäuferakten*
TA:HS	Westin, G. and Bergsten, T. (eds.), *Balthasar Hubmaier Schriften*, QGT, IX
TA:Gl.	Müller, Lydia (ed.), *Glaubenszeugnisse oberdeutscher Taufgesinnter*, I, QGT, III
TA:VMS	Muralt, L. von and Schmid, W. (eds.), *Quellen zur Geschichte der Täufer in der Schweiz, I:Zürich*
TA:Württemberg	Bossert, G. (ed.), *Herzogtum Württemberg*, QGT, I
ZSW	Egli, E. et al. (eds.), *Huldreich Zwinglis sämtliche Werke*; vols. 88 ff., *Corpus Reformatorum*
CWMS	Wenger, J. C. (ed.), *The Complete Writings of Menno Simons*; translated by Leonard Verduin
Handlung oder Acta	*Handlung oder Acta gehaltner Disputation uund Gespräch zu Zoffingen in Berner Biet den Widertäuffern*, 1532
Acta des Gespräch	*Acta des Gesprächs Zwüschen predicanntenn uund Tauffbrüderenn Erganngen*, Bern, 1538

1 INTRODUCTION

Definitions and Delineations

Independent dissent in the Protestant Reformation. The continental Protestant Reformation of the sixteenth century has been traditionally and almost exclusively identified with two major groupings: one related to the teachings of Martin Luther called Lutheran, and another, which found its chief spokesmen in Huldrich Zwingli, Martin Bucer, and John Calvin, called Reformed. Yet there also existed a sizable number of reform-oriented, Christian individuals and congregations who participated in the revolutionary break with the Roman Catholic organization and its sacramental system (and therefore must be considered Protestants), but who refused to be identified with either the Lutheran or Reformed churches.

In the sixteenth century, both Roman Catholics and Lutheran and Reformed Protestants generally lumped these independent dissenters together, indiscriminately and loosely, under the epithet "Anabaptist."[1] This initial tendency to fuse all branches of independent Protestant dissent into one broad, undefined entity readily led to the ascription to the whole of the heresy, fanaticism, antinomianism, excesses, and seditions of its worst elements. H. S. Bender has provided a sample list of the numerous vitriolic attacks which tended to conceal the existence of a distinctive and legitimate Anabaptist movement.[2] In addition, after 1528, it was almost everywhere illegal even to attempt to defend and thus distinguish legitimate Anabaptism or to present any kind of public rebuttal. It became common to identify, uncritically, "Anabaptist" dissenters with those who instigated the Peasants' War (1525) and with the notorious revolutionaries of Münster (1535).[3]

Such conditions, combined with the number and prestige of those (such as Huldrich Zwingli, Philip Melanchthon, Urban Rhegius, Johann Buder, and Andreas Althamer) who promoted the lumping together of all independent dissenters into one fanatical group, encouraged the incorporation of this distorted view into Reformation historiography. The very title of Heinrich Bullinger's book, *Der Widertäufferen ursprung, fürgang, secten, wäsen, fürname und gemeine irer Artickel* (1560), is an excellent example of the type of writings that became the principal sources for the appraisal of Anabaptism by most subsequent historians.[4] Few of them ever compared this negative polemical literature with the confessional writings of the dissenters themselves.[5] Consequently, well into the nineteenth century the term "Anabaptism" was still used by most historians, in this broad, undefined, and uncritical way.

In the mid-nineteenth century, the Old Catholic historian, Carl A. Cornelius, led the way toward a large-scale reappraisal of Anabaptism and sixteenth-century independent Protestant dissent.[6] His work, involving thorough research into the available Anabaptist sources, called for a major revision of the traditional, ill-defined, and derogatory understanding of Anabaptism. A host of detailed biographical studies of Anabaptist and other dissenter leaders followed, and continue to the present. By 1910, Adolf von Harnack could comment:

> Thanks to the research of recent years, the portraits of distinguished Christians from Anabaptist circles have been given us; and not a few of these honourable and strong-minded men are more comprehensible to us than a heroic Luther or an iron-willed Calvin.[7]

Finally, the collection and publication of several volumes of source material, some of it new, reflecting the views of the dissenters themselves (especially of the Anabaptists)[8] have forced most historians to concede to the inadequacy of previous descriptions of early sixteenth-century independent Protestant dissent in general and of Anabaptism in particular.

Introduction 21

At first, however, even most of the revisionists of Anabaptist history retained the assumption of some basic unity for independent dissent; but they began a more careful inquiry into the nature of this unity over against both the major Protestant groups and Roman Catholicism. Subsequently there emerged a growing recognition and even characterization of a variety of quite distinct and diverse groups within the total body of independent Protestant dissent. In turn, this led ultimately to questioning whether there were really sufficient common characteristics to justify even a broad lumping of the dissenters into one group.

Thus Ernst Troeltsch, in the initial phase of revisionism, attempted to identify the essential unity of independent dissent by coining the terminology for them of "sect type" (the close-knit society of believers) and "Spiritualists" (noninstitutionalists) in contrast to both the major Protestant groups and the Catholics, whom he calls the "church type" (with stress on the church as a universal institution).[9] More recently, Roland Bainton also still implies some kind of meaningful cohesiveness by labeling the dissenters "The Left Wing of the Reformation" and by suggesting several broad traits as typical of the whole.[10] At the same time, however, he recognizes major differences by identifying three fairly distinct groups within his "Left Wing": the Anabaptists, the Spiritualists, and the Socinians.[11]

Similarly, in his massive survey, *The Radical Reformation,* Williams still divides the continental Reformation initially into two parts: the "Magisterial" (Lutheran and Reformed) and the "Radical."[12] Under the term "Radical Reformation," which both implies unity and suggests something of the nature of that unity, he includes a vast array of sixteenth-century Protestant dissent. But then, parallel to Bainton, he too characterizes the distinguishes three major subgroups: Anabaptists, Spiritualists, and Evangelical Rationalists.[13]

J. C. Wenger's *Die dritte Reformation,* however, abandons any attempt to keep the various dissenting groups in one body. Wenger's "Third Reformation" describes an autonomous and much narrower movement than either Williams' "Radical Reformation" or Bainton's "Left Wing," because he confines it only to the "Anabaptists" as found in Williams and Bainton.[14]

Very recently, Leonard Verduin has added the designation "The Stepchildren" of the Reformation or "The Second Front;" but it is not quite clear whether he intends these names to encompass the whole of independent dissent or only a narrower entity, somewhat closer to Wenger. His source references are drawn mostly from Anabaptism and would suggest the latter. Also, Verduin correctly maintains the inadequacy, even inapplicability, of the terms "Left Wing" and "Radical Reformation," especially when applied to the Anabaptists. The Anabaptists, he demonstrates, were in some quite essential features much more right wing than Luther, and also in other matters they varied in *essence*, not just in greater *degree of radicalness* (as "Radical Reformation" would imply), from the major Reformers.[15]

It is apparent that as yet there is no satisfactory precise generic term or single set of criteria that can successfully unite the independent dissenters — except in the negative sense of being independent, that is, not being Lutheran or Reformed.[16] Rather, independent dissent is recognized increasingly as including several quite distinct movements.[17] Nevertheless, principally because of the wide acceptance and usage of the terms by others, this study shall employ, for convenience, the term "Magisterial Reformation" to designate the Lutheran and Reformed churches on the continent and, with even greater reservation, "Radical Reformation" to encompass but not describe most of the rest of Protestant dissent.

The distinctiveness of Anabaptism. Whereas the search for an inclusive definition and label for independent Protestant dissent has not proved very successful, significant advances are being made in delineating historically realistic groups within the Radical Reformation, by comparing them with each other, with Roman Catholicism, and with the Magisterial Reformation. Continuing research in each smaller grouping indicates that in those doctrines and practices of greatest concern to each, the difference between the principal groups within the Radical Reformation considerably outweigh any generalized similarities. On some issues, for example on matters such as the Trinity, the visible church, and the sole authority of the Scriptures, Anabaptism differs more from the other two groups most often included in the Radical Reformation than it does from the Magisterial Reformation.[18]

Several factors made the defining of Anabaptism initially difficult: especially the lack in Anabaptism of an all-encompassing organizational unity or administrative structure, the absence of one principal leader, since rarely did any leader survive long enough, before Menno Simons, to stamp his thought pattern on the movement as a whole, and uncertainty concerning which of the varieties of Anabaptism that developed had precedence and priority. However, these difficulties diminished as the volume, availability, and careful study of the source materials increased. Such research has led to a substantial consensus for Zürich as the founding center and for the Swiss Brethren as the original Anabaptists.[19] Moreover, the sources have also revealed that such factors as the concentration of Anabaptist preaching and teaching on a few decisive issues, the numerous imprisonments together of their leaders, which were used for mutual instruction, the many disputations on issues of concern to their opponents, the remarkable mobility of their leaders, and the composition and rapid spread of the Schleitheim Articles (1527) produced considerable uniformity in faith and practice in the Swiss Brethren branch of Anabaptism.[20]

The Swiss pattern was also substantially continued in the Mennonites (the Dutch Anabaptists after 1535), in the Hutterites, and to a lesser degree even in the more mystically inclined South German branch.[21] As a result a considerable consensus has now developed also regarding Anabaptism's most essential characteristics, a consensus which negates many of the criticisms made by sixteenth-century opponents and later historians who used the term Anabaptism in the broader, undefined sense.

Nevertheless, some disagreements persist. These include, primarily, the priority of importance of Anabaptism's various characteristics as an aid to clarifying the movement's ideological essence and uniqueness, the inclusion or exclusion of certain fringe groups, and the question of whether Anabaptism is most directly related: (1) to the Reformation, (2) to medieval, heretical sectarianism, or (3) to the ascetic reform movements in the late medieval church.

One of the most recent of the many historians who now grant primacy within the early development of Anabaptism to the Swiss Brethren, Torsten Bergsten, gives the following fairly typical summary of the major and distinctive characteristics of Anabaptism: exclusive biblical authority, church reform which reflects the primitive ideal of the church as a voluntary fellowship of believers who visibly manifest Christlike qualities, a baptismal confession of personal faith,[22] strong, congregationally controlled discipline, a "Sermon on the Mount" ideal of Christian conduct, and nonviolent principles, often totally pacifistic.[23] Most Anabaptist scholars would agree generally that these are essential and common characteristics, but disagree on whether there are others, and on which is the most vital or controlling one.

Several scholars have given primacy to Anabaptism's biblicism or, more accurately, to its hermeneutical system (that is, to the superiority of the New Testament, or the "non-flat" Bible).[24] Many other scholars have stressed its concept of the restitution of the New Testament model of the church as a community of convinced believers which Verduin calls a nonsacralist view of the church and society.[25] Bender agrees that the "non-flat" Bible and the nonsacralist church are important to Anabaptism, but finally presses on in his search for primacy to stress the principle of a voluntary relationship of radical, personal, discipleship to Christ, fulfillable only in accordance with the ethical principles of the Sermon on the Mount and in a disciplined brotherhood of baptized believers.[26]

Robert Friedmann, evaluating Anabaptism primarily from his extensive research on the Hutterites, adds to Bergsten's list of essential characteristics by arguing that Anabaptism's dominant characteristic is a radical separation between the world and the church, which he calls the theology of the two kingdoms.[27] Two additional characteristics, omitted by Bergsten probably because they are not exclusively Anabaptist, are nevertheless generally recognized as major elements and common emphases in the Anabaptist synthesis: the concern for the preservation of human responsibility (or free will) in relation to sin, salvation, and good works and the correlated emphasis on the experience of regeneration leading to holy conduct. Both contrast with Luther's stress on sovereign election and forensic justification.[28]

In summary, by synthesizing these characteristics into a meaningful whole (especially regarding hermeneutics, the church, discipleship, separation, and regeneration), Anabaptism evidenced a remarkable unanimity and expressed a significant uniqueness both from the Magisterial Reformation and from the rest of the Radical Reformation.[29] Even in those areas where Anabaptist groups (excluding the revolutionaries) seem to be most at variance with each other (such as, whether separation from the world also excluded them from the holding of political office, whether the love ethic and nonretaliation meant the total rejection of military service and private property, and whether the objective Scriptures share fully the authority of the spiritual Word), the differences seem to reflect *degree* rather than *essence* or principle[30] — even though some of these differences were institutionally expressed (for example, creating the Hutterite communities).

The second major area of disagreement relates to the subdividing of Anabaptism to include Evangelicals (mostly Swiss Brethren and Mennonites), Contemplatives (mostly South German), and Revolutionaries (Münster). Specifically, most recent Mennonite scholars, especially Bender and Friedmann, object to the revolutionaries as in any sense true Anabaptists. Rather, they consider such movements, even when they included many Anabaptists, as local and temporary aberrations caused by (1) non-Anabaptist ideas (for example, from Thomas Müntzer) contrary to the teachings of all the major Anabaptist groups,[31] (2) intense persecution and locally oppressive conditions which temporarily heightened eschatological fervor, and (3) both the martyrdom or imprisonment of key leaders and the disruption from extensive migrations which made it difficult to prevent some involvement by fringe groups in these fanatical aberrations.[32] Consequently, Friedmann combines the Evangelicals and the Contemplatives but completely excludes the Revolutionaries, who become a separate category. He then subdivides the resultant Anabaptism geographically into: (1) the Swiss Brethren and South Germans, (2) the Dutch Mennonites, and (3) the Hutterian Brethren and communal types in Moravia.

The exclusion of the Revolutionary category seems to be justified, if one accepts the consensus regarding the dominant characteristics of Anabaptism. All of these characteristics readily apply to Williams' Evangelical Anabaptists and to most of his Contemplatives.[33] But when they are applied to the Esslingen, Müntzer, Münsterite revolutionaries, serious contradictions appear, especially with reference to "Sermon-on-the-Mount" nonretaliation and quietism, to the love ethic with its corollary of sharing even with one's enemies, to separationism stressing the spiritual kingdom and heavenly citizenship and the suffering church, to the use exclusively of the ban in matters of conscience and spiritual discipline, and to the dominance of the New Testament over the Old Testament.[34] The inclusion of a Revolutionary subdivision under the term "Anabaptism" is highly questionable.

Consequently, this study limits itself to "Evangelical Anabaptism," which will refer primarily to the Swiss Brethren in the early years of the Reformation, but also to its most closely related continuations, the Moravian Hutterites and the Dutch Mennonites,[35] and, to a lesser degree, even to the less cohesive and more contemplative South German segment.[36]

The Origins of Evangelical Anabaptism:
An Historiographical Survey

Scholarly controversy continues not only over the essence of Anabaptism and over the inclusion or exclusion of specific groups but also over the problem of its intellectual origins and the degree of its continuity or discontinuity with other religious and reform forces. From the debate on origins and relationships, three distinct options have emerged: one advocating Anabaptism's essential origin in the Magisterial Reformation, another in medieval heretical sectarianism, and the third in the medieval Catholic ascetic tradition. These variant views constitute one of the most significant problems in Anabaptist research at present.[37]

Most historians uphold the view that Anabaptism originated both ideologically and structurally out of the Reformation milieu in general and out of the Zwinglian Reformation in particular. Thus Fritz Blanke insists that both Grebel and Zwingli had the same objectives and that both were biblicists.[38] He concludes:

> But so much is certain: the soil in which grew the new thinking [Anabaptist] . . . was not the Middle Ages, neither the Roman nor the Waldensian, but Zwingli's reformed teaching. . . . They desired . . . to carry forward the Reformation; they wanted to continue building on the foundation laid by Zwingli.[39]

Similarly, Bender concludes his biography of Conrad Grebel by asserting:

> That Grebel and his Swiss Brethren derived their faith solely and directly from the New Testament without any apparent literary or personal antecedents is one of the most striking things about the movement. Every attempt to trace connections to earlier sources has failed, whether to the Waldensians, or the Hussites as Ludwig Keller believed, or to the Franciscan Tertiaries as Albrecht Ritschl suggested.[40]

Concerning the description of Anabaptism as essentially radical Zwinglianism, Heinrich Bornkamm also comments that this conclusion is something that "today can be sure of general agreement."[41]

While Walther Köhler subscribes in general to this judgment, he also suggests that some aspects of Anabaptism seem to be adaptations of Erasmian humanism, especially the tendencies toward moralism, pacifism, tolerance, and spiritualism.[42] In contrast, Bender opposes specifically and strenuously any direct relationship between humanism and Anabaptism, except for the doctrine common to the Reformation as a whole that Scripture is the ultimate source of authority in faith and practice.[43] By investigating the question "Can Anabaptists be described as humanists?" Robert Kreider suggests something of a mediating position, that though certainly not classical humanists, some leaders were more influenced by humanism than Bender was willing to admit.[44]

Von Muralt also insists "that the Anabaptist movement in Switzerland had its origin in the Reformation" and that the Anabaptists considered themselves to be consistently carrying through Zwingli's own principles. But von Muralt also maintains the probability of a rather extensive preparatory role by Erasmus and that even the early Zwingli was more Erasmian than Lutheran. He significantly adds, however, that Erasmus mediated not so much humanism as the spirit of the *Devotio Moderna* to the Anabaptist leaders.[45]

Still maintaining the theory of Anabaptist origins in the Reformation, Hans Hillerbrand, primarily by comparing some selected ideological motifs, broadens the picture further by suggesting four major formative influences on the rise of Anabaptism: the Reformers (Zwingli and Luther), Erasmus, Carlstadt, and Müntzer.[46] Hillerbrand seems to give primacy to Erasmus and Zwingli, though this is not certain since he does not specifically weigh the importance of each nor does he consider which had priority of contact. Furthermore, he does not prove that Carlstadt's and Müntzer's contributions were either causal or foundational, rather than just stimulating or substantiating beliefs already held, with reference to any major Anabaptist doctrine. Hillerbrand does make the point, however, that "the movement did not come into being in a biblical or Zwinglian vacuum, but a variety of formative influences were operative.[47]

The second and contrasting theory, suggested by the Hutterian *Chronicle* itself,[48] that Anabaptism was part of a historic line of the true church which had survived "underground" through the post-Constantinian dark ages and which occasionally manifested itself in spite of persecution in such evangelical dissenters as the Waldensians and the Bohemian Brethren, has also retained its advocates. Ludwig Keller maintained that there was a close and direct relationship

28   Anabaptism and Asceticism

between Anabaptist origins and the Waldensians, by suggesting that Anabaptism frequently arose in localities where the Waldensians had been active and by taking the doctrine of the church as Anabaptism's most distinguishing characteristic (that is, the restoration of the apostolic church in the sense of "a voluntary community of brethren").[49]

Though Keller's own thesis has been judged generally as lacking in supporting evidence, the concept of "heretical" continuity has retained vitality.[50] For example, Vedder reasserts the relationship thus:

> The close correspondence in doctrine and practice between Petrobrucians and Waldensians, between Waldensians and Anabaptists, even in the absence of definite documentary proofs, warrants the conclusion that in these successive sects we really study the history of a single evangelical movement. . . . If such is the case, the Anabaptists of the sixteenth century are not so related to the Reformation as has generally been supposed.[51]

Quite recently Delbert Gratz also renewed the theory, in part, by asserting that rural Bernese Anabaptism was an older strain, independent of Zürich in origin, but with Waldensian ties.[52] Reexamination of Gratz' evidence by Fast and Bender, however, reveals no distinctly Anabaptist doctrine or practice anywhere in the Bernese area prior to the emergence of Anabaptism in Zürich (January, 1525).[53] Furthermore, all the Anabaptist leaders and preachers in the canton of Berne had previous contact with the Zürich Anabaptists.[54] That Anabaptism perhaps found a ready response in local areas preconditioned by Waldensianism does not constitute a theory of actual origins.

Another variation of the theory of medieval "heretical" origins relates Anabaptism to the Bohemian Brethren rather than the Waldensians. This argument is usually associated with the tenuous theory of Anabaptist origins in the Zwickau-Wittenberg area, rather than at Zürich, through the influence of Thomas Müntzer, who had visited Prague and possibly the Bohemian Brethren there in 1521 and 1522. An unpublished paper by Alexander Rempel has recently restated this theory.[55]

The most recent and most comprehensive work specifically advocating the "Anabaptist-medieval heresy" theory, by Leonard Verduin, attempts to demonstrate that Anabaptism is primarily a continuing expression of that specific kind of post-Constantinian, Donatistic dissent that repudiated the church as coextensive with society. Verduin calls the belief in the close relationship of the temporal and spiritual in a unified Christian society, including the parish pattern at the local level, "Christian sacralism." He ascribes it not only to medieval Roman Catholicism but also to the Magisterial Reformation, and focuses on it as the principal reason for their common rejection of Anabaptism. He maintains that "sacralism" is diametrically opposed to the "compositism" of the New Testament, many medieval "heresies," and the Anabaptists.[56]

However, not only does he fail to demonstrate any direct lineal connections between Anabaptism and the various medieval "heresies" that were antisacralist, but he also draws bits and pieces of data, to show an ideological parallelism, from a widely scattered and unrelated variety of groups and eras, ranging from Donatism to Waldensianism. More seriously, he fails to show how and why the sixteenth-century Anabaptists gathered and synthesized these various sources so quickly into one consistent bundle. Nor does he prove that Anabaptists either read or knew of these medieval antecedents in any detail. Furthermore, as John Oyer has commented, "The opposition of Luther to the Anabaptists' insistence on moral purity was hardly ever related to the church issue [sacralism] in his mind: it was preeminently a theological issue in its own right."[57]

Albrecht Ritschl was the first to clearly enunciate the third theory of origins. He suggests that Anabaptism was closely related to a late medieval, Catholic, ascetic reform tradition rather than to either the Magisterial Reformation or medieval heresy.[58] Ritschl vigorously denies that the Anabaptists were a radical extension of the principles of the major Reformers (especially of Zwingli and Luther). Rather, he insists that in spite of a brief association during the Reformation's early, fluid stage (because of common antipapal and pro-biblically-based ecclesiastical reform sentiments), they had fundamentally different expectations regarding the nature and results of the reform movement itself. He contends that the essence of the Anabaptist reform ideal is one with the ascetic, medieval reform movement as expressed by Francis of Assisi, by the Franciscan Spirituals, and as perpetuated, especially in the urban areas, by the Franciscan Tertiaries. Unfortunately, since Ritschl drew his portrait of Anabaptism largely from the biased accounts of Bullinger, he consequently overstated its parallel with the radical, mystical, and eschatological aspects of Franciscanism. The resulting errors in detail have tended to discredit the total theory and his work has received scant attention in recent Anabaptist research.

Nevertheless, some historians continue to note, usually incidentally, aspects of possible Anabaptist dependence on, and association with, various late medieval, ascetic reform movements. For example, von Muralt hints at a possible rapport and flow of ideas between the *Devotio Moderna* and Swiss Anabaptism through Erasmus.[59] Similarly, van der Zijpp and Hyma note the preparatory work of the *Devotio Moderna* for Dutch Anabaptism.[60] Bainton also says that in such matters as anti-intellectualism and antispeculative theology and the stress on practical piety, the Anabaptists were heirs of the *Devotio Moderna* and of the Spiritual Franciscans.[61] With considerable caution, Bergsten also suggests that

> the *devotio moderna* through Erasmus doubtlessly influenced Anabaptism. Without doubt, the piety of the middle ages has been of importance also in other ways for the rise of the Anabaptists. One does not intend to imply by this, however, that the Anabaptists had medieval origins, rather, merely to suggest that it was prepared for by these pre-reform and heretical movements.[62]

Similarly, in his theological summary, contrasting Anabaptism and Pietism, Friedmann concludes that Anabaptism was closer to the practical piety and moderate, devotional mysticism of the *Devotio Moderna*, whereas Pietism had closer affinity with Schwenkfeld and with purer, more esoteric, medieval mysticism.[63] Several writers have even confirmed some details in Ritschl's theory by asserting direct formative ties between South German Anabaptism and a moderately ascetic, practical, medieval piety which was mediated in part through the Franciscans, but especially through the publication of the *German Theology*.[64] Finally, Friedmann, looking at Anabaptism through his extensive research in Hutterite sources, also suggests that in some important aspects "Anabaptism almost converged toward monasticism."[65]

Though many generalized references suggesting ideological parallels with various expressions of medieval asceticism have appeared recently, scattered through numerous books and articles, there has never been a major examination of this whole third theory of origins, particularly as it relates to the *Devotio Moderna* in its Erasmian version, to late medieval practical "mysticism" or piety, especially as expressed in the *German Theology*, and to the means of transmission

Introduction 31

of the spiritual perspective and motifs of each to Anabaptism. The resources for such an examination on a broad synthetic scale in terms of the history of ideas are now available and such is the aim of this present work.

In summary, though the theory that Anabaptism is rooted in the Reformation itself still has not overcome the objection that Anabaptism's real essence is something more than just a radical extension of certain key Reformation ideals, and though the theory of rootage in medieval heresy still lacks adequate and convincing source evidence, remarkably, the remaining alternative, that Anabaptism is primarily a Reformation expression of the essence of an older Catholic, ascetic, reform tradition, has received little direct attention; though, as previously noted, several historians from other camps have observed possible connections at several points — and significantly at points which seem to be closest to the heart of Anabaptism.

Several factors have contributed to this inattention: (1) Ritschl's deficient understanding of the characteristics of Anabaptism, and also his lack of documentation, since his theory was only introductory to a larger work, led subsequently to a general dismissal of his theory; (2) much recent Anabaptist research has been done by Mennonite scholars who often possess strong pro-Protestant and antihumanistic and anti-Catholic sentiments; and (3) many Reformation historians, being Protestants, have difficulty adequately understanding the ascetic tradition within medieval Catholicism. They tend therefore to confuse the repudiation by the Anabaptists, in common with the Reformation, of monasticism, the dominant institutionalization of asceticism, with the repudiation of the ascetic ideal itself — an assumption which may be erroneous.

The Statement of the Problem

Clearly the problem of the intellectual origins of Anabaptism is still a wide-open issue. Thus Robert Friedmann has observed that while generally the immediate, institutional origins of Anabaptism have been traced to the Grebel group and the Zürich area, the longer-range intellectual and psychological *raison d'être* and antecedents for such a movement remain somewhat obscure.[66] Similarly Wilhelm Pauck has pointed out the need for analysis of the medieval roots of Anabaptism[67] and Heinrich Bornkamm, though accepting Fritz

Blanke's contention that Anabaptism was essentially a radical Zwinglianism, added,

> nevertheless the question that needs to be clarified, and which is not yet settled, is whether the advance preparation comes through the churchly or heretical forms of piety of the middle ages, not the question of origin out of some specific sect.[68]

The problem has been most pointedly posed by Heinold Fast thus:

> If the Anabaptists in decisive matters were pupils of the Reformers, especially Zwingli, wherein and on what grounds did they break with the Reformers? And indeed this is the real question: Did the Anabaptists merely radicalize Zwingli's theses, either because Zwingli had not remained true to his original views or because he did not proceed rapidly or logically enough, so therefore we must attribute the break between them to differences in character and background or perhaps to differences in education? . . . Or, is there an essentially different conception of the Christian message at the heart of the break? Wherein would the peculiar character of such a conception lie?[69]

Accordingly, it is the general aim of this study to reinvestigate the possibility and extent of a formative relationship between the initial Evangelical Anabaptism and the late medieval, ascetic reform tradition, especially as that tradition was expressed by the *Devotio Moderna*. More specifically, this investigation seeks to determine whether the emergence of Evangelical Anabaptism and the way its most essential and distinctive elements were expressed are adequately explainable as a partially Protestantized[70] reaffirmation of a still-vital current of ascetically oriented, reform idealism, and thus is a truer continuation of that pre-Reformation movement than any other major sixteenth-century Protestant group. Such a relationship would then imply that ideologically Anabaptism may have had much in common with the noninstitutional aspects of the Catholic Reformation[71] and that it differed in kind, as well as degree, from important aspects of the Magisterial Reformation, as Ritschl contended. There may well be a measure of truth in Capito's, Zwingli's, and others' references to Anabaptism as a "new kind of Monkery."[72]

Methodology, Sources, and Limitations

This study is concerned less with ascertaining lineal, institutional

Introduction 33

connections between Anabaptism and earlier movements than with analyzing potential lines of intellectual continuity by uncovering ideological parallels which were potentially preparatory to the most distinctive Anabaptist ideas.[73] It is also concerned with accounting for the extensive appeal which these Anabaptist ideas had in the sixteenth-century Reformation era, an appeal held in check only by a most rigorous repressive policy by both the Magisterial Reformers and the Roman Catholics in cooperation with the civil authorities.[74]

Any historian investigating the transfer of ideas from medieval predecessors to Anabaptism faces a serious problem with the sources. Due to their persecution, even the Anabaptist leaders had little time to write in depth; sermons were rarely written at all, and even their brief polemical pamphlets were published only with the greatest difficulty. Also, because of their self-conscious role as ardent biblicists because, in part, of the nature of their zeal for the restitution of the apostolic church over against Catholic traditionalism (which made them antagonistic to both historical precedents and ecclesiastical scholarship as norms of faith), and because of their conscious separation from "Babylon" (both Roman Catholicism and Magisterial Protestantism), they tended in their writings to avoid references to either influential historical antecedents or to contemporary influences.

But one must not therefore assume that there were none; rather, the task of discerning requires a broader approach. For example, one must ask not only what books their leaders read and with whom they associated in formative years, but also what patterns or presuppositions seem to affect their interpretations of Scripture and what mental, emotional, and spiritual preconditioning is expressed in their theological affirmations, religious life-style, and condemnations of their opponents.

In terms of the relationship of procedure to sources, the initial section of this study involves a general examination of the internal essence and the capabilities for ideological and institutional flexibility of the Christian ascetic tradition — especially a careful reexamination of its capabilities for variation, its vitality, reform efforts, and expectations in the era after Francis of Assisi, especially after the Council of Constance (1414-1418).

The second section is aimed largely at ascertaining the decisive area of discontent which provoked the earliest Anabaptist withdrawal from the Magisterial Reformation in order to discover whether there are ascetically oriented, predisposing influences. At this point the investigation will concentrate on the background, training, theological contacts, and conversion to Anabaptism of the formative and creative leaders of Anabaptism, that is, those who dominate Anabaptist leadership in the first two formative years of the movement. In spite of some limitations of the sources,[75] there is sufficient evidence to reveal both the strength of the ascetic ideal in the emergence of Anabaptism and the extent of its influence on the earliest and formative leadership. Also, there are substantial clues indicating the most probable progenitors through whom the ideal was mediated to Anabaptism.

The third section demonstrates that the dominant motif in Evangelical Anabaptist theology is the concern for holiness, and that its expression, theologically and institutionally, parallels in a general way traditional ascetic ideals and practices. This section is based on an extensive analysis of the theological writings primarily of the early Swiss Brethren leaders (the Grebel group, Balthasar Hubmaier,[76] Michael Sattler, Martin Weninger, and others) but also, by a limited extension of geographic and chronological range, on some testimony by some of the more influential leaders of later but closely related Dutch and Hutterite branches (for example, Menno Simons of the Dutch Anabaptists and Peter Riedmann of the Moravian Hutterites) and of some of the South German branch (for example, Hans Denck, Hans Hut, and Hans Schlaffer). To this is added the theological formulations from the major disputations relative to the Swiss Brethren, and relevant comments by the Magisterial Reformers.

The fourth section compares the distinctive theology, practices, and piety of Evangelical Anabaptism with the ideology of those specific, late medieval persons or groups which previous investigations, in this study and by others, indicate as probable agents for the mediation of the ascetic ideal to Anabaptism: namely, with the religious writings of Erasmus before 1525, the *Devotio Moderna*, Franciscan piety (as expressed by Francis of Assisi, the constitutions of the Third Order, and some late medieval preachers of reform and repentance), and the moderate mysticism of the *German Theology*. Also included is an evaluation of some of the means by which the transfer of ideas took place.

Translations in English of various sources were utilized for general overviews, but in problem areas, careful comparison with the best critical texts were made.[77] Accordingly, unless otherwise noted, the writer accepts responsibility for all translations used. Most quotations have been given in English translation unless there is some specific reason to leave the original (that is, for tonal purposes or to show various possibilities in translation).

In conclusion, the author expects to demonstrate that the emergence of Evangelical Anabaptism during the Reformation was substantially, though not exclusively, the product of a previously formulated and still vital, ascetically oriented reform predisposition, and that in its most essential elements, that is, its reform goals, its code of conduct, and the development of its theology, Anabaptism was dominated by an ascetic idealism. Furthermore, the ideological predecessors which most effectively influenced Anabaptism, both directly and indirectly, literarily and personally, were representatives of valid aspects of the medieval Catholic ascetic tradition. Finally, its institutional expression and many of its practices can also be explainable as reflections of the essence of late medieval Catholic idealism, especially as manifest in the Brethren of the Common Life and the Franciscan Tertiaries.

From a synthesis of these late medieval predecessors, with which they had adequate contact and whose concepts pervaded society, almost all that is uniquely and vitally Anabaptist can be derived, with the exception of the distinctly Protestant elements of the radical repudiation of the institutional authority of the Roman Catholic Church and its sacramental system.

2 THE CHRISTIAN ASCETIC TRADITION BEFORE THE REFORMATION

The theory that Anabaptism is best understood as a Protestantized form of the medieval ascetic tradition requires for substantiation that there be both discernible lines of continuity and also similarity of goals, ideals, and emphases in their basic understanding and practice of Christianity. Such requirements suggest the necessity, initially, of reappraising the essence and basic ideals of asceticism and of clarifying the varieties of expression, the flexibility ideologically and institutionally, of Christian asceticism over the centuries, especially its variations, trends, and vitality in the fifteenth century. The role and nature of Anabaptism, in relation to asceticism, can be adequately evaluated only after such a background is established.

A General Definition

Even the briefest survey of the history of Christian asceticism must begin with some definition. Basically, Christian asceticism refers to a particular way of defining and developing the spiritual life. There is substantial agreement concerning most of the ingredients which go into the formulation of this definition. For example, a long list of substantially similar definitions, by both Roman Catholic and Protestant historians and theologians, are given in the thorough treatment of the subject in the *Dictionaire de Spiritualité*.[1] From these definitions, one can readily isolate three primary characteristics of Christian asceticism.

First, there is a negative connotation involving renunciation, or the suppression of those ways of life considered dangerous to Christian virtue and therefore evil, mortification, both inner and exterior relating to the flesh, and penitence or penance of some kind.

Second, there is also a positive emphasis on methodical effort or exercise to develop Christian virtues and progress towards perfection. Even the term "asceticism," derived from the Greek *askesis*, meaning practice, training (athletic), and discipline, was used often by the early Christians to refer to the positive practice of spiritual things or to spiritual exercises performed for the purpose of acquiring habits of virtue."[2] Some Protestant writers incorrectly tend to make the first or negative characteristic, the total definition;[3] whereas, in its most comprehensive sense, asceticism refers to "everything which in the spiritual life involves effort, struggle, and exercise to control both oneself and external temptations and everything involving positive effort for the perfecting of our spiritual activities."[4] Both these negative and positive aspects relate to the pursuit of a certain kind of virtue or perfection.

This leads to the third aspect of a definition of Christian asceticism, namely the understanding of the unique ideal of perfection which undergirds both the positive and negative efforts aimed at its attainment. Therefore the goal is ascetic perfection or virtue, the advocacy of the other-worldly or spiritual ideal and value system for this life. It must not be equated with the methods, either of physical austerity or of religious exercises.[5]

Considering the phenomenon from its sociological perspective, Max Weber suggests that asceticism "endeavors not only to subject the natural instincts to the disciplined conduct of life but also and always presents a radical, ethical/religious critique of the relationship (of the faithful) to the social life of worldly society and to those virtues obviously more utilitarian and conventional than heroic."[6]

Another clarifying distinction comes from Ernst Troeltsch, who maintains that the ethic of Jesus and of the New Testament (true "Christian" asceticism) must be separated both from religious asceticism in general and from monastic asceticism in particular.[7] He conceives of this New Testament ascetic "ethic" as something more "heroic" than "ascetic." From his view of monasticism as the embodiment of a quite negative and deficient definition of "asceticism," he suggests that the "heroic" ethic is what the sects (especially the sixteenth-century Anabaptists) stress, in contrast to the more monastic understanding of asceticism in both medieval Roman Catholicism and Luther.[8]

Some historians recognize also that if we are to understand Christian asceticism correctly at least one more distinction is necessary. Christian asceticism should be distinguished from mysticism. That is, "asceticism is ethical; mysticism, largely intellectual."[9] In asceticism the stress is on moral virtue; in mysticism, on contemplation; though often they are "mutually cooperative."[10]

From the above, three factors emerge as essential ingredients for a balanced understanding of Christian asceticism: (1) negatively, the resistance to and struggle against the evil impulses of the "fallen" flesh, with separation from this-worldly society and its temptations as a corollary; (2) positively, the development of virtues that lead towards spiritual perfection; and (3) an otherworldly conditioned ethical and moral thrust (heroic ethics) which distinguishes it from mysticism.

The Biblical Foundations

Ultimately, all attempts at explanation of the phenomenon of Christian asceticism refer back to the foundational biblical texts for justification and validation (whether medieval-monastic asceticism, pre-monastic Christian asceticism, or Troeltsch's primitive, heroic ethics).[11] Biblical justifications fall into three categories. The first, though not the most significant, finds "ascetic" roots in the vigorous ethical standards and practices of the Old Testament, especially in the prophetic stress on the justice, holiness, and otherness of God.[12] Second, there is an appeal to the New Testament's advocacy of some measure of renunciation, which includes: the challenge by Jesus to radical self-sacrifice, which is repeated by the Apostle Paul,[14] and prescriptions for fasting,[15] sexual continence,[16] and some renunciation of possessions and materialism.[17] Paul writes that he controls and subdues his body similar to an athlete (1 Corinthians 9:27), and he expects the same of all Christians.[18] Third, and principally, there is the appeal to many positive teachings of perfectibility and to the advocacy of the Christian's imitation of Christ.[19]

The New Testament ideal of perfection, or the Christlike, virtuous life, extends much further and higher than legalism, or the fulfillment of (Old Testament) law, higher than a negative renunciation; it rises to belief in the realizability of a growing measure of inner and outer imitation of Christ, in the necessity and worth of striving to achieve "the image of Christ," and even in the possibility of experiencing some sort of preliminary spiritual union with Christ.

This third and positive aspect is fundamental. The taking up of the cross is in order to "follow"; the buffeting and subduing of the body is to "run the race" better and to triumph in the spiritual combat (1 Corinthians 9:24-27; 2 Timothy 4:7; Ephesians 6:10-18); the mortification (whether interior or exterior or both) is for the "cultivation of the virtues which the Creator intended man to possess."[20] Even suffering and martyrdom for Christ have a positive function and objective, as in the Beatitudes (Matthew 5:3-10; Romans 8:17 ff.).

Consequently one must conclude that Christian "asceticism," in so far as it is biblically based (and, as we shall see, both primitive Christian asceticism and the early monasticism of the Desert Fathers, rigorously claimed such for it), and even after undergoing later historical and environmental conditioning, is essentially a positive doctrine (or program) for advancing in spiritual perfection or, essentially, towards Christlikeness.[21] The imitation of Christ is the "means," and the image of Christ, or the Christ-life (Galatians 2:20), or spiritual perfection, is its supreme "goal."[22] Elements of renunciation, however institutionalized, remain at best one portion of the "means" to that "goal." A major question for our consideration is whether or to what degree throughout the history of Christian asceticism it is a flexible "means."

Asceticism's Ideological Structuring: Pre-Monastic

Pre-monasticism: degrees of change. Primitive Christian asceticism soon came under the conditioning influence of historical forces. Few historians, if any, would question the assertion that considerable variation in theory and practice took place between the first and third centuries. The questions are: how extensive and fundamental was this variation, how much of the change is due to foreign or non-Christian influences, and how much can be accounted for as legitimate variations of interpretation, application, and stress, to meet new conditions (that is, how much is the variation a valid evolution or adaptation, consistent with its essential biblical and apostolic foundations)?

40   Anabaptism and Asceticism

E. Troeltsch and H. Workman (and most Protestant writers) maintain that the changes in primitive Christian asceticism were fundamental, largely owing to alien influences (for example, Stoic, Gnostic, Pythagorean, Jewish, Egyptian, etc.),[23] but were also a reaction to radical environmental changes (for example, to persecution and martyrdom, to increasing social and ecclesiastical rigidity, and to spiritual compromises with society and with the state).[24]

On the other hand, Patrice Cousin (and most Roman Catholic writers) minimize alien, non-Christian influences and stress rather a natural evolution, attempting to show direct relationship between the asceticism of Jesus and the apostolic church and that of the Desert Fathers.[25] For example, the *Dictionaire de Spiritualite'* sees physical mortification, one of the basic ingredients of later monasticism, as a logical extension of the biblical concept of spiritual combat.[26] Moreover, one can expect the ascetic ideal to follow the general trend toward institutionalization, active within the church during the second to the fourth century, which produced a structuring of canon, creed, and episcopacy, and ultimately, when the state allowed it, of corporation.[27]

Pre-monasticism: nature of change. It is possible to illustrate and summarize the general nature of the change in Christian asceticism in the pre-monastic period, even though many details remain highly controversial. Quite early the imitation of Christ for the attainment of spiritual perfection began to be systematized mainly along three lines: "mortification of the senses, unworldliness, and detachment from family ties."[28]

In the second century, unworldliness did not mean monastic withdrawal of a few to isolation since persecution and careful catechizing maintained a substantial and practical demarcation between the society of the "world" and that of the church as a whole. Nevertheless, as early as the second century, one can find within the Christian communities certain men and women who reacted against what they considered to be the sexual debauchery of city life of the Roman Empire by gathering together daily for prayer, by charitable activity, and by practicing absolute chastity. Thus virginity gained in reputation in the churches as a mark of superior spirituality, second only to martyrdom.[29] Some writers consider this rise of the ideal of virginity to be more than just adaptation, but rather the influence of an alien philosophy resulting in a growing tendency to believe in a dualistic antagonism between flesh and spirit.[30]

Similarly, from the early second century, the church considered martyrs to be the most heroic Christians, the ultimate examples of ascetic self-sacrifice and mortification. Thus even before the end of the threat of literal martyrdom, but especially then, the prestige of the martyr may have encouraged a parallel kind of self-martyrdom by a voluntary and total renunciation of the world and the flesh for perfection's sake.[31] Ultimately this innovation becomes an accepted and important expression of Christian asceticism, especially in Egypt where persecution had been particularly severe.[32]

Thus, by the end of the third century, Christian asceticism was already showing some signs of organizational structuring, though it was still within the churches. There was considerable tendency toward ideological formalism, standardization and, especially by the Alexandrians, Clement and Origen, systematization of principles, but such is far from complete. The ascetic ideal was still capable of considerable variation of expression.

Ideological and Institutional Structuring: Monastic

The Desert Fathers. Monasticism, from *monachos* meaning "alone," is a specific, institutionalized variation of Christian asceticism which arose primarily to accommodate the complete withdrawal in the late third and early fourth century of numerous Christians from both temporal society and the organized church. Some of these ascetics sought by this radical withdrawal to avoid the risk of apostasy during the heavy persecutions at the end of the third century. Some also sought to avoid military service. In the early fourth century there was, in addition, a desire to avoid the effects of the "secularization" of the church under Constantine. But strongest of all was their search for freedom to develop their own spiritual perfection — by withdrawal to the aloneness of the deserts of Egypt or the forests of Asia Minor.[33] It appeared to be the only possible way to be faithful to their convictions.

The principal model for the earliest expression of monastic asceticism was the famous Antony or Anthony[34] (d. 356), and the chief agent of one of its earliest major variations was the almost equally famous Pachomius (cir. 286-346).[35]

The Antonian ideal of anchoritic monasticism, given great prestige by the personal piety and charismatic powers of Anthony himself, is expressed by flight from the corrupt world to find solitude and to live the simple life as a hermit. Both solitude and simplicity are considered most important aids to working out one's own salvation and perfecting one's own holiness.

There are stages in the Antonian type flight from the world and toward God and godliness. But in the pure Antonian anchoritic (or eremitic) ideal, the final and highest stage is always total, solitary communion with God. It is attainable by a practiced elite only.[36]

The nature of the life which this elite sought is described as "holiness" and its chief characteristics included total love for Christ. other-worldliness, spiritual courage, tranquility and inner joyfulness and composure, purity of soul and mind, humility and prayerfulness, and gentleness and courtesy.[37] While the hermits made practically no attempts at theological formulation, and rarely tried to analyze their own spiritual experiences, they effectively promoted this ideal of holiness by living according to it. It was "the seal of their sanctity . . . far beyond abstinence or miracle or sign."[38] This ideal of holiness with its pattern of values or characteristics will reappear repeatedly throughout this study and thereby assume major significance.

The Antonian anchorites considered worldly influences, fleshly appetites, and demoniac temptations to be the chief obstacles in the way of the attainment of their ideal. Such an attitude could and did lead at times to vigorous austerities and severe forms of physical renunciation. Helen Waddell gives an example of some monks who through ascetic deprivations unintentionally caused their own death. Their associates looked upon this kind of death as martyrdom.[39]

In addition to the fundamental renunciation of the world and its temptations (expressed by their solitude, chastity, and poverty), there were several other more positive means used by the Antonian hermit-ascetics to attain their goal of perfection or holiness. Of great importance was a life of prayer and the study of Scripture.[40] The memorization and recitation to oneself of Scripture also provided the means to maintain an unbroken communion with God for those who advocated continuing some simple work, such as making baskets, "in order to earn subsistence and to be able to give to the poor."[41] The Antonian ascetics emphasized a life of penitence, usually involving constant examination of conscience[42] and coupled with a moderately austere physical mortification (eating only once daily, abstaining from oil, meat, and wine and all luxuries and physical comforts).

A life of spiritual liberty, in the sense of not being bound to obedience to any other person, such as a superior, nor to any one place, was also typical. For them the pursuit of holiness meant involvement in a spiritual warfare, not only against one's passions and fleshly temptations (especially regarding chastity), and against melancholy and depression, but actually against "demonic" powers. Finally, their lives were typified by constant contemplation of the Divine by which they hoped to develop greater union or closeness or fellowship with God in this life.

Though the Antonian kind of anchoritic asceticism took on a fairly common pattern and gained widespread acceptance and popularity, aided by the prestige of Anthony, it was never a completely rigid code. Numerous exceptions and variations can be found in the anchoritic practices of the fourth century. A most significant variation from the pure eremetic ideal, contemporary with Anthony in time and place, was the development of the Pachomian monastic communities. They demonstrate early the potential ideological and institutional flexibility of the Christian ascetic tradition. Several aspects of Pachomian monasticism illustrate the nature of these institutional and ideological variations.

While total solitude remained the ultimate ideal for all, Pachomius sought "to formulate an ascetic way for average souls."[43] Institutionally, it meant the creation of communities of ascetics as a generally necessary, preparatory step to the anchorite ideal. This was not yet pure cenobism (communitarianism), since the community, in theory, was still not the final or highest expression of the ascetic ideal. Rather, it was an expedient variation, a temporary stage, for the sake of the average Christian while en route to the more advanced, eremetic life.

In the Pachomian revision, chastity and poverty remain essential, but solitude is temporarily mitigated. Instead, at the basis of the new communal life, obedience becomes the new mode of self-renunciation. "The monk voluntarily renounces his own will in order to do that of the superior."[44] Consequently, the community becomes hierarchically organized with the Superior-General at the top.[45]

Although Pachomius instituted some strong sanctions and a fixed "rule" to insure obedience, in general the new communal monasticism was more moderate in its practices and restrictions than was most anchoritism. For example, Pachomius allowed two meals daily and more fruit and vegetables but still no wine, oil, or meats. Similarly, group prayer was reduced to shortened sessions, three times daily, and the Eucharist to one celebration weekly.[46]

Another significant variation was the much greater stress on working with one's hands. For the Pachomian monk "this is an absolute requirement."[47] Consequently, many of the village communities became large productive centers (for example, Deir el Abiad had a population of about 2,200). The use of skills was encouraged, and varied according to aptitude. The products were sold in the neighboring cities, as far as Alexandria.[48] The work was usually done in silence while meditating upon Scripture. Thus work, as well as a life of prayer and contemplation, becomes a means to moral (ascetic) perfection.[49]

The Pachomian community further adjusted the anchoritic ideal, by stressing to a greater degree the social virtues of humility, patience, and brotherly love.[50] For example, the "chief concern," of the monks of Sceta is described as "the loving kindness which they show to one another and towards such as by chance may reach that spot...."[51]

From the beginning, then, monasticism exhibited considerable adaptability and flexibility of both ideals and structure. It could take either anchoritic or cenobitic forms; and it could express self-renunciation by varying degrees of solitude and abandonment of possessions or by obedience to the superior. The goal of holiness or spiritual perfection was the one constant. The trend, however, was for the ascetic road to holiness to be understood with increasing strictness and rigidity as poverty, chastity, and obedience (or solitude).[52]

Furthermore, both pure anchoritism and the variation of the Pachomian "community," but especially the latter, became extremely popular in the fourth century. One specialist in Egyptian history, J. Maspero, has estimated that there were up to 500,000 monks and nuns in the Eastern Mediterranean area by the fifth century.[53] Monasticism had become the dominant expression of the ideals of Christian asceticism.

Moreover, the new expression of Christian asceticism, monasticism, in both its anchoritic and semi-cenobitic forms, initially included renunciation of the institutional church. Workman emphasizes that monasticism became a veritable stampede from the institutional church to a "purer ideal that lay outside."[54] Sometimes church officialdom was even antagonistic.[55] If lay monks sometimes took "communion" themselves and confessed to their lay brothers, as Workman contends, this represents an anti-sacerdotalistic protest as serious as that of Montanus.[56] Early monasticism must therefore be recognized also as, in part, "the protest of the lay spirit against any conception of religion which excluded the laity from the highest obligations or supremest attainments."[57] The later gaining of official, ecclesiastical support was due considerably to monasticism's defense of orthodoxy against Arianism. This is suggested by Bishop Athanasius' writing of the *Life of Anthony*, which helped establish the monastic ideal.[58]

Cenobitism and its expansion in the West. Space does not permit a detailed elaboration of the triumph and expansion of cenobitic monasticism in Western Europe; again this section will attempt only to illustrate broadly those areas of continuing adaptability and flexibility within the Western monastic form of ascetic ideals and institutions.

The credit for setting forth cenobitism as a totally independent and in fact superior ideal to anchoritism is generally ascribed to Basil the Great. He claimed that anchoritism did not allow adequately or properly for the practice and attainment of the highest concepts of virtue. Fraternal correction,[59] through communal life and a "Rule," was not optional but necessary to the development of brotherly love, patience, and similar social virtues.

Martin of Tours, Jerome, Augustine, and Cassian continued the popularizing of monastic asceticism in the West and also continued to promote and develop the cenobitic ideal. For example, Columbàs writes that "the whole ideal of 'monk' " underwent "a profound evolution" in Bishop Augustine.[60] Augustine gave the idea of *monos*, meaning "one alone," a heightened cenobitic sense. He suggests that, "they who thus live together make one person so that they really possess what is called in Scripture 'one mind and one heart.' "[61] Augustine also laid extra stress on the social virtues of love and humility, as "the virtues attaching us most radically to God."[62]

Furthermore, while some Oriental ascetic writers conceived the ideal of "purity of heart" as a progressive extinction of passion to a state of absolute calm, passivity, and freedom from temptation, the West generally followed Augustine in rejecting any idea of the possibility of an earthly state of total freedom from sinning.[63] Similarly, though both Pelagius and Augustine were ascetics, they differed radically on the worth of human effort, on whether the human will had sufficient power in itself to avoid sinning and to progress in virtue. Cassian attempted to mediate by suggesting that there must always be some divine action, but that such is involved in the attaining of perfection only "as much as it is necessary."[64] Thereafter, some measure of conscious effort by each individual is retained within the monastic tradition.

The contributions of Jerome, Augustine, and Cassian brought into existence what can be considered a "theology of asceticism" in general, and of cenobitism in particular.[65] Thus, even prior to the Benedictine era, Western asceticism was becoming increasingly formalized. In general, it took the following pattern.[66]

From the negative side, such influential writers as Basil, Jerome, and Cassian were portraying the principle of "renunciation" increasingly as synonymous with "becoming a monk."[67] Cassian further defines a monk as more than one who relinquishes all personal temporal goods upon entering a monastery but also "a person who continues to renounce his whole life through. . . . It involves a full participation in the humility and poverty of Christ."[68] Withdrawal from the world, though not to absolute solitude, continued as essential to the monastic life.[69] Obedience to the superior and to the "Rule" of the community was increasingly accepted as superior to or a substitute for solitude. Spiritual exercises, moral effort, and suffering were essential elements in toiling for virtue.[70]

Some measure of physical austerity and practical self-discipline, usually quite rigorous, was always considered essential if the senses were to be controlled so that the soul could be humbled and purified.[71] The notion of combat, or involvement in a spiritual struggle as "soldiers of Christ," against both inner vices and external demons through the armaments of prayer, fasting, and mortifications, is maintained[72]; though this aspect seems to be less pronounced than it was among the Desert Fathers.

There were other renunciatory themes which these early monks (both anchorites and cenobites) regularly applied to themselves, and which reappear later, such as "slaveship" to God and Christ,[73] the "holy athlete," interior and daily "martyrdom," and taking up "the cross." Columbàs asserts that the theme of "cross-bearing" is "the one most frequently encountered in primitive monastic literature.[74] He also observes that "they sought above all to imitate Christ in His death."[75]

While the negative is the most obvious side of the development of early medieval monastic life and theology, again one must not overlook the positive ideals. From the positive side the goal remained holiness or perfection of life, aiming for fellowship with God, or "to acquire purity, liberty of soul, perfection, love," and "to be full citizens of that Jerusalem which is above."[76] Moreover, Cassian and others established that the ideal of perfection in cenobitism would include the "social virtues" previously mentioned. Even the striving for moral perfection is clarified, especially by Jerome and Augustine, so as never to be for its own sake but, positively, for love of God in order to please God and to become one with Him.[77]

The cenobitic ideal also retained the earlier, positive emphasis of the anchorites of dialogue with God through prayer and Scripture reading. Epiphanius writes: "The true monk should keep in his heart an uninterrupted awareness of the spirit of prayer and of psalmody."[78] Cassian also taught that the positive cultivation of "purity of heart" should be identified with "charity," which leads to the final goal of "eternal life"; but, he adds, "we can have a foretaste of the perfect contemplation of heaven even now."[79] He delineates two means: exterior works of charity on behalf of men and (for him, the better way) purity of heart by separation from the world.[80] John Chrysostom compares the monastic life to man in paradise before the Fall. "The faithful monk has returned to the garden of Eden."[81] Therefore many of the renunciatory practices have as their positive purpose, the bringing of the monk closer to his original, prelapsarian condition.

One of the most significant themes in the ideological structuring of early cenobitism, found in some of the most ancient texts, is the idea of the monastery or community as a "church." For example, Pachomius calls it "the house of God"; Basil, "the body of Christ." Again, according to Columbàs, Basil maintains that "the monastery is the church in miniature. . . . This deeply rooted conviction explains why Basil reproves the individual who withdraws . . . why he believes that there should be only one monastery in any given area."[82] Concerning the church in Jerusalem (Acts 2), Cassian writes "The whole church then was like those few now who can with difficulty be found in monasteries."[83] Apparently, early cenobitism consciously thought of itself as a restoration of the apostolic church. This is further indication of the inherent tension with the inclusive institutional church of the post-Constantinian era.

There are two additional examples of cenobitic variation which developed early in the West and further illustrate asceticism's

48   Anabaptism and Asceticism

flexibility. The first is the monastic establishment of Cassiodorus, a contemporary of Benedict of Nursia (sixth century), with its unique emphasis on intellectual activity and the *scriptoria* as legitimate activities conducive to spiritual development.[84] The second variation, also contemporary with Benedict, and only quasi-cenobitic, is Iro-Celtic monasticism, which dominated the Irish church by a remarkable adaptation of its structure to local clan conditions. Accordingly, it developed such unique characteristics as: abbots with authority over bishops; considerable mobility, especially through pilgrimages of penance in the form of missionary journeys; an active, monastery-centered, biblical and classical scholarship; and rather more rigorous and austere mortification practices than was typical of continental cenobitism in the West.[85]

The subsequent era, from the sixth to the twelfth centuries, is often designated "the Benedictine centuries," because during this period Benedictine cenobitism (promoted by Pope Gregory)[86] came to dominate Western monasticism and monasticism in turn became increasingly influential in Western society. Benedict's cenobitic "Rule" represented both a summarizing and consummation of the main trends of Western cenobitism and adaptability to the emerging society of the West.[87]

Actually, Benedictine asceticism exhibits few major institutional or ideological revisions, though there were some minor distinctive characteristics, such as: thoroughness of detail with reference to the functioning of a very ordered communal life (though the rule is relatively brief — 12,000 words); greater simplicity by reducing asceticism basically to fulfilling the three vows of poverty, chastity, and obedience, and to a threefold occupational pattern, chanting and prayer (*Opus Dei*), devotional study (*Lectio Divina*), and manual work (*Opera Manuum*); stability, in that the members were permanently bound to the one community (a somewhat unique element) under its abbot and "Rule," and functioned as one large family of God; and moderation in that the Rule is noticeably more lenient about physical austerities than most earlier expressions.[88] Nevertheless, the Benedictine goal was still charity (or perfection) but through a moderate, well-organized, common life of detachment, spiritual exercises, and work. And though Benedictinism dominated in the West, older forms of ascetic expression continued also, especially the Celtic and some anchoritism.

During the Benedictine centuries several new orders appeared, but these were for the most part non-innovative. Their "reason for being" usually was monastic reform by a return to the old principles and by an intensification of physical austerity and isolation. For example, the Cistercians (twelfth century) primarily emphasized a more austere cenobitism, and the Carthusians (eleventh century) added some anchoritic elements, such as separate cells, along with a renewed austerity, including hair shirts, rigorous fasting, and pilgrimages as penitential exercises. Cluniac Benedictinism (of the tenth and eleventh centuries) was also ideologically mostly conservative, but it did inaugurate some liturgical innovations and one major institutional variation, a significant departure from traditional cenobitic local autonomy. Cluny became a "mother-house" for many other "daughter" monasteries who came under its jurisdiction and supervision — a unique hierarchical system of organizational and structural unity in addition to the older unity through conformity to the same Rule.[89] Nevertheless, on the whole there is little change during the Benedictine centuries in the basic patterns which were already established for expressing Christian asceticism.

Between the late eleventh and fourteenth centuries, however, at least four relatively new forms of monasticism appeared to illustrate the continuing (or renewed) capacity of Christian asceticism to be innovative, flexible, and adaptable. First, there was the appearance of the remarkable military orders of the crusading era, for example, the Knights Templars and the Knights Hospitallers. Such orders are dramatic examples of both organizational flexibility and ideological adaptability. Monks who assumed military functions, or *vice versa*, were simultaneously under oaths of secular knighthood, the three major vows of monasticisim, and a "Rule,"[90] Organizationally, they lived in convent "barracks," and ideologically, they combined the obedience of the soldier with the submissiveness of the monk. After the crusading era, in some orders, the rule of celibacy was relaxed to allow them to marry once[91] — certainly another example of the degree of innovation possible within the monastic, ascetic tradition. Workman thinks that it even required a "new conception of holiness."[92]

Another major innovation was the rise of the Mendicant Orders. Workman describes the coming of the friars, of Francis and of Dominic, as "the rise of a new conception of monasticism so completely different that the friars were forbidden to enter within the walls of any monastery."[93] While the basic ascetic ideals, expressed as chastity, poverty, and obedience (or self-abnegation) continue, yet one can observe a switch in emphasis from the absolute solitude of the anchorite, from the rigid obedience of the cenobite, and from the contemplative way to purity favored by both anchorite and cenobite, to a greater stress on absolute poverty[94] (both individual and at first, in Franciscanism, also corporate), and on the attainment of personal perfection and selflessness through service to God in society, by means of active, altruistic deeds of love, preaching, missionary work, and teaching.[95] This ascetic variation radically diminished the older ideal of physical withdrawal from society[96] while retaining strong ethical earnestness and conductual piety. Moreover, the individual friar was not attached to any one monastery, place, or abbot; rather, he functioned within an Order with international connections under a Chapter General.[97]

The third important innovation in the ascetic life was the founding and approval of the Third Order of St. Francis, the Brothers and Sisters of Penitence. This order functioned fully "in the world, retaining the estate of marriage and most of the normal involvements of the life of the laity."[98] The ascetic goal of purity, holiness, virtue, Christlikeness does not change but the method of attainment radically changes. Not only is celibacy abandoned as a necessary element but even the renunciation of the world no longer demands a total, physical withdrawal from society. Poverty is changed to the responsibility to share one's possessions and to perform acts of charity. Physical mortifications are also much moderated.[99] Subsequently, the Dominicans, Augustinian Hermits, and the Minims also established Third Orders on the same ascetic pattern — a pattern which approximates a return to early Christian asceticism.

The era from the Mendicants to the Reformation is most paradoxical. On one hand the religious orders, especially the friars and Third Orders, successfully extended their ascetic road to piety "to the church as a whole," but simultaneously there was also rapid degeneration provoking a reactionary rigorism, a trend back to cenobitic monasticism and an "increasing tendency to multiply ascetic practices and forms."[100] Often these practices again accentuated such externals as pilgrimages, processions, genuflexions, repetition of prayers, and physical austerities, though the objective was still to cultivate a penitential attitude.[101]

The Brothers and Sisters of the Common Life, founded by Gerhard Groote (d. 1384), represent one of the last major ideological and institutional variations in the Christian ascetic tradition of the West prior to the Reformation era. They promoted the ideal of the restoration of primitive Christian asceticism, or the laicization of monasticism, begun by Francis of Assisi. Many of them became also Third Order Franciscans. Therefore Coulton refers to the organization of the Brethren of the Common Life as "a definite link between monasticism and the ordinary life." He adds that "it forms a landmark in monastic history. Here was the watershed — the moment when men were losing faith in the monks as they were and yet felt that the ideal must not be suffered to perish."[102]

Though Groote never rejects the value of monasticism for some, he does deny that the term *religio* can be restricted to mean only the regular clergy, the monks, and the nuns. He writes: "If devout women separate themselves from the world, and try to serve God in the privacy of their homes without taking monastic vows, they are just as religious as the nuns in their convents." He adds: "Truly religious men are not confined by place, time or manner of men." Rather, "all those who live aloof from the world to serve God, who despise temporal honors; leading chaste lives, obedient and poor: they are religious people."[103]

Though the Brethren were forced, for self-protection, into founding for some of their members a traditionally organized monastic order, the Windesheim Congregation of Augustian Canons Regular, the actual Brethren "houses" were never recognized "orders." They did have "Rule-like" constitutions but the three vows of Benedictine monasticism were not compulsory.[104] They lived in common, with shared possessions and maintained chastity but were not bound by oath to do so. Obedience was not to an abbot or office holder but to Christ only, in imitation of the Apostles. All were considered equal and it was permissible to admonish one another and to confess one's sins to one another even if each was a layman.[105]

The Brethren were active in the secular community not only by working but by teaching, publishing, and deeds of love and mercy. Accordingly, the Brethren at Zwolle, 1415, wrote: "We have decided to live in cities, in order that we might be able to give advice and instruction to clerics and other persons who wish to serve the Lord."[106] Their practices relating to ascetic mortification were also mild, although their food and clothing remained plain.[107] The basic ascetic goal of holiness and the means to it, the "imitation of Christ," were strong motifs in their teachings, but were strongly morally and spiritually internalized (more so in the Brethren of the Common Life than in Windesheim).[108] The best-known expression of this ideal of moderate, practical, internalized ascetic spirituality, *The Imitation of Christ*, was actually produced by a Windesheimer, Thomas à Kempis, probably utilizing an earlier "Brethren" work. The invention of printing widely diffused this book and its ideals in Western Europe in the late fifteenth century.

Nevertheless, in spite of its remarkable capacity to change and adapt, up to the Reformation the Christian ascetic tradition in the West also maintained several constants throughout its history. First, the *goal* was clearly the attainment of personal holiness, or the perfecting of one's own salvation.[109] The attributes of this ideal of personal "holiness" always included: a total love for, and allegiance to, God in Christ, a spiritual fellowship with Christ or a daily sharing of His life, work, and suffering, and the development of the image of Christ, or of Christlike virtues, especially purity of heart and mind, humility, selflessness, gentleness, loving-kindness, self-control, and peaceableness.[110]

Second, the *ideological means* to attain this goal of holiness also remained fairly constant. The aspect of total love for God demanded the elimination of its chief rival, the "world," by separation or detachment of some kind.[111] Fellowship with Christ called for self-surrender, self-denial, and self-crucifixion.[112] The gaining of virtue required the ability to triumph over the "old nature," the flesh and its lusts, and the cultivation of the Holy Spirit's presence, graces and gifts. The attainment of all three was aided by spiritual exercises, contemplation, and acts of love.[113] Success always required cooperation between individual self-initiative and divine grace through the Holy Spirit.

Third, while the *practical means* or external agencies by which the goal and the means to the goal became actuated also have some constant elements, this aspect of the ascetic tradition was clearly the most flexible and was capable of many variations, especially in form and in degrees of intensity.[114] For example, the principle of separation or detachment from the "world," when applied to society, family, and possessions, usually expressed itself externally as monachism, chastity, and poverty. But the principle changed its external expression successively from a separated church in the world to a church under persecution, living by its own "laws," and suffering martyrdom, to the limited withdrawal from both society and church by the third century "virgins," to the total physical withdrawal to solitude by the

The Christian Ascetic Tradition 53

hermit, to cenobitic "communal" withdrawal, and then back to a lesser degree of withdrawal by the Mendicants, Third Orders, and Brethren of the Common Life.

Between the third and sixteenth centuries, chastity expressed as celibacy is the one aspect of separation which had perhaps the least variation in application, though celibacy was not required of all Military Orders nor of the Third Orders. Theoretically, the ascetic tradition was also fairly consistent in requiring personal poverty of all but Third Orders, who had their own way to affirm and express the same principle. Except for the "Spiritual" Franciscans, however, renunciation of "communal" or "corporate" possessions was not practiced or required.

Similarly, the dominant means for expressing self-denial illustrates the flexibility and variability of the external agent. It changed from the solitude of the hermit, to obedience to an abbot by the cenobite, and then to obedience by the friars to Christ in sacrificial actions (that is, in missionary work, deeds of mercy, and all kinds of service for God). Again, the gaining of virtue and the conquest of the "flesh" tended to be achieved by the negative but practical means of practicing varying degrees of physical mortification, such as fasting, chastity, and various penitential activities.

Positive means to the same end included prayer, Scripture reading, and meditation by the individual, and worship, the sacraments, brotherly exhortation, and the discipline of the "Rule" by the individual within the context of the "church" or group. In each aspect, over the centuries there was also great variation in the amount and intensity of performance. To all of this there must be added God's gracious involvement, a constant factor without which, the ascetic tradition maintained (except for Pelagianism), there could be no success at all. This help was provided through the cross but made practical primarily through the aid of the Holy Spirit and the Scriptures.

Peifer aptly summarizes thus: "If monasticism has been such a long-lived phenomenon, is it not precisely because it was always ready to change structures and institutions which, because of changed conditions, were no longer the best means of expressing its inner nature?"[115] Accordingly, if Anabaptism is a valid continuation of this Christian ascetic tradition, it must hold substantially to the above ascetic ideal of holiness and to its associated ideological means for attainment, and that to a marked degree, *but* it does not need to hold as exactly to the practical means, to the traditional external practices and the institutional expressions. These could exhibit considerable variation, divergence, and revision. In fact, the fifteenth century provides suitable conditions, namely a growing frustration and disillusionment with institutional monasticism, but without an abandonment of the ascetic ideal, for the rise of a new variation.

Ascetic Vitality and Trends: Fifteenth Century

Continuous decline? Most writers of medieval monastic history designate the Mendicant revival of the early thirteenth century, though quite short-lived, as the last major resurgence of ascetic idealism before the Protestant Reformation.[116] The era from the late thirteenth through the fifteenth century is described by Knowles as "a gradual decline in the external maintenance of the spiritual ideals of monasticism," the Carthusians being the major exception. He maintains that after the twelfth century, "old Monasticism" became static and the spiritual dynamism passed to the friars. Then, from the mid-fourteenth century onward, the friars also underwent a "lowering of moral standards."[117] Concerning the fourteenth century, Knowles suggests that the agreement of Langland, Wycliffe, and Chaucer "as to the worldliness of the monks and the rascality of the friars is too remarkable to be dismissed," and that even for the fifteenth century "the picture . . . is not a bright one.[118]

However, one need not interpret the abundance of literature in the fifteenth century calling for reform and attacking abuses as an indication of further or continuous spiritual and moral decline. The turning point seems much earlier, coinciding more with the Avignon papacy and schism in the fourteenth century. The reforming movements of Franciscan Observants began in 1368 and the Brethren of the Common Life about a decade later. Following the Council of Constance (1414-18), several reform movements emerged demonstrating both concern for a revival of practical piety and personal spirituality and a still vital faith in ascetic idealism in the late fifteenth century. One cannot overlook the popularity of such ascetic works as the *Imitation of Christ*. The major theme of fifteenth-century monastic history is not that of an ever-deepening institutional degeneracy and a decline of the ascetic ideals, but rather the growing intensity of frustration over the seeming unfulfillable but increasing desire for reform.

Though numerous attempts at major reform were being undertaken by mid-century, some with the support of both the papacy and the temporal power, success was mostly local and of comparatively short duration. The failure of institutional reforms was due largely to ingrained institutional and administrative defects in the church related to its complicated church-state involvements, especially the system of granting benefices *in commendam*, that encouraged corruption and abuse.[119] Consequently, reform was often foiled by either hierarchical or secular resistance, or both. Such failures do not imply necessarily a lessening but rather a frustrating of ascetic idealism, leading to widespread despair.

Attempts at monastic reform: illustrative signs of reawakening, concern, and frustration. Pope Benedict XII made some efforts in the fourteenth century to effect a general monastic reform, but failed. That failure, plus the papal schism, redirected hope for a general reform of all of monasticism increasingly to the councils; and the whole issue was set specifically and at length before the Council of Constance.[120] The council did consider the problem and out of the "directives" of Constance subsequently came the monastic reform movements of Melk, Castel, and Bursfeld. The Council of Basel in turn attempted to use the Congregation of Windesheim as its chief agent of reformation.[121] Though these four fifteenth-century, northern, monastic reform movements were on a sizable scale, with expectations of a renewal of the whole church, unlike the more sporadic and isolated efforts of the previous century, these later efforts also failed to achieve a general reform of monasticism and through it of the Church.

The Windesheim Congregation of Augustinian Canons Regular, formed in 1387, was probably the most effective monastic reformative organization. It was originally established by some of the Brethren of the Common Life,[122] for their protection, but it soon became a major vehicle for conveying some of the "Brethren" ideals to many other monasteries, even in other orders. By 1419, Windesheim headed twenty reformed congregations; by the time of the writing of Johann Busch's *Chronicle* (cir. 1470),[123] it had eighty-one associated houses, and by the turn of the century there were over one hundred, influencing twenty-three dioceses in northwestern Europe.[124] In addition, the Windesheimers aided in the beginning of the Bursfeld reform.

According to the late fifteenth-century treatise, *De Reformatione*,

56 Anabaptism and Asceticism

by the Windesheimer, Johann Busch, the Windesheim influence (mostly within the monastic system itself) was directed toward such ends as: the restoration of the ideals of "true obedience, pure poverty or absence of private property, and chaste continence"; "a return to the Society of Jerusalem as mirrored in Acts . . . [implying] steady, sometimes violent, opposition to the world"; renewed "ideals of introspection and mortification"; constructive activity, especially book copying; simplicity in clothes and diet; self-abasement (that is, "The Windesheimer must be dead to himself and maintain this by continual practice"); and almsgiving and general beneficence.[125] Acquoy testifies that they especially read, and sometimes produced, lives of Christ, Passion books, and similar writings of simple edification, not only in Latin but in the vernacular.[126]

Though something of the ideals of its "Brethren" founders from Deventer continued to motivate and permeate these reforms by the Windesheimers, as is reflected in Thomas à Kempis' *The Imitation of Christ*, clearly by the late fifteenth century the practical means to achieve reformation was becoming increasingly traditional, little more than the advocacy of a rigorous, uncompromising return to one's traditional "Rule," thus "keeping themselves in all holiness of life and custody of the senses and discipline of manners. . . ."[127]

The once closely related Brethren of the Common Life tended to diverge considerably from the Windesheimers during the course of the fifteenth century. Though some houses of the Brethren were also affected somewhat by the same trend to greater rigorism and cenobitic rigidity, on the whole, the Brethren continued to stress the more distinctively lay and more moderately ascetic reformative principles of their founder, Gerhard Groote (1340-84), and of the school of thought to which the name, the *Devotio Moderna*, has been given. H. Daniel-Rops summarizes the original spiritual essence of the *Devotio Moderna* movement, which the Brethren sought to maintain, as: "a warm, pulsating and profoundly human way of seeking perfection; a spiritual technique based entirely on the inner make-up of the individual; a modest kind of mysticism . . . which subjected the whole soul to the imitation of Christ, the One Model."[128]

The "Brethren" scholar at the end of the fifteenth century, Gabriel Biel (d. 1490), still describes the lay ideal of the Brethren of the Common Life as "a life in the freedom of the Christian law, under the one abbot Jesus Christ, without obligation to observances above and beyond the precepts. . . . Everyone should remain in the state in which he is called." Biel placed their active life of simple piety over against the rigorous ideal of the Observantists, thus: "not exterior observances but a pure conscience marks the perfect monk."[129]

The "Devotio" writers were not interested in building theological systems; rather, they sought spiritual perfection through personal devotion, through "prayer, tears, meditation and supplication," through "a humble, simple life, soundly based upon discipline and temperate habits,"[130] and through charitable activity. By the last quarter of the fifteenth century, there were over fifty houses of the Brethren of the Common Life and more than one hundred houses of affiliated Tertiary women. These houses numbered from twenty to four hundred persons in each, "who are never idle but, bee-like, cease not to sweat importunately for their own salvation and the winning of souls."[131]

In the last half of the fifteenth century the Brethren devoted more energy and effort to their work as educators, educational chaplains, and publishers, and by these means their influence multiplied. "The fact is Münster and Deventer sent out so vast a host of really great scholars and teachers that it is quite impossible to enumerate them."[132]

In Bavaria, independent of the *Devotio Moderna* but parallel in time, a small Benedictine reform movement began at Kastel, in 1380, with the aid of some Bohemian monks. Later, it was encouraged to expand its influence by the Councils of Constance and Basel. Ultimately, about twenty other monasteries were helped, including St. Gall.[133] However, by 1450, the further spread of its reforming activities had halted. This movement indicates ascetic vitality but largely along traditional lines.

The abbot of Petershausen, also commissioned by the Council of Constance, convoked the Provincial Chapter of the Benedictines of Mayence-Bramberg, in 1417, for the purpose of reform. One hundred and twenty-six monasteries were represented. Their abbots took oaths to tighten regulations, especially according to the prescriptions of the *Benedictina* (of Pope Benedict XII, 1336). Although the Chapter was only partially successful in implementing this action, an important impulse toward a more extensive reform program and ascetic resurgence had begun.

More immediately effective was the reform resulting from the direct efforts of Duke Albert V of Austria. By importing some re-

58   Anabaptism and Asceticism

formed-minded monks to Melk in 1418, he made it a center of ascetic reform activity throughout Austria, Bavaria, and Swabia, that lasted until the Protestant Reformation.[134] However, the monasteries of the Melk "observance" never united themselves into an organized congregation, only into a fragile fellowship; and this may have weakened their total influence somewhat.[135]

A combination of factors brought into existence in northern Germany another fifteenth-century monastic reform movement, parallel to the Melk reform of South Germany, but on an even larger scale. The reform of Bursfeld, as it is called, rivaled Windesheim in breadth and depth of influence and owed much in its origin to this elder sister.[136] Johann Dederoth, a Benedictine monk of Nordheim near Göttingen, emerged from the Peterhausen attempt at reformation as a reformative leader. Aided by a commission from the Council of Basel (1430), plus some Windesheim monks, he successfully turned the monastery of Bursfeld into a reforming center in 1434. By 1446, a congregation of reformed monasteries was formed. It grew to thirty-six houses by 1469 and ninety by 1490;[137] and constituted a significant monastic renewal on the eve of the Reformation. Both Nicholas of Cusa (papal legate in 1451-52)[138] and Trithemius (1461-1516),[139] Abbot at Spanheim and Würzburg, were actively involved in its progress.

Nevertheless, the total impact remained limited and institutionally and traditionally restricted. In spite of Nicholas' great "visitation" work and his encouraging of both the Windesheim and Bursfeld reforms, Vansteenberghe notes that it left a sense of disappointment among his contemporaries and successors.[140] Similarly, Trithemius in an oration to the General Chapter of Bursfeld said of Benedictinism, at the turn of the century, "The greater part of our walls have fallen; for in many of them religion hath perished, devotion grown cold, charity hath expired. . . . A minority alone shine with reformation . . . minds still shrink from that Benedictine Rule which they profess."[141] Ascetic concerns were still alive but hope for major renewal through the reform of its anachronistic institutions was fading.

In France, there were numerous locally successful monastic reform efforts during the last half of the fifteenth century, such as, by Abbot Jean de Bourbon at Cluny in 1458 and by Jean de Cirey at Citeaux in 1476.[142] The latter attempted also a more general Cistercian reform but failed. Earlier, St. Collette (d. 1447) had made the reform of the Poor Clare nunneries, along traditional lines, her life's

The Christian Ascetic Tradition   59

work, with considerable immediate success. During her lifetime, reformed houses flocked to join her movement. Yet Daniel-Rops concludes that in the end it too was ineffective and St. Collette confessed disillusionment shortly before her death, saying: "Alas, I have toiled so hard and long for religion, and all my work will wither away in a moment...."[143] However, concern for more general monastic reform and renewal continued. In 1484, Charles VIII put it on the program of the Estates General at Tours, but again with little practical results. Also in 1485, Archbishop Salazar, at the synod of Sens, attempted unsuccessfully to legislate reform.

Some brief measure of success under Pierre du Mars (abbot, 1479-92) was achieved at Chezal-Benoit, near Bourges (which took its inspiration from the reform of St. Justin of Padua).[144] There were five reformed monasteries in the congregation by 1516. Of greater importance than the number of monasteries affected were their much publicized entreaties for reform, as illustrated by Abbot Guy Jouenneaux (of St. Sulpice) in his *Defense of Monastic Reform* written to gain the support of Parlement. In it he condemns monks for worldliness; namely, playing forbidden games, swearing, hunting parties, frequenting taverns, bearing the sword, and retaining private property. He presses for a return to the original ideals.[145]

The Brethren of the Common Life and the Windesheim Congregation were also involved in a reform movement in France. Through Jean Standonck they established a semi-monastic community of scholars and students near Paris, with eighty students by 1493, of whom it is said, "They seldom left the community except to enter some reformed monastery at his advice."[146] At the Great Commission of Tours (1493), these reformers pressed for moral and administrative changes. The growing concern for reform involving a revival of ascetic values is illustrated by Michael Bureau's treatise on Reform (1496), which comments, "The word *reform* has rung so loudly in men's ears that, with whomsoever we converse, this is a most ordinary subject."[147]

Through Standonck's urging, the monks, Jean Mombaer and Koetken, came from Windesheim (1496) to lead a program of conventual reform, at Chateau-Landon, then at Livry, and at Cysoing near Lille (they also made an attempt at St. Victor, but it was not successful till 1515). Finally, by 1509, they were able to set up a small reformed Congregation of Monasteries. In spite of these numerous efforts, giving evidence of much ascetic concern, by 1517 and the outbreak of the Protestant Reformation the number of Regulars within the ranks of reformed monasticism was only a fraction of the total, but ascetic idealism was clearly alive among the faithful.

The story of the friars in the fifteenth century, according to Knowles, begins with an expression of ascetic concern relating to a "lowering of moral standards." To the long-standing pattern of bitter rivalry between the Orders of Friars, there was added a "civil war" within the Franciscan Order, between the Conventuals and Observants, which continued throughout most of the century.[148] The "civil war" was due to the rise of the stricter Franciscan Observants, with their ideal of reform by a return to the "Constitutions" and encouraged by the Council of Constance. The Observants were further aided by numerous popular and influential reform preachers emerging from their ranks, including Bernardino of Siena, John Capistrano, Blessed James of the March, and Albert of Sarteano. Similarly, Raymond of Capua began an Observant type of reform among the Dominicans.

Actually, in spite of the negative impact of the rivalries, the emergence of the Observants resulted in "a modest revival of new foundations in the late fifteenth century," especially in France. Mostly they were Franciscan, of the "Observant" type, plus some by a new Mendicant Order, dedicated to very strict poverty and some anchoritic ideals, founded by Francis of Paulo (1416-1507), called the Minims.[149]

The Minims were only one expression of a more general revival of the popularity of the eremetical life. "England and Ireland swarmed with hermits . . . large numbers . . . built . . . outside the walls of Paris. . . . This rejection and abandonment of the world is highly significant."[150]

Thus, though the fifteenth-century picture with reference to monastic reform is a frustrating scene, it is certainly not the lowest point in the history of monastic asceticism. The numerous reform attempts reveal a still vital and growing belief in the ascetic ideals by many of the pious. However, the pattern of monastic reform seems largely limited to the adoption of more and more rigorous observances, and the restoration of traditional practices. There was even a return to the older eremetic ideal. Except for the Brethren of the Common Life, there was little attempt at renewal by a creative readaptation of the ascetic ideals to a new structure. Therefore, while a conservative and backward-looking attempt at ascetic reform grew in the fifteenth century, so did the frustration over the pattern of limited and local successes but of failure in the larger context.

The preachers of repentance. Equally important as monastic reform for appraising the vitality of ascetic ideals in the late fifteenth-century is the influence of revivalist preaching. While attendance at ordinary church services was generally poor, many preachers "possessed a fame reasonably akin to that which surrounds the stars of the modern cinema."[151] Their crowds were so large that sermons had to be preached in the fields or public squares. Vincent Ferrer (1357-1419), for example, often preached three or four times daily, and Nicholas of Cusa preached in the vernacular all over Germany. It is reported that he delivered eighty sermons in Brixen alone.[152] Equally popular were Bernardino of Siena (1380-1444)[153] and John Capistrano, who preached to vast throngs in the north, through an interpreter! At the end of the century, this phenomenal popularity of informal preaching was still maintained by Franciscan Observantine, Oliver Maillard, Geiler von Keysersberg, Girolamo Savonarola of Florence, and others. These "preachers of repentance," as they are sometimes called, continued to uphold the ascetic norms for personal morality, with considerable popular success.[154]

Most of these preachers were monks, and along with themes of hellfire and divine judgment they promoted ascetic views on the nature of sin and appealed for the imitation of Christ's sufferings and amendment of life. Responses similar to Savonarola's "Bonfire of Vanities" in Florence were not unique.[155] Maillard preached daily with the single aim of individual soul-saving. To further his goal he sought to dissociate himself most emphatically from what the multitude saw around them: the unworthiness of the clergy and the decay of the church. He emphasized both the church's need of drastic purification and the fewness of the number to reach heaven compared to the multitude heading for hell.[156] Geiler's sermons similarly called for renewal according to ascetic norms and some even anticipated that a general moral reform would come only through some climactic, imminent, divine action. For example, before Emperor Maximilian (1492) he warned that "things cannot last, *es muss brechen.*" On another occasion he prophesied: "Since neither Pope nor Kaiser, King nor Bishops, are willing to *reform their lives*, God will send a man to do this and to revive our fallen religion."[157]

62 Anabaptism and Asceticism

The Christian humanists of the north. Finally, the vitality of the ascetic ideal in the fifteenth century is reflected not only in the repeated attempts at monastic reform, in the activity of the Brethren of the Common Life, and in the popularity of the preachers of repentance but also in the works of many of the northern humanists. Erasmus, Agricola, Celtis, Mutian, and others, had ties with the Brethren of the Common Life and in Erasmus' "philosophy of Christ" the innovative, ascetic idealism of the *Devotio Moderna* is not only reflected but extended.[158] The simple, moderately ascetic, devout piety of the *Devotio Moderna*, coupled with humanistic biblical "primitivism" applied to asceticism and perhaps with some Neoplatonism, influenced Erasmus to support iconoclasm, sacramentarianism (a denial of the real presence), and even to reject music in worship.[159] This is a return to the "heroic" ethic of biblical Christianity. Similarly, his writings stressed, as he put it, the "more interior means of helping us to depart from this life with cheerfulness and Christian trust,"[160] also the "ethical-ascetic" demands of the gospel,[161] and the centrality of love.[162]

In all of his satire against the superstitions and abuses relating to many of the external practices of the church and of the monastic system, he does not appear to abandon the essence derived from biblical norms of the ascetic ideal; but rather to promote it independently of the traditional institutions and external expressions. He scores the discrepancy between the ideal and reality.[163]

Similarly, much of the northern "Christian" humanism of the early sixteenth century had certain distinctive and common elements which were derived probably from the impact of a still vital ascetic piety outside of monastic institutions. Spitz refers both to an increasing inwardness and individualism in religion with a strong personalized stoic and ascetic moralism stressing practical good works and the virtuous life and to a tendency to go back to *Christian* antiquity for norms of religion.[164] Furthermore, "to a man the humanists were sharp critics of ecclesiastical abuses and participated in every reform effort in the decades prior to the Reformation."[165]

Printing and Literature. A final factor, essential to an understanding of the vitality of ascetic idealism at the beginning of the Reformation, was the development of printing which made possible a more widespread dissemination in the late fifteenth century of the call for an ascetically oriented reform. As one example of many,

Werner Rolewinck, a Carthusian monk from Cologne, wrote a work advocating moral reform which, when it was published in 1474, became quite popular, quickly going through over thirty printings.[166] Daniel Rops refers to "the enormous success of various spiritual volumes addressed to the general public" (for example, Gerson's *Plain Man's ABC* and his *Treatise on the Ten Commandments*, Raymond Lull's *Art of Contemplation*, also works of Tauler, Ruysbroek, and Zerbolt).[167] The most popular of all was *The Imitation of Christ*, the handbook of the *Devotio Moderna*.[168]

Summary

In summary, though the efforts of the Christian ascetic tradition in the fifteenth century to reform its own institutions, and to elevate Christian morality generally, resulted in successes that were at best local and of short duration, yet the ascetic ideal is considerably stronger in 1500 than it was in 1400. There was a growing desire for reform, ascetically oriented, an increasing awareness of earlier and different expressions of asceticism, especially of primitive, biblical asceticism, and frustration with the failures of traditional, rigoristic, monastic reform methods and a willingness, even desire, for changes in form, not content. The desire of many was not to abandon ascetic ideals, but to reappraise how best to express them. Thus Knowles appraises the evidence correctly when he asserts that full reform by the methods which were used in the fifteenth century was clearly not possible with the tangled and complex church-state relations, as illustrated by the practice of commendations. But, at the same time, Spitz can also correctly refer to an "upsurge of religious feeling and seeking . . . characteristic of great masses of people"[169] in that era.

Generally, the direction of fifteenth-century reform had followed the dictum of the Council of Constance: "not new laws but ordinary respect for the laws which had existed for many centuries."[170] It tended to be highly conservative and traditional (though the anchoritism of St. Francis of Paulo and the Minims, recalls the ancient ideal of the Desert Fathers). The northern humanists' program of protest and reform, in essence "represented no real innovation,"[171] but did exhibit a willingness to subscribe to changes in the externals of the medieval pattern.

The trend towards a revived, primitive, biblical asceticism is

64   Anabaptism and Asceticism

associated largely with the *Devotio Moderna*, which upheld a moderation, laicization, personalization, and internalization of ascetic ideals and practices. Some of the late fifteenth-century reformers began to reflect considerable pessimism about the ability of renewing the existing institutions, without drastic revisions, or even of expressing the real ascetic ideals adequately through them. Michel Menot (d. 1518) asserts: "I have no great hopes for the church unless it be planted anew."[172]

It is particularly important to note that the hope for a general reform, frustrated by the failure of both Concilliarism and of the "Saints" of the fourteenth and fifteenth centuries, was becoming far more than just a desire for the elimination of institutional and administrative abuses; it consistently included a hope and call for "a revival of fervor, charity, asceticism and discipline" in the masses of individual Christians. The key word in much of the pro-reform writing and preaching was "repent."[173] As frustration increased, expectation grew that if and when the renewal and general reform came, it would involve by divine impetus a cataclysmic, institutional upheaval. Also, for many, the end product was expected to be a greater manifestation and fulfillment of the spiritual ideals which were still conceived to be largely ascetic.

Initially, many frustrated reformers accepted the early Protestant Reformation as the fulfillment of their radical expectations, by its total repudiation of a papal hierarchy, monasticism, and a scholastic sacramental system. But, as Luther himself admitted, it failed to bring about the substantial increase in general piety which was the second and equally vital expectation that also emerged in the fifteenth century. Many who had initially supported Luther noted this failure with concern, and as the next chapter will demonstrate, this concern becomes a major factor in the emergence of Anabaptism as an alternative, reform movement.

The Anabaptists accepted for the most part the radical institutional or "Protestant" revision of Luther but in their concern for piety they went further than the early Magisterial Reformation by also eliminating totally the entanglement of the state with the church and by insisting on behavioral evidences of individual piety as essential to a true spiritual reform or restitution — as essential to true Christianity! These two concerns, for individual piety and for ecclesiastical purity, are united in the Anabaptist Reform movement.

3 ASCETIC FACTORS IN THE EMERGENCE OF ANABAPTISM

In Pre-Anabaptist Dissent

The thesis that Anabaptism is largely Zwinglian in origin fails adequately to recognize the existence of a large, loosely related movement of dissent at the time Anabaptism emerged. It was pro-reform but dissatisfied with some aspects of Lutheranism. It maintained that Luther's teachings were deficient in some things, especially concern for piety, and exaggerated in others, especially election and predestination, Christian liberty, and an exclusively imputed righteousness. Some persons, who were associated with this broad movement of reform and dissent, were also antischismatic and never quite "Protestant."

A substantial portion of this broad movement favoring reform but not Luther's interpretation of it reflected the continuation of the ascetically-oriented reform expectations of the fifteenth century, reviewed in the second chapter; expectations of a total renewal of the church involving a moral purification of individuals. Such ascetic expectations were also clearly part of the program of Erasmian Christian humanism. Consequently, many of the Christian humanists, especially those associated with Erasmus, the bulk of Zasius' circle at Freiburg, and many of the circle of reform humanists at Nuremberg, though they too were reformers, refused to support Luther fully. Many other humanists who did support him at first, later returned to the Roman Church.

As Luther clarified his program, especially between 1521 and 1524, these same expectations gave rise to numerous independent Protestant groups and groups within Lutheranism and Zwinglianism that rejected the formulations of the major, Magisterial Reformers. Two notable leaders of such groups are Hans Denck, who later became an Anabaptist, and Thomas Müntzer, who did not. In both, however, their strongest and earliest expressions of dissatisfaction with the Magisterial Reformation, before January 1525, relate to their concern for a reformation that promoted ascetic norms of conduct.

Müntzer is noted for his coining of a number of slogans which were picked up by most of those who were dissatisfied with Luther. Many of them contain ascetic overtones; such as Müntzer's complaints that Luther made "the Christian faith too rosy, had proclaimed a honey-sweet Christ instead of a bitter one, and had said nothing about the commitment which one must make to become Christ's disciple."[1] He accused Luther among other things of freeing men from papal burdens but then leaving them "in carnal freedom" and not leading them on to God and the Spirit.

According to a contemporary opponent's pamphlet, *Die Historie Thomae Müntzers*,[2] Müntzer taught that "one must come to a genuine Christian piety: First one must desist from such public evils as adultery, murder, blasphemy, and the like. The body must be castigated and martyred with fasting and poor clothing. One should talk little, look sour, and not cut off one's beard. Such . . . he called the 'mortification of the flesh' and the 'cross' of which the Gospels write." Though this pamphlet probably exaggerates the details of Müntzer's teaching, the ascetic element is unmistakable.

Prior to the emergence of Anabaptism, the humanistically trained scholar, Hans Denck, already a follower of the new evangelical (Lutheran) reform, came to Nuremberg (1524) as Rector of St. Sebald school.[3] In Nuremberg, he associated with a group of humanist reformers who were expressing keen disappointment with the product of Luther's doctrines. Basically they agreed with Luther's criticism of the "old" system, but were uneasy about the "new" that he was proposing in its place. Piety was losing out in their opinion, and they did not approve.

Denck leveled his personal criticism primarily against Luther's interpretation of justification as totally "imputed." Luther seemed to imply the possibility of full forgiveness of sins regardless of the character of the believer's life thereafter. Denck reacted by insisting that "no one may truly know Christ except one who follows Him in life."[4] Denck's "Confession" (January 1525) contains similar assertions. He declares: "It is not the remission of sins which is the heart of the gospel, but the new life with Christ." It also contains many Erasmian emphases, especially his stress on both the essentially internal and life-transforming nature of faith.[5]

All of this illustrates the existence, or continuance, of a strong ascetic-reform predisposition within both the total movement for reform in the early sixteenth century and among many initial adherents of the Protestant Reformation itself, just prior to the emergence of Anabaptism. While some of these ascetically predisposed Reformers returned to the old church, though usually still as Reformers, others became leaders of various kinds of Protestant alternatives, one of which emerged in 1525 — Anabaptism.

Ascetic Factors in the Formation of the Earliest Anabaptists: The Swiss Brethren

To what extent were ascetic factors involved in the initial estrangement from the Magisterial Reformation of the earliest and most significant Anabaptist leaders? To answer this requires a careful investigation both into the kind of men who constituted the initial leadership of early Anabaptism and into the central issue in their break with Zwingli.

Among those related to the Zwingli Circle. Several of the initial Anabaptist leaders in Zürich[6] came directly out of a larger group of Reformers called the "Zwingli Circle." For several years this "circle" had been associated with Zwingli's reform program at Zürich. Zwingli lists some of the principal personnel, an "inner" circle, in a letter to Myconius in which he urges him also to come and join them at Zürich. He writes: "You will be with Utinger, Engelhart, and Rey, the congenial older men; with Erasmus, Zwingli, and Grossman who are by no means to be despised; and with Grebel, Amman, and Binder, the most excellent and learned younger fellows."[7]

To this substantial list of the inner circle one should add also Andreas Castelburger, Leo Jud, and by the end of 1522, Simon Stumpf and Felix Manz.[8] Though not in the inner circle, there were also several young, aggressive supporters such as Claus Hottinger, Heinrich Aberli, Bartlime Pur, and Wilhelm Reublin. Actually Reublin was quite a late addition, coming to Zürich late in 1522 after he was expelled in June from Basel for his reforming activities there. Thus he was less a direct product of Zwingli's teaching and influence than most of the others.[9] Why several of this number (Grebel, Manz, Stumpf, Castelburger, Aberli, and Reublin) broke away from Zwingli's program to support an alternative one defined principally by Grebel and Manz,[10] is one of the most significant problems in the history of the rise of Anabaptism and most relevant to the problem of origins.

H. S. Bender convincingly demonstrates that before October 1523 there existed no "radical party" in Zürich distinct from the Zwingli group, though some of the latter were somewhat more activist and impatient about reform that either Grebel or Zwingli.[11] In 1522, the Zürich reform movement appeared to be substantially united, but around a broadly defined, and still mostly theoretical, evangelical reform vision which was largely framed and taught to them by Zwingli himself.

The break between Zwingli and some of his closest supporters, led by Grebel, Manz, Castelberger, and Stumpf, involved at least three phases and three issues.[12] The first began with Zwingli's attempt in 1523 to put some of the practical implications of his theoretical program into effect. While, as a result of the "disputation" of January 1523, the City Council had opened Zürich to the preaching of the biblical gospel freely and therefore to the unrestrained presentation of Zwingli's theoretical reform program, it was not until the second "disputation," October 26-29, 1523, that Zwingli attempted to institute some major practical changes in the church's life and practice so as to bring them into conformity with an evangelical-biblical basis.

However, when Zwingli accepted an arbitrary decision by the Council to postpone action on the vital issue of the mass, some thought this indicated a willingness on his part (though he denied it, theoretically and repeatedly) to place even the religious aspects of the reform program under the control of the civil authorities, the City Council. They thought that he should insist that the program be determined only by the Word and the Spirit, that is, by the spiritual leaders who were committed to, students of, and obedient to the Word alone as the Spirit aided them to understand it.[13]

At this point, and on this issue, some of Zwingli's supporters, especially Stumpf and perhaps Grebel, became concerned and, at the disputation, openly objected. This initial concern slowly grew to a conviction that Zwingli was tending to compromise and to depart from his own previous principles.[14] Clearly some of the Zwingli circle understood Zwingli's original program to be opposed to any degree of "worldly" control over either the church's faith or its religious practices. This "control" many held to be substantially responsible for the inability of the church in the fifteenth century to reform itself. Therefore, they insisted on full and immediate obedience to the "known" Word and will of God by all Christians and by the Christian leadership of the new reform.

The "disputation" of October 1523 did not provoke immediately a schism, serious conflict, or even deep tensions within the Zwingli circle; probably due to Zwingli's quick denial of any intent of placing religious issues under temporal authority. Yet it seems that some element of suspicion remained; suspicion that the incident might indicate a weakness in Zwingli to compromise under pressure or even that they may have misunderstood Zwingli's program. It led some of the Zwingli circle eventually to a second and much deeper confrontation with Zwingli to determine more precisely his position and the correctness of their understanding of the nature of his whole reform program. Unity could no longer be assumed. Accordingly, Manz, Stumpf, and Grebel, and probably others, held several conferences with Zwingli, between October 1523 and September 1524, in which they sought reassurances and clarification. Only at this point can one come to grips with the real issues at the heart of the resultant schism and the emergence of the Swiss Brethren.[15]

Three highly significant problems directly related to this study relate to these conferences: What was the program expected by this considerable portion of uneasy personnel from Zwingli's intimate circle of supporters? How close were the Grebel group's expectations, enunciated in their program, to Zwingli's own position prior to 1523? What ascetic ideals and influences are contained in and how important are these to the formulation of the Grebel program?

No Anabaptist source has preserved explicitly the initial reform expectations of the Grebel group. However, there are some allusions to these expectations in the letters and writings of some members of the group, in the records of the Zwinglian reformation of the later disputations with the Anabaptists and of their testimonials at their trials, and in three accounts of Anabaptist origins in Zürich contained in Zwingli's polemical writings against them.[16]

The most explicit reference is in an undated disposition, probably late 1525 or early 1526, by Zwingli in which he refers back to several conferences with some of his associates in the months after the October 1523 disputation. In these, they tried to ascertain more clearly Zwingli's reform views and to win his support for their particular reform program. He testifies that Simon Stumpf of Höngy, Conrad Grebel, and Felix Manz had each come to him separately, and more than once, proposing that he set up a separatist church which should live *"aller unschuldigsten"* (most piously).[17]

"Separatist" was not necessarily understood initially as the separation of the church from the state to create the "secular" state but only a distinguishing of pious from impious or true Christians from false — it did not necessarily imply, at first, either that the pious church would be a minority or that it would not be directly involved in civil government; in fact, as we shall see, they initially expected the opposite. But, apparently without prior collusion (Zwingli reports they began only then to coalesce as a group by holding night meetings at the home of Manz's mother) substantially similar expectations concerning the ascetic nature of the reformed church already existed.

Concerning the content of these private discussions, Zwingli reports more fully (in a testimonial report):

> At a certain time Felix Manz came to him in front of Huyuff's shop and engaged in conversation with him again on the subject of the church and said that nobody ought to be in this same church except those who knew themselves to be without sin. And when Zwingli asked him about this point, whether he considered himself to be one of those, Manz did not give him any real answer.[18]

Zwingli also reports another discussion with Manz, again on the theme of the church ("von ein Christen volck"), but this time Zwingli endeavored to counter the pressure with a compromising and all-encompassing idea:

Ascetic Factors in Emerging Anabaptism 71

> Master Ulrich [Zwingli] asked whether one could not also secretly and by himself be a [true?] Christian. Then Manz gave M. Ulrich answer to this, saying, "No, for Christianity and brotherly love must be expressed publicly one to the other and cannot be secret [a private matter?]." Manz then pointed out how Paul wrote about it, designating that fornication, covetousness, adultery, and such like should not be tolerated among Christians and that Zwingli should announce and point out such things. Then M. Ulrich answered that Manz should do this himself and put out of the church those who had such vices in them. Thereupon Manz replied that it was not fitting for him that he ought to do such things since he was not a bishop like M. Ulrich.[19]

Here, Manz, is again advocating church reform in which open separation of true from false Christians, *in terms of standards of conduct*, is the dominant factor. Although Zwingli repeatedly exaggerated their position, to that of desire for an absolute perfectionism,[20] nevertheless, it is apparent that a concern for some relative kind of perfectionism, manifest holiness, or moral separation is in fact the central issue; not church-state separation, directly.

Zwingli's *Elenchus*, published later, contains another description of the 1524 expectations of the Brethren, and more details on the method by which they hoped to fulfill them, as follows:

> It does not escape us that there will ever be those who oppose the gospel, even among those who boast in the name of Christ. We therefore can never hope that all minds will so unite as Christians should find it possible to live. For in the Acts of the Apostles those who had believed seceded from the others, and then it happened that they who came to believe went over to those who were now a new church. So then must we do: they [the Manz-Grebel group] beg that we make a deliverance [statement] to this effect — they who wish to follow Christ should stand on our side. They promise also that our forces shall be far superior [numerically?] to the army of the unbelieving.[21]

Zwingli rejected this appeal on a biblical basis by interpreting the parable of the tares so as to support the inclusive church concept in its broadest sense, on the basis of expediency, or that "secession would cause confusion" and detrimental dissension, on the basis of its novelty, that no exact parallel existed to the situation in the Book of Acts, and finally on the basis of gradualness, that he expected something similar to result by the gradual influence of the proclaimed Word and thereby "without disorder."[22] Zwingli also implies that the dissensions and conflicts which centred around baptism were a later development.[23]

The *Elenchus* also reasserts that conduct and the application of the ban (that is, discipline, or, as Grebel termed it, "the rule of Christ") was the central issue; that Grebel's group wanted to "at once shut out from the church him who committed any wrong" (Zwingli fails, in his exaggeration, to add — if they refuse to repent and then to conform). Similarly, as the passage implies, these dissident Reformers were referring specifically to *disciplinary* measures when Zwingli, in exaggeration, accuses them of "asserting that they were without sin."[24] A doctrinal difference over absolute "sinless perfection" was not the issue at all.

Zwingli summarizes the reasons for his opposition as:

1. "They had attempted a division and partition of the church, and this was just as hypocritical as the superstition of the monks."[25] Zwingli discerns a parallel with monasticism, though putting it in the worst possible light.

2. While debate had been going on generally regarding the validity of infant baptism, Zwingli asserts that the Grebel group eventually went further than just a denial of infant baptism and had established "rebaptism," on their own.

3. They had become publicly critical, charging both ministers of state and church with vices; and some of their number, claiming charismatic authority, had "prophesied, as they call it, in the marketplace and squares" against the established clergy.

4. Finally, writes Zwingli, they rejected the Old Testament as equal with the New Testament as a basis for faith and practice. This last point becomes apparent only in the debates over baptism (after January 1525) and may well be a result rather than an initial cause of difference between the Swiss Brethren and Zwingli.

Grebel's publications, especially his correspondence, provide most of the information from within the Grebel group concerning the content and development of its ascetic reform expectations before 1524. On January 30, 1522, Grebel mentions forwarding some works of Tertullian to Vadian of St. Gall, and jestingly adds: "Take heed now that I make not a Tertullianus out of yourself.[26] This approving familiarity with Tertullian, an early third-century Montanist spokesman who stressed "a radical act of conversion" and expressed strong ascetic, moralistic, and charismatic sentiments, may indicate some influential significance by him in developing Grebel's predisposition to asceticism, though it is impossible to measure the degree.[27] However, in another letter to Vadian, Grebel also expresses anti-institutional and anti-ceremonial sentiments. He makes clear that he is in no sense sympathetic to institutional monasticism and he calls the Dominican order "a sect of perdition."[28] Also, Zwingli allowed Grebel to publish a poem, at the conclusion of his *Apologeticus Archeteles* (August 23, 1522), which expresses Grebel's expectations for a widespread, Gospel-initiated restoration of the true church in place of the corrupt, oppressive, and superstitious church of the bishops.[29]

Again, Grebel expresses to Vadian his concern for his mother with these words: "I fear for her salvation, unless she puts on Christ and becomes a new creature born again by the divine Spirit."[30] Something more than a forensic justification is indicated. Moreover, when this statement is considered in the context of his concern for her unforgiving attitude, it is clear that he was relating closely salvation to conduct. The true, regenerate Christian is discernible by a change in conduct.

Benedict Burgauer, a cleric of St. Gall who considered himself a moderate evangelical, was much criticized by Grebel and therefore is not generally representative of early Grebelian thought. But his letter to Grebel indicates the existence quite early (and by other Zwinglian supporters than the Grebel group) of concern about some of the interpretations of *sola fides*. On one point, he echoes later Anabaptist concern; that is, Burgauer asserts his opposition to the teaching that "we ought not to be diligently active in effort, nor work meritoriously in the vineyard of the Lord, for thus the suffering of Christ is superfluous, because the mortification of the body and [the striving to live] a life very similar to Christ's, is disbelief."[31]

As a final illustration of ascetic predispositions, Grebel, while waiting for the planned public disputation on baptism on January 1525, wrote to Vadian:

> For this cause may God grant us His perfect mercy that we may obey, that you may submit to the Word without condition and also obey the same. Otherwise it is quite to be feared that matters [concerning personal salvation?] stand not so well as

74   Anabaptism and Asceticism

we may falsely comfort ourselves. Narrow is the way; many things hinder the entrance thereon.[32]

He also closes with a greeting to the "beginners in the Word of God and the godly life." Clearly, Grebel is expressing the exclusiveness of the church (or better, a more restricted concept than the Magisterical Reformers of what constitutes "being a Christian person"); also the necessity of obedience to the Word as evidence of a true salvation and of entrance to the "Way." But there is no explicit rejection of the theory of the "unitary society," at this stage, except for the recognition that not all of sixteenth-century European society was Christian.

The main topic for the public disputation with the newly formed "Swiss Brethren" at Zürich on January 17, 1525, now was infant baptism. This did not mean a change of issue; rather, by then, and uniquely, the Brethren had tied their understanding of baptism into their ascetic definition of the church. Consequently, their interpretation of "baptism" also adds light to our understanding of the earlier (1523-1524) "reform-program" promoted by Grebel and Manz. For example, the first Anabaptist writing on baptism, the Manz "Protestation" (probably written late in 1524), asserts that the proper candidates for baptism are "only those . . . who reform themselves, begin a new life, lay aside their vices [die sich besseren, ein neu leben an sich nemend, den lasteren absterbend], are buried with Christ, and rise with Him out of their baptism into newness of life."[33] They also identify their baptism in part with God's sending of John the Baptist to call people to an awareness of their sins and

> to forsake them and reform [sich bessertend], for the ax is laid at the root of the tree and everyone who shall not bring forth good fruit will be cut down and cast into the fire. To those who wished to reform, he showed the Lamb of God that taketh away the sin of the world and baptized them. . . .[34]

Further, the "Protestation" contends that the apostles taught that "forgiveness of sins in Christ's name should be given to everyone who, believing on His name, should *do righteous works from a changed heart.*"[35] Again, it adds, that therefore baptism signified "inner cleansing and dying to sin."[36] Similarly, Bullinger notes this ethical content; writing that Manz, Grebel, and Reublin maintained that "baptism should be administered to those *wanting to mortify the* old Adam and live a new life."[37] The most precise interpretation tying together baptism and the ascetic separation of the church comes from the *Hutterite Chronicle*, which says of Manz, Grebel, and Blaurock:

> . . . they recognized that a person must learn from the divine Word and preaching *a true faith which manifests itself* in love, and receive the true Christian baptism on the basis of the recognized and confessed faith, in the union with God of a good conscience, [prepared] henceforth to serve God *in a holy Christian life with all godliness,* also to be steadfast to the end in tribulation. . . . *Therewith began the separation from the world and its evil works.*[38]

Clearly, their whole concept of baptism had become tied to *the principle of separation,* of creating a purified church of holy living Christians. Baptism became the most significant vehicle for their ascetic, moral-spiritual reform program.

In his last letter to the Brethren, written while awaiting execution, Manz maintains the view that the true church is perceivable on ascetic terms by insisting that the Savior came as "an example and a light"; in contrast, "false prophets and hypocrites . . . who with the same mouth curse and pray, whose life is disorderly [or improper] . . . destroy the essence of Christ."[39] But, he adds, "The sheep of Christ seek the honor of God . . . and allow themselves to be kept from it neither by possession nor temporal wealth."[40] Furthermore,

> . . . the lord Christ *compels no one* to His glory; but only those who are *willing and ready* reach it through true faith and baptism. When a man works the proper fruits of repentance, then heaven with eternal joy is purchased for him out of grace through Christ, and is won by . . . His blood . . . therewith He shows us His love and imparts to us the strength of His Spirit. *And he who receives and exercises the same grows and becomes perfect in God.*[41]

Finally, "He who cannot show love, finds no room with God." And, "Those who are hateful and envious cannot be Christians."[42]

Concerning Manz' advocacy of a separated church which was clearly visible by the conduct of its members, Krajewski comments:

> There is not in Manz a perfectionism which maintains a full sinlessness of the true Christian, but rather his viewpoint is that the Christian manifests himself by faith and works of love and he would use congregational discipline against especially coarse sins. Faith must be worked out in behavior also. Faith, which in general brings forth no fruit, is dead.[43]

The "perfectionism" label that Krajewski finds necessary to deny was unfortunately and insincerely suggested first by Zwingli, but its continuation to the present is perhaps a case of reading back subsequent theological issues: a procedure which seriously distorts the sixteenth-century situation.

It would seem that what Manz demands, and Zwingli objects to comes very close to the old idea of an ascetic conversion and a commitment to ascetic idealism with its concept of perfectibility or relative perfectionism. It is almost the equivalent of what was sometimes referred to as the first stage in renunciation. Only now it is required of all true Christians and not just a few elite souls, the monks.

In the fall of 1524, as it became clear that Zwingli was rejecting this ascetic expectation of reform, a disappointed group of not quite twenty reform leaders consolidated around Grebel and Manz and began to look abroad for others who might support or promote their program. Letters were sent to Carlstadt, Luther and Müntzer explaining their break with Zwingli and their understanding of Reformation. Unfortunately, the only letters which survive are one to Müntzer (which apparently was never delivered) and a reply to Grebel partly on Luther's behalf from Erhard Hegenwald in Wittenberg. These two letters contain some further indication of the nature of the group's program and understanding of reform as of the fall of 1524.

Grebel's letter to Thomas Müntzer, September 5, 1524,[44] on behalf of the Brethren, makes it clear in the opening paragraph that there was little direct contact with Müntzer's thought except that they were attracted by what they read in his two tracts, probably his *Protestation oder Empietung* (1524) and *Von dem getlichten Glauben* (1524), on the subject of fictitious faith.[45] Grebel's main concern is clearly centred on his conviction that the evangelical preachers (or the Magisterial Reformers) were proclaiming a "superficial faith, without fruits of faith, without a baptism of test and probation, without love and hope, without right Christian practices.

..." He also expresses concern for "the destruction of all godly life" and accuses the Magisterial Reformers of preaching "a sinful sweet Christ" (a "Müntzer" expression of moral concern). Much of the blame for these errors he ascribes to "antichristian caution," and a "false caution, the hiding of the divine Word, and the mixing of it with the human."

Grebel proceeds to illustrate by listing twenty-five points which, in contrast, he and his associates considered correct practice regarding the Lord's Supper. Two of these points are especially significant for this study: 1. He objects to any procedures that would "create a faith consisting in mere outward seeming" or create "an external reverence . . . and a turning away from the internal." Even external conformity to ascetic norms of conduct must be a reflection of internal reality to be valid. 2. He also requires that the Lord's Supper be closely associated with the ban. He insists that the Supper "is not to be administered without the rule of Christ in Matthew 18 . . . for without that rule every man will run after externals, and the inner matter, love [brotherly?] will be passed by. . . ." Here again his concern for the separated, disciplined church colors all other issues. If the true church is to be restored, it must be composed only of people who outwardly and voluntarily demonstrate the reality of their personal commitment and inner change. This church is not absolutely "pure," for the outward is still possible without the inward, but Grebel totally rejects any possibility of inner reality without external manifestation in terms of conduct. The intentionally impious and disobedient cannot possess true faith just by fulfilling the rites of the church. Grebel distinguishes between external ceremonialism which indicates nothing and external virtues which probably show true inner faith. At the end of the first section he reiterates this central point: "Attack (*züch*) with the Word and establish a Christian congregation with the help of Christ and His rule, as we find it instituted in Matthew 18 and applied in the Epistles."[46]

The second section of this letter to Müntzer, about baptism, is also consistent with previous testimony. He writes:

> The Scripture describes baptism thus, that it signifies the washing away of sins by faith and the blood of Christ (to him that is baptized, changes his mind, and believes before and after it); that it signifies that a man is dead and ought to be dead to sin

and walks in newness of life and spirit, and that he shall certainly be saved if by the inner baptism *he lives his faith* according to this significance...."[47]

The letter of Erhard Hegenwald to Grebel, January 1, 1525[18] follows an earlier exchange of letters which are now lost; therefore some of its allusions are vague. Before he went from Zürich to Wittenberg to study, Hegenwald was well acquainted with Grebel. For example, he edited the minutes of the January 1523 Zürich "Disputation" and apparently, at some time thereabout, influenced Grebel not to write a sharply critical letter to the preachers and doctor (Vadian) of St. Gall.[49]

Three issues in this letter of Hegenwald's support the argument for the importance of the ascetic factor in the dissent of the Grebel group: Grebel's letter had accused Hegenwald of attacking his insistence on "spirit, life, and work as *witnesses of faith.*" Apparently Grebel had asserted this as a basic necessity in an earlier letter. In reply, Hegenwald denies intending any such attack (*"mein ouch nit, dass ich das thun hab, so fern mir ze wissen ist"*) and suggests, rather, that he intended only to warn that one needs to be humble and cautious, for it is easy to be convinced that one is doing God's will and instead be deceived, deluded, and self-willed. He writes: "Man does many things to please himself, and which seem reasonable, right, and godly to him, but are really somewhat counter to the will, knowledge, and fear of God." He continues, ". . . this shameless hypocrisy that I call godlessness lies so secretly and deeply concealed in the heart of men that no man can recognize it properly in himself. . . ." Hegenwald's gentle reaction is still a pointed counterattack, based on the reassertion of Luther's doctrine of total depravity, and implying the need to uphold forensic justification. Then there follows three more full pages of much less subtle warning to Grebel about the personal dangers of spiritual pride.

The second relevant matter is that Hegenwald clearly implies that Grebel, in his letter, had attacked any toleration of obvious vices within the church. Hegenwald, apparently quoting Grebel, writes: "I do not call 'avoiding the externally wicked life,' walking without the appearance of ungodliness" (*On scheyn der gotlossheit wandeln heyss ich nit dass ässerlich böss leben myden*); but rather, "Piety, I call the knowledge of God which stands in Jesus Christ whom the Father commands us to hear" (*Pietatem heyss ich die erkantnuss*

Ascetic Factors in Emerging Anabaptism 79

gottes, welche stat in Christo Jesu, den der vater gibit zu hören). Again Hegenwald sounds very Lutheran; piety is more a matter of knowing than doing! He adds, "Paul also boasted that he knew nothing except Jesus Christ and him crucified" — Hegenwald seems to be implying that Grebel's theology tended to weaken the effectiveness and sufficiency of Christ's sacrifice imputed freely to the believer. This charge was also made by Zwingli in the *Elenchus*, two years later.[50]

Third, in reply to some assertion by Grebel about the Lord's Supper, Hegenwald makes the following significant warning against possible external legalism or pharisaism (especially significant because of the date and because it comes from a friend):

> But I say this, as soon as you want to hang Christ on any kind of external thing and insist that salvation must stand in works (faith excepted) and not otherwise (since Christ and the kingdom of heaven of which He is head in a concealed mystery, as Paul says), then you make out of Him a Moses.[51]

Clearly the objection behind all of these replies is to the apparent insistence by Grebel and his associates that the church membership be restricted exclusively to those who demonstrate *outwardly* the fruits of repentance and a manifest holiness, which they define in specifically ascetic terms.[52]

One must conclude from the evidence that the Grebel group's program of 1524 was a call for action to ensure the separation of the obviously ungodly from the outwardly godly and thus to restore the moral purity of the life of the church and the church's "image" and witness to the world. They wanted reformed churches that inwardly *and outwardly* coincided with the plain message and example of Christ. This meant a strict conformity to Scripture, as illuminated to the pious by the Holy Spirit.

The ascetic objectives of this reformation had several specific consequences. Henceforth congregations should be composed only of voluntary, sincere Christian believers who demonstrate their sincerity by Christian behavior; by continuously, outwardly exhibiting a new life of righteousness and holiness which was specifically and ascetically understood to mean the abandonment both of serious vices such as drunkenness and fornication and a worldly, disobedient spirit. After January 1525, they expected all true believers to demonstrate their submissiveness to the will of God by voluntary participation in a believer's baptism. Following the ascetic pattern the church becomes also a brotherhood of Christian love which must manifest itself in a willingness to share goods or hold possessions in common trust[53] and to abandon benefices,[54] compulsory tithing, and usury.

To preserve the whole program, the church must exercise strong congregational discipline over the morality and external spiritual life of its members, a discipline exclusively by the brotherhood, not involving the state. The means is exclusively the use of the ban, that is, of excommunication, according to the rule of Christ (Matthew 18). Apparently, at first, the Grebel group thought that this restored, apostolic church could cooperate, even integrate with civil government if such was composed of "true" Christians and set up by the church.[55] Later this idea was dropped owing to their failure at Zürich and perhaps to further study,[56] though it was never entirely abandoned by Hubmaier because of his successes in gaining governmental cooperation at Waldshut and Nicolsburg.

Grebel's letters to Vadian, December 15, 1523, and September 3, 1524, and the correspondence with Müntzer and Hegenwald indicate that for almost a year the Grebel group had tried to win Zwingli's support. Their proposals were apparently not rejected outright or immediately. But by September 1524, they conceded failure and designated Zwingli as one who, just as those in the Roman Church, was guilty of "the mixing of the divine Word with the human."[57] Zwingli two years later, on recalling the ascetic nature of their program, retaliated by charging the Grebel group with "self-righteousness and pharisaism, and that this was the basis on which they had withdrawn from the general church and the general society."[58]

What Zwingli and most of the early Reformers had thought was impossible had happened — division! Even while agreeing on the sole authority of Scripture, evangelical believers were disagreeing, openly now, about its interpretation and implementation. Once differences emerged over the nature of the reform which each expected (the reasons for which this study is probing), these led to a further development, out of the ensuing controversies, of differences in hermeneutics and to mutual intolerance and schism.

Along with the initial appearance of disagreement in the Zwingli circle, October 1523, and with the subsequent "conferences" between the Grebel group and Zwingli in 1524, a third issue, which encouraged defection and also relates to the formation of Anabaptism,

Ascetic Factors in Emerging Anabaptism 81

arose gradually during 1524 in the villages of Wytikon and Zollikon just outside Zürich. Some people, heeding the teaching and preaching of Reublin and Brötli, refused to baptize their newborn infants. Nevertheless, this initial rejection of infant baptism must not be overstressed. There is no evidence that it was an issue or even included at all in the original Grebel group's reform program.[59] Though Grebel's interest in the subject develops quickly, in the fall of 1524, as is evidenced by clear reference to it in the letter to Müntzer and the one from Hegenwald, and by his reading with approval Carlstadt's booklet on the matter in October 1524, these first intimations of his rejection of infant baptism give no indication that he had formulated as yet any alternative doctrine of believer's baptism. At this juncture his position of baptism was not essentially anti-Zwinglian. To reject infant baptism did *not* make one an Anabaptist, not in 1524.[60]

Nevertheless, infant versus believer's baptism, if baptism is also ascetically defined, provided the Grebel group with an ideal issue whereby it could make one more concerted effort to gain official adoption of their whole program. Zwingli fully recognized that the issue of baptism as subsequently and uniquely developed by the Anabaptists had taken on new and larger implications. For this reason he comments: "If infant baptism should be overthrown, then it would be fitting to introduce adult baptism and *with this rebaptism they would be able to establish their church.*"[61]

In the late fall of 1524, the City Council held a number of public and private discussions with concerned parents and some of the Grebel group. Out of these talks came the scheduling by the City Council of a major disputation for Tuesday, January 17, 1525, and also the composition of the "Protestation and Schutzschrift," a positive presentation of believer's baptism as the symbol of ascetic reform, by Felix Manz.[62]

By the time Grebel wrote to Vadian, December 15, 1524, the issues were clear and definite for Grebel too; he was able to view the situation realistically, to recognize the extent of the deviation in their program and goals from those of Zwingli, and to anticipate, resolutely, future persecution. The outcome of the disputation of January 17, 1525, verified Grebel's pessimistic analysis of the trends. Zwingli and the Zürich council officially retained infant baptism; but even worse, they instituted civil coercion to end any further promotion of the Grebel group's program. The result was open schism. On January 21,

1525, by rebaptizing themselves, the Grebel group became an organized separatist movement. The first modern free church, that of the "Anabaptists" or the "Swiss Brethren," was born.[63]

From this point, the Swiss Anabaptists began to preach and practice that only "believer's baptism" was valid. But what did it signify? Was the interpretation and presentation of biblical baptism consistent with their earlier reform program and even colored by it? The answer is positive on all points. Ascetic behavior as the necessary and prior evidence of true faith is dominant.

Bender describes their practice of baptism, after January 21, 1525, as "the symbol of the washing of repentance and putting off sin, the outward sign of the decisive entrance into a new and holy life."[64] Jacob Hottinger's description to the Zürich court confirms this judgment.[65] Again, in April 1525, Arbogast Finsterbach, of Oberwinterthur, asked Grebel what one had to do to be baptized. Grebel answered, "One must first give up fornication, gambling, drinking, and usury."[66] Grebel's teaching, while at Grüningen, is probably reflected in the *Grüninger Eingabe* of June 1527, which says: "Let everyone notice that baptism belongs to those believers who devote themselves to the Son of God and separate themselves from evil."[67] It adds concerning the "fruit of the Spirit," believers "who walk therein, *they* are the church of Christ and the body of Christ and the Christian church."[68]

In summary, the most distinctive issue in the Grebel group's program was not, initially, infant versus believer's baptism; that was only a later and a deeply significant vehicle for expressing a much deeper issue. Neither, at first, was the primary issue state-church versus free church (or, in Verduin's ponderous terms, sacralism versus compositism); though, in October 1523, the threat of a restored "temporal" control over the church did generate some initial suspicion concerning Zwingli's intentions. But the subsequent events, of 1523 and 1524, clearly indicate that the Grebel group still hoped for a sufficiently widespread acceptance of the "true" reform to permit their initial program to include close church-state relationships by means of a "Christian" senate.

The real essence of their protest centered on the nature of the whole sixteenth-century reform movement itself and on the effects anticipated. The dominant ideals and expectations for reform that motivated the Grebel group and those who, after January 21, 1525, evolved into the Anabaptist "Swiss Brethren" (and numerous others who though somewhat sympathetic to the Grebel group were unprepared to follow through to schism) are clearly ascetic. These ascetic ideals reflect strongly the spirit and aspirations of the late fifteenth-century Reformers.

Three expectations by these first Anabaptists concerning reform stand out: 1. They expected that any reformation that was truly divinely inspired would promote unquestioning obedience to the Word of God, without any compromise with existing institutions or traditions. 2. They expected and demanded a visible separation on moral grounds of church from nonchurch, the end of a morally mixed society called Christian but obviously not truly Christian. Also, they believed in the church as a *spiritual* entity, to be spiritually governed, with spiritual purposes. This is what led to the secondary notion that in its functional manifestation as churches it must be separated institutionally from "worldly" control whether papal or civil. 3. They expected the restoration of visible churches in which a spiritually vital and an ascetically holy Christian life would typify all members, individually and corporately.[69] The Anabaptist's concern for scriptural authority substantially accords with Zwingli's, but what of the ascetic expectations? This question raises the issue of Zwingli's role in the emergence of Anabaptism.

Zwingli: a reluctant progenitor of Anabaptism? From where did the Swiss Anabaptists derive their reform program? Many, especially Mennonite historians, suggest that it was latent in Zwingli's own original program. But was Zwingli's program, before 1523, really a latent Anabaptism? Was it in the ascetic tradition? Did he subsequently deviate, leaving the Anabaptists to carry on alone?

Certainly the Grebel group thought he deviated, and repeatedly accused him, in 1524 and 1525, of abandoning his former goals. On one obvious item, his initial rejection of the practice of infant baptism, Zwingli admits to reversing himself,[70] but the solution is less simple since to him this represented only a secondary matter. Zwingli maintained that his reversal was really consistent, that he was actually holding firmly to his original principle of the insignificance of the external sacraments. Believer's baptism had become totally unacceptable because of the interpretation put on it by the Anabaptists. He considered that his reversal was necessary for consistency. Therefore the solution requires a deeper inquiry. Did Zwingli substantially revise any major principles, especially relating to the nature of the "new" church, sufficiently to account for the schism in the Zwingli circle?

In a letter from Zwingli to Erasmus Fabricius (concerning Zwingli's defense before the Zürich senate at the visit of an episcopal delegation, April 7-9, 1522) several aspects in Zwingli's developing program emerge which are consistent with the later Zwingli and are not Anabaptist.[71] He objects to the church levying, contrary to the teachings of Peter and the New Testament, a heavier burden of prescriptions and ceremonials on its members than did the Old Testament on Israel. He therefore urges that many, such as the excessive number of prescribed fastings, should be abandoned. Nevertheless, lenten fastings were approved if done voluntarily. Then he reports: "I denied, however, that I was of the opinion that *no human prescriptions at all* ought to be kept or enacted."[72] This is not a Swiss Anabaptist sentiment even though he acknowledged that the sacred writings, as "the truth of heaven" were *above* human traditions and corrected them.[73]

He also insisted that a decrease in prescribed ecclesiastical ceremonies did not involve any decrease in respect for civil laws; that Christianity was an "instrument for the preservation of justice in general."[74] His faith in the power and norm of the gospel was overwhelming, so much so that he insisted that the gospel itself apart from ceremonials, legislation, or discipline could lead even the common people to all necessary truth. Further, and most significantly for our study, he adds: "They can believe; therefore they can also understand. Whatever takes place here is done by the inspiration of God...."[75]

Zwingli agrees that there is no salvation outside the church but denies that this "church" meant *any* institutional or visible structure, rather it encompassed all who confess Christ and believe in their hearts that God has raised him from the dead.[76] This understanding of the church does not call for the administration of ascetic tests by a close-knit community.

The lack of detailed explanations of many issues at this early stage, plus the human tendency to hear only what agrees with one's own strong predispositions, made it possible for some to interpret Zwingli's early program as more of an embryonic Anabaptism than it really was, to overlook the modifying remark, for example, that human prescriptions, though they cannot be above or contrary to Scripture, can otherwise be enacted. Similarly, while his internalizing and spiritualizing of the church seems Anabaptist, as far as it goes, it says nothing of what he anticipated to be the proper expression and organization of the visible church. In the same way many parts of this reform program can be extended to oppose the Anabaptist position as readily as to imply or foreshadow it.

Zwingli's "Warning to Schwyz Against Control by Foreign Lands" (May 16, 1522) provides similar examples. It condemns mercenary soldiering, war for power, greed, and gain[77] and to a degree the principle of war itself[78] *but* also it defends a just war, especially "for independence," and resistance against "insolent aristocracy."[79] Moreover Zwingli utilizes the Old Testament extensively and directly as the basis for his arguments. Thus this work does not really support the predominant Anabaptist position of total pacifism nor their insistence on the primacy of the New Testament.

In July 1522, Zwingli (and ten other preachers) wrote to the Bishop of Constance urging him to grant permission for priests to marry.[80] The underlying concern of the petition was not for a relaxation of moral ideals but the opposite, for improvement in holy living. They wanted to abrogate legislated celibacy for priests and monks, which led to rampant, tolerated, and hypocritical concubinage. In the light of greater awareness of the ethics of the gospel, they now believed that the expediency of concubinage was even more morally unacceptable than marriage. He writes:

> We are aware that our life differs all too widely from the pattern of the gospel, but is the gospel on that account to be abolished or done away with? Ought we not rather to devote ourselves vigorously to correcting our faults according to its standards? . . .[81]

Zwingli was still willing, however, to grant a superior glory or virtue to chastity, whenever such was possible.[82] From this, it is apparent that the whole Zwingli circle then shared in a heightening of ethical sensitivity owing to the impact of the gospel message and in a concern for the correction of conduct by the gospel; but later even this concern is shown to lack the priority of importance and degree of intensity of the Swiss Brethren.

Zwingli's *Archetelas*, or "Reply to the Bishop's Admonition," written in August 22-23, 1522,[83] must have been very well known to Grebel since Zwingli permitted him to append a poem to it. Even in this work Zwingli's position is not exactly Anabaptist. He insists that Scripture, as the "Words of God" through Christ, "the light

86   Anabaptism and Asceticism

of the world," is the only final authority, even over the views of the earliest church fathers and all human traditions. He adds: "Nay, if any set of men taught their own notions that . . . were quite inconsistent with the divine, I flung this saying of the apostle at them, 'We ought to obey God rather than men [Acts 5:29]'. . . ."[84] This is almost an exact replica of numerous, later Anabaptist assertions.

A closer examination shows, however, that Zwingli repeatedly makes clear that scriptural authority meant for him *both* the Old and New Testaments on an equal basis. He refers to them as "the two swords" given by Christ to His disciples.[85] Again there is no indication of the later and distinctively Anabaptist stress on the superior authority of the New Testament over the Old Testament by itself.

Zwingli also expresses again his belief that unity and agreement on reform would be the natural product of accepting the norm of Scripture. He had great confidence in the basic piety and spiritual capabilities of the common people. He writes:

> The common people, endowed with the harmlessness of the dove, will yield to the gospel alone; and the less they are vitiated with the dregs of human traditions, the more capable they are of receiving the heavenly teachings. . . . They are the really spiritual, for they depend wholly upon the spirit — that is the mind of God.[86]

Again:

> Scriptures can be compared together [interpreted] not only by those whose concern you say it is but also by those who trust in God and in His Word and who are pining with longing for Him.[87]

In addition, specifically in answer to the question of how to reconcile possible variances in interpretation, he insists, as did the Anabaptists, that the expected unity of interpretation and response required a pious attitude to Scripture.

> Do you not see that the Spirit of God is everywhere like unto itself and ever the same? The more unskilled a man is in human devices and at the same time devoted to the divine, the more clearly that Spirit informs him. . . . And as it is a Spirit of unity

Ascetic Factors in Emerging Anabaptism 87

and harmony and peace . . . it will inspire even the most ignorant, if they are pious, in such manner that they will understand the Scriptures in the plainest way according to God's purpose.[88]

There is, however, no place in Zwingli nor any instruments for dividing between "true" and "professing" Christians, except the direct action of the Word and the Spirit. The separatist principles in the Grebel program were not consistent with his perspective. Moreover, it is precisely the belief in unity, and the confidence in the willingness of the people to respond, that led to intolerance. Neither side could anticipate a legitimate, honest difference of opinion by the truly pious arising from their use of the "authoritative" Scriptures.

Zwingli expressly asserted that the gospel was the sole agency for the reform of a "wounded" church. Therefore, he noted that for three years he had concentrated on simply expounding Scripture, and in this order: Matthew (centering on Christ), Acts (the spread of the gospel), 1 Timothy (on Christian character), Galatians, 2 Timothy, 1 and 2 Peter, Hebrews (Christ as sole High Priest). He concludes: "This is the seed I have sown, Matthew, Luke, Paul, and Peter have watered it, and God has given it splendid increase."[89]

At the same time, he adds to the possibility of misunderstanding by also stating that human institutions must not conflict with Scripture. He writes:

> Therefore we ought to be constantly on our guard lest something be set up sometime that does not exactly square with the heavenly truth, which presents itself so simply that it can be easily grasped. . . .[90]

Yet, even this statement does not go as far as Grebel's position, in his letter to Müntzer, that one must abolish all that "one does not find in the exact words of Scripture."[91]

In reply to the bishop's contention that Zwingli's program was a threat to the political order, Zwingli gives the following summary of the nature of the Christian society which he envisaged:

> But that Christianity which I advocate is adapted to all cities, obeys the laws and the magistrates of the nation, pays taxes to whom taxes are due, tribute to whom tribute is due, rates to

88 Anabaptism and Asceticism

> whom rates are due. Under it no one calls any possession his own, all things are held to be in common; every one is eager to outdo his neighbor in kindness, to exercise all gentleness, to share his neighbor's burden, and relieve his need. For he regards all men as brothers, abhors blasphemy, embraces piety and helps it to grow among all.[92]

On one hand, this is very close to several elements of the early Grebel program; but on the other, it provides no indication of how Zwingli intended to establish this society. Nor does it imply the Anabaptist position that if the society as a whole fails to respond and submit voluntarily, then the true Christian community must act independently and function according to these ideals. The Anabaptists imply that the church is not necessarily coextensive with society at large. Its purity of life is of greater importance than the unity of society. Zwingli is not suggesting any such schismatic notions; rather, quite the opposite.

There are also strong intimations of Zwingli's basic position on the inclusive nature of the church in his policy of gradual reform. This policy comes out in reference to the presbyters, specifically: "Though I abominate them that are given up to their bellies, yet I forbear and suffer the weeds to grow up with the grain."[93] Again:

> Hundreds of times I have said openly: "I beseech you by Jesus Christ, by our common faith, not to make any change rashly, but to show to all men by your endurements, if in no other way, that you are Christians, in that, on account of the weak brethren, you bear things that by Christ's law you do not need to bear.[94]

There is some similarity to the Anabaptist position in Zwingli's stress on practical repentance. He asks: "Do I not teach long and great penitence, when I am continually crying: '*Metanoeite!*' [repent], 'Go and sell all that thou hast, and give to the poor' (Mt. 19:21) and 'Give alms, and all things shall be pure unto you' (Lk. 11:41)?"[95] But, even this emphasis must be balanced by Zwingli's very Lutheran-sounding insistence that ". . . Christ won the church by His own blood. For it is the formula for salvation. Whoever therefore confidently believes it, belongs to that church of Christ which He won by His blood. For faith alone is the ground of salvation."[96]

Issued just prior to the first Zürich "Disputation" (January 29, 1523), and included in that account, are Zwingli's "Sixty-Seven Arti-

Ascetic Factors in Emerging Anabaptism 89

cles."⁹⁷ Mostly, they only buttress what has already been demonstrated. For example, articles I and V reassert the independent validity and exclusive authority of the gospel; article II insists that the essence of the gospel is in the sacrifice of Christ; articles XIII to XV repeat Zwingli's expectation that the gospel, if made the norm, would work out its own program and effects, and agreement would gradually come to and typify the faithful; and articles III, XVII to XIX, XXI, XXII stress the all-sufficiency of Christ alone.

Two articles, however, more clearly foreshadow the later conflict. Article XXII states: "That Christ is our justice, from which follows that our works in so far as they are good, so far they are of Christ; but in so far as they are ours, they are neither right nor good." And, article LIV adds: "Christ has borne all our pains and labor. Hence whoever assigns to works of penance what belongs to Christ errs and slanders God." These two articles indicate that Zwingli held already a strong, "Lutheran" view of "imputed" righteousness. This doctrine is the basis for Hegenwald's later criticism of Grebel's position, and Zwingli himself also uses it later against Anabaptism.

Finally, in the "Disputation" itself (January 1523), there is further clarification of two important points in Zwingli's original position. First, concerning the nature of the church, Zwingli clearly stresses its noninstitutional aspects (in contrast to officialdom):

> But there is another church which the popes do not wish to recognize; this one is no other than all right Christians, collected in the name of the Holy Ghost and by the will of God. . . . That church . . . depends and rests only upon the Word and will of God. . . . That church cannot err. . . . That is the right church, the spotless bride of Jesus Christ governed and refreshed by the Spirit of God.⁹⁸

He also denies the right of the temporal powers (city council) ultimately to judge or determine the spiritual affairs of the church.⁹⁹ Second, when directly challenged about who is judge if and when conflict arose over scriptural interpretation, Zwingli reasserts his belief that the Holy Spirit would lead all pious students of the Scripture to the same truth:

> The Scriptures are so much the same everywhere, the Spirit of God flows so abundantly, walks in them so joyfully, that every

diligent reader, in so far as he approaches with humble heart, will decide by means of the Scriptures, taught by the Spirit of God, until he attains the truth.[100]

In summary, it is apparent from these sources that in 1522 and 1523 some aspects of Zwingli's program sound much akin to that of the Zürich Anabaptists later. Certainly they both shared a strong ethical concern for the moral reform of the church. Their expectations concerning the practical impact on the church of such a divinely led reform were also similar, up to a point. This common ethical sensitivity is also manifested by agreement on the need for the preaching of repentance. They shared the belief that the true church is made up only of sincere believers in Christ, a church which, in total, is spotless and cannot err.

They agreed that the Bible (the gospel) was the sole authoritative norm for all institutional and ceremonial reform and that explicit obedience to that norm was necessary and anything contradictory must be eliminated. Further, they believed that Scripture could be rightly understood, through the Holy Spirit, by all whose attitude was right, that is, humble and pious. Therefore, they expected those accepting this norm to come to a unity of truth; disunity could only mean that some alien influence was present.

But there are also clear references in the same sources relating to each of these same points that indicate serious incompatibility between even the early Zwingli and the earliest Anabaptist program. Zwingli kept his practical, ethical concerns subordinate to several other theological concerns; they did not dominate his program as with the Anabaptists. By the time he wrote his "67 Articles," Zwingli was emphasizing the theological primacy of the doctrines of a vicarious, all-sufficient atoning sacrifice of Christ and of imputed righteousness over against anything that implied works-righteousness, and even over concern for institutionally-manifest holiness and the necessity of external fruits of repentance.

There is also in Zwingli clear indication of his belief that the visible church is an inclusive church and only the invisible church is "pure." His reform program was to be brought to fruition gradually and by the power of gospel preaching and teaching alone. Therefore, Zwingli does not emphasize the use of church discipline (the ban) as an agency of reform, purification, and separation. Zwingli gives no indication of wanting to restrict the visible (in contrast to his "true") church to ascetically "tested" or externally holy and conforming believers only. Rather, he contrasts the "true" spiritual church with any and all organized institutional manifestations of it.

Even the "gospel" is somewhat different in Zwingli. It came from the Old and New Testaments without any clear distinction regarding levels of authority such as Anabaptism developed later. Further, he indicates considerable leniency toward religious ordinances and customs which did not actually contradict Scripture, even though they lacked any specific validation in Scripture. He never affirms the Anabaptists' contention that those living impiously should in no way participate in making decisions about any aspect of ecclesiastical and spiritual affairs and that unity among Christians must be based on a practical and discernible submission to the Word by all.

The evidence indicates that the Zwingli of 1524-25, who rejected the reform program presented first by some in the inner group and later by the Brethren, cannot be considered a revisionist who departed from his earlier "Anabaptistic" position. Rather, significant aspects of the reform program of Grebel and Manz (1524-25) were never really Zwinglian; the priorities were different even though many individual elements were common to both. From the beginning of the division there was an inherently different view of the nature of the visible expression of the "true" church, especially its ethical visibility and its relationship to society at large. Though their expectations of the ultimate product of the Reformation, the new Christian society, were similar, the means to achieve this goal were different.

The Anabaptist position gave primary priority to the principle of the purity of the visible church, including whatever institutional and individual moral separation was necessary to attain and preserve that principle. Thus the Anabaptists insisted that the true church must visibly express itself by living virtuously and functioning according to the rule of Christ (Matthew 18). All its members must willingly accept discipline and the church leadership must exercise it in conformity with an ascetically conceived, ethical code. The Anabaptists insisted that a true reform movement under the Word and the Spirit would produce a visibly functioning, biblically obedient, morally pure church.

If the unique, divisive aspects of the Grebel program, to which many of the Zwingli circle subscribed, did not ever coincide fully with

Zwingli's program, then the thesis that the emergence of Anabaptism can be adequately explained as consistent Zwinglianism, though radicalized and sharpened by private Bible studies, with little or no antecedent or outside influences, is found to be deficient.[101] Krajewski asserts that since the Anabaptists (especially Manz) subscribed to *sola scriptura*, and salvation by faith in Christ's sacrifice alone, not by the sacraments, therefore all attempts at relating Anabaptism to medieval Catholic influences are ruled out.[102] This assumes, however, and wrongly, that these specific doctrines are not to be found in any late medieval Catholic tradition with which the Grebel group may have had substantial contact.[103] Though the Anabaptists themselves give much of the credit to private Bible study to account for their uniqueness and rejection of Zwingli's variations,[104] this also partly begs the question. From where did they get their non-Zwinglian, distinctive, and apparently preconditioned, interpretive biases, held so strongly, clearly, and quickly?

Further evidence for non-Zwinglian origins and perhaps some clues to other possible antecedent influences on the development of the Anabaptist perspectives and program may be indicated by considering the rise of Anabaptism in its larger historical setting. Are the same predispositions with the same intensity present also among those founding Anabaptist leaders who were not connected with and nourished with the Zwingli circle? And, if so, did these concerns play a fundamental role in leading them to espouse Anabaptism?

Asceticism and the initial Swiss Brethren leaders outside the Zwingli circle. Some of those associated with the founding of the Swiss Brethren, January 1525, were not led to reform by Zwingli nor schooled by him to the same degree as were Grebel, Manz, and Castelberger; nor were they ever part of the Zwingli circle. Consequently, their rejection of the Magisterial Reformation and ready adherence to the viewpoint of Grebel and Manz as soon as it appeared cannot possibly be explained as simply a logical and consistent development of an earlier but misunderstood Zwinglianism. George (Cajacob) Blaurock is an important example[105] of an independent predisposition to Anabaptism, that is, of non-Zwinglian origin.

Blaurock, son of Luzi Cajacob, was born ca. 1492 in Bonaduz in the Grisons district in Switzerland. Several Swiss Brethren leaders, Brötli, Ulimann, and Castelberger, also came from that area. Unfortunately, the sources tell us almost nothing of Blaurock's youth or early education, except that he matriculated at the University of Leipzig in 1513.¹⁰⁶ Zwingli, at the disputation in March 1525, expresses disdain for Blaurock's education,¹⁰⁷ but this remark is made in such a charged atmosphere and highly polemical situation that its accuracy is questionable.

From 1516 to 1518 Blaurock was a vicar in Trins, in the diocese of Chur. The assumption that he was for a time a monk at St. Luzi has not been confirmed by the sources.¹⁰⁸ Blaurock probably decided to support the new evangelical reform in 1523 or early 1524. Actually, concerning the period between 1518 and 1524, the sources only state that he was married by the time he came to Zürich in late 1524.¹⁰⁹ Blanke suggests that Blaurock became a Zwinglian in 1523, but submits no specific evidence.¹¹⁰ The account of his arrival at Zürich, probably in December 1524,¹¹¹ of his consultation, brief association, and disappointment with Zwingli, of his turning to the faction led by Grebel, and Manz, and of his role in the decisive formation of Anabaptism, probably on January 21, 1525 (he was the first to request and receive "rebaptism") is preserved in the Hutterian *Chronicle*.¹¹²

The issue over which Blaurock became an Anabaptist and rejected Zwinglianism is clear. According to the *Chronicle*, on his arrival at Zürich he discussed the reform "at length" with Zwingli but was not satisfied with Zwingli's program, then began to look for some alternative and was told about Grebel and Manz, as "men more zealous than Zwingli." Consequently, sometimes just prior to the January 1525 disputation (since apparently by then he spoke for the Anabaptists but was still an unknown to the Zürich officials),¹¹³ according to the *Chronicle*:

> He inquired diligently for these men and found them, namely Conrad Grebel and Felix Manz. With them he spoke and talked through matters of faith. They came to one mind in these things, and in the pure fear of God they recognized that *a person must learn from the divine Word, preach a true faith which manifests itself in love, and receive the true Christian baptism on the basis of the recognized and confessed faith, in the union with God of a good conscience, [prepared] henceforth to serve God in a holy Christian life* with all godliness, also to be steadfast to the end in all tribulation.¹¹⁴

The element most stressed as the expected result of the true preaching and teaching of the Word of God and which apparently agreed with Blaurock's prior expectations is a "true faith" which is interpreted to mean a manifested and active faith; active in love, outwardly recognizable by others, and then confessed by baptism. Baptism implied also a declaration of intent to maintain thereafter a holy life, a life of godliness. The content of this last term was not yet as fixed as it later became but certainly it already had an ascetic content and included obedience to "the rule of Christ," as expressed by Grebel in his letter to Thomas Müntzer.[115]

Immediately after the momentous decision of January 21, 1525, to propagate actively, as a separatist group, their distinctive reform views, Blaurock is found in Zollikon attempting to convert a young man, Marx Bosshard. This action implies a conviction by Blaurock that many of those composing the contemporary Zwinglian church were still not really Christians. In fact, either loose living or disobedience to the Word, especially by rejection of Anabaptist teaching, was an indication to Anabaptists of a lack of the "true faith." In the words of Blaurock: "Marx, hitherto you have been a gay young man but you must now become a different man; you must lay aside the old Adam and put on the new one and reform [*dich besseren* — a favorite expression] your life." Marx, in reply, expressed a desire "for the grace of God, repentance, and a desire to do his best" to live a better life. Then Blaurock baptized him.[116] To Ruedi Thomann, an old man, Blaurock expressed similar demands for personal reformation and repentance. Again, and similarly, it was only after Hans Bruggback confessed with tears "what a great sinner he was" and professed a conversion that baptism was administered to him.[117]

Blaurock's proselytizing activities reveal that his primary concern was for the reform of the church by applying the Word to the personal salvation of men so as to bring them to a true, ascetic faith. He believed that this "conversion" required a personal acknowledgement of sinfulness and a willingness to receive grace, forsake sins (ascetically defined), and to live thereafter a new and holy life. Since an ascetic holiness becomes the ultimate evidence of salvation, its importance to Anabaptist theology and practices becomes fundamental. Blanke refers to these "conversions," and to several others in Zollikon that were similar, as illustrative of "a unique movement of repentance."[118] There are as yet no explicit references to an ideology of separation of church and state, that is, to anti-"sacralism" as Verduin describes it, though this principle developed quickly, perhaps stimulated by the ensuing persecution.

Two other leaders of the first Brethren group, Wilhelm Reublin and Johann Brötli, were also "outsiders" with reference to the Zwingli circle. Though perhaps more influenced by the Zwinglian reform than Blaurock, since they came to Zürich earlier, in 1522 and 1523 respectively, their background and, to a degree, their involvement still exhibit considerable independence from the Zwingli circle itself.[119]

Johannes Brötli had been a priest at Quarten in the Grisons area where he espoused the new evangelical reform movement sometime before he came to the Zürich territory in the summer of 1523. Almost immediately he assumed the duties of an assistant pastor and preacher at Zollikon, a village of Zürich, though in a somewhat unofficial capacity, that is, without salary.[120] In the summer of 1524, he openly objected to the practice of infant baptism[121] and by September, though the details of the process of his break with the Zwinglian reform position are not known, he is fully within the dissenting circle led by Grebel and Manz. His name appears also as a cosigner of the dissenters' letter of 1524 to Müntzer. It can be assumed that he was among the inner group who, by their "new" baptism, initiated the Anabaptist-Brethren movement on January 21, 1525, since the following day he, in turn, baptized the first Zollikoner convert to the movement, Hans Schumacher. Schumacher testifies that he replied to Brötli, "All right, Hans [Johann], you have taught me the truth. I thank you for it and ask you for the sign." The principles implied by this testimony, that baptism follows instruction, and is a sign of some personal inner commitment, coincide with the examples of baptism by Blaurock that same week.[122]

In association with Blaurock and Reublin, Brötli continued to work strenuously in the formation of the first Anabaptist congregation in the village of Zollikon until his banishment from the canton of Zürich by the Zürich council became effective on January 29, 1525. Toward the end of January, he appears at Schaffhausen traveling and proselytizing together with Reublin and Grebel. Then he went to Hallau where he successfully established an Anabaptist congregation which flourished until it was suppressed following the Austrian (Imperial) take-over at Waldshut in December 1525.[123] Brötli was martyred in 1528.[124]

As with Blaurock, Brötli left few written works or testimonials to enable one to trace the reasons for his break with Zwingli and espousal of Anabaptism. As a cosigner of the "Müntzer" letter he must have shared in the attitudes expressed by it. Also his baptizing activities, in association with Blaurock and Manz at Zollikon, suggest that he shared their ascetic interpretation of baptism. There are also two letters by him sent in February 1525[125] to Fridli Schumacher and the Brethren at Zollikon. These letters also confirm that he shared fully in the motivating principles of the new movement as expressed by Manz, Grebel, and Blaurock, principles which went much beyond simply the issue of the age of candidates for baptism. For example, he addresses the Brethren at Zollikon as "pious Christians" ("frommen Christen"), as those "called of God" and "gathered at Zollikon" — all of which indicates a clear understanding of the church as a separated, holy, called-out company of believers. Also, an early non-Lutheran and non-Zwinglian attitude to "election" is indicated by his assertion that "you are God's and He is yours and you are saved, but if you fall away, then you are children of damnation and God is far from you...."[126]

Reublin emerges as a most remarkable but rather distinctive Anabaptist leader, with a long and turbulent "ministerial" career. His road to Anabaptism is quite different from that of the others which we have been considering. He was born between 1480 and 1484 in Rottenburg on the Neckar, and died probably in Znaim in Moravia sometime after 1559. He was educated at the University of Freiburg while Balthasar Hubmaier was there. Following his ordination to the priesthood he went to Tübingen in 1509. Between 1510 and 1521, there is no known information about him. The record resumes when he appeared in Basel as *Magister*, in the spring of 1521, and became the "people's [presiding] priest" at St. Albans Church on June 24, 1521.

His popularity grew as a promoter of a biblically-based reform program, which in theory was quite similar to the early program of his contemporary, Zwingli. He too preached against the "abuses" of vain ceremonies and nonbiblical regulations. But he was more outspoken than Zwingli, especially against the mass. As a result, he was expelled by the council on June 27, 1522. That he was already a more activistic and radical reformer than Zwingli is illustrated by his involvement, in 1522, in the Corpus Christi procession, in which instead of the customary relics he carried a Bible with a sign containing the words: "This is the true shrine, the others are only dead men's bones."[127]

When he joined the Zwinglian reform movement at Zürich in

the fall of 1522, it was with a well-developed, radical reform program and outlook of his own.[128] Accordingly, soon after his arrival in Zürich, he began to agitate again for a faster and even more thorough reformation. By November 1522, he was already defying the fasting ordinances and calling church images, idols.[129] He was given a ministerial office (Christmas, 1522) by the village congregation of Wytikon in spite of objections by the church officials of Zürich.[130] At his church he continued to criticize celibacy outspokenly and to castigate in strong language various abuses of the old clergy and even of the magistrates. In contrast, he upheld the common people as quite pious ("frombs purli").[131] All of this was before the Grebel group was formed in Zürich and the themes represent a radical Zwinglianism, not distinctive aspects of Anabaptism.

Is it possible to detect what factor most strongly influenced Reublin to adopt Anabaptism? Unfortunately, though he is frequently named in the sources (1521-31), there are very few clues given concerning his "conversion" to Anabaptism. Superficially the pattern of his religious evolution though independent of Zwingli's direct influence seems to parallel that of Grebel. He too moves from a period of association with the evangelical reform, in general, to a crisis of dissatisfaction, and finally to Anabaptism.

The reasons for his eventual break with Zwingli, however, do not parallel those of Grebel, Manz, and Blaurock. He does not seem to have been associated with the Grebel group's initial dissent or their alternative program of 1524, although he was already recognized in Zürich as a radical Reformer. He was even imprisoned in August 1524 for his open opposition to infant baptism. Neither is he a signer of the Müntzer letter of late 1524, nor is he mentioned as part of the group who were first baptized on January 21, 1525, and who subsequently began to proselytize and baptize around Zürich and Zollikon. The first sign of any association with Anabaptists is his involvement with them in trial and banishment of January 17, 1525; apparently because he was still against infant baptism.

Reublin had taught early in 1524 that if one "wanted to be a true Christian and lead a Christian life, then there was no need of [infant] baptism" and that "if he had a child he wouldn't have it baptized until it came to maturity, when it could choose its own godparents."[132] While these statements reflect some concern by Reublin that a true Christian profession must be tied to godly living, there is no evidence that he subscribed to a doctrine of believer's baptism which embodied a whole ascetic reform package, as was developed by Grebel and Manz. Neither does his rejection of infant baptism in 1524 imply an espousal of an Anabaptistic sectarianism, either as behavioral separatism or separation of church and state. Rather, his rejection of infant baptism is only a more radical expression of a thorough biblicalism and of a rejection of *ex opere operato* definitions of the sacraments — again, only a radicalized Zwinglianism.

Therefore, unlike Blaurock and Grebel's group, Reublin appears to have been pushed into Anabaptism by circumstances, especially the persecution by the Zürich council for his reckless radicalism earlier and for his opposition to infant baptism. Initially he was not associated with the Anabaptist founders for whom a strong ascetic desire for a true church which manifested holiness of life by disciplinary separatism was fundamental.

Apparently Reublin accepted the distinctively Anabaptist position only later through association with the Brethren leaders early in January 1525 and also possibly through the influence of his close friend and neighboring priest, who became a founding Anabaptist leader, Johann Brötli. Though he was originally a radical Evangelical Reformer, as an Anabaptist, he is noted, rather, for his moderation.[133]

Clearly, not all who joined the first Anabaptists had the same motives. Moreover, though Reublin is a good example of the conversion to Anabaptism of one who was a radical Zwinglian, even becoming an Anabaptist leader, it is also evident that he had no definitive or formative influence, ideologically, on the initial development of the central features of the Anabaptist synthesis. Neither did he exercise any ideological leadership in the subsequent development of Swiss Anabaptism, 1525-27. After 1531, he adopted something of an enigmatic "lone wolf" role in the history of Anabaptism.

It is evident that dissent from Zwingli's reform program, which developed between 1523 and 1525, took several forms. Along with the majority of Zwingli's circle, who continued to support him, there was the dissenting group from the Zwingli circle who had decidedly and distinctively ascetic expectations for reform. These ascetic dissenters drew other Reformers with similar convictions and predispositions, to them, such as Blaurock, and together they established the basic tenets of Anabaptism.

But there were also other dissenters who broke initially with Zwingli more over the timing and thoroughness of the implementation of his reform than over ascetic concerns. These were the

Ascetic Factors in Emerging Anabaptism 99

real "radical" Zwinglians and they are not necessarily Anabaptists. Some of these radicals, such as Reublin, were converted to Swiss Anabaptism only after their break with Zwingli. Some others, such as Ludwig Haetzer (who was also against infant baptism and was also banished from Zürich in January 1525) never joined the Swiss Brethren. In 1525 Haetzer had rejected both Zwingli's reform and Anabaptist rebaptism and hoped instead for a "second" or true reformation yet to come.[134] If Haetzer later became an Anabaptist, and this is doubtful, the association was a tenuous one, and with the freer, more mystical variety of Hans Denck.

The evidence thus far confirms that the Anabaptists' founding predispositions and initial program were not derived primarily from Zwingli nor were they identical to Zwingli's. Anabaptism's emergence cannot be explained as simply a more radical and consistent Zwinglianism. Anabaptism contained a unique ascetic element which was embodied in their interpretation and practice of believer's baptism and was symbolized by it.

Asceticism in the Expansion and Consolidation of the Swiss Brethren

After January 1525, and the formation of the initial Anabaptist group in Zürich, the Swiss Brethren, numerous other reform leaders also abandoned the Evangelical (Magisterial) Reformation program and cast their lot with the Swiss Brethren. Some of these subsequently play a major role in helping formulate and consolidate the basic patterns of Evangelical Anabaptism. Were the predispositions which influenced such leaders toward Anabaptism also ascetic as they were in the original group? To answer this question there follows a close analysis of several such leaders and spokesmen, namely: Balthasar Hubmaier, Martin Weninger, and several ex-monks who also contributed substantially to the movement, Wolfgang Ulimann, Hans Altenbach, Johann Krüsi, and Michael Sattler. These are chosen both for their significance as formative leaders and the availability of relevant data.

Balthasar Hubmaier. No discussion of the predisposing issues relating to the emergence of early Anabaptist leadership could pass over the outstanding figure of Dr. Balthasar Hubmaier.[135] He is among the earliest significant converts to Anabaptism resulting from direct contact with the Zürich Brethren, that is, with Anabaptism as those led by Grebel and Manz initially formulated and institutionalized it. Some indications that an ascetically oriented conditioning contributed to his adoption and subsequent interpretation of Anabaptism, are present.

In the Catholic period of his life, Hubmaier had already become a competent scholar and was associated first with the faculty of the University of Freiburg (1511), then with the University of Ingolstadt, from which he received his doctorate in theology in 1512. He was also made vice-rector in 1515.[136] However, his preaching skill was also so impressive that he left Ingolstadt and academic life to become the chief preacher in the cathedral at Regensberg on January 25, 1516.

While at Regensberg (1516-1521), his pastoral concern for certain local social problems led to the preaching of numerous strong sermons against usury, to an anti-Jewish stance, to resistance to Imperial pressures and governmental interference in local religious affairs, and to an initially deep involvement in the "pilgrimages and miracles" revival which accompanied the building of the church, Zur Schönen Maria. These sermons and his local involvements reveal him at that time as both a loyal son of the Roman Church and also a devout and reforming leader who tended to become activistically involved in the problems of the church.

Hubmaier felt a vigorous compulsion toward reforming whatever items within the orthodox framework presented themselves to him as social and spiritual abuses.[137] Also, there is evidence of a growing pastoral concern for the promotion of popular piety and an anxiety for whatever tended to increase popular impiety. Bergsten points out that it was not only the unpleasantness of the jealousy expressed by the older local monastic foundations in Regensberg (especially the Dominicans) toward his success and the obvious increase in abuses and impiety associated with the local pilgrimages which led Hubmaier to leave Regensberg to begin a soul-searching reevaluation of his faith, but also that concern over both was made more acute by an already disturbing awareness of some of the newer Evangelical (Lutheran) reform criticisms.[138]

Although his decision to go to the small parish of Waldshut to reconsider his ministry and its future was in part sparked by his growing awareness of Luther's reforming movement, the major in-

Ascetic Factors in Emerging Anabaptism   101

fluence in determining the subsequent direction of his reforming concern is not Luther directly but the renewal of his contacts with Christian humanism and especially with Erasmus. His interest in Christian humanism went back to the University of Freiberg which had been a major center of reform from the perspective of Christian humanism during Hubmaier's stay there.[139] Bergsten suggests that Hubmaier's poem (1516) in praise of John Eck is humanistic and indicates that Hubmaier had an early interest in Christian humanism.[140] However, the more decisive period is 1521-22.

Even while on his journey from Regensberg to Waldshut, he began to renew his humanist contacts. In early 1521, he stopped at Ulm where he had a circle of friends among whom was a humanist medical doctor, Wolfgang Rychard. From Rychard, Humbaier obtained a copy of Oecolampadius' book *Judicium* which favored Luther and the new Evangelical Reformation. Rychard is known also to have expressed Evangelical and Lutheran sympathies as early as January 1521, that is, during the time Hubmaier was there.[141] Shortly after, Hubmaier was in correspondence with another humanist Evangelical, Beatus Rhenanus, and sent him a copy of the *Judicium*.[142] On October 26, 1521, he wrote to Johannes Sapidus expressing a desire for more contacts with humanist and Evangelical Reformers.

The letter also reveals several typically Erasmian traits: an interest in both biblical studies and the classics, a repudiation of scholastic formulations, some praise for Luther, and some criticism of Pope Leo X and of abuses in the church.[143] Hubmaier had quickly moved into sympathy for the Evangelical reform in general but he had not yet worked out the details. As yet there is no sign of awareness of differences or tensions between Erasmianism and Lutheranism.

Hubmaier's letter to the humanist (and Lutheran) doctor Adelphi (June 23, 1522), indicates that by then Hubmaier was busily engaged in intensive, personal study of the Pauline Epistles and was also reading Luther. The former seems to have been much influenced by his trip to Basel (June 1522) where he met Erasmus, Glarean, and Pellikan whom he now calls his "best friends." He was personally instructed by Erasmus on the subject of purgatory and on the interpretation of the key verse for new birth theology, John 1:13, that is, that the Sons of God are born "neither of the will of the flesh nor of the will of man."[144] Apparently, on the matter of purgatory, Erasmus took a clear Evangelical position and on the interpretative issue he pressed for a strong emphasis on inner regeneration.

The significance of this "Erasmian" influence went much beyond further encouragement for Hubmaier to intensify his own study of Scripture. Hubmaier also now recognized the Christian Scriptures as the ultimate norm for all religious reform.[145] Consequently he turned to public expository preaching[146] and to public questioning of the moral and spiritual worth and correctness of many traditional ceremonies, institutions, and even of the sacraments.[147] This questioning of rituals and rites was closely tied to his new emphasis on personal regeneration. There is little doubt that by late 1522, Hubmaier was a convinced Evangelical Reformer, in a broad sense; somewhat more Erasmian than Lutheran. He had been greatly influenced by Christian humanism and especially by Erasmus personally; then these influences were verified by his own study of Paul's writings in the New Testament.

He also sympathized with some of Luther's early writings, as did most humanist Reformers up to 1521. Bergsten concludes: "Humanism had influenced him in his development to a Reformer and an Anabaptist, and the impress was permanent."[148] One must recognize, however, that this influence does not refer to humanism in general but primarily to the ideals and piety associated with Erasmian Christian humanism. Hubmaier even noted a discrepancy between what Erasmus taught personally and what he was willing to put in writing. It caused him to express some antipathy toward Erasmus' character but not toward what Erasmus taught.[149]

That Luther remained less influential than Erasmus is suggested by the failure of even Hubmaier's study of the Pauline Epistles (Romans) to lead him ever to express the Lutheran terminology of exclusively forensic justification. Furthermore, Hubmaier's later writings on free will imply a constant position which was closely parallel to Erasmus' but in opposition to Luther's.[150]

A complete review of Hubmaier's continued activity and development as an Evangelical Reformer, 1523 and 1524, is not essential to this chapter, except to note the pattern and issues that led him to Anabaptism. His initial concern to apply Scriptural norms to the reform program, was tempered by a very Erasmian caution. He was no radical. He attempted to test his private biblical interpretations by disputation and discussion before making practical changes. He also sought to prepare the way for change and avoid strife by careful teaching and preaching of the gospel, and by a patient concern

Ascetic Factors in Emerging Anabaptism 103

for "the weaker folk" in the congregation.[151]

Perhaps this procedure for reform indicates some direct Zwinglian as well as Erasmian influence; it closely parallels some of Zwingli's pronouncements.)[152] In addition, Hubmaier appears to have adopted essentially the early Zwinglian view of the sacrament as an external sign only and as a *Wiedergedächtnis* (a "commemoration").[153] Yet one must be cautious not to label him either a Zwinglian or a Lutheran even though he, at first, often praised Luther and personally aided Zwingli, as a friend and colleague, in the second disputation (October 1523) at Zürich. For as we have seen, he never espoused what he considered to be Zwingli's and Luther's views on the bondage of the will, on predestination, and on exclusively forensic justification; and later openly repudiated them.[154] Moreover when, in 1525, he finally accepted the ascetically oriented Anabaptist view of the church and of its sacraments and membership, this also indicates the dominance of Erasmianism in his theological preferences.

Since many of these later theological issues were as yet not defined to the point of contention, Hubmaier in 1523-24, even as Grebel in 1523, still felt himself closely united to the whole Evangelical reform movement.[155] He shared a general conviction that all true followers of the Word would arrive at a unity of interpretation.

Hubmaier's decision to join the Swiss Brethren was much more than reaching a settled conviction that infant baptism was unbiblical and therefore should be abandoned. Such a narrow definition of Anabaptism is not based on the source evidence. Hubmaier opposed the baptism of infants as early as 1523 (even before Thomas Müntzer visited the area).[156] In his *18 Theses*, he insists that "every Christian should believe and be baptized for himself."[157] Yet his relations with Zwingli were warm through 1524 since he was not yet associating baptism with the "pure" church concept, as the Anabaptists did. Hubmaier uses the parable of the tares (Matthew 13) in *On Heretics*, to prove that coercion should not be used against heretics just as Zwingli uses it later against the Swiss Brethren's demand for a purging of the church.[158]

Many Evangelical Reformers were questioning whether the rite of infant baptism had biblical validity. Both Oecolampad and Hofmeister also expressed concern at this time about its lack of biblical warrant. Though Grebel and Reublin claimed that Hofmeister was "of one accord with us on baptism,"[159] though this was only half true. Apparently, Hofmeister, though doubting infant baptism, never accepted the Anabaptist alternative. Similarly, though Grebel correctly said in Hubmaier in January 1525 that he was "against Zwingli as far as baptism is concerned" (that is, against infant baptism), Hubmaier was not yet an Anabaptist.[160] Zwingli made very little effort to defend infant baptism, biblically, when Hubmaier came to Zürich in 1523 and personally expressed his doubts about it to him.[161] When Hubmaier's questionings produced a similar inadequate response by Oecolampad and Hofmeister, in 1524,[162] Hubmaier was convinced of the need to abandon infant baptism and began to do so, late in 1524.

While in general Hubmaier's *Theses Against Eck* (September 1524) contain, according to Vedder, "nothing . . . that foreshadows any serious difference of opinion between Hubmaier and Zwingli,"[163] yet Hubmaier stresses one doctrine in it which is different and which he later incorporates into his baptismal theology, namely that an open or public confession of personal faith is essential. He emphasizes that "with the heart one believes unto righteousness but with the mouth he makes confession unto salvation." A further development of a more positive position on baptism is evident in his subsequent letter to Oecolampad, on January 16, 1525.[164] Hubmaier writes that though Zwingli and Luther say that baptism "is a mere sign," he now asserts in contrast that baptism "is to be considered more than a sign." Rather, he terms it "a pledge of faith until death." He concludes:

> This meaning has nothing to do with babes, therefore infant baptism is without reality. . . . I believe, yea I know, that it will not go well with Christendom until baptism and the Supper are brought back to their own original purity.[165]

Though this begins to sound more Anabaptist, it is still not the equivalent of the interpretation given to baptism by Grebel and Manz. There is in Hubmaier not yet any stated tie between baptism and an ascetic conversion and holy living by which one can empirically distinguish true believers from the false pretenders; neither does he associate baptism with the ban, the agency for the church's purification.[166]

Though Hubmaier's "witness" baptism is more than Zwingli's "sign" and doubtlessly helped prepare the way for his acceptance of Anabaptism, primarily he is still cautiously and consistently applying Erasmian Evangelical principles for a biblically based ceremonial reform. Accordingly, he is still willing in January of 1525 to go slowly and even to create a substitute rite for infants, a kind of religious dedication and naming ceremony in and by the church. Believer's baptism for Hubmaier is not yet an espousal of sectarianism. He reports to Oecolampad that he is still willing even to baptize infants, if the parents insist, as an accommodation to their weakness.

Hubmaier's "Open Appeal to All Christian Believers" (February 2, 1525), calling for a public disputation on baptism, expresses firmer opposition to infant baptism but adds no new positive, alternate principles.[167] Similarly his *Conclusions Concerning the Mass*, published about the same time, do not suggest the tie with the ban and church discipline as is stated in Grebel's letter to Müntzer but rather individual, self-examination: "Let every man test himself." But for the first time he does add some social and ascetic norms for proper participation and he broadens the essentially symbolic meaning, thus: "Even so [in imitation of Christ] should our body and blood be at the service of the other brethren. . . . Let every man test himself whether he be so inclined toward his neighbors . . . else we should not profess ourselves to be Christians."[168]

He is beginning now to link his understanding of the sacraments to the traditionally ascetic theme of the imitation of Christ. Hubmaier also equates obedience to the Scriptures explicitly with a correct "following of Christ." If anyone understands better Christ's will about the Supper, he asks, "For God's sake show me from the Scriptures, for as he thus follows Christ, I will also, gladly with all my heart and with great thankfulness."[169]

Then, in the early spring of 1525, Reublin and Grebel separately visited Hubmaier, seeking his conversion to "Swiss Brethren" Anabaptism,[170] apparently with success; though Hubmaier stalled making an open profession until Easter. Perhaps he wanted time to consider the implications of his decision or, more likely, he simply waited for the most effective and opportune moment.[171] When Reublin visited him again, at the Easter season, Hubmaier openly accepted Anabaptist baptism for himself and began to teach and then to baptize his followers at Waldshut.[172]

After consultation with the Anabaptist leader Heinrich Aberli, and after another meeting with Grebel which he requested especially to discuss baptism,[173] Hubmaier published *The Christian Baptism of Believers* (July 1525) in reply to Zwingli's tract of May 28, *On Baptism, Rebaptism, and Infant Baptism*. Along with this booklet, Hubmaier also wrote a tract summarizing the Christian life. In these two booklets Hubmaier clearly expounds a theology of baptism and the church that now closely parallels the teaching of the Swiss Brethren. In identical terms he insists that baptism must relate to "amendment of life"[174] and living "according to the rule of Christ."[175]

Hubmaier, in the booklet *A Summary of the Christian Life* (1525), suggests that for him, now, the key to Christ's teaching and becoming a Christian is contained in the words "amend your life [*besserend ewer leben*] and believe the gospel" (Mk. 1:15).[176] He then explains this rendering of the biblical passage as involving three stages: Through the teachings of the Word comes first the awareness of need, sinful disobedience to God, helplessness, and a total despair of one's own ability to save oneself. Then comes awareness of the provision of help from Christ, the Physician, who "has come into this world to make the sinner righteous and godly" *(Das ich der Artzt sey, der kommen ist in dise welt, den sünder gerecht und fromb zemachen).*[177] This emphasis on Christ as the Physician who makes one righteous is not Luther's imputed *Rechtfertigkeit*, or forensic justification, although the person must respond with faith.

Hubmaier also defines this faith as a trust which includes personal and practical submission of the will, a willingness to obey the Word. It is more than just trust in Christ's sacrificial and vicarious provision for sin and much more than just correct belief or mental assent. Faith is closely tied to repentance and does not exist without it. Repentance is the negative repudiation of sin; faith the positive side of essentially the same internal attitude, that is, submission and trust and obedience.[178] To be saved, one must "trust (or submit) himself to the Physician" [*ergibt sich füran an den Artzt*] and "surrender himself as far as it is possible to His will." Then the Physician will "help him and advance him to the extent that he may follow God's Word and commands."[179]

As with the Zürich Brethren, especially Manz, repentance is associated with John the Baptist's message and must come first.[180] Hubmaier describes repentance as putting on "the rough coat of John the Baptist before one can, in Christ Jesus, overcome weakness and idleness. Then does a man surrender himself sincerely from the heart, and propose to lead a new life according to the rule and teaching of Christ . . . from whom he derives his life."[181]

The third stage he describes as "after a man inwardly and by

Ascetic Factors in Emerging Anabaptism   107

faith has surrendered himself to the new life, he must bear witness to it, outwardly and openly before the church in whose fellowship he enrolls himself." Baptism is this public witness of his pledge "to live another and better life" and to accept the discipline of the church henceforth "in accordance with the law [*Ordnung*] of Christ," Matthew 18. He adds concerning disciplinary power by the congregation: "Whence comes this power except only from the obligation of baptism."[182] The association of baptism and the Supper with "living according to the rule of Christ" henceforth occurs repeatedly in Hubmaier.[183]

All of this closely paralleled both the theory and the practice established by the Zürich Brethren. He concludes, in *Von der Taufe*, by quoting a favorite passage, almost a slogan, in the Swiss Brethren reform program: "The axe is laid to the root of the tree." He had accepted Anabaptist separation.

The *12 Articles*, written in a Zürich prison early in 1526, clearly express the completeness of the merger of his baptism theology with the wider implications of Anabaptist ecclesiology. He writes that without the proper baptism and Supper "we have among us neither faith, love, church, oath, brotherly discipline, ban, nor exclusion, without which things it will never be well in the church."[184]

Clearly Reublin and Grebel had converted Hubmaier not simply to believer's baptism but to their full ascetic-ethical interpretation of baptism and its close tie with the concept of the disciplined church. Both are now essential for Hubmaier also, not only to the *bene esse* (the well being) but in practice almost to the *esse* (essence) of the church.

Hubmaier's acceptance of Swiss Brethren theology was now almost complete. He resigned his "prebend" and was instead "elected" as pastor by the newly "baptized" congregation at Waldshut.[185] He also mentions abandoning lutes, pipes, and organs in worship, apparently a reflection of his espousal of Anabaptism, though Zwingli also adovcated this idea earlier.[186] On the other hand, since Hubmaier successfully won the support of the Council and people of Waldshut for his program, whereas the Grebel group failed at Zürich, he maintains a position closer to Grebel's initial proposal of 1524 with reference to the magistracy and the sword. He does not follow Grebel and Manz who subsequently discredit all cooperation and put both outside the pale of Christian participation.

To overemphasize this one area of deviation from Grebel and

Manz, at this stage and thereby refuse to identify Hubmaier with the early Swiss Brethren,[187] is to assume too much rigidity within the Swiss Brethren too soon. For example, Jacob Gross, who was closely associated with Grebel in Grüningen in 1525, is in 1526 still willing to "hold the spear" and "stand watch," even "build fortification" but says that he could not "kill anyone."[188] Aberli, a founding leader of the Swiss Brethren at Zürich, does not object to the use of Swiss military help in defense of Waldshut against the emperor. Before the Schleitheim Confession of 1527, the total rejection of the sword and magistracy was not entirely settled among the Swiss Brethren.[189]

While Hubmaier, and to some degree many others, had been led to an abandonment of infant baptism by the application of the basic principles of the Evangelical Reformation, especially *sola scriptura*, there are indications that his subsequent acceptance of the distinctive Anabaptist position was the product of much more than the persuasive powers and expository skills of Reublin and Grebel. Rather, there was a lengthy process of conditioning toward the Anabaptist's ascetic interpretation of the Scriptures and their distinctive expectations for reform; a conditioning which is derived much more from Erasmus than from Zwingli or Luther.

His turning to Anabaptism probably reflected an increasing disillusionment with Luther since by then he was no doubt aware of the rift of 1524-25 between Erasmus and Luther. Hubmaier, as noted above, was concerned that the program of the Magisterial Reformation was failing and would continue to fail to produce the truly purified church that he expected. His ideals for the Reformation coincided with the more ascetic norms of the Christian life and the interpretation of Scriptures advocated by the Zürich Brethren. Finally, there seems to be nothing in Hubmaier's evolution to Anabaptism that would in any way suggest either contacts with or influences on him by medieval heretical strains.

Ex-monks as Anabaptists. Vasella has pointed out that the "new faith," or the initial Evangelical Reformation in the Swiss towns, had from the beginning a dual origin: the city councils and the cloisters.[190] As examples of the latter, he lists the canons of St. Nicklaus, the Benedictine foundation, "Alterheiligen," in Schaffhausen, and the Praemonstratensian foundation of St. Luzi in Chur.[191] As early as 1521, Abbot Schlegel of St. Luzi was openly sympathetic to the reform movement (and, incidentally, was at this time in correspondence with Conrad Grebel).[192] However, disillusionment appears to have set in during the following year and led to the reversal of Abbot Schlegel's sympathies.[193]

This pattern of sympathy followed by disillusionment was typical of a number of monks who initially supported the Reformation. But some others instead of turning back on the whole Evangelical reform movement looked for a more compatible alternative and became a fruitful source of early Anabaptist leadership as that movement spread outward from Zürich. A number of ex-monks[194] were deeply involved both in the solidifying of doctrine and the early expansion of the Swiss Brethren.

Hans Altenbach of Luzern early in 1525[195] received believer's baptism at Waldshut; apparently he was among the earliest converts of Hubmaier. His trial testimony in Basel also reveals that from the time of his new baptism he was an active Anabaptist leader, preacher, and missionary. Altenbach had been a monk for nineteen years, had held the office of subprior, and had a baccalaureate degree in theology;[196] not an insignificant background.

He testified that he "found so much that his Order did which was not for God but against God" that he left without permission and forsook his vow "because it was against God." The term "against God" appears to be used by him to mean, contrary to the Word of God, the Scriptures.[197]

Only a few hints appear concerning the attitudes which led him to his adoption of Anabaptism. He insists that "one must believe before baptism" if it is to be true Christian baptism, and then elaborates a required sequence: first, belief, then the inner baptism of the Spirit, and then water as the sign of the spiritual baptism. He also adds: "One must previously hear about repentance, accept it, and bring forth works [wurken] and not until after the [evidential] works [wirkung], break and eat the bread. . . ." But at St. Martins "they only hear the Word of God, make no repentance, and go to the table and many are still in their sins. . . ." He also comments that Branschnider's son-in-law had not yet accepted baptism because "he didn't know himself to be upright yet."[198]

Johannes Krüsi (also called Hans Kern)[199] of St. Georgen near St. Gall was also a former monk.[200] He too was won to the Swiss Anabaptist cause early in 1525 and became one of its most active and influential leaders for a short time. He proselytized with great success in the city of St. Gall (until banished from the city), then at the abbey of St. Gall, and then in the canton of Appenzell where he "won over the Reformed congregation at Teufen to himself."[201]

He appears to have been working in close cooperation with two other ex-monks, who also turned to Anabaptism, Sebastian Ruggensberger and Wolfgang Ulimann.[202] Both Krüsi and Ruggensberger were from Klingau, near Waldshut, and came under Hubmaier's influence.[203] After being captured at his native town of St. Georgen, Krüsi was taken to Lucerne and executed there (about the end of July 1525)[204]

In spite of his short time at Teufen, his impact was such that the town continued for several years as an important Swiss Brethren center. An Anabaptist council was held there in 1528 and the congregation successfully resisted influences toward fanaticism.[205] The next year, 1529, the Teufen Anabaptists were still active enough that the Appenzell clergy held a disputation with them.[206]

Unfortunately, the report of his testimony, in the Lucerne *Ratsbuch*, tells us little about his distinctively Anabaptist concepts. He refers to his association with Grebel at St. Gall and to getting a handwritten booklet from him.[207] He says also that "Ulimann and Rupersberger [Ruggensberger] had also been his comrades and that they walked together and instructed one another."[208] In fact, he mentions that four of his Anabaptist colleagues had previous monastic associations, but he does not tell us the name of the fourth one.[209]

Krüsi's testimony of faith includes repeated brief assertions that belief should precede baptism and, if it is real, such belief "will persevere" (*behalten*). He also insists that "one should be subject to the Word of God," and that "everything should be in common in the love of God and in faith." He approves of Ulimann's iconoclastic activity and of his decision to live solely from voluntary gifts of food and money.[210]

Specific information about Sebastian Ruggensberger and his role as an Anabaptist leader is even more limited than about Altenbach and Krüsi; that there is any record at all indicates considerable influence. We know that he was previously not only a monk but also the prior of the monastery of Sion in Klingau, near Waldshut.[211] From 1523 to 1524 he sympathized with the Evangelical reform, as a close associate of Hubmaier; then as the issues clarified he too became an Anabaptist in 1525. Apparently, he took an active leadership role in association with Ulimann and Krüsi in the promotion of Ana-

Ascetic Factors in Emerging Anabaptism   111

baptism in the St. Gall area. Both Ruggensberger and Ulimann were banished as Anabaptists from St. Gall on January 22, 1526.[212] According to Peachey, he finally recanted and left Anabaptism (cir. 1528).[213]

Wolfgang Ulimann (or Uoliman — his real name was Wolfgang Schorant) appears to have been the most active leader in this group of four ex-monks (Altenbach, Krüsi, Ruggensberger, and Ulimann). He had been at the monastery of St. Lucius in Chur but abandoned the monastery, under the influence of early Evangelical reform teaching, probably by 1523.[214] After returning to his hometown of St. Gall, he was further influenced toward reform by the teaching of Johannes Kessler and began to preach the Evangelical gospel in the open air.

Late in 1524 while at St. Gall, Lorenz Hochrüttiner who was a friend of Grebel instigated a discussion of the relationship of baptism to the death of Christ (Romans 6).[215] Apparently this discussion promoted not only a criticism of infant baptism but also the distinctly ascetic interpretation of the Brethren.[216] Ulimann was sufficiently impressed that later he sought out Conrad Grebel for more instruction, after which in the early spring of 1525 he eagerly received believer's baptism from Grebel, by immersion.[217]

As a result, on March 18, 1525, Ulimann publicly called for separation from the official "reformed" church. Summoned before the Council (in April 1525), he defended believer's baptism by saying that "adult baptism implied the obligation to die to vices, live to Christ, and be obedient." Here again there occurs the same ascetic pattern as in the original Zürich Brethren.[218] After two more debates, the Council adopted a policy of suppression (June 1525) and Ulimann was banished on July 17, 1525,[219] but later he was pardoned on his oath not to proselytize in St. Gall.[220]

That Ulimann nevertheless continued to actively proselytize outside St. Gall is evidenced from his involvement in the November 25 disputation at Zürich,[221] his appearance at Basel in 1527 to aid the Brethren there, and finally his banishment from Basel also, on August 26, 1528.[222] Subsequently, he led a group of Anabaptists to Moravia and was finally martyred in Swabia late in 1528 while attempting to lead a second group to Moravia.[223] Though many details are missing, this data is sufficient, when compared to our scanty knowledge of most of the Anabaptist leaders of 1525-27, to indicate that his contribution to the development of early Anabaptism was impressive.

112   Anabaptism and Asceticism

In summary, these four ex-monks are among the foremost Swiss Anabaptist leaders and clearly played an important role in the initial expansion of the Swiss Brethren, especially in Switzerland. The information available is inadequate to determine their influence on the development of doctrine. All four first espoused the Evangelical reform but were not satisfied, and moved on to Anabaptism very readily, even eagerly, when news of the new movement reached them. It is impossible to determine the exact motivations for the change since they left no doctrinal or polemical writings, but each seems to be a faithful follower of the original tenets of the Grebel group. None were fanatics, and there are no known ties with any medieval heretical group.

By 1527, the chief surviving leaders of the Swiss Brethren still included Blaurock, Reublin, Altenbach, Ruggensberger, Ulimann, and Sattler. One must conclude that the common monastic training, and the continued sympathy with ascetic values by so many leaders, were major factors in sustaining and expanding the ascetic element in Swiss Anabaptist development.

The sources mention briefly several other monks and friars who also became Anabaptists but they were apparently lesser lights. For example, we can ascertain from the trial record at Bern, May 1527, that the Anabaptist Peter Breit had been a Franciscan; and after his recantation in 1527 apparently still rejected the Magisterial Reformation and returned to Franciscanism again.[224] He asserts that his decision to be baptized as an Anabaptist was based on the conviction that faith and teaching must precede baptism. It does not say when he received believer's baptism or anything concerning his subsequent activities. One may assume that he exerted little influence on the early Anabaptist movement. Yet this record is significant in that it suggests considerable affinity or sympathetic interaction between his two lives, as a Franciscan and an Anabaptist.

Some predisposition to sympathize with Anabaptism is also observable in Dr. Sebastian Hofmeister, another ex-Franciscan monk who early promoted the Reformation at Schaffhausen and sided with Zwingli in the 1523 disputations. Brötli, Hubmaier, and the Schaffhausen Council all witness to his sentiments favoring believer's baptism which he apparently set aside for the sake of wider "love" or unity. He almost persuaded Hubmaier to this viewpoint in 1526.[225]

There is also an interesting letter from the Anabaptist Nicolaus Gulden of St. Gall to "the sisters in the cloister" at Arrau.[226] The four "sisters" named were apparently not only still in religious Orders but also were "sisters" in the Anabaptist faith; he calls them "my beloved sisters in the Lord Jesus." This letter includes two other significant statements: First, he refers to baptism as "the water of repentance . . . with which we have been incorporated into the body of Christ." Here again is the close tie between repentance and baptism. Then, he urges them: "O remain in the fear of God and repentance [thunt bus] and bring forth the fruit of penitence for the axe has already been laid to the tree."[227] This is a typical and widely used Anabaptist "slogan" drawn directly from Grebel and reflecting the late medieval conviction that God was about to restore and morally purify His church by a drastic judgment on and replacement of the religious (and perhaps social) order.

The last and most important leader representing direct monastic involvement on the early development of the Swiss Brethren is Michael Sattler, the ex-prior of St. Peter's near Freiburg in Breisgau. Sattler is credited with a major role in the refining and solidifying of much of both the doctrine and practice of the early Swiss Brethren movement in Switzerland.[228]

Michael Sattler was born at Staufen in Breisgau, near Freiburg, about 1490.[229] It is not known when he entered the Benedictine monastery of St. Peter's near Freiburg but he rose to the office of prior, second only to the Abbot.[230] As is so often the case with even the most notable Anabaptists, the sources tell us nothing specifically about his youth and education, except that he was well educated,[231] he could use Latin, and possibly was familiar with the original biblical languages, Greek and Hebrew.[232] If he knew Greek, his training must have been humanistically oriented, probably at the University of Freiburg.[233] His later associations with Capito and other humanistically oriented Reformers indicate some degree of common scholarly ground, even though Sattler's interests and attitudes were not as humanistic as Denck's or Grebel's.

Out of the strong center for humanistic studies which developed at the University of Freiburg, 1505-1515,[234] there emerged a group of young Reformers who were much influenced toward Christian reform by Zasius and Erasmus, including: Urbanus Rhegius, Jacob Otter, Simon Stumpf, Peter Engelbrecht, and many others. Between 1517 and 1521, Luther's writings were also widely disseminated in the group and through the area[235] so that by 1522 the impact of Luther's Reformation was beginning to be felt extensively.[236] An

Imperial decree of November 1522 initiated a period of active repression by the city Council resulting in the dispersal of most of the more radical of the humanist Christian Reformers.[237] For example, by 1523, Jacob Otter was preaching at Kenzington in Breisgau in the manner of the Evangelical reform; similarly the ex-monk Otto Brunfels at Neuenberg and Peter Spengler at Schlatt.

Probably about this time, 1522 or 1523, the new Evangelical reforming ideas reached St. Peter's and its prior, Michael Sattler. According to the *Martyrs Mirror*, as with most Reformers, Sattler was much concerned about the prevalent institutional abuses in monasticism and the low moral standards of many of the priests and monks. From this background of reform interest he began a personal study of the Pauline Epistles.[238]

Exactly when he espoused the Evangelical Reformation, left the monastery, and married is not know, but possibly late in 1523 or in 1524.[239] Early in 1525 he adopted the Anabaptist interpretation of the church and the nature of true reform. Sattler's wife also became a fervent Anabaptist and died as a martyr.[240] Anshelm reports that the wife which Sattler chose was a Beghuine.[241] Her training as a Beghuine was an excellent preparation for her conversion to Swiss Anabaptism[242] and may have influenced Sattler also in that direction. The Beghuines were very close to the Franciscan Third Order. In 1453 Pope Nicholas V actually decreed that all Beghards and Beghuines were to belong also to the Third Order.[243] McDonnell comments concerning Beghuine spirituality that "from a European-wide perspective, it is one facet of a profound reform program, lay in appeal, and abiding by the ascesis of the primitive church. . . ."[244]

Ferdinand I not only decreed (first at Nürnberg, November 1522, and again in 1523)[245] the extirpation of heresy in his lands, including Breisgau, but pressed for effective action. Apparently this forced Sattler to flee early in 1525, if not sooner, to the Zürich area. By February or March of 1525, very shortly after the birth of the Swiss "Anabaptist" Brethren (January 21, 1525), Sattler was already associated with the Anabaptist movement.[246] Gustav Bossert gives Rueblin credit for his conversion. If so, Sattler had probably not yet reached Zürich but perhaps was in the Schaffhausen, Waldshut, and south Breisgau area, where Reublin was preaching. Myron S. Augsburger notes the continuing closeness of Reublin and Sattler; for example, they were together in Strassburg in 1526 and were coworkers in South Germany until Sattler's arrest and execution in

1527.[247] Reublin wrote a moving account of Sattler's trial and execution.[248]

The sources give us no specific reasons for Sattler's conversion to Anabaptism. However, by March 25, 1525, he must have already fully espoused Swiss Anabaptism since at that time he appears in prison in Zürich as an Anabaptist in company with George Blaurock, a number of Zollikon Brethren, and some other founding leaders.[249] After his release, he apparently continued teaching and preaching for the Brethren cause in the Ufter area, in association with Mumprat of Constance, Conrad Winkler, and Carli Brenwald.[250] In October, he joined Blaurock, Grebel, and Manz at Grüningen.[251] They were imprisoned at Grüningen and were taken to Zürich for trial and for the November disputation. Sattler was expelled after taking an oath of nonretaliation (Urfecht) and paying a fine.[252]

To this point, the indication of an initially strong ethical ascetic sensitivity which was partly responsible for leaving the monastery, and the circumstantial evidence of a quick and close association with the founders of Swiss Anabaptism, only suggest the possibility of ascetic sympathy as the primary reason for Sattler's abandoning, rather quickly, the Evangelical reform movement to espouse wholeheartedly Swiss Anabaptism. But further confirmation comes from a scrutiny of the later documents of his life.

He next appeared as a guest in Capito's home in Strassburg in the fall of 1526.[253] At Strassburg, Sattler entered into friendly discussions with the Evangelical Reformers, especially Capito and Bucer. From these discussions,[254] and also the differences between Sattler and Hans Denck which became apparent upon the latter's arrival in Strassburg,[255] one can perceive more clearly the basis for Sattler's strong and ready adherence to the principles of the Swiss Brethren and something of his chief objections to the Evangelical Reformation.

After consultation with the other Swiss Anabaptists in Strassburg, he wrote his "20 Articles"[256] for presentation to Capito and Bucer. In this document one can readily detect the main thrust of Sattler's concern, which is ultimately embodied also in the Schleitheim Confession (1527) and so mediated to most of the enduring branches of Anabaptism.[257] His principal concern is for the preservation in true Christianity of moral earnestness and ascetic idealism. His ascetic convictions are so strong, perhaps even stronger than those of the original Zürich Brethren, and expressed so clearly and forcefully at Strassburg that one must conclude that they are at the heart of both his initial and continuing rejection of the Evangelical Reformation and his espousal of Swiss Anabaptism. This conclusion coincides with Walter Koehler's studied observation that Sattler's "entire work was the pursuit of one goal: the formation and purification of a church of believers and saints. As an Evangelical, he was able to find his standard only in the gospel, especially in the Sermon on the Mount."[258]

Articles 7 through 20 especially, in his "20 Articles," advocate a strong ascetic dualism. They contrast walking in darkness with walking in light, they emphasize the "enmity" of the flesh against the Spirit, and they polarize this worldly citizenship over against the heavenly. They also stress that the believer is "chosen out of the world" and predestined to "conformity to the image of Christ," and that only "they are true Christians who do the teachings of Christ with works." The document concludes with a summarizing pronouncement that "Christ and Belial have nothing in common." The whole document is nothing less than a manifesto for moral separation on lay, ascetic terms.

Sattler's "Letter to Capito," explaining his departure from Strasburg, and also Capito's later letter to the council at Horb (after the martydom of Sattler) confirm that the ascetic issues in the "20 Articles" were the primary areas of actual disagreement between "Sattlerian" Anabaptists and the Strassburg Magisterial Reformers.[259] Apparently Bucer and Capito did not think these differences were deep enough to warrant a breach of friendship or of Evangelical unity. Bucer later still referred to Sattler as "a dear friend of God although he was a leader of the Anabaptists; but much more skilled and honorable than some."[260] But for Sattler the differences were vital. He believed that Capito and Bucer incorrectly wanted to make obedience to the Word less important than unity and love.[261] Capito comments on the situation and also illustrates Sattler's great concern over behavior, in his letter to the council at Horb, thus:

> This Michael is known to us here in Strassburg and he was somewhat in error, which we showed him through the Scriptures; but since he saw a lack in our preachers and in other preachers of the true doctrine, especially in the outward life of the congregation . . . his method and his articles of faith we always kindly rejected.[262]

Doubtlessly Sattler, the ex-monk, with his strongly ascetic pre-

Ascetic Factors in Emerging Anabaptism 117

disposition and program, made a deep and enduring imprint on the development of Anabaptism through his close personal association with the founding leaders of the Zürich Brethren. His close friendship with the leading Evangelical Reformers also, and their respect for him, indicate the quality of his piety, the consistency of his convictions, and the strength of his personality. He provided the leadership for the 1527 Schleitheim conference, the first organized attempt to delineate a basis for unity for the whole Swiss Brethren movement.

The clarity of the seven brief articles which Sattler composed for the Schleitheim conference, which were adopted by it for all the Swiss Brethren, plus the impressiveness of his martyrdom, the record of which, along with the Seven Articles, was rapidly printed and widely disseminated,[263] added much to the strength of his influence. This was aided also by the lack of other theological writings, apart from Hubmaier's among, the Swiss Brethren due to both the forced mobility of the leaders and often their very brief life-span — as a result of persecution and execution.

By his absolute application of the ascetic ideals to additional practical details of the Christian's social life (for example, to the bearing of arms), Sattler enhanced ascetic separation among the Swiss Brethren and their offshoots in Moravia and the Netherlands. Jan Kiwiet even suggests that after Sattler's "Schleitheim Articles" the Anabaptists were separated from other Christians and united together less by theological differences than by their religious life, their asceticism.[264] Sattler's vital role in further defining and consolidating the ascetic nature of this "religious life" was not in any sense a departure from the initial principles of the Brethren movement that issued from Zürich, but rather he was developing, defining, and extending them.

Martin Weninger. A tract by the Anabaptist leader, Martin Weninger (also called Martin Lingy or Lingki), summarizes well this portion of our investigation into the ascetic factor in the early development of Anabaptism. Weninger, a weaver from Schaffhausen, was won to Anabaptism by Grebel during Grebel's February-March (1525) sojourn at Schaffhausen. A few months later, in November 1525, Weninger was imprisoned with a number of the most active leaders of the Zürich Brethren, including Blaurock, Manz, Grebel, and Sattler.[265] These imprisonments together were usually times of mutual sharing, stabilizing, and unifying of their doctrinal views. After the

118   Anabaptism and Asceticism

trial, both Sattler and Weninger were expelled from the canton of Zürich.[266]

Weninger continued his active leadership and promotion of the Swiss Brethren cause. Evidence of his missionary work appear mostly in Basel, Bern, and Solothurn area,[267] but there is reference also to a brief stay at Strassburg.[268] Bernese officials specifically asked the Solothurn authorities to send him to the Zofingen Disputation of 1532. This request indicates both that they considered him a major leader and probably also that he had spent considerable time proselytizing in that area.

At the "Zofingen Disputation"[269] he was one of the principal speakers for the Anabaptist cause. Bertold Haller, the reformed leader at Bern, referred to him as a "learned man." In October of 1532, he was apparently preaching again in the Zürich area[270] but persecution and threat of execution had intensified to the point of making effective proselytizing almost impossible in Switzerland. He then returned to Schaffhausen, and under pressure (imprisonment) finally recanted and submitted to the Magisterial Reformation shortly before 1538.[271]

Weninger's *Vindication (or Rechenschaft)*,[272] 1535, probably written to Galle Hafner, an Evangelical clergyman at Schaffhausen, at his request, clearly summarizes what seems by then to be the standard Swiss Brethren response to the question why they separated themselves from the Magisterial Reformation and became Anabaptists. He maintains that the contemporary Evangelical clergy were "teaching sins and hardening people in their sins with their frivolous teaching. . . . They minimize to the people the shadow of the wantonness of their life of sin (Jeremiah 8:6; 2 Peter 2), saying peace . . . to those who ridicule God with their doings and walk after the lust and desire of their evil heart, and they themselves are servants of corruption to sin. They are called Christians who walk in darkness. . . . By such evident witness it is now clear that the doctrine of the priests [Evangelical] is not of God. . . ."[273] He continues: "[Their] preaching does not help, people are getting worse and worse, no one is improving."[274] Why? because there is no "ban to make any difference whether a person does good or evil."[275] He concludes: "Now since they do not preach . . . the doctrine of godliness, Paul teaches us to shun them."[276]

Clearly, the Brethren could not recognize any congregation as a true church of Christ whose leaders tolerated carnality (as defined by Anabaptist, ascetic standards)[277] among both clergy and laity. Once again it is evident that manifest holiness of life is the decisive issue. From Weninger's writings, Wenger concludes: "Fully aware of their own depravity, the Brethren nevertheless felt that unless a believer lived a holy life, he was not one of Christ's disicples."[278] Thus the findings thus far from this analysis of formative Anabaptist leadership answer affirmatively the original questions, that is, (1) whether the necessity for Christians to live a "holy life" was the central issue in the Anabaptists' break from the Magisterial Reformation, and (2) whether this life was ascetically motivated and defined.

In Anabaptist Preaching

The thesis that Anabaptism's dominant and distinctive conviction is that a transformation of conduct, according to the traditional ascetic norms, must visibly typify all Christians is buttressed further by considering the principal thrust of early Anabaptist preaching. The Anabaptist Brethren of Zürich went out to the villages as "John the Baptists," calling on all who would hear to forsake sin and demanding a personal conversion that included active, manifest penance or amendment of life. In this, they follow rather closely the traditional pattern of the medieval "preachers of repentance" of the previous generation, such as Savonarola or Geiler von Keysersberg.

One of the most influential, evangelist-missionary preachers during the first years of Anabaptist expansion was George Blaurock. Blaurock's preaching proclaimed: "Therefore, ye children of men, forsake your sins . . . now that you can find the Physician who can heal all infirmities."[279] To those he was trying to convert, such as Marx Bosshard in Zollikon (1525), Blaurock demanded a change in one's conduct: "You have hitherto been a frivolous [frölich] young man and now you must become a different man; put off the old Adam and put on a new one, and be changed."[280]

The reference to putting off the "old Adam" (or the fleshly nature) also coincides with the traditional, ascetically oriented call to repentance. Blaurock's success in winning the more mature and aged also may be an indication of the traditional nature of his message. The appeal was compatible with their ascetic presuppositions regarding the Christian life. Blaurock reasserts that the only way to be acceptable to God, to be truly a Christian, is to "be changed" (*dich besseren*) and to adopt a life of holiness in conduct, in contrast to worldliness and frivolity.

Blaurock's preaching calling for the personal espousal of ascetic norms of conduct is consistent with that of Grebel's. While Grebel was preaching in the Grünigen area, in the early fall of 1525, an invitation to preach came from Dürnten. He declared himself ready to do so "if the people there would turn away from sin and from drinking and carousing."[281] Similarly, Blanke describes the conversion of Jörg Schad as basically an agreement to begin a new life and to live according to the Sermon on the Mount. It was on this basis that Schad "requested the sign of brotherly love," or baptism.[282]

Thus, even Anabaptist preaching and teaching on believer's rather than infant baptism is, as Zwingli recognized it, actually a subsidiary issue; the real objective is to elicit an ascetic conversion. The norm of the Sermon on the Mount, which occurs so often,[283] is also very much a part of the older ascetic code. It coincides with Blaurock's proclamation: "This is what God requires: that the whole human race shall love and fear Him, that they should follow [imitate] His Son Jesus Christ, and observe His divine doctrine."[284]

Though some Anabaptist preaching had an intense sense of eschatological urgency, even this was understood in an ascetic framework; that is, it anticipated the complete destruction, soon, of this temporal, evil "world-system," to be replaced by the kingdom of God. Their message of repentance and obedience to the Word of God was preparatory to the sorting about to take place in the final judgment. The quotation, which occurs repeatedly in Anabaptist preaching and teaching, that "the axe is laid to the root of the tree" illustrates the urgency and intensity of their expectations of eschatological purification.[285]

Accordingly, Anabaptist preaching was *not* generally directed toward either social reform or revolution, but rather toward withdrawal from worldliness and toward a moral preparation for Christ's coming in judgment to punish the evil and reward the good. Even though the South German Anabaptist leader, Hans Hut, had previous ties with Thomas Müntzer and retained a very strong eschatological emphasis in his preaching, many of his followers readily adopted Hutterian communitarianism, the most ascetically structured branch of Anabaptism, as the proper preparatory role while awaiting the final eschatological event.

Unfortunately, Anabaptist sermons were rarely written and even more rarely preserved or published. One important exception is an anonymous Anabaptist sermon, "On Jeremiah," which was published in 1527, coupled in one pamphlet with Eitelhans Langenmantel's tract, *An Exposition of the Lord's Prayer*.[286] Langenmantel may have written both works but the evidence is not clear. At any rate, Langenmantel had been baptized by Hans Hut early in 1527, and the pamphlet, with both tracts, stems from the formative years of this South German branch of Anabaptism.

Though not the product of the original Swiss Brethren, this sermon on Jeremiah corroborates fully the previous indirect evidence concerning the objectives of Anabaptist preaching. Its text and theme, from Jeremiah 7, asserts: "God says: 'Amend your ways and your doings, then will I dwell with you in this place; and let no one deceive himself.' "[287] The sermon asserts that God "demands" that the whole world fulfill the "command of Christ," that is, "recognize Christ's teaching" and His "words" and "do them," and, that it "forsake sin and henceforth sin no more."[288] It adds that the first plank in building an enduring Christian house (or life) is: "Desist from sin";[289] later this exhortation is ascetically rephrased as: "Desist from deceptive wealth and from the superfluous cares of this world."[290] It concludes by asserting that no one is born into the kingdom of God unless he not only receives the Word in his heart but is willing to do and obey it.[291]

In Anabaptist-Magisterial Polemics

Criticism of the Magisterial reform. The Anabaptists' primary, continuous, and explicit criticism of the Magisterial Reformation also focused on the conviction that it lacked adequate ethical convictions. This criticism was directed against both the Magisterial clergy and laity. Grebel protests that "in our time everyone hopes to be saved . . . while remaining in the old life of sin."[292] He also asserts during the course of his trial that "no avaricious person, no usurer, no gambler . . . shall have a place among the Christians."[293] In his last letter to the "Brethren," Felix Manz calls the Magisterial Reformers "false prophets." His reason for this assessment is plainly given: they are those who "curse and pray with the same mouth, and whose life is disorderly."[294]

Hubmaier echoes the same refrain. His criticisms also reveal the

122   Anabaptism and Asceticism

ascetic,moralistic framework behind the Anabaptist dissent. He protests that while all Evangelicals appeal to the gospel, the Magisterial Reformers, or "would-be Evangelical people,"

> claim to be good Christians and Evangelical . . . [but] *nothing can be seen* except drinking, reveling, blasphemy, usury, lying, deceit, extortion, cheating, violence, robbery, arson, gambling, dancing, courting, idleness, fornication, adultery, rape, tyranny, assaults, murder. Everything is *frivolity and insolence of the flesh.*

He adds, that the [Magisterial] Reformers are doing nothing to correct this situation because the old Adam in them "wants to be a Christian and yet go without correction." In contrast, he writes: "Christ Jesus our Lord and Savior always took great pains to *uproot and combat sin* among His people."[295] Significantly, Hubmaier also condemns the system which combined ecclesiastical and temporal powers because it produced an unholy, worldly clergy.[296]

Michael Sattler during his discussion with the Strassburg Reformers, and in subsequent tracts concerning the nature of true Christianity, also expressed anxiety over the unholy conduct of many associated with the Magisterial Reformation and charges them with deficient faith and unwillingness to exercise discipline.[297] In his letter to the magistracy at Horb, Capito sadly acknowledges some validity to Sattler's observations concerning the lack of manifest piety.[298]

Perhaps the most direct and mature attack, written in 1535 in dialogue with a Zwinglian clergyman, is Martin Weninger's *Vindication*. It reflects the continuing adverse reaction by the Anabaptists to the continued lack of manifest holy living among the clergy and laity of the Magisterial Reformation. He protests: ". . . their preaching does not help, people are getting worse and worse, no one is improving," and they "draw the wanton people to themselves and harden them in sin . . . and they themselves are servants of corruption and sin."[299] Such carnality was considered valid proof that the churches of the Magisterial Reformation were not true representatives of the church of Christ. This is consistent with the earlier Swiss Anabaptist statement, at the Bernese Debate of 1528, charging that within the Reformation church "no beginning was made toward true Christian conduct."[300]

Various Anabaptist spokesmen at Marburg, in 1538, especially Hans Kuchenbacher,[301] Jörg Schnabel,[302] and Jörg Leinhardt,[303] continue to press the same criticism. The Hutterian *Chronicle* sum-

Ascetic Factors in Emerging Anabaptism 123

marizes the ultimate conclusion of the Anabaptists when it labels the Magisterial Reformation as "the new Babylon, because no amendment of life was perceived in them at all." It also comments further that the Anabaptists believed the Magisterial Reformation program to be deficient because it was satisfied essentially with external, institutional, and ceremonial reforms, but not sufficiently concerned about piety.[304]

The Anabaptists blamed the ethical failure of the Magisterial Reformation not directly on political issues, such as separation of church and state, but on religious deficiencies. Wenger maintains, specifically, that they accused the Magisterial Reformers of theological deficiency with reference to faith and repentance and with disciplinary failure owing to a lack of spiritual commitment.[305] For all three issues (faith, repentance, and church discipline) the Anabaptists define the failure of the Magisterial Reformation in terms that reflect their own ascetic presuppositions.

Theologically, they consistently condemned any concept of justification by faith which would eliminate from faith the necessity also of good works, obedience, and love. In "Concerning the Satisfaction of Christ," Sattler complains that the Magisterial Reformers "reject works without faith in order that they may set up faith without works. They wish to obey God only with the soul and not also *with the body*. . . ."[306] He repudiates any interpretation of Scripture on justification that weakens moral effort and responsibility, or that suggests "a person could be saved through Christ whether he does works of faith or not."[307]

Similarly, Hubmaier ascribes beliefs to the Magisterial Reformers that he rejects as "half truths," namely that "faith saves us, and we can do nothing," and that "there is no free will, God acts sovereignly in salvation." He maintains that people had learned these "half-truths" or articles of faith "without any amendment of life" and that such ideas had become an excuse for producing a situation in which "no Christian works are practiced and brotherly love is extinguished in all hearts." For this reason, he continues, "the world is worse than it was 1,000 years ago."[308]

Parallel with the Anabaptists' rejection of any definition of the content of faith which would divorce it from good works and conduct was their conviction that the Magisterial Reformers were also ignoring the necessity of repentance in their doctrine of salvation. They maintained that the Magisterial Reformers were preaching forgiveness without requiring the intent of amendment of life. A testimony at the Bernese Disputation (1538) illustrates the point well. It asserts that while in the Reformed Church, "We were aware of a great lack in regard to repentance, conversion, and the true Christian life. It *was on these things that my heart was set* . . .[but] true repentance and Christian love were not in evidence." He refers to Grebel and his associates as those "who had surrendered themselves to the doctrine of Christ by conversion. With their assistance a congregation was formed in which *repentance was in evidence.*"³⁰⁹ How they defined repentance will be discussed in chapter IV.

The third major deficiency to which the Anabaptists attributed causality for the moral failure of the Reformation was the Reformers' unwillingness to utilize the ban in the church to ensure proper Christian conduct, in accordance with Matthew 18. The Anabaptists repeatedly refer to this failure as a justification for continuing their institutionally separate existence as a church.³¹⁰ For this attitude, the *Vindication* provides one of the fullest and clearest explanations:

> Dear one, how many are now Christ's brethren who do God's will? Therefore your fellowship is not a brotherhood [bruderschafft] of Christ. For you have as brethren: adulterers, heavy drinkers, blasphemers, misers, usurers, dancers, carnival [masqueraders], alley ruffians; without a ban to make any difference, whether a person do good or evil. Dear one, why? For this reason, that the priests who ought to discipline the people are just like the people. Therefore Paul teaches and admonishes us to keep clear of such people (2 Timothy 2).³¹¹

The above passage may explain, in part, Calvinism's success in replacing much of Anabaptism in the Netherlands since Calvin did add the need of applied discipline through the ban to his definition of the church.

Jörg Schnabel in his debate with Bucer at Marburg in 1538 specifically selects these same three deficiencies (the lack of adequate doctrines of working *faith* and *repentance* and the lack of the external application of moral *discipline*) as the "most important" reasons for his initial withdrawal from the Magisterial Church and for his continued rejection of it. Schnabel points first to his concern over the failure of many who professed faith to exhibit Christlike conduct, such as their callousness regarding the poor in the practice of usury. Then, he adds the second and related doctrinal criticism that "the teachers had forgotten repentance." Finally, he refers to their lack of

Ascetic Factors in Emerging Anabaptism 125

effective discipline, to their neglect of the ban. He claims that the leaders refused to take disciplinary action to "stop sinning" (according to their Anabaptist code) even when such was pointed out to them. He expresses the typical Anabaptist, ascetically oriented reform expectations clearly: "Although this church [Magisterial] was to be better than the papist . . . avarice is now double in the church."[312] On the basis of this threefold failure, Schnabel concludes that the Magisterial Church is not the true church of Christ and union with it is impossible for Anabaptists.[313]

Criticism of the Anabaptists. The opponents of Anabaptism went a step further and specifically and repeatedly asserted that there was an essential affinity between Anabaptist aims and ideals and medieval Catholic, monastic spirituality. As early as January 1525, Hegenwald's letter, replying to Grebel, raises the issue of identifying Anabaptist moralism with legalism. In opposition to Grebel he writes: "I do not call the avoidance of the externally wicked life 'walking without the appearance of evil.' " He adds: "Herein you are lacking," and then pointedly suggests that Grebel was failing to recognize that the details of both external practices and conduct are unimportant as long as faith is present.[314] Grebel apparently had insisted that whoever really believes will obey the Word of Christ completely, even in external things. Finally, Hegenwald in Lutheran fashion, and similar to Luther's and Zwingli's criticism of the monastic system, explicitly accuses Grebel of insisting that salvation stands on external works, including a legalistic code of conduct, thus making Christ a "Moses." He adds that real piety is a humble trust in the cross and not in anything else.[315]

Similarly, Zwingli, first in his initial conversations with Stumpf, Grebel, and Manz in 1524, and then again in the later disputations at Zürich with the Swiss Brethren leaders, repeatedly accused his former colleagues of perfectionism, of requiring that only "holy" people be considered true Christians, and of trying to set up a church "without sin."[316] Also, in his *Elenchus* of 1527,[317] criticizing the "Schleitheim Confession," he maintains that the way Sattler advocated the use of the ban implied a kind of perfectionism in which Christian piety is pressed to the extreme of an impossible separation from all worldliness. Zwingli asserts that they "think of themselves so finely that they boast that they are the people who have been called of God from the world. As if . . . all mortals were not worldly."[318] In addition, Zwingli considered that the "Schleitheim Confession's" demand for separation implied a "works-righteousness."[319] He concludes that the Anabaptist position is a "new monkery," adding: "For the foolish men assume what the monks used to assume, viz., that they are in a state of perfection, although they do not use these words."[320] It is important to remember that when Zwingli accuses the Swiss Brethren of reasserting a "monkish" concept of perfectionism, that must not be confused with "perfectionism" in modern Protestant theology.

Moreover, while Zwingli exaggerated the Anabaptist position at times, other less antagonistic witnesses also agree with his overall evaluation of Anabaptism. For example, the Anabaptist leader, Hubmaier, commenting on "the fear of God" and its relationship to works, admits: "Concerning this fear of God I have so earnestly preached up to this time that many people hate me therefore, and say that I want to make monks and nuns of them. That I can prove by many hundred men."[321] The context of this statement makes clear that its purpose is not to deny the relationship suggested but rather to uphold it.

Again, though Hubmaier reacts negatively to Zwingli's whole charge that they permitted baptism only to those who confess they are "without sin," agree to "live" and "be dressed according to your standards" and thus "compel with baptism as if it were a monkish vow," yet he fails to respond specifically except for the weak rejoinder that all Anabaptists choose baptism voluntarily. This silence seems to indicate acceptance of some aspects of the charge since he had been countering Zwingli, clause by clause, up to this point.[322] In fact, on at least one other occasion Hubmaier asserted that they did "command baptism [with its external significance] to others,"[323] and this comes close to verifying even Zwingli's charge of "compulsion."

The reaction by the Strassburg Reformers, Capito and Bucer, to Michael Sattler's presentation of Anabaptism was based on their high personal regard and continued friendship for him; it is not tinged with animosity or bitter conflict. Yet Capito also rejected Sattler's position on discipline and manifest holiness and considered it to be conformity by coercion. Capito also describes it as a "new monkery."[324] Johannes Kessler of St. Gall remarks in his diary that the Anabaptists insisted "even more vigorously than the papists on righteous works."[325]

Luther and Calvin made the same accusations. Luther reacted strongly against the Anabaptist assertion that baptism was not a work of God unless the recipient was a believer in the personal, ethical sense of which the Anabaptists defined such. He considered them blatant legalists in the Roman Catholic tradition. Thus he wrote: "So also the papists still to this day insist on works and worthiness of the person, contrary to grace, thus giving strong support (in words at least) to their brethren, the Anabaptists. . . . While they outwardly profess to be great enemies, inwardly they think, teach, and defend one and the same against our only Savior Christ, who alone is our righteousness."[326] Calvin's remarkable reference to the Anabaptists "and their companions, the Jesuits" is based on his understanding that the Anabaptists demanded repentance before the signs of grace, and that they even "prescribe to their young certain days, during which they must exercise themselves in repentance."[327]

Summary

The early history of Anabaptism substantiates Ritschl's assertion that the first leaders were primarily motivated by ascetic ideals which still permeated much of early sixteenth-century society owing to the vitality of the late medieval ascetic reform movements. Therefore, they relate primarily to the larger "rightist" reaction to Luther which began to reveal itself increasingly among many Evangelical Reformers, especially in the era of 1520 to 1525. Some, reacting against both the lack of theological motivation for ethical reform and the schismatic tendencies in Luther, returned to the old church. Others, though accepting the validity, even necessity, of a break by the Reformation from the former institutional Catholic Church, were still deeply disillusioned by the ethical deficiencies and by some of the theological definitions of the Magisterial Reformers.

Some of these latter dissenters created new "reformed" syntheses — one of which was Anabaptism. The concern for manifest holiness, traditionally and ascetically conceived, coupled with the Reformation accent on biblical authority, spiritually and devotionally apprehended, became the twin foci for a unique "Protestant," Anabaptist theology and institutionalization. This alternate reformed synthesis can perhaps be characterized best as a Protestantized continuation of an ascetic, biblical theology of holiness.

In their effort to demonstrate doctrinally the Evangelical orthodoxy of Anabaptism, some Mennonite historians tend to minimize the differences between Anabaptists and Magisterial Reformers.[328] Wenger's contention that their differences were mostly in such matters as baptism, separation of church and state, liberty of conscience, rejection of the oath, and nonresistance rather than in essential theology, overlooks the real essence of Anabaptist uniqueness. Rather, the fundamental differences involved such vital matters as the goal of the whole reform movement, the way of salvation itself, including justification, penance, grace and voluntavism, and individual and corporate perfectibility,[329] In Hubmaier's debate with John Faber in 1527, "Hubmaier . . . could more easily make concessions to Catholic Faber than . . . to Protestant Zwingli, for example, on the freedom of the will and the importance of good works."[330]

The Anabaptists' zeal for holy living led to more than external variations on Luther and Zwingli, and to more than just a greater tendency to moralism and legalism; it led to a fundamentally different theology.[331] As Bender noted, the Anabaptists' charge of *Scheinglauben* brought the counterchange of *Scheinheiligkeit* by the Reformers[332] — an indication of deep internal differences. These observations suggest the need of a further analysis of Anabaptist theology in terms of their prime objective or *raison d'être* as a movement.[333]

Furthermore, our study has already provided some preliminary insights into the problem of the origins of the distinctively Anabaptist synthesis, especially its ascetically oriented, theological, and conductual predispositions. Anabaptism reflects the lay, ascetic ideals and the "Imitation of Christ" tradition of the *Devotio Moderna* of the fifteenth century; possibly mediated partly through Erasmus, and certainly through the influence of the many ex-monks, including some Franciscan Observants, who assumed substantial leadership roles in the formative years of Anabaptism. There is, however, no evidence for any significant connections with medieval heresies.

4 THE DOMINANCE OF ASCETICISM IN THE STRUCTURING OF ANABAPTIST THEOLOGY

Among the many and varied attempts to categorize and characterize the theology of Evangelical Anabaptism,[1] three have made major, preparatory contributions to the approach of this chapter, namely; Ethelbert Stauffer's "Theology of Martyrdom,"[2] Harold Bender's "Theology of Discipleship,"[3] and Robert Friedmann's "Doctrine of the Two Worlds."[4] These three discussions, each trying to isolate the essence of the Anabaptist faith, actually complement each other and are subsidiary and closely related facets in a well-established theological pattern in the medieval church, the ascetic theology of holiness. That Anabaptist theology may be best expressed as a theology of holiness coincides also with one of Myron S. Augsburger's generalizations following his detailed study of Michael Sattler. Augsburger comments: "Sattler's thought finds its major premise in God's holiness and an Anabaptist/Mennonite theology would be a ... 'theology of Holiness.' "[5]

Elements Comprising an Ascetic Theology of Holiness

At least three ingredients are essential to the existence of a Christian theology of holiness or perfection in its broadest compass:

First, there must be a conviction that the development and attainment of actual sanctity, of Christlikeness in inner spirit and outer conduct in the individual Christian disciple, is both a possibility and at the same time the supreme object of the redemptive purposes of God.[6] Second, every person hoping for salvation is required to actively pursue and, in some measure, attain in this life some similitude of this otherworldly perfection — based on Christ's words: "Be ye therefore perfect, even as your Father which is in heaven is perfect."[7] Third, if the ideal of the pursuit of holiness is to become a full theology of holiness, it must be demonstrably the determinative interpretive principle for understanding and expressing all other aspects of Christian doctrine and practice.[8] It must have become the "crown" of all moral and dogmatic theology.

A theology of holiness may be identified further by contrasting it with the Luther-type theology of forensic or "imputed" justification, which stresses justification and assurance of salvation by a trusting faith, or belief, alone. In Luther and Zwingli, each believer is legally accounted righteous, even perfect, before God solely by the merits and perfection of Christ which are imputed fully to the believer by faith alone. The believer remains in some sense an actual and practicing sinner throughout his life; he remains ontologically unchanged.[9] As Zwingli asserts, "Our works insofar as they are good, so far they are of Christ, but insofar as they are ours, are neither right nor good."[10]

In Luther and Zwingli this doctrine of imputed righteousness is logically combined with and supported by the doctrines of total depravity, the bondage of will, and sovereign, unconditional election. In such a pattern, justification and actual sanctification are separated and, especially in Luther, the former becomes dominant; the latter tends to become secondary.[11] Thus, for Luther, assurance is a matter of a trusting faith in the promises; for a holiness theology, assurance requires that the trusting faith be evidenced by the fruitage of actual holiness in life.

Similarly, a theology of holiness can be distinguished from a theology of external sacramentalism, or of salvation by institutionalized rites and submission to ecclesiastical authority. The latter type of theology tends to limit the extent and range of necessary, personal, spiritual involvement and, as in the medieval era, to produce the idea of a large body of laity who are adequately obedient but often quite spiritually passive. Consequently, those reform movements in the medieval church, such as that of Francis of Assisi, which aimed at the advance of personal holiness for the whole church, maintained at times a somewhat tenuous union with the institutional program. They reconciled the tensions by dramatizing, spiritualizing, and asceticizing the sacraments, especially the mass, and by emphasizing the inner, devotional attitude of the recipient. Many historians have noted the latent tendency by such reform movements to minimize, even bypass the external agencies of the institutional church in favor of piety through personal devotion to Christ as an adequate road to salvation.[12]

When the adjective "ascetic" is added, the resultant designation, "an ascetic theology of holiness," is even more precise. It implies all the additional limiting distinctives and characteristics of the ascetic tradition, as outlined in chapter two. Also the contrasting of an "ascetic" theology of holiness with a "mystical" theology of holiness, and with what may be described as a "secular" theology of holiness, contributes further clarification to the topic. The value of making these particular comparisons will become more apparent as this study progresses.

The "ascetic" approach appears to be distinguishable from the mystical, though they are not necessarily mutually exclusive, primarily with reference to the agencies for the attainment of the desired perfection; also sometimes with reference to the ultimate goal itself. An ascetic theology of holiness stresses the practical, daily, outward struggle for the mortification of sin and the flesh, and also those practical exercises and activities aimed at the cultivation of the inner virtues; whereas the mystical stresses more directly the internal, especially the contemplative and ecstatic.[13]

While the goal of both is perfection,[14] the ascetic stresses perfection as active conformity to Christ, as the imitation of Christ, an externally effective, otherworldly value system, or as a union with Christ in the sense of a practical conformity to the divine will and purpose, but maintaining generally some humanness and self-identity. The mystical often has neoplatonic tendencies which move beyond a renunciation of the evil self-nature, the evil flesh, and the evil world system to a negation of the physical itself, and beyond conformity to Christ to a spiritual union with, or an esoteric vision of, the divine by contemplative ecstasy which ultimately ends in something closer to total absorption into the divine.[15] Furthermore, while the ascetic way may be either individual or communal, the mystical tends to be strongly solitary, subjective, and private.

Basing his interpretations on Thomas Aquinas and John of the Cross, Garrigou-Lagrange maintains that Christian ascetic and Christian mystical theology though not identical, are nevertheless closely related, even complementary aspects within the theology of the spiritual life and the pursuit of perfection.[16] Lagrange also presents the ascetic, or purgative, as simply the initial, lower, and renunciatory stage on the road to perfection, and a moderate, Christian mysticism as the third, or highest, or unitive stage. Then, he suggests, the two, the ascetic and the mystical, overlap and fuse in the middle stage, the stage characterized by the positive aspects of the imitation of Christ.[17]

Other scholars, using a wider range of historical data, suggest that an ascetic theology may remain distinct, and does not necessarily lead to the mystical; is involved by definition as much with positive, spiritual development as with renunciation and purgation; has internal as well as external concerns; and often claims to include in itself *all* that is necessary for the attainment of perfection and true union with Christ.[18] This viewpoint, therefore, rejects the idea that the ascetic way is restricted to being only a preliminary and inferior stage in an essentially mystical way to holiness; rather, it maintains the complete sufficiency of the ascetic way and the necessity in true spirituality of a continuous correlation of the internal and spiritual with the external and practical, at all levels.[19] Orthodox Christian mysticism and Christian asceticism, though related, at times overlapping, and having a similar but not identical goal, are nevertheless separable and distinguishable in both theory and historical expression.[20]

An ascetic theology of holiness also contrasts with a theology of secular holiness, such as is found in Luther. The latter teaches not only sanctification as vicarious and imputed by faith, and the actual unfulfillability in this life of the law, but also the acceptability of living out the Christian life in civil society, and in one's calling.[21] Luther's combination of "secular holiness and imputed sanctification eliminates a rigorous ascetic sense of alienation from civil society, much of the compulsion for progress in personal and otherworldly holiness, and much of the necessity for personal effort in its attainment that are typical of ascetic spirituality. Actual sanctification is also considered a gift of God in Christ, essentially attained after death; one's major concern in this life is to serve God acceptably in the common occupations. Williams has noted the divergence of Luther's doctrine of vocation in the world from the religious vocation of the

The Dominance of Asceticism   133

medieval ascetic with its radical withdrawal from the world.[22] In the ascetic tradition, "calling," even when laicized is still essentially religious, and work is primarily for religious purposes. Work may have value for developing holiness or as an aid to fulfilling a religious end, as in a lay missionary, but it is not itself generally equated with holiness; holiness is not secularized.

When the characteristics of the ascetic theology of holiness in the Christian ascetic tradition prior to the sixteenth century, especially in the twelfth to fifteenth centuries, as outlined in chapter two, are coupled with the above distinctions, they constitute a sufficiently constant and precise set of norms and categories for a comparative evaluation of the essence, character, and pattern of early Anabaptist theology and practices. The most discernible, essential, and constant characteristics include a distinctive goal, several distinctive supporting principles, and some distinctive practical expressions, briefly summarized as follows: The primary goal of the ascetic Christian life is for an ever-increasing realization and manifestation in the individual and the group, in this life, of the Christ image, or, of holiness with a strong moral and ascetic definition. The most constant characteristics of holiness appear positively as a total love for God and for one's fellows, total obedience to God, and an otherworldly value system; and negatively as the elimination of sin which is identified primarily with a corrupt human society, the flesh, and the devil. The consummation of this pursuit of holiness, in the eternal state, constitutes full and true salvation.

The most obvious of the several fundamental supporting principles by which the goal is attained, and the pursuit activated and manifested, is both inner and outer renunciation, to eradicate sin's power. This principle incorporates also mortification of the flesh and its lusts, the death of self-will or total submission to the divine, and separation from this present evil world system or society — from its goals, its values, and especially its materialism.[23] It implies a deep pessimism and antagonism toward this present evil world system. Persons are redeemable but this world system is not; rather, it is predestined for destruction and replacement by a divine kingdom.

A second principle for the attainment of holiness is the development and practical manifestation of positive virtues. The correct virtues are those modeled by the life of Christ, the perfect Man, and those enjoined by Him, especially in the "Sermon on the Mount." These first two principles imply that orthodox Christian asceticism generally has a strong sense both of human degeneracy and of man's domination by sin due to the fall, that is, a strong belief in the powers of sin and the devil, and in the hopelessness of betterment without the aid of divine grace in Christ.

Here a third principle appears, a constant insistence that though betterment is possible through grace, it always requires some individual moral effort, and a man has some degree of capacity for such effort — at least after the reception of some measure of initial grace. Always the development of the holy life, even though principally by divine power and grace, in one way or another still demands some cooperative effort by man. The ascetic tradition stresses that every Christian is responsibly involved in a holy war against evil. In medieval ascetic theology there is also complete agreement that absolute perfection is not possible in this life; rather, perfection itself has a progressive connotation; there is always more progress possible while in this life.[24] However, a "relative" perfection, at various stages of development, is considered attainable.

Finally, by the sixteenth century, another principle reaches full evolution, that the ascetic way is not only the best but also the only way to salvation for all Christians. Throughout the medieval centuries the principle generally had been that the ascetic way was the best and superior road, but it was only for the select few; in turn, it tolerated the institutional, ecclesiastical road, but with some suspicion. When Francis of Assisi revised the structures of the ascetic ideal so as to make it both a possible and desirable road for all Christians, the next step followed: that is, since it was no longer only the superior way possible to the few, it becomes the necessary, exclusive way for all who wish to attain salvation.

The related practical agencies, practices, and institutionalization by which the goal is to be achieved and its supporting principles activated and expressed in their ascetic theology of holiness are similarly distinctive and discernible. Such elements as spiritual exercises (praying, Bible study, and worship), fasting, work, simplicity, plainness or poverty, foot-washing, communal discipline, and deeds of charity are among the many standard expressions. As noted in chapter two, much flexibility and variation are possible in this area. In the fifteenth century, the tendency in ascetic expression was either toward a more rigorous traditional monasticism or toward laicized, voluntary brotherhoods with a moderate, external asceticism but with its ideals renewed and vigorously internalized.

Using these categories of the distinctive goal, supporting principles, and practical agencies as a guiding pattern for an understanding of what is an ascetic theology of holiness, it is now possible to analyze the Anabaptist sources to ascertian whether or to what degree Anabaptist theology conforms to this pattern and therefore should be designated as an ascetic theology.

Certainly, the polemical and homiletical concerns for piety and conduct, ascetically conceived, which chapter three already indicated as fundamental to the rise of Anabaptism, suggest that the doctrine of ascetic holiness may be the clue to unfold the inner structure of the whole of Anabaptist theology and practice. Accordingly, the rest of this chapter focuses on three problems: 1. What was the essence or nature of the holiness or perfection envisioned by the Anabaptists? Was it ascetic and related to a specifically ascetic code of conduct? 2. Did Anabaptism follow ascetic principles, ideologically and in their practices, for the attainment of the goal? 3. Does holiness actually function as the central interpretive principle affecting and determining the whole range of Anabaptist theological understanding and development?

Anabaptism as an Ascetic Theology of Manifest Holiness and Relative Perfectionism

The theological primacy of the pursuit of holiness. As with all Christians, personal salvation in the sense of the attainment of eternal life was recognized by the Anabaptists as the ultimate objective of God's redemptive involvement in history.[25] However, this goal of eternal life or salvation involved for them not just forgiveness of sins, not just a quantitative but also a qualitative conception of eternal life which must begin in this life.[26] Hubmaier combines these two aspects by commenting that true Christians "become holy [*heilig*] and receive . . . eternal life."[27] Thus the attainment of eternal life, holiness, and blessedness are almost made synonyms.

Similarily, the Anabaptists' understanding of the work of Christ in providing salvation included some measure of actual elimination of the power of sin in this life. Sattler argues that the purpose of the atonement by Christ was to restore a holy-living people. The atonement was to provide more than forgiveness and the assurance of heav-

136 Anabaptism and Asceticism

en but also, and they cannot be separated, "wholeness of being" as in Isaiah 53.[28] He refers to the extirpation of sin in the new filial relationship that one enters on becoming a Christian.[29] In his "20 Articles," the first, which is almost a title for the whole list, says: "Christ came to make holy [selig] all who believe in Him alone (1 Tim 1:15 f.)." That *selig* means "saved" in the sense of "holy (not "blessed" in this case) is clear from the scriptural references which he uses for Article One and again in Article Twelve: the devil seeks to destroy, Christ to make holy [selig] (Mt. 18:11, 1 Pet. 5:3)."[30]

But whether using *selig* or *heilig* or other similar terms, the Anabaptists repeatedly referred to Christians as being "made" saved (machen) or "made" holy; they rarely, if ever, used the typical Lutheran terminology of *rechtfertigen* and its derivatives, *Rechtfertigkeit*, or *Gerechtfertigung*, signifying being reckoned righteous, or forensic justification.[31] Rather, the Anabaptists stressed biblical passages such as 1 John 3:7, 8: "Little children, let no man deceive you: he that doeth righteousness is righteous, even as he is righteous. He that committeth sin is of the devil."[32] Clearly actual moral and spiritual healing, rather than mere judicial or forensic justification, is their understanding of God's purpose in providing salvation through Christ.[33]

Ultimate salvation and present holiness of conduct arising from sincere inner intent were inseparable. Weninger could, and did, assert that one is saved "not by doing wrong but by doing right."[34] Similarly the testimony of an unknown Anabaptist associate of Hottinger, in the Grebel circle at Zürich (1525-26), declared: "Indeed if one wishes to be a Christian and be called a brother, the condition is that he learn to know God, that he desist from sins and desires to experience a reformation [bettering], and that he afterwards allow it to be evidenced by baptism, improvement [of conduct], and a new life."[35] Sattler, in his "Articles" for Capito and Bucer, specifically asserts that only "they are true Christians who do the teachings of Christ with words."[36] Clearly individual holiness of life, beginning in this life, was inseparably joined to salvation and eternal life as both the goal of the redemptive work of God and the assurance of its reality.

Augsburger's careful study of the theology of Sattler makes clear that Sattler understands the entire Christian life as basically a life of holiness.[37] He maintains that Sattler's ethic, even his love ethic, is an ethic of holiness.³⁸ While Sattler is the clearest exponent among the early Anabaptist leaders of the primacy of holiness, his position was not greatly innovative. Weninger, for example, also specifically labeled the true gospel as "the saving words of the doctrine of godliness."³⁹

How did the Anabaptists define holiness? What was the nature of the perfection expected and demanded? What norms or criteria underlaid their conceptual framework? Though the expected effects of the redemptive work of God were described by several figures of speech, the end expectations were essentially the same. The Evangelical Anabaptists conceived of the goal of holiness, or godliness, as a limited kind of "divinization" (participation in the divine nature) of man by a restoration through a regenerative and healing process in conjunction with one's conscious, voluntary emulation of Christ. It is a restoration to true humanity, just as Christ was the true man, and is therefore limited and must be called a creaturely "divinization" or holiness.

Similarly, when they described the redemptive process as a restoration, they usually meant the perfection of the created, Adamic, prefall state — again a limited, dependent and creaturely perfection.⁴⁰ Since what was damaged most by the fall was the "divine image," its restoration and healing, which they expected, is also a kind of divinization.⁴¹ So also their references to regeneration referred primarily to a rebirth of the spirit or the coming to life of a new nature. This new nature is also related however to the "human" aspect of Christ as the second Adam, who came to rectify the damage done by the first Adam.⁴²

Therefore true man as originally created in God's image, the restoration of which is the object of divine redemptive activity, is conceived to be what Christ was; but it is Christ's *human* life, work, teachings, and His relationship to God and to His fellowmen which became the model for the expected "perfection." In the Anabaptist goal, the perfect man does not become God; he is conformed both by regeneration and emulation to the image of Christ as the true Man.⁴³

Although there is often a mystical deepening of the concepts of conformity to and imitation of the human Christ, to include an increasing participation in the divine nature and to an identification or union with the risen, glorified Christ,⁴⁴ nevertheless the awareness of one's creatureliness, of an eternal "distinctiveness of being" from ultimate Deity, is never lost.

Another way by which Anabaptists conceived the nature of God's

138 Anabaptism and Asceticism

intended perfection for man was to relate it to the concept of the kingdom of God. The divine redemptive goal becomes a transference by the new birth into the new kingdom with a corresponding assumption of its citizenship, ideals, laws, and life. Holiness therefore becomes equated with both the ideals of the kingdom, as lived by Christ, and obedience to its laws as established by Christ.[45]

Accordingly, the Anabaptist ideal of holiness, whether as a limited divinization through regeneration and emulation or as a new birth to a new citizenship in the kingdom of God, is completely Christ-centered with reference to pattern and requirements. Salvation is equated with holiness, and holiness is equated with receiving the Christ-life and with living in accordance with Christ's laws.

This ideal was expected to express itself in terms of both the absolute preeminence of a devotional, loving relationship with God and holy, virtuous and moralistic, fraternal and interpersonal human relationships. The former set forth a love for God in which concern for His praise and glorification and for submissiveness (*Gelassenheit*) to His will are its foremost attributes,[46] but also coupled with a substantial measure of fear.[47] Rosella Duerksen observes that the principle of Christian love is treated more frequently in Anabaptist hymnody than any other single idea. Only he who has Christian love is truly born anew of God.[48] Sattler expressed the same concern by his assertion that he could consider as Christians only those "who truly love and follow God (others, I do not know). . . ."[49]

This concern for a personal, subjective relationship to God, of love and fear, was never for Anabaptists satisfactorily expressed by contemplative, emotional, or esoteric experiences. Devotional, spiritual love must have visible, objective expression, through loving one's brethren and one's neighbor[50] and through works of love.[51] Works of love usually meant being kind, just, liberal in giving, or sharing, compassionate, and not returning evil for evil. For the Anabaptists, holiness could never be a purely private or subjective relationship to God.[52]

Equally vital, in Anabaptist thought, for an acceptable or holy relationship with God was the requirement of a spirit of submissiveness and obedience.[53] Sattler refers to filial obedience as perfection's "end and completion."[54] Such obedience also required active commitment to service, a sharing in the redemptive task, the fulfilling of the moral admonitions of the gospel regarding virtuous, interpersonal human relationships with one's brethren and neighbors, and the stewardship of life in this world.[55]

It is partially the insistence that a Christian's internal holiness must be expressed in such practical, conductual, interpersonal relationships, and be developed by external disciplines, that gives Anabaptist theology much of its ascetic flavor. Since Anabaptists were not anchoritic, they maintained that only in the manward social relationships could the full range of the virtues of the holy life, as manifest by Christ and produced by the Holy Spirit, be developed and expressed.[56] The attributes of virtue were not theologically formulated, nor minutely categorized and analyzed, but were expressed in simple biblical terminology to elicit action; generally there is only a listing of the fruit of the Spirit from Galatians' chapter five,[57] or a reference to the moral teachings of the Sermon on the Mount,[58] or to the pattern of the life and conduct of Christ.[59]

Among Anabaptists, holiness as virtue also had its negative perspective; again expressed in biblical terms and parallel to the ascetic tradition. They emphasized the renunciation or repudiation of the evil world, the evil flesh, and the devil, and a dying to the sin nature. They were most precise about what holiness was not and in their denouncing of the related specific sins and vices.[60]

From the beginning, in the Grebel group, the Anabaptists conceived of holiness, whether positively or negatively defined, as almost identical to a quite precisely articulated and decisively applied code of conduct, the norms of which were derived from the same biblical passages traditionally emphasized in ascetic spirituality. While the Anabaptists' code espoused the usual attributes for a good Christian, such as prayerfulness, a forgiving spirit, patience in tribulation, and the fruit of the Spirit (Galatians 5), more distinctively it took literally and seriously the positive standards of the Sermon on the Mount and the negative injunctions of Scripture to renounce the world, the flesh, and the devil.[61]

Specifically, most Anabaptists repudiated utterly the bearing and use of weapons, all physical coercion in the community of Christians with reference to matters of faith, and even retaliation against one's enemies.[62] They upheld also an intense opposition to materialism, to usury, to worldly frivolity, to sensuality, and to anything of a physically immoral nature.[63] Equally intense is the demand for total submission and obedience in conduct to God's Word and Spirit and to the discipline of the group of believers.[64] What was true of the Grebel group relative to holiness as a code of conduct was further elaborated and established by the writings of Michael Sattler and the "Schleitheim Confession," and was then followed by Anabaptism generally.[65]

To Anabaptism's understanding of holiness as essentially a personal inner, redemptive concern, but which required an external behavioral manifestation as part of its kingdom relationships, was added the ingredient of Christian brotherhood. The brotherhood was viewed as either the visible extension of Christ's body or as His bride, and in both cases as possessing the power of "the keys." Therefore, the brotherhood itself became an agency of redemption and of holiness.[66] Holiness again, as in much of medieval asceticism, took on a corporate nature, concern, and expression similar to cenobitism.[67] Accordingly, Anabaptists stressed the Pauline description of the church as holy, "without spot or wrinkle or any such thing (Eph. 5:27)."[68]

Holiness, as conceived by Evangelical Anabaptists, was also integrated with their understanding of the redemptive plan of God as part of a cosmic, spiritual struggle, creating a radical dualism. Friedmann has written a thoughtful article surveying this aspect of the subject.[69] However, since he admits that the doctrine of two kingdoms in conflict is only "implicit" in the sources, it would seem that he attempts too much in trying to make of this dualism the key to the understanding and structuring of the whole of Anabaptist theology.[70] Rather, the pursuit of Christian holiness seems to be the key presented most explicitly with which to comprehend the essence of Anabaptist theology.

Nevertheless, a cosmic dualism, and a radical juxtaposition of the two kingdoms, is certainly a vital, underlying, and related aspect which is much more explicit in the sources than even Friedmann's article suggests. For example, the "Grüninger Eingabe," which reflects the thought of the Grebel group, demands a rigorous distinction between the fruit of the Spirit and the fruit of darkness, which is defined as "all the lusts of the flesh"; only those who walk in the former are the church of Christ.[71] Most explicit is the presentation by "M.S." (probably Michael Sattler) of radical dualism as related to hermeneutics. He sets forth, as the key to understanding God's purposes, two long columns of antagonistic and contrasting topics, such as: Old Man — New Man, Death — Life, Sin — Piety, Enmity — Love, Darkness — Light, Hell — Heaven, Evil — Good, and so on. The work concludes: "The earthly Adam corrupted and lost it all. The heavenly Adam restored and sanctified all through the Holy Spirit who proceeds from the Father to all newly-born people (John 3, 1 Corinthians 15).''[72]

In Sattler's "Letter of 20 Differences,"[73] in the Schleitheim Confession,[74] in Zwingli's criticism of the Schleitheim Confession,[75] in the Bernese Disputation of 1538,[76] and in Menno Simons[77] there are similar, even identical, explicit, and extensive references to this radical dualism. One very clear example comes from the Schleitheim Confession: ". . . all creatures are in but two classes . . . Christ and Belial . . . none can have part with the other."[78] Once again, although this relationship between holiness and dualism does not originate in Anabaptism with Sattler, he is the strongest exponent during the formative years (1525-27), and his influence was extensive.[79]

In summary, the Anabaptists derived from their dualistic orientation the following schema:[80] There are only two kingdoms relevant to human existence: the kingdom of God under the leadership of Jesus Christ, of which the visible church is a limited expression, and the kingdom of Evil, including this present world order, which is dominated by Satan and is destined for destruction. These two kingdoms or "orders" are radically distinct from each other, in every essential detail. The kingdom of God is eternal and heavenly oriented, dominated by the spiritual, and submissive to the rule of God; but the kingdom of Satan is temporal, this-worldly oriented, dominated by the fallen flesh, proud, and disobedient to the rule of God. The Anabaptists' attitude to the flesh and its role in this schema brings their dualism even closer to that traditionally expressed in medieval ascetic spirituality.

Moreover, the kingdom of God is not something completely future or transcendental, but it has a necessary, present expression. Salvation means accepting the life and laws of the kingdom and an initiation or entrance into the kingdom, the receiving of new citizenship. So stanza seventeen of Blaurock's hymn, "Gott führt ein recht gericht," typically stresses the life of the Christian here as a pilgrimage;[81] Christians are foreigners and pilgrims, only passing through — again the strong accent on this theme is in accord with the ascetic tradition. Accordingly, salvation is not exclusively forensic justification, or a present assurance of an entirely future expectation or hope, but also a present, actual new birth, a present transformation, and a literal

142   Anabaptism and Asceticism

and immediate transference of allegiance unto a kingdom which is characterized by holiness of life and obedience to the rule of God, which is exhibited here and now, while still in this life. Since, from the Anabaptist viewpoint, both the Roman Catholics and the Magisterial Protestants were mixing the two kingdoms, they were inevitably degenerate. Any restoration of the true church called for a purifying by radical separation, and a reestablishment of the church as unique and distinctive in the midst of this present evil world society.[82]

As much as possible, commensurate with the church's redemptive task of reaching out and calling people into the divine kingdom, and out of the evil one, Christians live out the new life within the separated brotherhood or fellowship of believers. Secular occupation, though not rejected, as it was not by the Desert Fathers nor by medieval cenobitism, had a subsidiary role. Since the two kingdoms are involved in a cosmic conflict, the true church and the present evil world system, as limited expressions of these kingdoms, will also be in conflict. Each uses weapons peculiar to its own nature, therefore the Christian conquest is not through physical and carnal weapons, but spiritual only. Though the world will use violence against the church, it must be borne patiently. The cosmic struggle is also expressed in the sphere of the inner conflict within the individual Christian; the struggle between the impulses of the spirit and those of the flesh. The ultimate conclusion to both the church-world and the spirit-flesh conflicts is eschatological, namely death — or perchance the parousia, the Second Advent of Christ. This dualistic conflict, cosmic, corporate, and personal, creates a dualistic approach to the meaning of history and life. Moral choice, or separation by taking sides, is the ultimate and necessary decision by every person.

Finally, life in the kingdom of God represents a totally different order of things. It demands that life here and now, for Christians, be lived according to kingdom values as reflected by the life of Christ and the Sermon on the Mount. It is either opposed to or highly suspicious of the values and culture typical of the present world societies; it is suspicious of its moral perspectives, economic values, power arrangements, and educational and cultural achievements.

Therefore holiness, as conceptualized and defined by the Anabaptists, follows the traditional pattern of ascetic expression and includes: *internally*, the supremacy of love for God and one's fellows, and a kind of relativistic, creaturely "divinization" which involves regeneration and a new citizenship; *externally*, the development of Christlike virtues, and the renunciation of vices according to an ascetic code of conduct in a social and corporate context; and a radical sense of separation related to cosmic, dualistic tensions.

Not only is the primacy of holiness, in Anabaptism, indicated by its synonymity with salvation, and by the comprehensiveness of its conceptualization, but also by their viewing of holiness, personally and corporately, as a condition partially, and to that degree necessarily, accomplishable in this life and partially in the eternal realm. Most Anabaptists either follow directly Hubmaier's description of the three stages of development of the "this-life" aspects of holiness, or the differences are superficial enough to warrant using it still as a general example, namely: (1) an initial transformation of man's nature, relating to the spirit and soul, sufficient to permit an effective willing to do good and live holily, which he calls the inner baptism; (2) a placing of oneself into the care and discipline and fellowship of a brotherhood by the pledge of baptism, which is the outer or believer's baptism; and (3) a baptism of blood, or suffering and persecution, which, as a mortification of the flesh, works a developing purification in the yielded Christian and which terminates only with death. Hubmaier saw salvation and forgiveness of sins as the product of this total process of becoming holy.[83]

Only a relative holiness is achievable, or necessary now; the corrupt, sinful flesh, though no longer dominant in the true Christian, remains present and troublesome throughout life and is eliminated or transformed to incorruption only at the resurrection.[84] In the eternal state, the end product, the perfect Christian, united with Christ seems to achieve glorification to a state which may be even above that which man originally had in Eden's Paradise. Then it is that the Anabaptists look for the ecstatic vision and the contemplative union.[85] The final judgment also is the final purifying of the church when those whose outer profession approximated reality, but who were internally "tares," are separated from the "wheat" and the church is completed corporately as the pure bride of Christ.

Since the Anabaptists conceived of salvation as almost synonymous with the striving for and attainment of holiness, holiness became the dominant element not only in their practical concerns, polemically and homiletically, but also in their theological framework. Furthermore, it was a holiness conceived much more in ascetical than in mystical terms, and more actual than forensic or imputed. Their ideal appears to coincide generally with that of traditional monastic spirituality. However, this initial apparent parallelism needs further confirmation by a more thorough examination of those supporting and subsidiary principles which buttress and extend the ideal of holiness, and provide the ideological pattern for its attainment.

Supporting principles: renunciation and separation. Directly out of the Anabaptists' relating of holiness to the principle of radical dualism, evolves the subsidiary and supporting principle that fundamental to the pursuit of holiness is the renunciation of, and radical separation from, the world, the flesh, and the devil. The two kingdoms must be kept poles apart. Entry to the one, declare several of the formative leaders, demands the total rejection of the other.[86] Hubmaier reminded Oecolampad that Christ taught that His truth would bring division. Hubmaier also concedes that this involves a much more drastic narrowing of Christ's kingdom than was traditionally the case.[87]

Separation from evil was conceived of as both personal and corporate. For example, in his letter from prison to the congregation at Horb, Sattler urges both personal and corporate separation from idolatry, sensuality, and the abominations of the world. He concludes: "Finally beloved brethren and sisters, sanctify [set apart] yourselves for Him that made you holy. . . . Flee the shadow of this world."[88] With reference to personal evil, Anabaptists referred repeatedly to the necessity of the mortification of the flesh, and of the repudiation of self-will to disobedience.[89] Each individual's life must be "changed," the life of the "old Adam" renounced and put to death.[90] Also renounced are all the institutions and practices of this world system which nourish such unholy attributes as pride, greed, lust for pomp or power, hate, revenge, violence, lust, and so on. Capito noted this intense otherworldliness when he remarked: "I testify before God that I cannot say that on account of lack of wisdom they are somewhat indifferent towards earthly things but rather, from divine motives."[91] As in Francis of Assisi, personal separation was often expressed as an antimaterialism. Sattler scorns any Christian who would maintain that "we never through faith in Him renounce our supposed possessions and our own selves. . . ." Rather, Sattler proceeds to affirm such renunciation by quoting numerous scriptural passages which were typically used by the ascetic tradition, for example, the rich young ruler of Matthew 19.[92]

With reference to corporate separatism, the establishment of the separated church or brotherhood was not an optional matter for the Anabaptists. It was a vital expression of the spirit of obedience, a necessary milieu for practicing the love ethic. Manz affirms his efforts to gather out of the existing mixed and worldly society of Christendom those willing to follow Christ.[93] It was the same corporate, called-out, separatist emphasis that caused Zwingli to condemn the movement as sectarian and socially disruptive.[94] The same factor is an important key for distinguishing Evangelical Anabaptism from Schwenkfeldian spiritualism, and from Pietism. Anabaptists believed that God wanted not only holy individuals but a holy church; furthermore a holy individual was not achievable apart from his participation in a separated, holy community.[95] Although the external manifestations of this corporate separation differed somewhat in various branches of Anabaptism, as reflected by the Swiss Brethren on one hand, and the Hutterian communities on the other, *the underlying principle* of moral, spiritual, and some measure of physical separation, and the setting up of a corporate entity, *remains constant* and closely parallels the principle that also undergirded similarly varying expressions of the cloister ideal over its long history.

Supporting principles: freedom to choose. Continuously stressed in Anabaptist writings, and also emerging from their dualistic concept of life, is their affirmation of the capacity and responsibility of all men to choose for themselves the way of righteousness and holiness. This affirmation of free choice must be considered as one of Anabaptism's primary supporting principles in formulating their theology of holiness. For the Anabaptists, if the pursuit of holiness, in terms of repudiating the evil world and its god for the divine, was to be morally meaningful, it required this right of free choice. There could be no holy life, no beginning of salvation at all, apart from such a responsible choice.

Thus, in contrast to Luther's *Bondage of the Will*, and to almost all the early Magisterial Reformers, every major Anabaptist leader explicitly or implicitly espoused the principle of some human free will, and some capacity for responsible choice, when one is confronted with the message of the gospel.[96] In particular, early in the movement's history, in 1526-27, following the Erasmus-Luther controversy on the subject, two influential leaders, Hubmaier and Denck, wrote booklets explicitly outlining their theological and moral opposition to Luther's advocacy of unconditional election.[97] Since several others have analyzed these works by Denck and Hubmaier on free will quite carefully,[98] and there seems to be little disagreement regarding their import, only a few emphases of particular relevance to this thesis need to be mentioned here.

From the beginning the Anabaptists rooted their belief in the possibility of some measure of free choice in their dual concern for God's holiness and justice and for man's moral responsibility. God's just nature could not allow for an arbitrary election to heaven or hell.[99] Rather, each man is responsible for his own final destiny[100] and every man is eligible for salvation.[101] This potentially universal provision for salvation led to occasional charges against the Anabaptists of universalism.[102]

Hubmaier is typical of Anabaptists generally, in the first years, 1525-27, in opposing with much vehemence any idea that salvation is compelled, or that human moral choices whether good or bad happen out of necessity. Such false notions, he asserts, produce much "evil and filth" and are destructive to moral progress and to "fasting, praying, and almsgiving."[103]

Closely related is their conviction that God's precepts on repentance and holy living must be actually fulfillable.[104] Sattler asks regarding conduct: "Why should God make known His will if He would not wish that a person do it?"[105] Furthermore, Hubmaier insists, what God commands, man can perform, with His help, if he desires to do so.[106] A just God does not demand the impossible.

Wrong choice and the essence of the Anabaptist view of sin are closely correlated. Not exclusively, but primarily, internal sin is conceived of as disobedience to the will of God, an act or state of the will;[107] even as Adam's sin which produced the "Fall" was essentially a disobeying of God.[108] This idea of sin as willful disobedience is then extended to imply both that man's higher and proper will has come under the domination of the fallen flesh,[109] and that there is a defect in man's unaided understanding which distorts the capacity to know what is good.[110] Since sin is primarily and firstly a matter of the will, and the will in fallen man is dominated by the flesh, sin takes on an ascetic perspective; sin is closely correlated with the desires and demands of the flesh and its worldly orientation.[111]

Though Anabaptists subscribe to the doctrine of the Adamic fall, whereby all men are sinners, and to the dominance of the will by the flesh with an ensuing corruption and sickness to the point of helplessness to save oneself, yet, in contrast to Luther,[112] they also insist on the retention of some initial freedom of choice.[113] This freedom is limited to be sure. While it is sufficient to make each man responsible for his destiny, to make him eligible for further grace and greater freedom, or for damnation, yet it is totally without capacity, power, or knowledge to achieve anything, redemptively, unaided by special grace. This is a most important point.

Not all Anabaptist writers account in the same way for this minimal, morally necessary freedom, and some are not explicit about it at all, but it seems to be implicitly assumed by all.[114] Explicitly, at least three theories were formulated among early Anabaptists to account for this initial, limited ability to choose. In Hubmaier, for example, the depravity of man resulting from the Fall is not quite total. Some vestige of the image of God remains in all, through an imprisoned and powerless but unfallen spirit. This vestige is enough to enable the initial, limited choice, the cry for grace, but never enough to earn or effect salvation.[115] In Denck and Marpeck, only slightly different than Hubmaier, the initial freedom is due to some kind of common or prevenient grace by God — a kind of dim light of conscience or divine, inner Word or Spirit, or an immanence, or even a natural law, common to man since the Fall, but expanded by Christ and the gospel.[116] Melchior Hoffman suggests a liberating grace, common to all, resulting directly from the universal and immediate effect of the atonement of Christ.[117]

It is not necessary to explore the details of these slightly varying theories; rather, only to note that all three arise for the same purpose: to give to all men the initial, morally responsible capacity of choice, the capacity to incline toward or to refuse the greater workings of grace, which in turn frees the will for the pursuit of holiness and the attainment of eternal blessedness. Hubmaier tries extensively to clarify this important difference between advocating an initial and limited freedom to choose or respond to grace and a Pelagian view of free will. Anabaptism is not Pelagian; the will is really freed only after the reception of divine grace.

Even though Hubmaier left more theological writings than most early Anabaptist leaders, especially on this subject of the will, he is still somewhat vague about the source, nature, operation, and limits of this initial capacity for free choice in salvation. In *Concerning Free Will*, he discusses in detail the prelapsarian condition of man, the postlapsarian condition, and the post-"new birth" restoration. But he omits any direct mention of this first step in the process of transition from a fallen sinner to the first reception of special grace creating the restored or regenerated Christian.[118]

That there is a distinct initial step involving the exercise of a limited freedom to choose is implied in several places and ways. In general, Hubmaier sees man in his fallen state as having lost his freedom to choose good and evil, but since he also maintains that man has a tripartite nature, body, soul, and spirit, each with its own capacity to "will," he distinguishes different effects for the "Fall" in each part. The flesh "has lost its goodness and freedom irrevocably and has become utterly worthless and helpless. It can do nothing except to sin. . . ." Here he agrees with Luther.[119] But the spirit of man is not affected *per se*, only indirectly; it is helplessly imprisoned in the fallen flesh. The soul shares partially in the corruption of the flesh and is thereby "maimed" and "wounded," and is totally incapable of judging good and evil correctly. It cannot of itself do good or choose correctly. Though the soul is helpless, there remains within it the capacity for uncoerced initiative or desire, even though lacking ability. Here is the heart of the matter. Man is helpless, with absolutely no ability to do good or save himself; but the freedom, actually only the capacity, to *desire* what is right and good remains.[120] He refers to the situation as being "half dead," even unable to recognize good and evil properly but able to respond to or refuse the initial call of God from His Word.

Accordingly, the change that takes place in regeneration also centers in the soul.[121] This change is described as being "awakened by the Word of God," being "made whole through His dear Son," being able "to know again what is good and evil," recovering one's "lost liberty," and the soul becoming "now," freely and willingly, able to be "obedient to the Spirit and choose good. Just as it could in Eden."[122]

Hubmaier seems to be suggesting an initial but very limited freedom, by the soul's will, to respond positively or to reject God's gracious initiatives through the Word, but of itself totally incapable of effecting anything, redemptively. Only if the soul responds positively is it then aided by more grace, called direct or special grace, and man is thereby given freedom of the will for both the soul and spirit, and thereby the ability to override and control the will of the still-fallen, corrupt flesh.

This distinction between an initial, limited freedom of choice and actual free will is quite clear and distinctive. Hubmaier refers to it precisely by commenting that after God draws men through the Word on the merits of Christ, "*if they desire it*, free choice is restored, they are born again . . . as in Paradise, save for the flesh. . . ."[123] The flesh however is never transformed or freed, *per se*, in this life; it can only be forcefully subdued until death. It must wait for the change to incorruption at the resurrection. Hubmaier concludes his booklet by asserting that arguments denying personal moral responsibility for the initial choice, and for subsequent actions in the pursuit of holiness and salvation, "are wicked, cunning, blasphemous deviltries. I do not know that Satan even set up any worse ones on earth to oppose kindness, piety, and godliness."[124]

Moreover, for the Anabaptists, there can be neither compulsion nor favoritism in the matter of election to eternal salvation. Hubmaier makes it perfectly clear that while God wills man's salvation, yet "God wants him unconstrained, under no compulsion."[125] Such voluntaryism also implicitly demands a free, moral acquiescence which is prior to and underlying even the Anabaptists' strongest protestations of belief in the necessity of divine enabling if one is "to will to do His will." This stress on voluntaryism, and the capacity for some kind of morally responsible choice, is completely consistent with the general pattern of the medieval ascetic tradition.[126]

Supporting principles: synergism. Anabaptist insistence on some universal human capacity for free choice leads Anabaptism into the camp of synergistic theology, dominant in the medieval church. But there are variations and degrees of synergism, and it is questionable whether all can be lumped together as Pelagianism — as Luther does. Because of the many variations and complexities, to discover and unravel the exact nature of the principle of free, human cooperation with grace for the "attainment" of salvation[127] which permeates the Anabaptists' soteriological formula is vital to any attempt to isolate its intellectual antecedents.

Again, articulating precise theological definitions in Anabaptist theology is difficult because most of the Anabaptists' theological writings are not systematized treatises but hastily formulated, popular, polemical tracts and confessions. Also, since they were often speaking or writing directly to the problems of the moment, their statements seem at times contradictory, especially on this subject. Occasionally they stress *sola gratia* in the fashion of Luther, but at other times they demand moral effort in a way quite foreign to the main thrust

150   Anabaptism and Asceticism

of the Magisterial Reformation. They accent a strong doctrine of grace when debating the criticisms by their opponents in the Magisterial Reformation, but in their own literature the emphasis is on choice, repentance, responsibility, and moral effort.

These variant emphases have produced similarly conflicting interpretations of Anabaptist theology by subsequent historians. Depending on which passages are given prominence, one may conclude, as does Lüdemann, following Luther, that Anabaptist theology is outright Pelagianism;[128] or, conversely, as in Wenger, that the Anabaptists are not weak on grace at all; rather that they maintained that the initiative in salvation is all of grace and that they are therefore in accord with Reformation theology in its basic position on justification by faith and grace alone.[129]

Is there a possibility of reconciling these conflicting views? What exactly did the Anabaptists mean when they ascribed salvation to grace and to the merits of Christ alone, and to faith alone, yet also just as expressly to repentance, love, and works? Is the principle of reconciliation, if there is one, consistent with any part of the medieval ascetic tradition?

For several reasons, Hubmaier again provides the best source in which to find the essential features of early Anabaptist "synergism," and the key to the reconciliation of the apparent conflicts. For example, Hubmaier himself repeats the same, seemingly contradictory statements, but without any apparent awareness of genuine conflict or contradiction.[130] In Hubmaier this is significant since he represents a high level of theological training, possessing a doctorate in theology, and his writings are not only the most extensive but also the most theologically organized and consistent of any Anabaptist leader prior to Menno Simons (an Anabaptist after 1536). Also, in 1525, his initial period of writing, Hubmaier was in close association with the Swiss founders of Anabaptism. In many places in his writings during this period, he echoes the fine points, even the tone and vocabulary, of the Grebel group.[131] In subsequent years, 1526-27, he is involved more with the South German and Moravian branches of Anabaptism. Thus, his works represent an important bridge. Moreover, during the years, 1525-27, there is little if any controversy within the whole of Evangelical Anabaptism over the soteriological aspects of Hubmaier's writings. His writings were known and widely used by leading Anabaptists such as Leonard Schiemer and Pilgram Marpeck of the South German branch, and by Peter Ridemann of the Hutterites.[132]

As already noted, Hubmaier made an important distinction between an initial freedom of response and full free will; or between a capacity to choose, in the restricted sense of responding positively or negatively to God's grace, and the ability to know and perform the good. The ability to know and perform, requiring the freedom of the wills of both the soul and spirit, is not possible at all, apart from divine grace which is provided only by Christ's atonement.[133] Thus, from the perspective of human ability, power, or meaningful effectiveness, Hubmaier could and did proclaim that salvation is wholly of grace, by the provision or merits of Christ alone, through faith.[134] But at the same time, he could and did reject any idea that grace was irresistible and independently operative, or that election was predetermined, or that man was irresponsible, or even totally bad as a result of the Fall.[135] Some measure of voluntary free response was necessary for any application of either an initial "calling," or non-coercive grace, or of effective regenerative and perfecting grace. Hubmaier specifically asserts that God draws men through the Word on the merits of Christ, but only "if they desire it, free choice is restored, they are born again. . . ." He then repeats the medieval maxim, "Man, help yourself, and then I will help you."[136]

To a degree, even this initial favorable response is an almost inseparably cooperative matter, according to Hubmaier. That is, this initial capacity to respond, though present in all as a kind of first or prevenient grace, is latent until awakened by the gospel or "new grace." Hubmaier's "new grace" by the Word and the Spirit which leads those willing to be led of God to true repentance, and to achieving a regeneration in cooperation with the human will, is called the second stage of his three stages of grace — the first being natural or common grace, giving limited capacity to the soul to respond to God, and the second and third, called regenerative grace and sanctifying grace, are phases of "special" grace, relating directly to Christ's redemptive provisions.[137]

Both stages two and three involve the principle of cooperation all along the process to be effective.[138] That is, grace through the Word and the Spirit is never a compelling grace, even though it is grace alone that effects the awakening of the soul.[139] Hubmaier seems to infer that if the initial positive response is maintained, "special" or "new" grace increasingly deepens and informs that initial, helpless, but positive response until it becomes true repentance, belief, and faith which then are grounds for the new birth or regeneration.[140]

Thus, in this second or regenerative stage, special grace is the sole effective agency; human powers effect no change. It is grace on the condition of willing cooperation that first awakens the latent capacity of the soul and elicits an uncoerced response.[141] Then it takes the submissive soul and informs it to the point of contrition or repentance, which leads to belief and faith.[142]

On the basis of repentance and faith a regeneration takes place in which grace frees the soul's and spirit's will from bondage to the fallen flesh,[143] and provides the knowledge of good and evil[144] so that man's will becomes, except for the flesh, as fully free to make moral choices and live a holy life "as it could in Eden."[145] Grace by the Holy Spirit not only transforms the inner nature of man, but also pardons sin up to that point, and provides the resources to enable one to follow Christ obediently and overcome the flesh, if one desires to. This is the "comfort" of the gospel for Hubmaier.[146]

Hubmaier repeatedly associates the "grace" operative in regeneration (stage two) with the Word of God and the Holy Spirit — the two working in close combination. The Word, possibly because it is more external and observable, is given the most attention. He refers to the fallen soul as remediable "through the Word of God,"[147] as "coming to life," and being "awakened" by the "proclamation of the holy word."[148] The soul is "healed," made "free and whole" by a rebirth . . . by the power of His Word."[149] When referring to the full work on inner regeneration, the Holy Spirit is specifically added as the effective Agent. Hubmaier attributes forgiveness and regeneration, or the creation of the new creature in Christ, to the "Word" and "the Spirit of God working inwardly in the heart of men."[150] Finally, he identifies regeneration as an "inner baptism" performed "by the Holy Spirit through the living Word of God."[151] These two elements, the Word and the Spirit, constitute the primary agencies both for the call of God and the accomplishment of regeneration.

While Hubmaier insists that "if our souls are to be healed," there "must, must, must" be such a rebirth,[152] an inner baptism of the Spirit,[153] yet even this is only a stage in a still incomplete process of attaining salvation. Regeneration does not assure ultimate salvation, though making it entirely possible if the now fulfillable conditions are actually fulfilled. Hubmaier rejected Oecolampad's view that if inner baptism is completed, one "will never be condemned"; therefore externalities, even water baptism, are not of major importance. For

Hubmaier, inner baptism is not completed salvation; outer baptism and other external evidences of faith and obedience do not save either; but both together are part of an ongoing process now made possible, and none of which may be bypassed.[154]

Man's contribution to this cooperative process of regeneration, sometimes called inner baptism, is an active "purpose" to change; it is constantly assumed, repeatedly asserted,[155] and considered absolutely necessary; but clearly it is never considered an independent or meritorious or enabling power. The whole process demands, for success, a dynamic fusion of human desire and divine power, which is hard to separate, and they were rarely concerned to try.

As previously noted, in the beginning stage when the soul is awakened by the Word, if it responds positively, it is further informed or aided by the Word (especially the law) and the Spirit, producing sorrow and fear. If the "positive" set of the will is still maintained, freely, the further interaction of the Word and Spirit, transforms fear and sorrow for sin to true repentance. According to Anabaptism, the evidence or assurance for the completion of this stage seems to be primarily a resultant willingness by the repentant one to be obedient to the Word, and a change in conduct which reflects a transformation of nature, a regeneration.

The exact nature of this process, especially the role and nature of repentance in regeneration, is never analyzed in detail by the early Anabaptists. Again, Hubmaier comes closest to putting it into a theologically, intelligible framework.

There is also an element in Hubmaier's view of repentance for which man is responsible, and in which he is actively involved; though even here a measure of cooperation, noncoercive initiative, and assistance by grace is required. Initial repentance becomes possible only after the law brings an awareness of sin and need.[156] This awareness is rooted in the exercise of such limited freedom of will as then exists, nourished but not compelled by the Word. Hubmaier notes that one can still "through our perverseness bring ourselves again into condemnation."[157]

Hubmaier makes a brief attempt at defining the essential nature of effective repentance in response to his rhetorical question: "What is repentance [buss]?" He replies: "To deplore one's sins before God, beg His forgiveness for them, and do the like no more. The best repentance is namely, to guard oneself in the future against sin, to walk according to the word of God."[158] In this statement, Hubmaier

154   Anabaptism and Asceticism

is actually repeating a typical medieval contritional maxim.[159] Similarly in his *Summary*, Hubmaier describes "amendment" (or repentance) as concern for one's sins, through the teaching of the Word; a confession to God of disobedience, since sin's essence, in Anabaptism, is disobedience more than unbelief; and a coming, in despair of oneself, to Christ for help.[160] He further defines the confession involved in repentance primarily as direct confession to God; but also as private confession, to someone who has been wronged individually; and public, before the whole congregation, "if by a mortal sin [*tödsind*] he steps on, outrages, and dishonors the church and her members."[161]

Hubmaier also distinguishes *Reue* (remorse), *Leid* (regret), and *Busse* (contrition, repentance), though all three are required. He writes: "Every man is obliged to have remorse and regret, also to effect contrition [*buss zuwircken*] concerning his sin." To illustrate the meaning of *buss zuwircken*, Hubmaier puts forward John the Baptist's demands for fruit worthy of repentance (Matthew 3:8, 10), Zacchaeus' willingness to make restitution (Luke 19:8), and the repentant woman (Luke 7:37) who afterward gives herself into active service for Christ, as "the effect (evidence) of a Christian repentance [*busswirckhung*]."[162] He also refers to prayer and action (deeds) as expressions of the "highest contrition."[163]

Repentance is also considered a necessary ingredient at all stages of the redemptive process. Again Hubmaier asks, rhetorically, if a Christian falls into sin after regeneration, how does he find release? He answers: "Through repentance and prayer to God."[164] In another tract, he adds the comment that the congregation has the keys to "open to the sinner the gates of heaven, as often as he feels sorrow for his sins and repents. . . ."[165] He concludes: "In summary, God is merciful but He wants no less than, if the man has committed sin, that he through remorse, regret, and contrition according to the condition of his sin make a payment to His godly and offended righteousness."[166] Repentance is not a single act but a continuous attitude of the will leading to repeated repentance; man's role is therefore one of continuous cooperation.

On the other side of the picture, Wenger declares that "repentance" for Anabaptists was totally of divine initiative. "It is nothing which the sinner can initiate himself." Wenger then quotes from Menno Simons: "Do you think . . . that you can receive faith, repentance (*Busse*), sorrow for sin, and the grace of God whenever it suits you? Oh, no!. . . ."[167] Is there a contradiction here? Not

The Dominance of Asceticism   155

at all. When this quotation of Menno is put into its context, he is advocating the necessity of hearing "the divine Word" before one can respond. This grace is still not irresistible, and the responsibility of human choice and response remains. The principle of cooperation prevails in the vital doctrine of repentance.

The last phases in the regenerative stage, which seem to involve man's free will in a cooperative process, are contained in the terms "believing" and "trusting." In reference to man's role, Hubmaier asserts that Christ's command is both to "amend your life [*besserend ewer leben*] *and* believe the gospel."[168] Belief in this context seems to designate a narrower concept than that which is generally implied by "faith," which will be discussed later. Rather, belief seems here to mean a recognition, understanding, and acceptance that Christ alone and all-sufficiently provides the desired salvation.[169] By salvation Hubmaier does not mean just an imputed (forensic) justification but the full resources for the attainment of holiness and blessedness. Thus, in the same context, he refers to Christ as "the Physician" who "has come into the world to make the sinner righteous *and* godly."[170]

Hubmaier places trust after belief — at least logically, if not an actual distinction in time and experience. His word for trust is really submission, or surrender; that is, after repentance and belief, one "submits himself to his Physician [*ergibt sich füran an den Artzt*]";[171] again the human involvement comes to the foreground. Thus belief is activated. He continues: "One will surrender *himself, so far as it is possible,* to His will [*will sich ouch, als vil ainem verwunten müglich, in seinen willen ergeben*]."[172] The cooperative aspect of this stage in the regenerative process is quite explicit, as indicated by the italicized phrases in the previous question. Hubmaier adds, even more explicitly: "What the wounded man out of his own strength cannot do, *that* will the Physician do to *help him* and advance him, to the extent that he may follow God's Word and commands," or attain holiness.[173]

For Hubmaier, the regenerative aspect of salvation is by faith, but not by "faith alone," to cite Luther's definition of faith, since Hubmaier adds to true faith the necessity of hope and love; though all three are actuated by grace.[174] The precise meaning of the inner faith ingredient is not easy to pinpoint in Hubmaier or in the Anabaptists in general. He uses "faith" in at least three ways: simple faith or simple belief; true or regenerating faith including inner trust

156   Anabaptism and Asceticism

and obedience; and a larger continuous, all-encompassing faith which is the equivalent of holy living and brings one to and assures one of ultimate salvation. With reference to simple faith he writes: "Simple belief is not sufficient for salvation . . . Romans 10 . . . nor can we be only mouth Christians . . . but rather we must prove our faith with works of love for God and our neighbor." He continues: "Simple faith [der bloss glaub] is not worthy to be called faith, for true faith [ein Rechter glaub] may never be without works of love."[175]

With reference to regenerating faith or true faith, he sometimes refers to it in terms sounding very much like Luther, that is, as an inner, trusting, belief or confidence in the promises and provisions of the gospel. For example, in his *Handbook of Christian Doctrine*, Hubmaier states that faith follows from the gospel; that "faith is a recognition of the unspeakable mercy of God and of His gracious favor and goodwill which He has given to us through His beloved son, Jesus Christ . . . whereby we with confidence of heart may call Him, 'Father'. . . ."[176]

But, on the other hand, Hubmaier is clear that even faith as inner trusting belief is not adequate for salvation if it is inner only. In a debate with Zwingli on this issue, Hubmaier writes: "It is not enough for us to believe in Christ in our hearts. We must also confess Him before man *by every means* by which one can profess himself a Christian."[177] Faith to be fully operative must be an actively obedient faith and must include open confession, especially by believer's baptism.[178] He writes concerning trusting, inner faith: "Although faith alone makes one holy [regenerate], it alone does not save [ultimate salvation], for outward profession must be there (Matthew 10, Luke 4, Romans 10)."[179] Hubmaier can be said to adhere to salvation by faith alone only if the definition of faith is broadened much beyond Luther's meaning. It must include active obedience and works of love as part of its expression.

It is also significant that in his *Handbook* (or catechism), Hubmaier considers "repentance" immediately *prior to* the question of faith.[180] This is probably meant to indicate that faith is built on, grows out of, and is dependent on the cooperative involvement in repentance. His insistence on the active quality of faith suggests that for true faith, in its large sense, he incorporates repentance and submission, with necessary external manifestations into the idea of trusting belief. Ultimately this alone constitutes true, saving faith. Therefore, in true faith, the cooperative principle and the voluntary involvement of the human will with grace are again fused. It is this cooperation that transforms belief and trust into true active faith. It is from one side of this larger kind of faith that he could assert that "a man attains salvation through his own faith. . . ."[181]

Throughout his writings, Hubmaier's main concern was to negate any identification of saving faith with simple mental assent, or even with an inner belief or trust that failed to change conduct and promote holiness of life. Saving faith is an inclusive term; it embraces all the proper, free human responses to God's grace. It is a regenerating faith that also perseveres. It is a gift of grace but it is contingent upon cooperative responses. Thus faith too is a dynamic concept, based on and infused with the synergistic principle.

Hubmaier's views on the principle of synergism in regeneration have been presented as generally typical of early Evangelical Anabaptism, though they are much more detailed in most aspects than those of most of the other Anabaptist spokesmen — though Denck also wrote substantially, and in general agreement, on the more limited theme of free will.[182] Yet there is adequate testimony from the writings of the Grebel group, Sattler, and subsequent Swiss apologists to show generally their support for Hubmaier's position. The following are a few confirmatory examples.

Neither the early Grebel group's testimonials, nor the Sattlerian writings, nor the later Swiss apologists and debaters, including Martin Weninger's *Vindication* and Zofingen (1532) and Bernese (1538) debates, have much to say about the actual initiation of the redemptive, regenerative process. None elaborate a theory such as Hubmaier's tripartite man with three wills and each varyingly affected by the Fall; but they imply something similar when they refer often to the need of dying "to the will of the flesh" and "walking in the mind of the Spirit" if one is to be a true Christian.[183] All also assume the capacity for some kind of free response to God's approach in grace, the capacity to accept, reject, or even reverse one's decision, which also parallels the purposes underlying Hubmaier's theory. The Lord "compels no one to come"; men must "turn" from sin, "believe" in Christ, and "obey" the gospel.[184]

Also, in basic agreement with Hubmaier, the Swiss Brethren assert the absolute necessity of a divinely wrought regeneration or inner baptism effected by special grace, if man is to have any capacity or power to perform righteousness and attain salvation. This enabling grace is for them as in Hubmaier centered in the work of the Word and the Spirit and represents a special grace made available and effective by Christ's atoning work alone.[185] They assert also the absolute necessity of repentance prior to belief and faith — a repentance defined as active contrition in the same general terms as Hubmaier.[186] They recognize that in some way, grace and free human cooperation through repentance are in constant fusion and jointly involved in all phases of the regenerative process, and must be kept thus.[187]

As in Hubmaier, faith incorporates both human and divine elements in dynamic fusion. Moreover, since all the actual power to know good correctly and to do it is from the divine side alone, and since the creation of true faith is impossible by the human side alone, therefore faith is truly a gift of God.[188] But they also insist, as did Hubmaier, that true faith is an active, working, obedient faith and forgiveness of sins depends on doing "righteous works from a changed heart."[189] Finally, the anticipated effects of the regenerative process are the same: forgiveness of sins, actual moral and spiritual healing, a new nature, a restored freedom to do good, and an available supply of divine power to enable one to live a relatively holy life.[190]

Hubmaier's treatment of faith in relation to regeneration is one facet which is also quite extensively developed by the other early Swiss Anabaptists, especially in the tract "Concerning the Satisfaction of Christ"; a tract generally ascribed to Michael Sattler or a close associate.[191] The purpose of this tract is to contrast both the Catholic sacramental system and Luther's "faith" principle with the Swiss Anabaptist understanding of how Christ's provision of a redemption which satisfied the demands of God is appropriated by, and mediated to, the believer.

The author of the tract agrees with the Magisterial Reformers that, according to the New Testament, justification or righteousness is provided, sufficiently and freely, by Christ's sacrifice of Himself and is mediated through faith. However, both the terms justification and faith are given distinctive definitions akin to those of Hubmaier.

While the author accepts a limited forensic imputation of righteousness as one valid aspect of Christ's gracious provision, acknowledging that according to 1 Peter 2 men can be pronounced forgiven and just through the sacrificial merits of Christ, such is presented as only a part of the larger regenerative process.[192] Accordingly, the author rhetorically asks whether justification happens either by rites, *ex opere operato*, or by faith alone, "whether or not they believe on

The Dominance of Asceticism 159

Him, or whether or not they turn from sin, whether or not they have a change of mind, as the work-saints [Roman Catholics] and scribes [Magisterial Reformers] think?" He answers: "That is far from the truth."[193] He denies that one can "be saved by Christ whether he does the works of faith or not."[194] Thus the definition of faith is the key which changed simple forensic justification into and incorporates it with an actual transformation of life. In actuality, the process becomes almost justification by "works of faith" and holy living.

As in Hubmaier, the tract carefully distinguishes true faith as the appropriating principle of justification from both external works or rites of the sacramental system, which it describes as "works without faith," and the seemingly fruitless mental assent of the Magisterial Reformers, described as "faith without works."[195]

The faith that brings righteousness is based on "doing," not only "hearing" the law. It is a working, renunciatory, and submissive faith. The tract presents a long list of New Testament passages stressing the cost of discipleship and demanding effort, self-improvement, self-denial, and renunciation for salvation.[196] As in Hubmaier, true faith is tied to repentance; it presumes it and incorporates it. The tract makes clear that no one is "pronounced free" without turning from sin, changing one's mind, and believing.[197] It adds, "So also one must speak of faith, namely that repentance is not apart from works, yea not apart from love (which is an unction). . . . Again, one must preach works of faith, that is, a turning back from works [of law and ceremonial], possessions, and yourself. . . ."[198] Thus again forensic justification is only one aspect of a larger regenerative process involving free human cooperation with grace in repentance, belief, and works of faith.

Faith, out of its prerequisite of repentance, takes on, in this tract also, the added and continuous dimension of active obedience. The author notes that forgiveness is "to follow Him [Christ] according to the demands of faith"; a faith that is described as not apart from works, love, and obedience; a faith that is "constant," that involves being *prepared* to take up the cross and follow Jesus Christ even to a martyr's stake.[199] When such implications of human effort are coupled with the specific statement relating to the divine activity that "He [Christ] *makes known* to us the true obedience by which alone the Father is satisfied,"[200] then the cooperative principle is operative also in faith as obedience.[201]

As in Hubmaier, faith becomes the agency for mediating the obedi-

160   Anabaptism and Asceticism

ence necessary to satisfy God. Not only is obedience a forensic imputation of the perfect obedience of the historic Christ but also the creation of conditions whereby Christ can actually repeat that obedience in the life of the believer. True faith therefore not only mediates regeneration but assumes and partly produces a cooperative attitude by the individual with the indwelling power and Spirit of Christ.[202] The tract upholds the necessity of "allowing" God to work obedience within.[203]

Again, the author comments that though Christ has taken on Himself the sin of the world He wishes to be understood that this means "insofar as the word surrenders to Him in faith."[204] The surrender must be maintained, it must be continuous; the author also uses the term "constant" if faith is to be sufficient for salvation.[205]

Therefore, again as in Hubmaier, while the author could insist that faith is, in one sense, wholly of grace, "of God inasmuch as the will and the ability to turn back to God are the gift of God through Jesus Christ our Lord,"[206] and is without merit in that works of faith are not of man's own strength but only performed through the enabling of Christ,[207] yet also, in the earlier portion of the same statement faith presumes a free and continuous human cooperation involving repentance, self-surrender, and works of faith. Then he comes back again, that though man's part is uncoerced yet it is "not as though a man could do this of himself but he is able to do it through the strength of faith."[208] Clearly there is a dynamic interaction here, similar to that in Hubmaier's writings. Moreover, the only kind of faith that must and will satisfy God, and is substantially and actually produced by Him, is one which manifests itself in holy and spiritually fruitful conduct.[209]

Thus, this Sattlerian tract from the Swiss Anabaptists, along with other scattered allusions in their writings and testimonials, represents a view of faith and repentance which though less theologically organized and more limited in scope is fully in harmony with Hubmaier's treatment of the subject. Here too the faith principle for appropriating regeneration is both synergistic and ascetic. It is synergistic in that it requires more than mental assent but also active, continuous, voluntary cooperation in repentance, surrender, and obedience, even though the light by which to choose rightly, the power to attain full freedom of will and actively to obey, are provided by grace alone, contingently through Christ by the Word and the Spirit, and perhaps to a degree by participation in the Christian brother-

The Dominance of Asceticism   161

hood. Though Sattler's acceptance of the full sufficiency of Christ's atonement was apparently acceptable to Bucer,[210] there was a definite divergence centered on this matter of synergism in its appropriation.

Ascetic elements enter into Anabaptist soteriology both in relation to repentance and to the nature of the expected fruitage of faith. The renunciation of possessions and of oneself is vitally involved. For example, the author of the "Satisfaction of Christ" asks, rhetorically, "Must we never through faith in Him renounce our supposed possessions and our own selves and suffer for His sake?" He answers positively by quoting several passages from the New Testament which were traditional favorites for promoting asceticism; passages which demand the complete renunciation of self and of material things, such as the young rich man of Matthew 19.[212]

The close theological agreement, especially on the necessity and nature of repentance and works of faith, in the "Satisfaction of Christ," the Schleitheim Confession, and Sattler's "20 Articles" is one factor supporting the suggestion of a common Sattlerian authorship. But more important for this study is the wide influence and substantial acceptance of their ideas, especially those in the Schleitheim Confession, by the Swiss Brethren as a whole and by other and later branches of Evangelical Anabaptism. Zwingli, in his *Elenchus*, written in the summer of 1527, testified to the widespread distribution of handwritten copies of the Schleitheim Confession among the Swiss Brethren.[213] Copies of Sattler's "Acts" and "Letters" were prepared soon after his martyrdom and went through numerous printings and were widely distributed in the brotherhood.[214]

Research by Delbert Gratz notes the strong influence of these works, especially the Schleitheim Confession, on the Bernese Anabaptists and even on the Dutch.[215] In his dissertation on Sattler, Augsburger maintains that the Sattlerian writings became substantially determinative, theologically, for the essence of the whole Evangelical Anabaptist cause, including the Swiss Brethren, the early Dutch Mennonites, the Hutterian Brethren, and to a lesser degree the South German branch.[216] The Schleitheim Confession and several other Sattlerian tracts were published early in German as a *Sammelband*, and a translation of it was made into Dutch by 1560, giving further evidence of the unity and importance of these writings.[217] Thus it is not surprising to find in later Swiss Brethren disputations, and by their apologists, the same theological expressions and concerns, the same seemingly contradictory assertions as in Hubmaier, the Grebel group, and Sattler, and still without a sense of tension or contradiction regarding grace and the gift of faith on one hand, and self-effort, repentance, and salvation by works of faith on the other.

Von Muralt lists several references to both grace and repentance at the Zofingen (1532) and the Bernese (1538) debates,[218] but he tends to overaccent the grace-faith aspects from the divine side, leading to the overdrawn conclusion that the Anabaptists held substantially to the Magisterial Reformers' position on justification by faith in the message of Christ.[219] Certainly they held to the all-sufficiency and sole sufficiency of Christ's atonement, but the appropriation principle of "faith" has the same distinctive definition already noted in Hubmaier and Sattler. At the Bernese disputation, the Anabaptist spokesman, Hotz, insisted on not only salvation by faith in the provisions of the atonement, but also on the necessity of belief plus repentance if there were to be true Christians and a true church.[220]

These Anabaptists also specifically expressed their concern that the doctrine of repentance was being ignored by the Magisterial Reformers. They upheld that the evidence for true repentance is that it expresses itself in a new life of holiness.[221] Similarly, Hans Luti testified to the Anabaptists' conviction that not only is belief necessary for the new birth and baptism but, as he states repeatedly, one must also "demonstrably repent" (*thund buss*).[222] He continued that eligibility for the Lord's Supper is based both on belief "and sincere improvement of life" (*und Rechtschafne besserung thud* . . .).[223] Only babies are saved automatically, without a voluntary cooperation of the will, by the imputed merits of the death of Christ.[224]

The Anabaptist apologist, Martin Weninger, likewise asserts the importance of "doing" God's will, and the absolute necessity of the "power" of grace in order to do so. But, one is also obliged to "oppose the devil by the firm faith of Christ."[225] That is, grace is here equated with enabling power, but with the implication that this "power" is only made effective as one uses it and cooperates with it.

One possible exception to the synergistic principle is the testimony of Peter Tesch at the Marburg disputation, but even here the context is too limited to be sure of the full meaning of his reported statements.[226] Trying to set forth Anabaptism in the best light possible to the Magisterial Reformation, Tesch describes the initial regenerative aspect of salvation as "without any . . . contribution by man . . . solely through faith . . . in Christ Jesus." That he meant this statement to be at least close to the typical Anabaptist sense of enabling power, however, is suggested in that he too still defends the Anabaptist and ascetic, synergistic concern by going on to describe this faith as subsequently cooperative: "However, this faith must be engaged in all good works through love, which it is *capable of* doing in Christ, *all things being possible*, even light, which were previously unpleasant and arduous."[227]

Actually no further information is forthcoming from these later testimonials as to how the reconciliation and fusion of divine grace and human effort (or willing) was to take place. Grace continues to be the dominant, effective factor in regeneration in that the provision by the atonement for salvation and the power or enabling to repent, have faith, and do works of faith are both wholly of grace. Both faith in Christ and love, which bring salvation, are gifts of grace in that they are impossible to human effort alone. But these gifts are given on conditional terms, on the basis of the voluntary and uncoerced acceptance, obedience, and active cooperation of the believer. True faith must include and incorporate repentance and the Word of God. The synergistic principle is maintained throughout but it is nevertheless far removed from Pelagianism. Significantly, the same kind of synergism appears again, with but minor variations, in the extensive writings of the Dutch Anabaptist leaders, Dirk Philips and Menno Simons, and in Hutterite confessions.[228]

In the foregoing analysis of synergism in the Anabaptist doctrine of regeneration, though there is a latent capacity for free, responsible response in man, the initiative seems clearly to be with grace — usually through the hearing of the Word and the activity of the Holy Spirit, but in some representatives also by some natural or common grace. None of the Anabaptist leaders surveyed grants any possibility whatever for self-salvation apart from grace, nor even for any meritorious acts by natural human powers. The initial free will is only enough to allow for moral responsibility, and the subsequent freeing of the will by regenerating grace is only to encourage moral earnestness and striving, but in both stages such efforts are totally ineffective by themselves. Though their concern is dominantly for man's involvement and for Christian conduct, in reaction to Luther's *sola gratia*, still grace emerges as the overwhelmingly predominant partner, the real enabling factor in true repentance, true faith, and true love, and in all that is embraced by the concept of regeneration.

But grace never functions redemptively apart from the contingency of free human cooperation to the extent possible, small and weak though that cooperation may be. Grace never coerces. The power and ability to be saved and pursue holiness is assured by regeneration, but ultimate salvation is not; it is never inevitable. There is always the need of responsible and free cooperation. This minute initial free capacity to respond, and the ensuing pattern of synergism, is a significant distinctive that provides an important clue for the search in Chapter V for medieval intellectual antecedents.

In the foregoing analysis of synergism in the experience and process of regeneration, it becomes apparent that even regeneration, in spite of its many benefits, does not imply for Anabaptists that salvation is already achieved or that cooperative effort is finished. Rather, regeneration only signifies that an ongoing process of sanctification which enables one to attain salvation has become now, and only now, genuinely possible, and also therefore necessary. There can be no assurance of salvation apart from the ascetic and holy life. In his discussion of baptism, Grebel notes the necessity of believing "before and after it [baptism]" and that baptism should signify that a man is dead to sin and walking in newness of life. He adds, one "shall certainly be saved, *if* by the inner baptism *he lives his faith* according to this significance."[229] A continuing conditional factor, the necessity of continued human cooperation, is thus readily apparent.

Though the Anabaptists do not divorce regeneration, including justification, from sanctification, to the same degree or in the same way as Luther, since they maintain the essential unity of the whole process with reference to salvation, nevertheless, water baptism which is considered generally necessary by Hubmaier does constitute something of a distinguishing point between the two within the process. Hubmaier refers to three distinct baptisms as three successive aspects in the process of salvation: the inner or spiritual baptism of regeneration, the outer or water baptism which is a pledge and confession, and the ongoing baptism of blood and suffering which is sanctification.

Sometimes water baptism is described, even by Hubmaier, as also the first voluntary or initiatory step at the beginning of the cooperative process of sanctification, rather than as a phase in itself. Similarly, sanctifying grace, or third grace, is often terminologically distinguished from first, common, or prevenient grace and from second, special, or regenerating grace. Nevertheless, Hubmaier and the Anabaptists in general insist that all are but parts of one ongoing process, the purpose of which is that "thus our sickness is healed and we receive forgiveness of sins."²³⁰ Ultimate forgiveness becomes the product of a process of actual deliverance or healing, not the immediate and forensic result of a single decision of faith.

The third phase, the ongoing process of sanctification involving the actual living out and development of the potential and resources available to the truly regenerate, is also dependent upon the continuous cooperation of the individual. Such synergism is illustrated particularly well by the voluntary nature and necessity of water baptism²³¹ and also by two ideas, appearing repeatedly in Anabaptist writings, *bussfertigkeit* and *gelassenheit*. The former is used more often by the Swiss Brethren and the latter by the South German Anabaptists, but they are not mutually exclusive; nor are they identical ideas, though closely related.

As noted previously, repentance in regeneration was not just an attitude expressed at one point just prior to and as a prerequisite for true faith, but rather, as with true faith itself, it is a dynamic, necessary, and continuous element in the regenerative process in salvation. It is one of the unifying elements in the process and it is defined ascetically by the Anabaptists. *Bussfertigkeit* is the term they used to express the continuous aspect of repentance, especially as it related to sanctification. The term is not easily translatable but seems to mean a necessary, continuous, and voluntary attitude of revulsion toward sin and of submission and humility toward God; it designates the attitude which produces a totally penitential life.²³²

The term came into use in Anabaptism only gradually. The earliest leaders seem to have stressed more the immediately necessary, practical results of the initial repentance as part of regeneration or of becoming a Christian. Thus, while Manz, typically, asserted that forgiveness is on one hand the provision of grace alone, on the other he adds that the provisions of grace through Christ are dispensed only to those "who wished to reform" and baptism is for those who bring forth fruits of repentance.²³³ Hubmaier, in reference to the restoration of a brother excluded for sinning, also demands genuine, observable repentance: by turning around, making amends, improving one's life, and confessing one's sinfulness with the intention of avoiding repetition.²³⁴ Hubmaier is here referring to necessary and repeated instances of specific repentance related to specific sins by Christians; each repentance is similar in nature and content to that which initially brought about regeneration, and though these instances would be a product of the continuous attitude implied by *Bussfertigkeit,* they are also distinguishable from it.

This combining of a distinguishable continuous inner attitude with external acts of penitence becomes clearly evident in Hubmaier's final writing, the *Rechenschaft.* Here he refers to the continuous life of piety, the necessity by all Christians of "making payment to God's outraged righteousness . . . through prayer *and action,* which is the highest contribution [*welches die höchst buss ist*]."[235] Even more clearly, in one of Sattler's hymns there appears the ascetic idea of a penitent life as the necessary and only true preparedness or watchfulness whereby one attains to eternal salvation.[236]

By the time of the Zofingen disputation (1532), the idea of a distinct, necessary, and continuous attitude of penitence is fully formulated. The Zofingen Anabaptists spoke of the necessity of "conversion from the world to God and from unrighteousness to a penitent [*bussfertig*] life."[237] In the record of the Bernese disputation of 1538, the term *bussfertigkeit* is now used repeatedly to refer to the penitent life.[238] They argued that simply to say one believes is not sufficient; the true Christians are those who couple faith and *bussfertigkeit.*[239] Therefore, the church should admit into membership only "on the basis of a repentant life [*durch ein bussuertig lebenn ufgenommen werden*]."[240] These Anabaptists insisted that Christ came to lead men to *bussfertigkeit*[241] and that the church is built on the foundation of *bussfertigkeit.*[242]

That the ascetically oriented concept of the penitent life had become very early a fundamental aspect of the Anabaptist understanding of the true church, though its terminology developed slowly, is made very clear by the testimonial by one of the Anabaptist spokesmen at Berne. In an attempt to explain his earlier espousal of Anabaptism, he centers attention, significantly, on the importance of the idea of *bussfertigkeit* to the whole initial presentation of Anabaptist thought:

> No beginning was made toward true Christian living [in state Protestantism] . . . true repentance and Christian love were not in evidence. . . . Then God sent His messengers, Conrad Grebel and others. . . . I found them men who had surrendered themselves to the doctrine of Christ by repentance [*bussfertigkeit*]. With their assistance we established a congregation in which repentance was in evidence by newness of life in Christ.[243]

The Dominance of Asceticism 167

Thus, for salvation, the Anabaptists required not just the initial repentance leading to a regeneration, but also a synergistically oriented, continuous attitude of repentance, the penitent life, which would then express itself in repeated acts of specific, public, or private penance, and confession for restoration after sins were committed.

A potential for such a continuous attitude of repentance, as noted previously, was a necessary factor even in Hubmaier's description of the regeneration phase. That is, regenerative penitence, or conversion, begins with sorrow for sin (roughly equivalent to *attritio*), develops into willingness to confess sins (not priestly confession) and to abandon them, and finally — if it is true and full repentance (*contritio*) — it must reach the penitential attitude of continuous and loving submission to God and to His laws and be reflected in an outward expression of ascetically penitent conduct as the fruitage of true penitence.

Water baptism becomes both a witness to conversion through personal repentance and faith, and a pledge of one's firm intention or desire to continue in the penitent life. Thus baptism itself takes the form of a penitential exercise, both a first fruit of repentance and a first step of obedience in the penitential life.

Furthermore, this penitential attitude is not automatic. The will is freed in regeneration by grace, and a potential enabling is provided by grace, but the penitent life also requires the continuous free cooperation of the individual. Cooperation is a prerequisite for the effective operation of sanctifying grace, which in turn is essential for perseverance, for the development of holiness, and for the attainment of ultimate salvation.

The Anabaptist position on penitence and on the exercises and the fruitage of penitence comes remarkably close to the practice of the apostolic and early ante-Nicene church, as described by Poschmann; especially in Clement, where postbaptismal repentance was also considered to be continuous rather than repeated.[244] This continuous aspect entered the monastic tradition, after the fifth century, when the monk's initiation vow was represented as an act of penance, a second baptism, which led into the subsequent life of the "religious" which was considered in turn to be a kind of continuous private penance of an ascetic nature.[245] Thus the idea of penance as more than specific and repeated acts of penance relative to specific sins but rather as a kind of ascetic life-style, reflecting a constant inner attitude, entered the medieval Catholic, ascetic tradition.

168 Anabaptism and Asceticism

On the other hand, repeated acts of private penance which were nonsacramental or priestly grew in Celtic Christianity. The idea of the therapeutic value of works of penance was also extended; primary stress being placed on works of prayer and fasting, then on almsgiving and various renunciations of the flesh.[246] However, the Irish monastic penitential books made clear "that the performance of penance is only efficacious where there is sincere contrition and conversion."[247] These northern monks were largely responsible for reintroducing into medieval Christianity the idea of repetitive acts of private penance, and also of renewing the stress on "penance as the most elementary requirement of the gospel."[248]

When, in repetitive private penance, the elements of confession, imposition of acts of penance, and absolution combined into one procedural rite, about AD 1000, the stage was ready for the development to dominance of sacramental penance.[249] Nevertheless, the possibility of nonsacramental penance was not entirely ruled out prior to the Reformation. Various theories existed, attempting to define the relationship of sacramental to the nonsacramental and of the parts within sacramental penance to each other and to the whole. In the nonsacramental, forgiveness was consistently recognized as dependent on contrition; the other facets of penance, such as restitution and absolution, were only evidential, declarative, and subsidiary. Grace was necessary to transform an inadequate, human *attritio*, sorrow for sins out of fear, into effective *contritio*, renunciation of sin out of love for God.[250]

In sacramental penance, according to Thomas Aquinas forgiveness was dependent on the whole procedural rite which provided the grace for the required contrition, and on the exercise of the ecclesiastical power of the keys; both are necessary. In Scotism, forgiveness depended on contrition alone, which was still considered to be sufficient of itself, if possible to achieve, plus only the intention to participate in the whole of the sacrament; but the full sacramental procedure was also acceptable and more certain since it would assure the augmentation of grace and the change from what was probably an inadequate *attritio* into an effective assurance of forgiveness.[251]

Moreover, the Scotists, and to a lesser degree the Thomists too, maintained that the doctrine of penance had a voluntaristic basis. Forgiveness derived from grace, for the sake of the merits of Christ, but was contingent upon the cooperation of the sinner. *Attritio*, as an ineffective and inadequate but preliminary sorrow for sin, was possible to the natural powers of fallen man; effective *contritio* was *attritio* matured or advanced or formed by grace alone. *Contritio* always required some infusion of grace. In Scotus, this needed grace could be mediated, *ex opere operato*, through sacramental penance, but effective contrition was always also possible extrasacramentally — though attained thus only with difficulty, and still lacking in assurance since no absolution was provided. The intent to confess and to amend were considered necessary constituents of a valid contrition.[252] Thus penance as a sacrament is separated from penance as a virtue, and private penance from the ecclesiastical authority of the keys.

Gabriel Biel, an exponent of both nominalism and the *Devotio Moderna* at the end of the fifteenth century, made contrition not only essentially independent of the keys of ecclesiastical authority but also the sole means or cause of forgiveness. For Biel, *attritio*, regret unformed by grace, even with the addition of all of the procedures of sacramental penance, was always an imperfect penance. Only true contrition, through grace, including the detestation of sin and a firm purpose to amend one's life out of love for God, could bring forgiveness of sins. Biel nevertheless maintained, but only because the teaching of the church said so, that true contrition would include the intention of participating in the sacrament as part of obedience, though denying that the sacrament was inherently causal of forgiveness or that absolution could create or assure contrition.[253]

Luther's rejection of both free will, including the Roman Catholic teaching on contrition which seemed to involve personal merit in forgiveness, and the priestly power of the keys, eliminated *both* the virtue of penance and sacramental penance itself from his system.[254]

In contrast, the Anabaptists retained the power of the keys for the congregation in regard to discipline, and also retained public repentance for public and grievous sins after baptism. Also, they turned water baptism into a declarative, penitential work, and turned the continuing obligation of private penance into something quite similar to the monastic concept of the penitential life. That is, while they rejected sacramental penance, as did Luther, they retained the virtue of penance, the ideal of the centrality of repentance in the gospel, and contrition as synergistic, continuous in intent, and the sole cause of forgiveness; repentance was a prerequisite to true faith. Thus, again they reflect an abandonment of the scholastic, Catholic sacramental system but not of the underlying medieval Catholic, ascetic ideal.

The term *Gelassenheit* was also used, largely by the South German Anabaptists, to describe a necessary attitude of the mind, an attitude of submissiveness and surrender to God's will growing out of a true regeneration.[255] As previously mentioned, there is considerable similarity between this idea and some aspects of the Swiss concept of *Bussfertigkeit* (penitence) which also includes the requirement of submissiveness.[256] The difference seems to be only a matter of emphasis and degree. Whereas repentance, even as *Bussfertigkeit* or the penitent life, seems to stress somewhat more the negative aspect of sorrow for sin, dying to sin, and renunciation of sin and self and worldliness, though contrition always demanded also the positive intent of amendment and improvement, *Gelassenheit* stresses more a positive acquiescence and obedience to God's will. However, Hubmaier also uses it negatively to refer to a resignation in the sense of a renunciation of the devil and his works, of which water baptism is a public witness. This again brings it very close to the Swiss Brethren "repentance."[257]

Friedmann distinguishes three ingredients of *gelassenheit* and its synonyms, as used by the Anabaptists: a yielding of one's members to active service for God, a submissiveness to the discipline and admonitions of the brotherhood as stated in the baptismal pledge, and an acceptance of suffering due to the antagonism of the world.[258] Accordingly, Friedmann prefers to coin the word "yieldedness' in preference to "resignation," as the best translation since the latter tends to imply a more mystical kind of passivity than the Anabaptists usually meant; though some degree of passivity is present also in Anabaptism where the influence of late medieval German mysticism was strong, especially in the South German branch.[259]

Gelassenheit, as with repentance, was both part of the initial conversion which relates to regeneration[260] and part of the ensuing process of sanctification as a required, continuous attitude. Hubmaier uses the term to mean yielding oneself to the enabling power of God so strongly as to include a continuous readiness to suffer and die with Christ in the faith for the sake of attaining eternal life.[261] When the term is used by the South German Anabaptist leader, Hans Denck, the same continuousness is present; it involved a lifetime.[262]

The stress on the necessity of continuous, free, self-surrender adds another contingent dimension to the synergistic interaction with enabling grace whereby the required new or holy life is achieved. Denck states it succinctly: ". . . it is a cheap excuse to say we are unable to surrender ourselves. . . . We are free to surrender, but unable to achieve anything."²⁶³ Similarly, Hubmaier asserts: "The sinner will, as far *as it is possible* for a sinful man, yield *himself* to the Lord's will...."²⁶⁴

Because the early Anabaptists' primary concern was to affirm the necessity of regeneration with its concomitant behavioral improvements, the nature of the subsequent Christian life, especially the pattern of progress and growth in sanctification, is not theologically explained in great detail. The necessity of constancy and continuation is stressed clearly, as noted; but is there also progress and growth? If so, how does the cooperative principle relate to this phase? Is perfection attainable in this life?

There are a few, brief references that imply both the possibility of post-regenerative growth and something of the means by which they expected spiritual growth to take place. An example of both comes from Hubmaier's prayer that "*beginning* faith, hope, and love toward Christ Jesus our Lord may be *increased* and strengthened" in those to whom the work is dedicated, and by the work itself.²⁶⁵ However, it will be seen that the primary agency is again grace, and again only in cooperation with moral effort and desire. The goal itself and its ascetic nature is summarized well by the Swiss Brethren minister, Hans Marquart, as "dying to sin, to the flesh, and to all evil desires" and walking "in the will of the heavenly Father."²⁶⁶

As in the regenerative process, the Holy Spirit and the Word of God are considered to be the chief agencies of sanctifying grace without which no progress is possible. Marquart writes of attaining the goal "through the grace of His Son, Jesus Christ, in the power of the Holy Spirit."²⁶⁷ Hubmaier prays for the Holy Spirit to undertake the task of enabling the believer's will to become "in all things submissive" to God's "fatherly will."²⁶⁸ Walter Klaassen notes the "surprising agreement in all branches of Anabaptism" regarding the role of the Holy Spirit as the major empowering and guiding Agent in both regeneration and growth in perfection.²⁶⁹

Similarly, regarding the role of the Word, the Anabaptists at the Zofingen debate (1532) insist that in true Christians, the "Word of Christ grows and bears fruit."²⁷⁰ Hubmaier also observes the need for teaching and instruction *after* baptism, as well as before, because "there are still deficiencies in matters of faith" which need exterminating.²⁷¹ As one "learned repentance and amendment of life"²⁷² for regeneration, by the Word and the Spirit, so one learns to grow in the penitent life. The Word and the Spirit are closely allied;

the Word informs as the Holy Spirit makes it alive.²⁷³

Hubmaier places a definite synergistic condition on the effectiveness of all aspects of sanctifying grace; both the work of the Word and the Spirit are contingent upon human cooperation and response.²⁷⁴ Concerning the Spirit he writes: "He helps our spirits, witnesses to them, strengthens them to fight and strive against the flesh, sin, the world, death, the devil, and hell."²⁷⁵ Similarly Manz, concerning the receiving of Christ's love, grace, and "the power of His Spirit," says that such is conditional upon bringing forth fruits of repentance. He adds, concerning the power of the Spirit, "Whoever receives and uses it grows and is made perfect in God."²⁷⁶

The nature of the human involvement or response to the divine Word and the Spirit in growth in sanctification seems to rise largely out of the previously discussed principles of separation, continuing repentance, and obedient submission, when these are aided by and fused with grace.²⁷⁷ Specifically, the human involvement in the development of sanctification bears a strong resemblance to some of the principles underlying the ascetic, penitential exercises. For example, there is the repeated emphasis placed on the need for constant personal moral and spiritual striving and on continual spiritual conflict and struggle. Sanctification was never automatic or just "imputed" or without diligent moral effort by the believer.

The overall testimony of the Anabaptists on the necessity and nature of the human involvement is clear. The Grebel group maintained that the believers must "strive" for perfection constantly,²⁷⁸ that they must fight sin, and that they could "overcome it."²⁷⁹ This latter remark illustrates that the Anabaptists had much more optimism than Luther regarding the actual attainment of the holy life; regeneration and grace provided both the power and the will.

Michael Sattler, the most probable author of the tract *Two Kinds of Obedience*, refers to the necessity of even "filial" obedience "striving" for perfection and, he also adds, it "attains" it.²⁸⁰ Hubmaier too stresses the existence of spiritual enemies that need to be "resisted and exterminated . . . even after baptism."²⁸¹ For him, baptism must signify an intent to "fight and strive under His [Christ's] banner until death."²⁸² These, and many similar expressions throughout the writings of the Anabaptists ²⁸³ reveal a stress in reference to moral and spiritual conflict that finds its parallel only in the long history of the ascetic tradition.

The necessary struggle and conflict in the progress of sanctification is also aimed at the typical foes of the medieval ascetics: the devil, the world, and the flesh. Weninger urges that *true* Christians must "oppose the devil by the firm faith of Christ."[284] Anabaptist opposition to the world represents only a slight modification of the poverty ideal of the Franciscan Tertiaries, and includes the rejection of creaturely comforts, luxury, materialism, and private possessions.[285] The necessity of "taming," subduing, conquering the flesh by the restored soul is especially strong in Hubmaier's tripartite anthropology.[286] Regeneration frees the soul from the domination of the fallen flesh and places divine powers at the soul's disposal making possible the subduing of the evil flesh. But since the flesh remains fallen and corrupt until the resurrection, the struggle to control the flesh is continuous throughout this life.[287]

The cooperative principle also reappears in the struggle and conflict in sanctification. Hubmaier promises that God "*helps our spirits* . . . to fight and strive against the flesh, sin, the world, the devil, and hell";[288] but the restored soul in its new freedom may still fail to use its resources and therefore fall to the fleshly temptations. If it does, "it shall die."[289] Clearly, in Hubmaier, for the successful waging of the conflict, there must be free, sustained, moral effort by the regenerate soul's will. Even Menno Simons, who tended to stress the role of grace as much as possible, noted the necessity for the true Christians to "strive" for the penitent life, including opposing evil and seeking righteousness "with all their might."[290]

It is probably the above ascetically oriented conviction of the necessity of continual moral and spiritual struggle against asceticism's traditional foes of the flesh, the world, and the devil which more than any other caused Anabaptism to retain several features that bear a strong resemblance to the older penitential exercises which also functioned as agencies of sanctification. For example, the Anabaptists did not hesitate to use the term "mortification," especially in reference to the controlling of the flesh, that chief agency of the devil which, after regeneration, continues to hinder the Christian from "advancing" to God.[291] The Grebel group called for a spiritual mortification as the essence of the Christian warfare on the road to eternal rest;[292] Sattler, for the crucifixion of the flesh with its passions and lusts;[293] and Hubmaier, for a "daily mortification" of the flesh because the flesh continues to resist the newborn soul and the spirit and tries to "prevent a man from doing that which he would do according to the Word of God."[294]

174 Anabaptism and Asceticism

How does the regenerate conquer? Hubmaier says by the Spirit of Christ, but also: "The man must *exercise himself* day and night in all things that concern the praise of God and brotherly love. Thus the old Adam is *tortured, slain, and buried.* That is the sum and correct order of the whole Christian life which then begins in the Word of God."[295] Furthermore, Hubmaier assures his followers that the evil lusts and sinful desires continuously arising from the unregenerate, corrupt flesh "cannot damn one if he confesses them to God with grief and does not walk after them but *controls* the devils of his flesh vigorously, *crucifies* them, *martyrs* them ceaselessly."[296]

While the foregoing gives conclusive evidence of the Anabaptists' assertion of the need for an ascetic kind of self-mortification of the flesh, a self-crucifixion, there are also numerous references which indicate something of the means. To achieve such penitential mortification, they refer primarily to confession or self-examination, and to daily exercises of devotion, brotherly love, charity, and suffering. Each one needs closer analysis for what it can contribute to our understanding of Anabaptist penitential exercises.

The penitential exercises of confession and self-examination appear clearly to be retained in principle by the Anabaptists. Hubmaier specifically asserts that the penitential life, which is quite distinct from occasions of public confession before the church, relating to restoration after public sins,[297] requires that "we should constantly confess and accuse ourselves of sin before God . . . but priestly confession I hold to be a vain thing."[298] This kind of penitential exercise, apparently associated with controlling private and not "grievous" sins and attitudes,[299] was closely, though not exclusively, tied by Hubmaier and by the Anabaptists in general to the Lord's Supper. He instructs concerning participation in the Supper: "Each man should at the beginning examine himself and confess his sins before God."[300] He adds that this confession may be expressed collectively in prayer. Also, in addition to confession and self-examination which is personally public to the brotherhood, collective and private to God, Hubmaier specifies another type of confession, to someone we have wronged.[301] This strong emphasis in Anabaptist theology and practice on various forms of self-examination, self-accusation, and public and personal confession indicates again Anabaptism's affinity with the Christian ascetic tradition.

Another expression of a sanctifying penitential exercise in Anabaptism is its emphasis on daily devotions, including prayer,[302] contemplation, adoration, and praise,[303] and fasting.[304] The purpose of these devotional exercises is expressly stated as to "finally come, without spot or impurity, into eternal life."[305] They placed great emphasis on the penitential therapy and value of prayer in particular, both private and congregational.[306] Its ascetic character and sanctifying intent is indicated by statements such as: believers need "sincere sighs and prayers to God that He may increase their faith . . . and brotherly love,"[307] and the sinners not only must yield to God's will but also must "call on Him daily for healing and purification."[308] Here, the initiative of calling and praying, though not the power, seems to be the responsibility of the restored, free, human will. At the conclusion of a discussion on the fusing of grace as the empowering factor with "our own powers" in the production of good works, Hubmaier asserts: "The highest theology of all is diligent prayer without ceasing to God who gives mouth and wisdom."[309]

Also considerable formalization of the devotional exercise of prayer is apparent in Hubmaier, akin to the practices of Franciscan Tertiaries.[310] Hubmaier maintains:

> I have admonished the people to pray faithfully and without ceasing. Also in all my preaching I recited with the people loudly and kneeling a public confession, the Lord's Prayer, and a psalm. I have also again restored the ringing of the bells, evening and morning and midday, when it was earlier done away by other preachers and for the people. I have indicated the ninth hour of prayer.[311]

Similarly, their retention and advocacy of fasting, which joins together prayer and a practical mortification of the flesh, represents an even stronger ascetic and synergistic orientation. Fasting, however, was expressed in a way consistent with the modifications of the laicization process by the Franciscan Tertiaries and the Brethren of the Common Life, and with the Anabaptists' own emphasis on the penitential life. Therefore Hubmaier confesses to the value of fasting "daily" and "continuously," but in the sense of "suppressing all excess," and "using food and drink with moderation so as not to feel the old Adam and he begin to cause one to fall . . . into the mire."[312]

The third type of penitential exercise, acts of charity, is closely related to the works of devotion to God and springs from such. Since, says Hubmaier, one cannot actually "do" anything for Christ, directly,

176 Anabaptism and Asceticism

to demonstrate love, Christ "points us to our neighbors, especially those of the household of faith, on whom we may work works of thankfulness, both physical and spiritual. . . . He [Christ] will receive these works of kindness as if we had done them to Him."[313] One aspect of the basic surrender to God in the regenerative process or stage, and to which water baptism was considered a witness, was the promise of intent by believers to "surrender *their members* to God the Lord and be devoted servants of righteousness in obedience so that they may become holy [*heylig*] and receive the goal which is eternal life, a gift of God in Christ Jesus our Lord."[314] Thus penitential service becomes an important contributor to the ongoing sanctification process.

Several statements by Hubmaier illustrate the necessity, role, and nature of these works of mercy and charity. In answer to the question, "Of what do real good works consist?" Hubmaier replies, "Works of mercy for which God will demand an account . . . at the last day." Furthermore, he emphasizes the condition that eternal life is "for all believers in Christ who have done deeds of mercy to their neighbor."[315] Emphasizing the necessity of this positive, active penitence, Hubmaier writes: "Further, know this, O pious Christian, it is not enough . . . to forsake sins and die to them. We must also do good to our neighbors."[316] Without being too specific, Hubmaier identifies these good works as only those deeds which "God Himself has designated for us and for which He will demand an accounting at the Last Day (Matthew 25)." He goes on to state that the deeds done for our neighbors are in imitation of Christ, doing as He did, "offering our own bodies, lives, property, blood for their sakes."[317]

The analysis of the sanctifying role of works of charity leads into the whole issue of Anabaptism's adoption of the "imitation of Christ" tradition which was so strong in the Brethren of the Common Life in the fifteenth century. Many Anabaptist historians have noted it and have fixed on it as one of Evangelical Anabaptism's most dominant characteristics.[318] Michael Sattler emphasized it, noting that part of Christ's mission was to leave an "example that ye should follow in His footsteps."[319] In his letter to Capito, Sattler claims that the only true Christians are those "who truly love and follow God (others I do not know)."[320] Even believer's baptism was defended as an act of obedience in imitation of Christ.[321] The same theme abounds in the Grebel group, in Hubmaier, and most Anabaptist writers of all branches.[322]

The "imitation of Christ" theme encompasses the whole positive side of the penitent life. Again synergism appears. There is a dual involvement in the renewal of the divine image in the believer; both regeneration and a voluntary, practical imitation of Christ.[323] In both, the human and the divine must constantly cooperate for success. The sign of one who follows Christ is that one takes up his cross "daily."[324] But true "imitation" is also impossible without grace. This represents far more than a humanist moralism; rather, it relates to penitential exercises and their sanctifying powers.

Furthermore, the imitation of Christ as a penitential exercise meant taking the commands of the gospel seriously. As Jesus obediently fulfilled the will of God so must His followers try — and by God's help, succeed.[325] Sattler asks, "Why should God make known His will, if He would not wish that a person do it . . .[Christ] makes known to us the true obedience by which *alone* the Father is satisfied."[326] In the plainest words possible, Hubmaier asserts: "The plain and simple will of God is that we hold before our eyes His dear Son, Jesus Christ, and follow His life and teaching. Thereon hang all the law and the prophets."[327]

The gracious acceptance of suffering and persecution for Christ's sake must also be considered a sanctifying penitential exercise. Reublin insists that "apart from suffering and the cross one cannot be saved."[328] The importance and necessity of this theme takes on major proportions in Anabaptist literature and therefore must be reviewed, even though treated extensively by numerous scholars, especially Ethelbert Stauffer.[329]

Stauffer maintains that in Anabaptism the themes of persecution and suffering are identified with the Old Testament's presentation of the suffering "remnant," which is also closely allied with the ascetic stresses on dualism, separation from the world, antagonism from the world, and the smallness of the number of the saved. These themes initially appear in the Grebel group, but are extended by Sattler, Menno, and others. Expectations of persecution and suffering are also tied to the "imitation of Christ" motif with reference to the necessity of a right attitude towards one's persecutors; a Christian must not retaliate but be submissive for Christ's sake.[330] Stauffer traces the history of the theology of martyrdom from Judaism through the New Testament into the early church Fathers; but then, strangely, he relegates the concept almost exclusively to the "underground" movements through medieval times up to the Reformation.

Even though Stauffer recognized the close alliance of the martyr theology with the whole "imitation of Christ" motif, nevertheless he fails to note the assimilation of the whole theology of martyrdom and of spiritual conflict through suffering by the Desert Fathers, and thus through them its transmission into the whole monastic traditon.[331] Verduin also identifies "cross bearing" Christianity and the exaltation of martyrdom almost exclusively with the "tradition of heresy" beginning "with the Donatists" — an unjustifiable exclusiveness.[332] There is no necessity to look outside and no justification for ignoring Catholic ascetic tradition in carefully searching out intellectual antecedents.

There was even an upsurge of both the theology of martyrdom and the motif of "the imitation of Christ" in the early years of the Reformation, in Albrecht Dürer's *Diary* of 1521, Luther's comments and his martyr's hymn of 1523.[333]

It is of particular significance to this study to point out a somewhat overlooked aspect, namely, that the right acceptance of suffering was also considered by the Anabaptists as a means to sanctification and to ultimate salvation and that therefore, to some degree, it too must be categorized as a penitential exercise. As a necessary work of penitence, the Christlike, submissive acceptance of suffering is, first, closely related to those penitential exercises which promote the mortification of the flesh. Hubmaier specifically calls it "a daily mortification of the flesh continuing until death," and in some cases it included death or martyrdom itself.[334] In fact, he considers it as something of a replacement for, and a truer expression of, extreme unction which also had traditionally the characteristics of a penitential exercise.[335]

This self-mortification by submission to suffering and persecution, Hubmaier also calls a third baptism or a baptism of blood. Although finding its fullest expression after the second or water baptism, it seems to have an earlier beginning in the anguish and suffering of guilt in the early stages of the first baptism of faith or of the Spirit. It continues as an inner temptation to avoid suffering and persecution for Christ's sake. The Anabaptists often gave falling before this temptation as a cause for the Magisterial Reformers' rejection of Anabaptism.[336] The temptation to avoid the way of suffering ends only at death, often by martyrdom but is then followed by sure and certain glorification.[337] The Grebel group also uses the symbolism of a "baptism" of suffering to express their insistence that true Christians must be prepared to suffer and die as sheep among wolves.[338] Sattler similarly urges the acceptance of suffering and persecution as a sanctifying "chastening of the Lord." He considers unwillingness to accept such patiently as an indication of lack of true surrender, and as carnality.[339]

Second, the patient acceptance of suffering must be included in this category of penitential exercises not only because it promotes sanctification through mortification, but also because of its close relationship to the "imitation of Christ." Both Sattler and Hubmaier insist that Christians must always act according to the example of Christ's life on earth. Both specifically tie together the concepts of suffering and the imitation of Christ. For example, Hubmaier advocates that the Christian, in following the pattern of discipleship set by Christ (*im nachfolge den weg*), must accept suffering and the cross just as Christ did.[340] Sattler agrees, quoting 1 Peter 2:21, that Christ's suffering for us is as an example, and all who are called are to follow in His steps.[341] Sattler adds that the way of suffering is in contrast to ruling.[342] The making of the acceptance of suffering antagonistic to Christian participation in the military, civil rulership, or the magistracy is strong in Sattler but Hubmaier does not apply it in this way.[343] Sattler even includes in his following of Christ in suffering the necessity of renouncing our "supposed possessions and our own selves" for His sake.

The redemptive nature of suffering in Anabaptism has been noted briefly by Friedmann,[344] but this aspect of suffering still needs further investigation in terms of its relationship to sanctification and the penitential pattern. According to Hubmaier, the acceptance of suffering is rooted in *gelassenheit*. That is, one must yield himself so completely, initially, to the enabling power of God that this submission includes a continuous lifelong readiness to suffer and die with Christ so as to attain eternal life.[345] While Sattler varies the metaphors and refers to suffering as a "chastisement of the Lord," the purpose is the same: salvation.[346] Repeatedly, Hubmaier urges a rejoicing in and patient acceptance of suffering, especially of persecution, for Christ's sake because it is the "right path that leads to eternal life," the path that even Christ had to go and whoever seeks another path "will fail to reach the door of heaven."[347] Elsewhere, he makes even more clear the redemptive character of suffering and martyrdom:

180   Anabaptism and Asceticism

> What is the nearest way by which one can attain to eternal life? Through anguish, distress, suffering, trouble, persecution, and death for the sake of the name of Christ. He Himself had to suffer and thus enter into His glory (Luke 24)....[348]

In one of his hymns, Blaurock expresses the typically ascetic idea that this life is only a pilgrimage toward the eternal kingdom, and he equates this pilgrimage with the path of suffering.[349] Even stronger is the assertion of Reublin to Pilgram Marpeck that "apart from suffering and the cross, one cannot be saved."[350]

Probably the most remarkable extension of the role of the acceptance of suffering in Evangelical Anabaptist theology is the notion, expressed by some, that the Christian's suffering is an actual continuation of Christ's atonement. This doctrine appears at the very beginning of the movement. The Grebel circle comments to Thomas Müntzer, concerning their anticipated persecution: "Thou knowest well that it cannot be otherwise. Christ must suffer still more in His members."[351] Sattler elucidates this remarkable idea, that the Christian's righteous suffering is a participation or sharing in an unfinished and continuing atonement, in the tract, "The Satisfaction of Christ." Here he moves from a discussion of suffering as renunciatory and part of the "imitation of Christ" to the following assertion:

> Yea indeed, if Christ therefore did enough by His passion which He suffered at Jerusalem and nothing was uncompleted of His suffering, why then does Paul say in Colossians 1, "Now I rejoice in my suffering which I bear for you and fill up in my body that which is lacking in the afflictions of Christ?"[352]

He then goes on to identify implicitly such suffering as one of the meritorious works of faith which are necessary for salvation.[353]

The meritorious aspect of suffering in Anabaptism is best illustrated by its most extreme form, martyrdom; though this is considered only the ultimate expression of a continuous, necessary martyrdom of the "devils of one's flesh."[354] That the Anabaptists ascribed exceptional merit and personal reward to martyrdom, though they did not espouse the notion of a reservoir of extra and dispensable merits by these saints,[355] is amply illustrated by their typically medieval description of miraculous events which were supposed to have accompanied their more exceptional martyrs; a good example is Reublin's account of the martyrdom of Michael Sattler in 1527, the details of which were published and circulated widely.[356]

This analysis of Anabaptist penitential exercises leads to the problem of the relationship of merit to works in Anabaptist thought. Most recent Mennonite historians, concerned with defending a strong view of grace for Anabaptism, to counteract Luther's charges that Anabaptism was Pelagian, or with attempting to demonstrate the theological closeness of Anabaptism to and its derivation from the Magisterial Reformation, treat the problem superficially. These writers quickly relegate all "works" in Anabaptism to an important but strictly evidential functioning.[357]

That the problem is not resolved that easily has been illustrated by the foregoing study on the role of works as sanctifying exercises of penitence. Hubmaier makes this clear by his strong objection to the popularized Lutheran idea that "we can do nothing good." He calls that a "half truth" which had produced the regrettable consequences that people "have not prayed, or fasted, or given alms for a long while...."[358]

Most important is the statement that appears in Hubmaier's *Rechenschaft* that it is necessary to make "payment to God's outraged righteousness ... through prayer and action, which is the highest repentance."[359] That is, works of devotion, mortification, imitation, and deeds of charity embody saving contrition; they are redemptive. This can be reconciled with frequent Anabaptist denials of works-righteousness when these denials are properly understood as repudiations of sacramental Roman Catholic or of Pelagian works. The Anabaptists' "saving" works were not equated with *ex opere operato* rites or external, ceremonial obedience; nor were they the product of natural human effort. They must be the product of the regenerate nature and synergistically performed. Thus Peter Rideman's *Confession* could summarize the issue: "We know that all our work, in so far as it is *our* work, is naught but sin and unrighteousness; but in so far as it is of Christ and done by Christ in us ... it is ... loved of God and well pleasing to Him."[360] Manz refers to "righteous works from a changed heart," and Sattler to works "out of faith" which are "made known" by Christ from the Word. Weninger asserts that "right [deeds] done from the fear of God are acceptable to Him."[361]

Synergism is again the key. True works are more than just evidential because, if "true," they must be so fused with grace as to become almost synonymous with grace. Apart from works, though the enabling and the freeing of the will to choose between good and evil is of grace, there is no salvation. Since grace operates in and through works, and since works are not compelled, they are more than evidential.[362] Hubmaier suggests that though works unaided and unfused with grace are utterly worthless, God works in the Christian as if the works were ours, and therefore rewards are promised for them.[363] Without such works both the assurance of salvation and its attainment, since salvation is a process, are impossible. Without works of faith there is no true, saving faith, only false faith, a delusion.[364]

Again, though repentance, belief, and submission are works which are possible only in cooperation with grace, they have a casual function, not just evidential. They produce faith, and they purchase the possibility of salvation; for example, Manz asserts: "When a person produces the right fruits of repentance then the heaven of eternal joy is purchased and secured for him by grace through Christ. . . ."[365] Furthermore, faith and love grow and increase by works of faith and love, and such growth is redemptively necessary. And, since the Christian is not free from the law of Christ,[366] and fulfillment is required for salvation — being "saved" and "keeping God's laws" are equated —[367] then works of obedience are a necessary part of the process of salvation.

For Luther, love and works are strictly only a fruit of saving faith. They are not causally or even necessarily evidentially related to a redemption which for him is completed, forensically, by the gift of faith and thus are totally of unmerited grace. The contrast between Luther and the Anabaptists is great. It simply is not correct to imply that their differences were only matters of emphasis and degree, and that both agree that faith alone is sufficient for salvation, and that works are only the fruit of faith.

To conclude this discussion of various factors and agencies suggesting the possibility of and means for progress in sanctification, one must also consider the role of association with a brotherhood; though the functioning of the brotherhood is not exactly a penitential exercise. The Anabaptists were convinced of the necessity of the believers' close association in a brotherhood if the individual Christian was to fulfill the plan of Christ, properly develop and express the holy life, and finally attain to salvation. Friedmann points out that they really rejected any notion of salvation apart from the brotherhood and held that "one cannot come to God [that is, attain salvation] except as one comes to Him together with one's brother."³⁶⁸

Similarly, Hubmaier and the Grebel group reject any concept of secret or private belief.³⁶⁹ This represents a repudiation of both the eremitic ideal in the ascetic tradition and the internalized individualism of the mystic and spiritualist. Among the Hutterites, part of the mortification of the self-life was through "self-less identification" with the Hutterite society. And that holds true for all Anabaptists, in principle.³⁷⁰ Here again, though directed more to the brotherhood as a whole than to an abbot, the cenobitic monastic ideal of obedience and submission as a sanctifying thing, is retained.

The brotherhood concept, as a sanctifying functioning, required that "each helps the other to overcome the inclination to sin, and to carry on the difficult task of purity."³⁷¹ Accordingly, the brotherhood must be considered as not only an agency for spiritual progress but also an aid in perseverance an analysis of this latter aspect comes later in this chapter.

As an agency of progress in sanctification, the brotherhood functioned in at least three ways: First, as an agency of spiritual discipline, restraint, chastisement, and correction. Concerning the curative powers of brotherly discipline Hubmaier writes: "Hereupon, O pious Christian, it is necessary, because men are by nature the children of wrath, evil, and baseness, to administer wholesome medicine to them. . . ."³⁷² He also refers to the value of "fraternal correction according to the institution and ordinance of Christ (Matthew 18)," and to the need to allow oneself to be chastised, admonished, and "punished" [disciplined] by his brothers and sisters according to the rule of Christ.³⁷³ Similarly Sattler urges the use of discipline according to Matthew 18 in order to maintain right conduct, acceptance of suffering and persecution, and the necessary separation from the world.³⁷⁴

The willingness to submit to such group discipline is part of the promise or vow of submission which must be voluntarily rendered at baptism.³⁷⁵ That without such submission, one's salvation is in jeopardy is indicated by Hubmaier's insistence that a true conversion must include a "purpose [bewilligt], in the strength of our Lord Jesus Christ that from now on we will regulate our lives according to His rule [nach seiner Regel]."³⁷⁶ Hubmaier identifies the promise and intent to live by the "rule of Christ" as part of true faith.³⁷⁷

This demand for submission to brotherly discipline and correction according to a "rule" bears a strong resemblance to the cenobitic, ascetic tradition which also required a perfecting submission

184 Anabaptism and Asceticism

to some "rule." The Anabaptists use the same type of terminology over and over with but the one singular change: it is no longer the rule of some specific monastic order, but directly the rule and ordinances of Christ from the Word which must be followed; the procedure is taken from Matthew 18, and the regulations from the evangelical "counsels," of the New Testament.[378] Therefore, to the brotherhood corporately, as the agency of discipline, is ascribed the power of the keys[379] and the task of excommunication and restoration with reference to public or serious (mortal) sins.[380] Without brotherly discipline, properly practiced and enforced, the Anabaptists were convinced that it was "impossible for things to go aright and stand well among Christians on earth."[381] Even gospel preaching and the right form of baptism were futile without the application of the rule of Christ.[382] Hubmaier asserts that unwillingness to humble themselves to the rigors of fraternal discipline is one of the main reasons for the rejection of Anabaptism by the Reformers. He adds: "It is very hard to set up a Christian rule among them."[383]

Second, the brotherhood contributed to the believer's progress in sanctification from justification. Similarly, they emphasized regenerating as a necessary agency of instruction, inspiration, and worship. Sermonizing, in spite of the wide distribution of the printed Scriptures, retained its vital place in the Christian life of the church. Hubmaier points out that the sermon aided progress in sanctification: by its ability to arouse the brethren, "by earnest contemplation of His [Christ's] bitter suffering and death, to adoration, love, and thanksgiving" and by "instruction in brotherly love."[384] There is need for instruction, after faith and baptism, writes Hubmaier, because "there are still deficiencies in matters of faith."[385] Sattler, similarly insists on the maintenance of ministers or shepherds in the brotherhood.[386] Therefore, preaching and teaching within the brotherhood and as a function of it, relate to growth in faith and sanctification.

Moreover, after the sermon, the meetings were often given over to a time of mutual exhortation, correction, and encouragement. Any member was allowed to speak and exhort for the common good — a kind of charismatic happening based on 1 Corinthians 12 to 14.[387] Similarly, united prayer and prayer for one another also functioned to aid in progress toward the goal so that they all may "finally come, without spot or impurity, into eternal life."[388]

Third, the brotherhood provided the chief loci for performing acts of service, sanctifying works of charity, and expressions of love to

The Dominance of Asceticism   185

God. Hubmaier insists that practical expressions of love made to neighbors, especially of the household of faith, are received by God as if done unto Him directly.[389] Also, since the brotherhood was understood to be more than just a local organization, but rather a partial actualization of the kingdom of God, it is within this context that one's entire kingdom and social responsibilities are centered. The brotherhood is a society in which the ethics of the kingdom, both personal and social, are developed and expressed.[390]

Accordingly, in Anabaptist thought, apart from the "brotherhood," salvation or progress in the attainment of holiness is virtually impossible.

Sixteenth century and most subsequent critics of Anabaptism have largely overlooked sanctification as progress in Anabaptist thought because the theme of perseverance was given much the greater prominence in Anabaptist writings. Anabaptists sought to counter popular Magisterial Reformation preaching by emphasizing the unity of the total process of salvation; they refused to radically separate sanctification from justification. Similarly, they emphasized regeneration as having already produced the "new creation" with a freed will and the presence of a new Power. These considerations led to an emphasis in their polemical literature on sanctification as perseverance to such an extent that they created the impression that there was little real concern for growth and development.[391] A few examples will illustrate this point.

Grebel's letter to Thomas Müntzer emphasizes the Christian life after baptism as a maintaining of the faith already achieved by the inner baptism according to this baptism's initial "significance," namely, that such a person "is dead and ought to be dead to sin. . . ."[392] This emphasis on having died completely to sins already in regeneration leads to the repeated use of such terms as "hold fast," "abide," "persevere," "endure," in Swiss Anabaptist writings and hymnody.[393] The notion of perseverance is even applied to the necessity of the keeping of His commandments.[394] There are similar strong passages in Sattler and Hubmaier. Sattler writes:

> Now since you have so well understood the will of God which has been made known by us, it will be necessary for you to achieve perseveringly, without interruption, the known will of God.[395]

Similarly, three times in article five in his *Rechenschaft* Hubmaier expresses the necessity of maintaining a constant, good conscience; that is, one is responsible, in thoughts, words, and deeds "to stand continually [*unterlass*] with a good conscience before God."[396]

In many other passages, one's ultimate salvation seems dependent primarily upon perseverance in the first principles rather than on progress and development. Blaurock makes receiving the eternal crown contingent upon holding fast and "keeping oneself unspotted from sin."[397] Those who are ready for the "heavenly supper" are not those who were called and once received the white, divinely given wedding garment but rather those "who in all sorrow *adhere* to Christ *unto the end* even as He steadfastly suffered for us on the cross . . . and thus it is with all . . . who shall *keep their wedding garment*. But he who is not clothed in this garment . . . shall be . . . cast into outer darkness."[398]

To add to the difficulty of distinguishing sanctification as progress, perseverance also is conceived synergistically. One is exhorted to do the holding fast, the persevering, the overcoming, and one is held morally responsible to do so. But the same divine agencies operative throughout in sanctification as progress are also necessary to perseverance. God's goodness and grace are extolled as "preserving us from sin"[399] and as giving daily renewing and strength "that we may continue in the narrow way." The enabling is "in the power of the Holy Spirit."[400]

Again, in both sanctification as perseverance and as progress, the brotherhood plays an important role. The administration of group discipline and admonition, and of excommunication to the offender, acts also as a preserving warning and deterrent to the others and as a means of restoration for the fallen.[401]

The resolution of the seeming tension between sanctification as growth or progress and as perseverance is that what is received in the beginning, at a true regeneration, and which must be perseveringly held on to and maintained, are attitudes that must manifest themselves in actions. These actions and attitudes are in turn those that produce moral and spiritual growth. Therefore steadfastness and some measure of progress seem to be coexistent, but there may still be varying rates of growth even while maintaining a basic perseverance. Therefore, sanctification in Anabaptist theology involves both progress and perseverance, and they are distinguishable even though Anabaptist polemical involvements tended to encourage particular

The Dominance of Asceticism   187

stress on the latter. Something of this combination may be implied in Weninger's comment:

> Those who hold fast to the beginning of the nature of Christ (as He then has imparted His nature in those things, for those who are God's from youth to the end of life), they partake of Christ (Hebrews 3).[402]

Luther, Zwingli, and the Strassburg Reformers charged the Anabaptists with proclaiming and upholding a doctrine of perfectionism. If the charge meant, as some historians have assumed, that they believed in the possibility of achieving some kind of permanent state of absolute perfection or sinlessness in this life, such a charge is readily refuted by simple reference to the Anabaptists' stress both on the need of the ban and on its restorative function.[403] But once absolute sinlessness is thus shown to be untenable, the opposite tendency is either to present the Anabaptists' concept of perfection as only a somewhat more serious recognition of the Christian's need to strive outwardly toward perfection,[404] or else as simply a rejection of what Verduin calls the "conductual averagism" of an inclusive or sacral society.[405] Neither of these alternatives really do justice to the sources.

Sinless perfection as an issue is essentially a "straw man." The sources show abundantly and clearly that the Anabaptists rejected any exaggerated charges of this type. Actually most charges only accused them of demanding a monastic, not an absolute, perfectionism. As Friedmann demonstrates, no Anabaptist ever claimed to have reached ultimate perfection in this life; in fact, they expressly deny it.[406] Yet they require more than just a negative attitude toward "conductual averagism." The Anabaptists seem to maintain the possibility of some kind of perfectionism, of living without sinning, in this life. The problem is to reconcile properly their advocacy of some kind of perfectibility and sinlessness with their denials of any absolute perfectionism.[407]

Several aspects of Anabaptist thought seem to substantiate a charge of perfectionism, if perfectionism is not pushed to some extreme form. First, the Anabaptists not only demanded a regeneration at the beginning of the Christian life but interpreted the resulting ontological change in fallen human nature to mean at least a completed potential for perfectibility in this life; but a perfectibility which at best is both relative and limited. This potential perfection from regeneration is limited in that, as noted previously, the flesh per se remains corrupted and sinful, until death and the resurrection. Therefore temptation remains until death, and all one's best fleshly works are somewhat deficient and tainted by "inborn weakness and imperfections." But these "weaknesses" are not held against one to "damnation," for "in Christ we have received all perfection," providing one is otherwise willing and working obedience.[408] Thus, there is an "imputed" perfection covering the flesh problem in part; but only the flesh problem, and only in part. They also held that the flesh need not and must not normally dominate the attitudes and actions of the truly regenerate believer.[409]

Even the freeing of the soul from the dominance of the flesh does not necessitate or make possible actual perfect sinlessness but only the elimination of known, willing sinfulness by free choice aided by grace — a potential, relative holiness.[410] Regeneration is not itself perfection but rather the partial restoration of pristine freedom, a potential for perfection and goodness by the soul and for control over the flesh. Hubmaier insists that the free restored soul can "master the flesh, tame it, dominate it. . . . To be sure there are imperfections . . . in all its acting and suffering . . . yet these are not fatal or destructive to the soul. . . ."[411] Therefore, the first limitation in Anabaptist theology on "absolute" perfection is the flesh itself. This problem is covered, redemptively, by "imputed" perfection and, in action, partially by the flesh's domination by the regenerated soul.

Furthermore, even the potential for achieving practical goodness is limited by one's lack of knowledge of God's will; this knowledge must be progressively increased as it is derived from the Word. Regeneration is, therefore, a completed potential for a "relative" perfection only; one is then expected to obey God fully, up to the level of understanding and maturity present. Sattler illustrates this relativity by exhorting the brethren at Horb to *further* sanctify themselves "for Him who made you holy."[412]

The possibility of maintaining a relative perfection along with a potential for growth in perfection toward ultimate perfection in the eternal state correlates with the Anabaptist emphasis on sanctification as perseverance, but counteracted by the presence of the added dimension of sanctification as growth or progress, and requires that the Anabaptist's definition of realizable perfection to be relative. This doctrine of a potential for growth in relative perfection resolves

The Dominance of Asceticism 189

the problem of the Anabaptists' teaching of sanctification as both progress and perseverance in a way fully consistent with medieval ascetic theology. Thomas Aquinas also suggests that perfection is relative in this life, and only absolute in the world to come, that perfection is attained by the practice of Christian virtue and by additions of grace to one's weak, infused, beginning grace.[413] The Anabaptists grant much more to regenerating or beginning grace and therefore place more stress on perseverance, but progress by the practice of virtue is present too, and the underlying principle is similiar.

If regeneration provides both the possibility for an immediate perfection of desire and a potential for growth in the perfection of performance, and perfection is therefore both maintainable and able to be matured at the same time, then the repeated assertion in Anabaptist writings of a distinction between sins, which are mortal because they are willingly and openly performed though contrary to the known laws of God, and failings, or "inadvertent" misdeeds, becomes more understandable.[414] To commit the former type means loss of status as a Christian and loss of salvation until there is a full renewal of repentance and a complete abandonment of the sin and desire to sin. But the latter type are possible in the life of the continuing Christian. These lesser "sins" are defined as external and temporary failings, done contrary to one's true will and immediately repented of, thus not invalidating the inner penitential attitude, and apparently, therefore, not shattering the maintained internal "perfection."

Therefore, while regeneration does not imply a potential for absolute sinlessness, this distinction in sins also suggests that the attitudes necessary to attain regeneration aided by grace result also in the possibility of living without any conscious intent to sin thereafter — a kind of relative perfection. That is, their differentiating of sins implies that to be a Christian one can and must possess and maintain a kind of permanent inner soul-sinlessness. A misunderstanding of this point would seem to account for some of the charges of perfectionism leveled against the Anabaptists. For example, Heinrich Hottinger of Zollikon wrote to the Zürich council urging them,

> not to believe every liar who slanders me and others. For some time a report has been spread that some of us teach that one may live without sin, also that we boast of living without sin.

And now it has been asserted that I have taught that to commit murder, adultery, or theft is not sin. Thus I am being slandered. . . .[415]

While the inner, relative perfection is being maintained — which acknowledges the capacity for "failings" but rejects the domination of the soul by the flesh while still a Christian — then, and only then, does the imputed perfection also come into effect. This recognition of an imputation of perfection also negates any charge of absolute perfectionism.

Friedmann rightly observes that the Anabaptists used primarily such terms as *Fromm-Machung* or *Gerechtmachung* rather than *Rechtfertigung* or *Gerechterklärung;* that is, unlike Luther, they do not consider justification and sanctification as solely or primarily a divinely declarative imputation rather than an actual deliverance from sin. Nor do they accept, to the same degree as Luther, that the believer is an incorrigible sinner throughout this life;[416] the flesh does remain sinful but it does not rule. Yet the Anabaptists do recognize that a complete perfection in Christ is imputed to the believer providing a genuine internal and relative perfection is being maintained and externally manifested. Sattler, in the "Satisfaction of Christ" comments that if there is true, constant faith, not apart from works, then this "is reckoned for righteousness."[417] Similarly, Hans Hotz testifies to continual "difficulty and temptation" arising from the flesh; but he adds that such for the true Christian who has constant, inner repentance "is reckoned not as sin but rather is covered and purified through the blood of Christ."[418]

The implication again is that true Christians are relatively sinless in terms of desire,[419] but not entirely in act, though desiring such, because of the flesh. But such acts are then called failings and are cared for by the imputation of Christ's righteousness. This combination of actual, relative, and inner perfection and imputed justification and perfection is more clearly expressed by Hubmaier, as follows:

In summary: God wants to have from us the will, words, and works of brotherly love and allows this neither to be met nor dismissed by words. But whatever inborn weaknesses and imperfections of the flesh are involved in our actions or omissions, He will not *reckon* [*zurechen*] to us for eternal damnation through the grace of our Lord Jesus Christ. For *in Christ we have received all perfection* and *in Him we are already saved.* What more is lacking in us?[420]

The Dominance of Asceticism 191

Again, in reference to a proper attitude to one's neighbors, Hubmaier says we should ask God both "that He give it to us *and* that He reckon not to us our failings and imperfections, to our eternal damnation...."[421]

Finally, the Anabaptists' repeated insistence both on the possibility of complete victory over the flesh in the constant conflict with sin, and on the capacity, in fact the necessity, of keeping the law of Christ and fulfilling the demands of the gospel in this life, implied a kind of perfectionism foreign to Luther. Concerning the expectation of actual victory, for example, Weninger, though denying that absolute sinlessness was meant because of the realitites of the flesh and temptation, then added: "But that I should let these reign, I answer, no."[422] Concerning law-keeping, even more pointedly, Weninger writes:

> They [the Protestant clergy] teach, contrary to Paul in Romans 6, that one may not be free of sin and live in righteousness, that "one must sin to the grave and no one can keep the commands of God," *which is not true.* 1 John 3 — 5. The apostle of God testifies, Christ bore our sins on His back that we might be without sin and live in righteousness. How can the priests dare to say that no one can do right *and not live without sin*?

Weninger proceeds also to quote a series of biblical passages to support his contention that Christians can live victoriously over sin and the flesh; that is, he too advocates a kind of potential, though relative, perfectionism.[423] This same optimism regarding the actual overcoming of sin took rise in the beginning in the Grebel group,[424] and is found also in Hubmaier, who writes that the true Christian, in the power of the gospel, "can and will do all that he is bidden"; he can fulfill the law of Christ, or live sinlessly. Again: "And when Christ says to a man keep my laws, leave evil and do good, from that time the man receives in faith, *power and ability to will and to do it* in the strength of Christ."[425]

It is clearly false to suggest that the Anabaptists in general taught an absolute sinless perfectionism in this life, though some extreme teaching of perfectionism does appear in a few marginal groups in central Germany.[426] But to affirm therefore that there is no doctrine of perfectionism at all in Anabaptism must, from the same evidence, be recognized as an overreaction. Even Bender, who presses Anabaptist affinities with Reformation theology, recognized that they "did not harbor the gloomy anthropology which taught that the Christian could never really break the bondage of sins and live in true holiness, which seems to characterize Luther."[427] But Bender still failed to see that an ascetic doctrine of relative, inner perfection, that must be expressed by a life of practical victory over the flesh and of progressive deepening of holiness of life, is implied, and that such is capable of reconciling the seeming contradictions in the writings of the Anabaptists on the subject. Therefore, Zwingli's assertion that Manz taught that none should be admitted into the church unless he "knows himself to be without sin" is correct; it becomes false only if Zwingli was implying that Manz meant an absolute sinless perfectionism.[428]

Supporting principles: brotherhood. The remaining principles can be summarized more briefly since they have already been treated in part in the previous survey of santification. One such is the principle of the separated, "brotherhood" community; that is, that there must be both withdrawal from worldliness and, at the same time, a collective rather than solitary means for the development and expression of holiness.

The visible brotherhood, or community, is not optional but absolutely essential to the realization of the Anabaptist concept of holiness. Love, sharing, forgiveness, humility, and other social virtues necessary to salvation could only be experienced in the objective, social involvement of a brotherhood. From the beginning, the Anabaptists absolutely rejected any notions of a private or solitary Christianity. When Zwingli asked Felix Manz to have the group hold their beliefs secretly, "just for oneself," Manz replied: "No, because one must demonstrate openly to the other a Christian and brotherly love so that it cannot remain secret."[429] The Hutterites, representing the most extreme form of communal institutionalization among Anabaptists, denied that one could be a Hutterite outside the community — a principle, to a lesser degree, held by all Anabaptists.[430]

The brotherhood was conceived as a redemptive community, though primarily in relation to the development and maintenance of santification, as has been discussed previously. As Friedmann puts it, the Anabaptists held that "one cannot find salvation without caring for the brotherhood. . . ."[431] The brotherhood constituted the primary area for the operation of the love ethic and the agency of necessary discipline without which neither the true expression of the church nor true holiness were possible. Thus, the tie between brotherhood and holiness is strong. For example, Weninger rejected the validity of the church organizations of the Magisterial Reformation as true brotherhoods because, in his opinion, they failed outwardly to "do God's will"; therefore, he charges, "your fellowship is not a brotherhood of Christ."[432] Furthermore, though it is varyingly institutionalized, all Evangelical Anabaptists saw the brotherhood as a separated, holy community, an expression of the kingdom of God, living in the "perfection of Christ."[433]

The Anabaptist insistence on the principle of brotherhood for the expression of holiness and true faith contrasts markedly, according to Friedmann, with the intense individualism and subjectively both in mystical spiritualism and in later Pietism. Unfortunately, Friedmann traces this brotherhood stress primarily to the "old Evangelicals" (a medieval heresy) and completely fails to notice that it was only a variant expression of the fundamental cenobitic ideal in the ascetic tradition.[434]

Furthermore, the Anabaptist concept of sanctification through the separated brotherhood rather than, as in Luther, through secular vocation, is also essentially a laicization of the ascetic idea. Williams writes:

> What Luther elaborated as the doctrine of vocation in the world, as a consequence of justification by faith alone over against the purely religious vocation of the medieval ascetics and clerics, the radicals also construed as "laic" but not in the world: rather for the world to come.

He continues that the essence of such, for the radicals, was an "eschatological vocation of programmatic self-deprivation or communal self-discipline."[435] In addition, he suggests that whereas Luther endowed "licit labor" by "all ranks and classes of society" with a religious and moral significance formerly reserved for the vocation of monks and clerics, the Anabaptist understanding of salvation as holiness led to an ascetic withdrawal from the world and to the concept of the attainment of sanctification not in secular vocations but in brotherhoods of mutual aid, love, and discipline.[436]

Supporting principles: internality. To enunciate a principle of internality for Anabaptism seems almost contradictory in the face of the Anabaptists' strong stress on water baptism, external manifestations of conductual holiness, and the brotherhood. But while externals could not be ignored or neglected, they were worthless by themselves. They had to express internal realities to be genuine or meaningful. In the Grebel group's letter to Thomas Müntzer, underlying its listing of twenty-five points of correct, external Christian practice, there are two clear foundational principles: First, the letter asserts that the Christian must obey the Scriptures explicitly in all matters of Christian practice as well as doctrine — with a further assumption (not followed to the same degree by all Anabaptists) that one ought to practice nothing that fails to have biblical sanction.[437] Second, there must be maintained a simplicity in externals in order to avoid allowing externals to become a substitute for the internal reality. For example, point two in the letter objects to anything that "will create a faith consisting in mere seeming."

Similarly, point fifteen objects to creating "an external reverence and veneration of the bread and a turning away from the internal." Point 25 insists that brotherly discipline must be associated with the practice of the Lord's Supper in order to avoid a ceremonial externality devoid of internal reality.[438] Grebel goes on to assert that while the Old Testament law was written outwardly, the New Testament is to be essentially internal, written "on the heart." The only thing granted external validity, per se, for Grebel, is the Bible, concerning which he comments: "only the external Word is to be so used...."[439]

Similarly, though asserting the importance, even necessity of the external water baptism of believers, if water and a baptizer are available,[440] the Anabaptists always insist on the prior necessity of inner spiritual baptism, of having already inwardly submitted to the rule of Christ, and already inwardly pledged to live a new life henceforth.[441]

Similarly the Anabaptists condemn works-righteousness but, at the same time, demand works "out of faith" or with the right internal motivation. Manz insists on the necessity of doing "righteous works from a changed heart,"[442] and Sattler, in the two tracts "The Satisfaction of Christ"[443] and "Two Kinds of Obedience,"[444] similarly stresses the internal base and that neither the inner nor the outer can be missing, in contrast to a pure legalism.[445] The latter tract is particularly insistent that true filial obedience, while it must express itself externally, nevertheless must originate in internal love and not in conformity or legalistic self-seeking.

Finally, the essentially internal nature of Anabaptist faith is illustrated by the fact that even their stress on the necessity of the brotherhood-church as an external visible institution,[446] even in its rigorous Hutterite communal form, was conceived as simply the normal expression of more basic inner principles. Friedmann isolates three inner motivations: brotherly love in action, involving sharing and togetherness; *Gelassenheit*, involving the surrender of oneself and of one's temporal possessions to God through the brotherhood; and unconditional obedience to God, expressed in part through accepting the discipline of the brotherhood.[447]

In his "Vindication," Weninger summarizes well this principle of internality: "Therefore, as the kingdom of Christ is internal (Luke 17), firmly within us, we have grace to do God's will and service, and to please Him with discipline and fear."[448] This stress on essential internality, while maintaining the need for external manifestation, also parallels some groups in the ascetic tradition; it is especially close to the *Devotio Moderna*, Erasmus, and the preachers of repentance. Also, the inner, spiritual motivations for the brotherhood closely parallel the earlier justifications for cenobitic life and for its vow of obedience.

Supporting principles: necessity. In Anabaptist thought, manifest holiness, derived from an inner transformation and continued cooperation with grace, was not optional but necessary for salvation. Weninger insisted that unless a believer lived a holy life, he was not one of Christ's disciples.[449] This is a startling assertion. What is implied is that the Anabaptists not only proclaimed the Reformation doctrine of the priesthood of all believers, but also the "monkhood," in its laicized sense, of all true believers. This is the older Franciscan ideal from the ascetic tradition taken to its logical and ultimate conclusion. Not only is the ascetic life now possible and encouraged for all Christians, but it is *required*, absolutely necessary, as the only road to salvation.

Regeneration, including a willingness to abandon sin, submit to discipline, and to live the holy, penitent life according to ascetic norms, becomes essential for salvation.[450] Similarly believer's baptism, as the Christ-ordained witness, pledge, and initiation into penitent life, also becomes generally a "must" for salvation.[451] Thus, the ascetic way, somewhat tempered organizationally and adapted to the necessary conditions of the life of the laity in this world, but

196   Anabaptism and Asceticism

still substantially retaining the ascetic principles, becomes now the exclusive Christian way. No longer is there an easier way, either by the sacraments or by "faith-alone," for the masses; nor a higher, specialized, monastic way for a few select souls. Also, there is still no salvation outside the church, but for the Anabaptists the only true church is the cenobitic, separated, holy brotherhood.[452]

Ascetic Forms in the Practical Expression of Anabaptist Theology

It is not the intent of this chapter to analyze exhaustively the external practice and institutionalization of the ascetic ideals in Anabaptism. However, one can readily demonstrate that at several vital points a considerable and significant degree of parallelism with the ascetic tradition did actually exist. Even where minor divergences appear, often these are at least also anticipated in the trends toward laicization already strongly affecting some branches of the medieval ascetic institutions.

In the first place, the principles of separation and dualism in the theology of the ascetic tradition, when applied to worldly society, found their primary practical manifestation in monasticism, either eremitic or cenobitic. Later, as was outlined in Chapter II, various attempts were initiated to apply these two ascetic ideals to the whole Christian laity, especially through the establishment of the tertiaries and by the recognition of various semimonastic brotherhoods, such as the Brethren of the Common Life.

The Anabaptists, though repudiating both the cloister and the hermitage, also accepted the underlying principles of separation and dualism. But institutionally they pressed forward a laicization of those ideals, according to the trend which had already begun in lay tertiary and brotherhood movements, to the conclusion of the necessity of an association, voluntarily, with a disciplining brotherhood by every true Christian. This brotherhood, separated from and often persecuted by the secular society, is considered to be the only true expression of the church.

Some ascetic forms of institutionalization in Anabaptism, such as the Hutterian communities, actually approached rather closely both the cenobitic experiments, noted in Chapter II, by the fourth-century "Desert Fathers" and some of the more cloistered lay brotherhoods

The Dominance of Asceticism 197

of the fourteenth and fifteenth century. All similarly justified their practice by appealing to the pattern of the first church in Jerusalem as described in Acts 4. But, the basic, common requirement by all the Anabaptists was that all true Christians must place themselves under the strict discipline of some sort of separated brotherhood-community through which the kingdom of God finds expression on earth. In spiritual purpose and meaning such a demand retains, in lacized form, much of the purpose of the traditional monastic vow of obedience. Furthermore, while for most Anabaptists separation did not extend to a total, cenobitic, physical withdrawal from society, it was applied to several areas: especially to worship, including complete withdrawal from both the churches of Roman Catholicism and of the Magisterial Reformation; to conduct, involving the rejection of the frivolity, festivities, amusements, and much of the "worldly" dress of society;[453] to social fellowship, including the maintenance of varying degrees of social distance from those outside the brotherhood; and to certain civic and social obligations such as the rejection by many of oath-taking, of holding of civic office, and of the bearing of weapons.[454]

In terms of vocation and the support of the community-brotherhood, the Anabaptists, rejected begging; work was required. Shirking or laziness made one eligible for discipline and the ban.[455] In general, the Anabaptists worked at normal "secular" vocations. Even those in Hutterite communal brotherhoods could work outside the community. However, all legitimate work was considered to have penitential morally corrective, and spiritual disciplinary value — an ascetic attitude toward work. Precedent, both for the rejection of begging and the use of secular employment for ascetic spiritual ends, can be found in the ascetic tradition, in the Brethren of the Common Life, in the Franciscan Tertiaries, and in some of the communities of the "Desert Fathers." It is quite unnecessary to appeal to the Waldensians, who also opposed begging, for antecedent relationships.[456]

The early Anabaptists do not seem to directly specify which kinds of work the members of the Anabaptist "holy" community could most fittingly engage in.[457] Some limitations are implicit, however, in their rejection of certain amusements such as the drinking house,[458] of usury,[459] bearing of arms and warfare, and the holding of civic offices. In these specifics also the restrictions are similar to those of the tertiaries.

Whereas the monks, in applying the principle of separation from all entanglements with this present evil world and the positive pursuit of moral purity, stressed, by the required vow of chastity, the spiritual superiority of virginity and total sexual abstinence, laicized monasticism long before the Reformation made some modifications and reinterpretations of the idea; the laicized ascetic way began to allow for the retention of marriage and family under certain stringent conditions. The Anabaptists seem to have adopted a laicized concept of chastity similar to that of the tertiaries. While the Anabaptists allowed for marriage and family in the brotherhood, they also set up stringent conditions and priorities, as follows: primary loyalty always must be to Christ; the union with Christ transcends any earthly marriage. One must be willing to forsake family, leave all, and follow Christ, if necessary, and "hereby is revealed who the chosen ones of Christ are."[460] Absolute faithfulness in a strictly monogamous marriage was demanded; there could be no divorce except for adultery.[461] An acceptable marriage contracted after conversion must always be "in Christ," that is, between believers only.[462] Emphasis was placed on the spiritual rather than the physical aspects of the union.

In spite of their acceptance of marriage under such ascetic conditions, some Anabaptists, initially, still esteemed actual chastity. This is illustrated by Hubmaier's strong assertion that actual virginity was to be commended as contributing to Christian spiritual development, though not to be considered compulsory.[463]

Ideally monasticism expressed the principle of separation from material things, explicit in the vow of personal poverty, by the total abandonment of personal possessions and property. In actual practice, several modifications of the ideal and varying interpretations of the degree of application were acceptable. As the basic monastic ideals spread to the laity living outside the cloister, the ideal of poverty found expression in the practice of laymen turning their property over to a monastery, but then retaining the use and care of it. A further laicization among the tertiaries created additional practical variations. They upheld the need of austere living and the wearing of plain clothes and of fraternal sharing without the necessity of taking monastic vows or a total giving up of one's goods, though some also formed religious communities in which they practiced communal living for greater perfection.[464]

The Anabaptists clearly upheld the same ideals of an inner renunciation of all desire for worldly, temporal posessions. They looked with open suspicion on the personal acquisition of goods.[465] In some observable way they required an abandonment of any concept of personal ownership of property or possessions. This abandonment could take either the stronger form as among the Hutterites of actually turning over all one's possessions to the brotherhood community,[466] or it could involve retaining personal direction and usage of them but with a strong sense of stewardship or trusteeship. Anabaptists maintained that all possessions belong really to God and must be used only according to His will, especially for the whole brotherhood and for the needy, and thus for the glory of God. Again, this is much like the practice of "usage" in laicized monasticism and the attitude of the tertiaries.[467]

Accordingly, from Grebel on, the Anabaptists overwhelmingly condemn usury, which was prevalent by the early sixteenth century, or anything that brings profit from another's distress or misery, as inconsistent with the Christian love-ethic and their belief in either the community or the stewardship of goods. This was part of a total repudiation of personal and "irresponsible ownership."[468]

The strong conviction in Anabaptism against materialism and greed and for simplicity of life-style, an expressed love-ethic and community of goods, are all reflections of the medieval, Christian ascetic tradition. Again, one need not look to medieval heresy for antecedents.

Thus, when one recognizes that there was already an officially approved trend toward the moderation and adaptation of the threefold monastic vow of poverty, chastity, and obedience by the lay ascetic tradition, then one must affirm that these vows and ideals are far from being negated or rejected within Anabaptist practice; rather one must conclude that they are essentially retained, even reaffirmed, in principle. This is further substantiated by Anabaptism's most distinctive practice, believer's baptism. The Anabaptists repeatedly interpret baptism as a pledge or initiatory vow involving the acceptance of the new life of purity and devotion to Christ; their expression of chastity.[469] It was also a pledge of submission to brotherhood discipline; their vow of obedience.[470] It included a renunciation of private possessions in favor of either the Christian stewardship of or the community of goods; their vow of poverty.[471]

In addition to its institutionalization in the threefold vow, the ascetic principle of separation from the world was given practical expression in medieval piety by society granting privileges to the monastic orders, namely: exemption from the duties of political officeholding, from bearing and use of weapons in military service, and from the taking of oaths. In varying degrees, in varying localities and times, these exemptions were also extended to the laicized forms of monasticism, especially to the tertiaries.[472] Accordingly, when these same exemptions are espoused by most Anabaptists,[473] such an espousal is consistent with their basic ascetic ideals of dualistic separation of the carnal from the spiritual, and of church from the world.[474] With so much historical precedent in the mainstreams of the ascetic tradition, it is again entirely unnecessary to postulate, as does Verduin, antecedents in the camp of medieval heresy.[475]

It is probable that since the allowing of exemptions and privileges consistent with the ascetic ideals was, even in official "lay-monasticism," never fully defined and rarely more than partially applied, such a lack of antecedent consensus may account in part for some of the irregularities and variations of their application within the Anabaptist movement, too. From the beginning of Anabaptism the tendency to require the ascetic exemptions was clear but actual application was varied.[476] Sattler, as an ex-monk, pressed for total exemption from all such social involvements,[477] but even the members of the Grebel group took oaths on certain occasions and under certain conditions.[478] The differences between Hubmaier and Sattler over the bearing of arms and holding civil offices are well known and have been carefully researched; they were not over the basic principle, but only over the degree of its application.[479]

Anabaptism also institutionalized their principles for the development of the inner spiritual life in ways compatible with the ascetic tradition. Since much of this institutionalization has been substantially described and analyzed earlier in this chapter, especially as such practices relate to penitential exercises, to works of charity and devotion, and to obedience to the "rule" within a communal context, a few predominant examples will suffice to illustrate and summarize.

As a practical manifestation of the ascetic principle of renunciation of the flesh and its desires, most Anabaptists advocated an outward and practical expression of simplicity, including wearing dark and plain clothing (homespun), avoidance of gluttony and intemperance of all kinds, and a humble and frugal life.[480] Verduin correctly observes that this "high appraisal of frugal living was quite nonexistent in the camp of the Reformers and therefore did not take its origins in the events that began in 1517."[481] Unfortunately, Verduin then concludes, again unnecessarily, that its antecdents must be in medieval heresy, such as the Poor Men of Lyon. However, these same practical concerns are strongly present in the fifteenth century in the tertiaries, in the Brethren of the Common Life, and in Erasmus.

Other outward, penitential exercises among Anabaptists, designed to aid in the mortification of the flesh and in promoting submission, conquest of self-will, and spiritual growth, included traditional ascetic practices such as fasting, though not as a perfunctory, external, prescribed rite[482] but rather "without outward pomp and show."[483] Hubmaier notes that all days are fast days for Christians, in the sense of eating and drinking only with moderation and thanksgiving; nevertheless "a man may mortify his flesh and in order to have some day for prayer he may manage to set and choose for himself a special day."[484]

Similarly, the simplicity of their outward worship had ascetic and anti-worldly overtones. For example, initially Grebel (like Zwingli) was against both singing and musical accompaniment in worship.[485] Later, he seemed to moderate to allow for singing only, and Blaurock and later leaders wrote numerous hymns.[486]

Their dualistic antiworldly sentiments were expressed not only in the nonviolent, antimagistracy, and antiwar ideals, and in expressions of charity and love through the sharing of goods, but also in almsgiving.[487] Hubmaier's rejection of Luther's bondage of the will and predestinarianism is, in part, a concern lest such destroy practical piety, including "fasting, praying, and almsgiving."[488] Again, the same pattern appears, an extensive parallelism with the more laicized forms of the medieval ascetic tradition.

In summary, the foregoing analysis strongly affirms that both medieval asceticism in its monastic and lay expressions and Anabaptism saw the primary goal of the Christian life as a conscious, responsible pursuit of holiness, perfection, or Christlikeness, which involved also a practical outward renunciation of worldliness, the fallen desires of the flesh and of all evil, and the disciplining of all material and physical aspects of human life. Salvation, though not requiring a perfect holiness for its attainment, at least required the desire for holiness of life and a voluntary and constant involvement in the process of its development. In monasticism, ascetic goals of holiness and salvation are achieved by "the withdrawal of the ascetic from society and its corrupting temptations and distractions"; but in Puritanism it is by "the severe control of social life so as to make the environment suitable for the ascetic to continue to live in the world."[489] In terms of this classification, Anabaptism, since it normally did not seek to control society (Münster is a possible exception) but rather sought through separated brotherhoods to witness to and exemplify the "perfection of Christ," finds its strongest kinship with a laicized monasticism.

Holiness as the Dominant Principle of Interpretation

Holiness, ascetically conceived, functions as the single, overarching, interpretive principle which dominates the whole ecclesiastical perspective and theological formulation of Evangelical Anabaptism. Augsburger in his analysis of the thought of Michael Sattler and the Swiss Brethren concludes that their doctrine of God appears to regard holiness as the "supreme attribute, structuring rather than being subordinate to sovereignty. . . ." He adds that Sattlerian thought, and Anabaptist-Mennonite theology as a whole, finds its "major premise in God's holiness."[490] Similarly, the general Anabaptist concern to preserve a measure of human free will is explicitly based on their strong convictions about the inviolability of the justice and holiness of God in His punishment of evil.[491]

The soteriology of Anabaptism also takes its uniqueness from its interaction with the dominant theme of holiness. Explicitly Anabaptism's definitions of who and what is a Christian is basically and consistently conduct centered. The initial dispute between the Grebel-Manz group and Zwingli was precisely over this issue. Similarly, the Schleitheim Confession of 1527 is less a confession of faith than the statement of a minimal test of conduct, ascetic in nature, for the identifying of the true Christians. The Sattlerian ascetic, test-"standard" in the "Schleitheim Articles" includes as its principles: the repentant spirit, amendment of the external life by the abandonment of gross sins and by a positive effort toward the imitation of Christ, absolute submission to the will of God as revealed in the Scriptures and to the discipline of the brotherhood, and the sacrificial and practical practice of brotherly love.[492] The same stress on an ascetic test for the recognition of a true Christian is found in Weninger; that is, a Christian is one who "does right."[493] Similarly the testimony at Zürich by an unknown associate of Hottinger (cir. 1525-26) describes a Christian as one who "desists from sins and desires to experience a reformation or bettering of life and conduct."[494]

Since, for Evangelical Anabaptism, the provision for salvation includes taking seriously both the precepts and counsels of the gospel, especially the command, "Be ye holy; for I am holy" (1 Pet. 1:16) and an accent on regeneration which enables one to do so,[495] a conduct-oriented holiness becomes the primary norm for distinguishing the godly from the ungodly, true Christians from the non-Christians, the true church from the false church and the world.[496] The *Satisfaction of Christ* elaborates on the point that the all-sufficiency of Christ's atonement is operationally effective only on condition of the exercise of an ascetically practical faith.[497]

Also, a repentance-centered doctrine of conversion is central to Anabaptist soteriology,[498] and this repentance includes a continuous will to holiness or the penitent life, a kind of mortification.[499] Though generally subscribing to justification by faith, faith is always in conjunction with or even subsequent to repentance, and includes typically ascetic elements such as attitudes of obedience, surrender, and self-renunciation. Repeatedly the life of Christ and His atonement are given ascetic purposes: an example for the development of holiness and the actual extirpation of sin in this life. The Christian is "to make known the obedience or righteousness of His Father not only in words but also with works."[500]

While Evangelical Anabaptists can in a general way be categorized as holding the Zwinglian view that the sacraments of the Lord's Supper and baptism are essentially symbolic signs[501] and as rejecting both Christ's physical presence and any *ex opere operato* definition of sacramental functioning, yet they also insist that these signs were valid for believers only, and that they involved more than just memorial rites or even testimonials of grace.[502] These additional, distinctive aspects in their sacramental interpretation reflect the domination of ascetic concerns and an interpretive interaction with the primacy of their theology of holiness.

From the earliest beginnings of the movement, Manz insisted on an ethical basis for the valid administration of believer's baptism.[503] He required that it be administered only to those "who reform, take on new life, lay aside sins. . . ."[504] He rests his doctrine of baptism on, first, the idea that John the Baptist was the divinely appointed forerunner to Christ, and therefore the essentially ethical nature of John's baptism indicates the necessary and prerequisite preparation for the proper receiving of the Christ.

Second, he insists that the same ethical interpretation which characterized John's baptism carries over also as the prime significance for Christian baptism, as was taught by Christ, and this the church was commanded to maintain thereafter. Manz writes:

> Also, just as John baptized only those who reformed, forsook evil works, and did good . . . so also the apostles received from Christ . . . the command . . . [to] teach . . . that forgiveness of sins in His name should be given to everyone who believing on His name should do righteous works from a changed heart . . . so they also were poured over with water externally to signify the inner cleansing and dying to sin.[505]

Baptism is here presented as a sign or testimony of an ascetic conversion which in turn equates with the Grebel group's norms for what constitutes a true Christian. Accordingly, Manz continued further by accenting that baptism derives its primary significance from Paul's words, in Romans, chapter 6, that baptism represents a death to the old life and a rising to a new. Manz also insists that "Christ baptized no one without external evidence of readiness."[506] Thus the Anabaptist's espousal of believer's baptism and their rejection of infant baptism was not based primarily on the problem of the relation of faith to the infant, a problem which caused many Reformers to hesitate over infant baptism, but by an ascetic interpretation of the baptism's significance which precluded infants. This is what is essentially Anabaptist and it is never Zwinglian. Zwingli correctly recognized that to accept the Anabaptist's position on baptism would lead to the acceptance of an ascetic theology.

Third, Manz bolstered his case for believer's baptism by a direct appeal to the ascetic ideal of the imitation of Christ. Manz writes: ". . . infant baptism . . . is also against the example of Christ who . . . was baptized at thirty years. . . . Now Christ has given us an example that as He has done so also ought we to do."[507]

The evidence for a close relationship between Anabaptist baptism and their demand for an "ascetic" conversion is extensive and most significant. There is the example of the decidedly ascetic conversion of Jorg Schad in response to Anabaptist teaching; he subsequently requests baptism as the "sign" of it.[508] Similarly, the Anabaptist spokesman at Bern, Hans Luti, repeatedly uses the term *thünd buss* (literally, do penance) as the basic prerequisite, along with belief and the new birth, for baptism. Baptism should signify that a conversion had already happened within the individual.[509] The same themes appear in the written presentation in early 1527 by the Anabaptists of Grüningen, which doubtlessly reflects the direct instruction they received earlier from the Grebel group.[510] This document insists that baptism, for Jesus, was a "righteousness" based on repentance. Again, it is the inability of an infant to personally repent that invalidates infant baptism.[511] Again, the tie is made between baptism and Romans 6:2-4, 19, which stresses baptism's significance as a testimony to the death of a life of self-will and sin and to the espousal of a new life of obedience in the service of righteousness.[512] Asceticism is expressly asserted by the statement: "Let everyone notice that baptism belongs to believers who commit themselves to the Son of God and separate themselves from evil."[513]

Not only was baptism the external witness to a strongly ethical interpretation of the nature of a true Christian, and closely tied to a necessary and previous ascetic conversion, but in several ways it went beyond an external sign and testimony to continuing significances which are also ascetic. First, Hubmaier emphasizes that baptism involves a confession of, and an initial act of, a continuously intended self-surrender or *Gelassenheit*.[514] Hubmaier also often uses derivatives of the term *ergeben* (to yield) in relation to baptism. He asserts that baptism implies "that one has already surrendered himself [*sich schon ergeben hab*] to live according to the Word, will *and rule of Christ*."[515] Thus the decidedly ascetic significance of living under a "rule" is tied to baptism. Second, both Beachy and Armour have elaborated on the Anabaptist concept of baptism as an initiation "pledge," or covenant, or an act of placing oneself henceforth into, and under the discipline of, the brotherhood.[516] Hubmaier expressly states that the brotherhood's authority for discipline and admonition comes "from the baptismal vow."[517]

Another ongoing element in their understanding of baptism as a pledge, covenant, or vow is the close relationship between baptism and the acceptance of suffering and martyrdom as a principle of Christian life in this world.[518] Later, as noted previously, the Anabaptists developed the idea of three baptisms, the inner and spiritual, the subsequent external ceremony and pledge with water, and finally the baptism of blood or suffering and perhaps martyrdom. Thus the middle or external baptism both looked back to the inner, the spiritual, and forward to renunciation, submission, and suffering.[519]

206 Anabaptism and Asceticism

The documents of the Marburg Anabaptists add another ascetic interpretation to baptism. These Anabaptists questioned prospective members and those requesting the "sign" of baptism thus: "If need should require it, are you prepared to devote all your possessions to the service of the brotherhood and do you agree not to fail any member who is in need and you are able to help?"[520]

Moreover, it appears to have become general practice among the Anabaptists to maintain something of a probationary novitiate before baptism. It was an interval of testing and instruction. Verheyden gives several examples of candidates for baptism having to wait for several years because, according to Dureck Lambrecht's testimony, "One has to reform his life beforehand," that is, before being eligible for baptism.[521]

This whole pattern, including the requirement of a personal ascetic commitment and an indefinite period of prior instruction, is found in the classic Anabaptist statement in the Schleitheim Confession (1527):

> Baptism shall be given to all those who have learned repentance and amendment of life and who believe truly that their sins are taken away by Christ, and to all those who walk in the resurrection of Christ and wish to be buried with Him in death, so that they may be resurrected with Him and to all those who with this significance request it of us and demand it for themselves.[522]

In summary then, the meaning of baptism for the Anabaptists included several unique, ascetic features. It was a voluntary witness to a personal, ascetic conversion; a voluntary commitment or pledge to the penitent life and to acceptance of the rule of Christ, including placing oneself under the authority and discipline of the "keys" of the brotherhood; and a voluntary commitment to place one's possessions at the disposal of the brotherhood when need arose. It also required a prior period of probationary scrutiny and opportunity for instruction.

These ascetic elements demonstrate clearly the close parallel between Anabaptist baptism and the monastic initiation vows. This parallel has been suggested by others but without specific evidence. For example, based on his Hutterite studies in general, Friedmann observes that Anabaptist "baptism *might perhaps* be compared to a monastic vow."[523] More recently, Michael Novak advocates the same idea but bases it only on the previous comments by Friedmann and Littell rather than on analysis of the sources, and on his contention that in general "Anabaptism represents a laicization of the Catholic monastic spirituality."[524] Specifically, he suggests only that there is a voluntary aspect in the pledge of both, that the "dynamism of living faithfully to a freely taken religious vow . . . appears to be very like the dynamism of living faithfully to believer's baptism," and that obedience in a communal situation is common to both.[525] Friedmann's reaction is that Novak's assumptions are only phenomenologically correct, that there are substantial differences of motivation.[526] But Friedmann bases his objection on an approach to the monastic tradition which is too narrow. He fails to do justice to its ascetic concepts of conversion and to the breadth of its "imitation of Christ" theology which, as we have seen, certainly includes motivations of love, discipleship, and a visible embodiment of the kingdom of God, as well as just aiming at the "perfect self-effacement" of the Lord.[527]

Poschmann points out that there was even a Catholic view, especially in the ascetic tradition, which conceived of baptism as an act of penance,[528] and which interpreted the vow of the "religious" as a kind of second baptism, a *conversio* to a life of ascetically defined and perpetual penance. Concerning the expression "second baptism," Pourrat comments that it

> is grounded on the entire renunciation of the world implied in the monastic profession. This renews and completes the renunciation of the devil and the world which is promised at baptism. Medieval theologians taught further that religious profession might remit all penalties due to sin.[529]

With a remarkable parallelism of terminology, Hubmaier refers to Anabaptist baptism as a "necessary renunciation of the devil and his works."[530] Hubmaier actually states that the vows of monks and nuns came in historically when the genuine Christian duty of baptism of believers was abolished and that baptism has a significance similar to when "youths are inducted into orders." Again, he writes, "Because we do not realize what baptism means, and what baptismal vows demand, Satan has started conventual vows."[531] It is perhaps significant that Zwingli was also aware of the same figure and imagery with reference to baptism.[532] He compares baptism to the "cowl" that introduces initiates into a monastic order. Moreover, Erasmus, of the imitation of Christ tradition, had previously emphasized that baptism "pledged" one to the Christian or penitent life.[533] Thus, much concrete evidence verifies that there is a close tie between Anabaptist baptism and the vow of the religious.

Are there similar ascetic overtones in the Anabaptist understanding of the Lord's Supper? While the symbolism changes, the answer is positive since even a cursory analysis reveals the same uniquely ascetic approach as appeared in their understanding of baptism. A few examples are sufficient to substantiate this parallelism.

For Grebel, the observance of the Lord's Supper reflects primarily a continuing personal commitment to the brotherhood as the visible body of Christ. He insists that there could be no *true* observance, rather only an outward and ritualistic observance in which "love will be passed by," unless the "rule of Christ" is functioning effectively in close association with its administration. Also, the right discernment of the body of Christ, he continues, requires a willingness by the participant to live and suffer for Christ *and* for the other members of His body in the brotherhood. He adds that if one eats, "who will not live the brotherly life . . . and dishonors love," he eats "unto damnation."[534]

In addition, a further asceticization is clearly asserted in their interpretation that the Supper was more than just a remembering of or memorial to Christ's sufferings but was actually a pledge or commitment by the participant to a present involvement in suffering. The *Satisfaction of Christ* affirms: ". . . did not Christ chiefly establish the Lord's Supper for this reason, namely, that they had to suffer as Christ their head?"[535] Similarly, Hubmaier calls the Supper a "pledge of love," a pledge that each participant is prepared to die for the other, even as Christ died for them.[536] The Anabaptists' stress, obviously, is on the continuing existential relationship to Christ, activated, made vital, real, and internal by a practical involvement, according to an ascetic pattern, in love, sacrifice, and suffering for and in fellowship with the visible body of Christ, the brotherhood.

The Schleitheim Articles specify the need to limit participation in the Lord's Supper strictly to those united beforehand by a baptism which conforms to their ascetic understanding of that sacrament. The Articles go on to explain that this limitation means that the only worthy participants are those separated from the works of darkness. The Lord's Supper is for a brotherhood of the ascetically separated.[537] The two, baptism and the Lord's Supper, are thus conceptually,

The Dominance of Asceticism   209

intimately linked together. Similarly, eleven years later, the Anabaptists at the Bern "disputation" assert that eligibility for proper and acceptable participation in the Supper is based on both belief *and* evidence of righteous improvement of conduct (*"und Rechtsschafne besserung thud"*).[538] Hubmaier adds yet another ascetic element by urging that each individual should "examine himself" before participation in the Supper.[539] Finally, even as Melchior Hoffman viewed baptism as the symbolizing of the believer's betrothal, or self-surrender, to Christ[540] so, similarly, he portrayed the Supper as the marriage and the marriage feast, as "the symbol of the closest possible union with Christ."[541]

Clearly, the close relationship in Anabaptist sacramental theology of the Lord's Supper to baptism, to fraternal love and discipline, and to the ascetic nature of both conversion and the separated life in the brotherhood, elevate the ascetic factors to a uniquely dominant role.

Although ritual foot washing is rarely mentioned and apparently had little significance in the earliest writings of the Anabaptists, there is some evidence that it was practiced quite early in some groups along with baptism and the Lord's Supper. Where practiced, it was given at least a semisacramental interpretation. Since excellent treatments of the significance of this ceremony among the Anabaptists is given elsewhere,[542] it is sufficient for our purposes to note that its dominating emphases, equality and humility, also represent a continuation of major ascetic virtues.[543] Significantly, the practice of foot washing was sustained through the Middle Ages primarily though not exclusively within the monastic tradition.[544]

The Anabaptist doctrine of the church also is molded around and dominated by a theology of ascetic holiness. The following is mostly a summation since considerable primary evidence has already been presented confirming this point.

First, the pervasiveness of ascetic holiness in relation to Anabaptist ecclesiology is illustrated by their understanding of what constitutes the proper basis for membership in the church. All their ecclesiology is based on the fundamental point that the church be reconstituted so as to be made up only of repentant, spiritually regenerate, and voluntarily baptized believers, who then function corporately as a holy living, disciplined brotherhood.[545] Zwingli understood the objectives of the original Grebel-group to be the creation of a church composed exclusively of those "living piously."[546] The church, then, is a family, a brotherhood of the reborn, and conduct is the sign which must validate the reality of the rebirth. Conduct, by which the familial relationship is demonstrated, is also consistently conceived according to traditional ascetic norms.[547]

Second, this ascetic requirement for membership is then extended to encompass the essential character of the church's corporate image. The Anabaptists rejected, corporately as well as individually, any notion of an exclusively internal holiness, or of an invisible church, which failed to have a corresponding external, holy manifestation. They refused to recognize any congregation as a valid expression of the Christian church if its corporate conduct was widely divergent from the biblical ideal of the holiness of the mystical church. Thus, there is a sense in which the Anabaptist "brotherhood-church," as Zwingli recognized clearly, represents not only a fellowship whose goal is the perfection of its individual members but also a fellowship which must exhibit, corporately and at all times, a measure of outward perfection in reference to the conductual ethics of the gospel. The church must not be an obviously mixed society.[548] It must not tolerate open sin. As Hans Kuchenbacher testified: "We cannot believe that this present evil society . . . is the Christian church and the congregation of God."[549] Such an assertion is in direct contradiction to Zwingli's affirmation that no one can be righteous or fulfill the command to love God and one's neighbor.[550] For the Anabaptists, the true church must externally manifest its inner character. As they emphasized repeatedly, it must constantly strive to be, corporately, the bride "without spot or wrinkle."[551]

On the other hand, their brotherhood-church does not demand, or claim to have attained, absolute perfection or purity; a distinction which Zwingli overlooks in his polemics. Tares are still possible, but are so hidden as to be known only to God.[552] There is to be no ignoring of open sin, no toleration in the church of those who willfully defy the laws and standards of Christ. Anabaptists fully recognized the existence of weak and immature Christians but even these must submit to, and reflect, the "perfection of Christ" by living under, and by being aided and sustained by, the "Rule of Christ" (Matthew 18) and the brotherhood.

The dominance of the ascetic is illustrated further not only by the Anabaptists' understanding of the nature of the church's membership and of its essentially holy character, but also by their understanding of its purpose. They emphasized the individual's need of the brotherhood-church for personal spiritual growth toward perfection and to ensure holy living; this, too, has obvious cenobitic overtones. The brotherhood was uniquely the place wherein the gifts of the Holy Spirit to each believer were operative to the common profit of all. All members shared together in a mutual, spiritual interaction for the purpose of edification and also correction.[553] Hubmaier pressed the importance, even the necessity, of brotherly discipline and correction for both personal perseverance and growth in the faith. He saw this right to discipline as emerging from and grounded upon the individual's baptismal vow which, as was previously noted, also substantially parallels the monastic vow of initiation.[554] Only the "ascetic" brotherhood-church was recognized as having the keys of binding and loosing, with its concomitant power of the ban, by which the holy conduct of both the individual and the church was ensured.[555]

Their doctrine of the holy church is also inseparable from the ascetic doctrine of separation. Therefore, the brotherhood provides the necessary means for expressing at least a partial social withdrawal, and it is from this base of separation through the holy brotherhood that Anabaptists give visible witness to the body of Christ as the kingdom of God.[556] At this point of witness through separation they activate also the social norms and virtues and the love ethic of the ascetic tradition. For example, they assert that a true brotherhood must manifest "obedience to Christ . . . not alone with mouth and heart but also with works and love . . ."[557] especially "brotherly love."[558] Augsburger maintains that, in the Sattlerian circle at least, there is "an ethic of holiness structuring the ethic of agape," or love, and that separation in the Schleitheim Confession is the basis for their commitment to nonviolence and noninvolvement in civic offices.[559] Zwingli also understood their antimagistracy position as a return to monkish perfectionism.[560] Thus from their separated base, the brotherhood, they were all, not just an elite clergy, to actively exemplify life in God's kingdom by deeds of love and goodness and mutual aid.

The brotherhood was intended also as a base for the proclamation of the gospel everywhere.[561] That is, the Anabaptist church was a "sealed band of athletes of the Spirit,"[562] whose goal was not only to manifest the perfection of Christ, individually and corporately, but also a specialized agency for spiritual service and mission. All of these throughout the Middle Ages in the West was also closely associated with the ascetic tradition.

Thus the Anabaptist understanding of the purpose of the brotherhood-church is that it is the locus for individual growth in holiness and for witness to the ideal of corporate holiness and separation; it is also a specialized agency for spiritual service and mission. All of these are also dominant motifs within the ascetic tradition throughout its history.

Ascetic characteristics and ideals also pervade Anabaptist patterns of worship. Three basic ideals stand out: simplicity, fellowship, and total, even prophetic, participation. Simplicity in worship, both in reference to ceremony and to such externals as buildings, was a characteristic in the traditions of both the Franciscans and the Brethren of the Common Life, and is also evident among Anabapitsts; it is clearly expressed in Leonard Schiemer's "Church Discipline" of 1527.[563] Schiemer, Rideman, and others, encouraged numerous meetings, several weekly if possible, for mutual admonition, biblical exhortation, extensive reading of Scripture, hymn singing, and prayer.[564] The Hutterites developed early a daily prayer hour, around six in the afternoon.[565]

But the focal point of Anabaptist worship and fellowship was their participation in the Lord's Supper. In it they emphasized their brotherly fellowship; the Supper was a demonstration of unity, intimacy of fellowship, and mutual love and concern.[566] The Lord's Supper was also the primary occasion for the exercise of mutual brotherly admonition and for public confession and public correction of serious sins, especially sins against the brotherhood.[567] The third ingredient in their ideal of worship, namely, open and total participation, included more than group involvement in hymn singing or recitations of some kind. According to an Anabaptist work, quoted by Bullinger, they held that the Apostle Paul's order for church worship (in 1 Corinthians 14) gives all members the opportunity to speak individually in church, if such is for mutual edification. The Anabaptists took this seriously and criticized the state church for silencing this right of "lay" prophetic participation for all.[568] Thus a laicized worship and the ascetic fellowship of the brotherhood are closely interrelated and are the controlling factors.[569]

Anabaptist eschatology is also molded by ascetic idealism. Novak has characterized it as an "eschatology of the cloister."[570] This classification seems to be substantiated at several points. The "coming again" of Christ is generally conceived by Anabaptists in terms of the culmination of the continuous but intensifying spiritual conflict between the kingdoms of God and Satan. This conflict is

The Dominance of Asceticism   213

to reach a dominating crisis in the last stage of history. Christ's return is then understood as primarily a time of validation and vindication for the true Christians for their otherworldly loyalty, citizenship, and conduct and for bearing suffering for Christ's and righteousness' sake in this life. A new age of the reign of Christ through the establishment of a spiritual kingdom[371] for the presently persecuted, martyred, separated, waiting, true church was thought to be at hand.[372] The martyr and the faithful bearer of persecution for Christ's sake are the true soldiers of Christ now, spiritually fighting the powers of the darkness and waiting for the *eschaton*, the triumph by Christ at His coming.[373]

This eschatology is radically different from Müntzer's. Rather, the Anabaptists' expectancy is proclaimed strongly as the grounds for a patient acceptance of persecution, the maintenance of holiness of life and conduct, for separation, and for mission and vigorous proselytization. It is consistently an ascetic, not militant, eschatology.

In his letter to the Anabaptists at Horb, Sattler presses the urgency of preaching and the harvesting of souls because the final sorting, "the time of threshing is nigh at hand (Luke 10)" and because the world rises up against those who testify the truth to it. He also urges diligence in persevering in assembling together to promote personal and corporate holiness "because the day of the Lord is approaching." Finally, he ends his plea by urging that they "sanctify" themselves, since the end, with its rewards for separation and for those "clothed in white," and the Shepherd are "nigh at hand." Therefore, he urges, "Flee the shadow of this world."[374] Christians must strive to be found "unspotted from sin . . . at the coming of the Lord Jesus."[375]

Thus, their eschatological perspective becomes predominantly a motivation to ascetic conduct, to perseverance in the spiritual struggle, to patient bearing of suffering, and to the obedient fulfillment of Christ's commands; it becomes primarily the time of the vindication of such a life — typical of the expectations and emphases in the ascetic tradition.

Finally, and perhaps most significantly, the proposition that Anabaptist theology was structured predominantly around ascetic idealism also holds true for their basic hermeneutical principles. In common with the Magisterial Reformers, the Swiss founders and the vast majority of Anabaptists adhered to the Bible as divinely inspired, *en toto*, and as the sole and final authority for Christian faith and

214 Anabaptism and Asceticism

practice.[576] Among some of the South German Anabaptists, especially Hans Denck, a tendency developed toward a greater stress on the mystical, inner Word than on the external Scriptures, but often this difference has been exaggerated by reading into it theological implications and nuances from the twentieth century. The distinguishing of both an inner and outer Word was to some degree present in all of Anabaptism, and even in Denck both were kept closely related, actually inseparable, in practice and usage; though Denck made somewhat more polemical use of the theological distinction than the Swiss Brethren and the Dutch branches.[577] Beachy credits the difference in usage and terminology to the greater influence of German mysticism, especially Tauler and the *Theologica Germanica*, on Denck and the South German branch.[578] In practice, all sought for a great conformity by the Christian community to the plain teachings of Scripture.

The significant issue is that in spite of some differences of stress among themselves on the nature of the authority of the external Scriptures, there is a oneness in the way they read the Scriptures, or in their basic interpretive attitude to what the Scriptures say, an attitude quite different from that of the Magisterial Reformers.[579] This unity of attitude becomes a recognizable and distinctive hermeneutical pattern, though again with some minor variations among themselves in the specifics of its structuring the formulation.[580]

Along with Zwingli, they held that the Scriptures were rightly understood only by the Holy Spirit's inner witness, but never, not even in the South German branch, was God's will to be discerned by some inner light independent from or totally separate from the Scritpures. The Holy Spirit must illumine and make alive, but the Scriptures function as a "regulation of the Spirit."[581] Thus they avoid both a sheer, cold literalism and a subjective, individualistic spiritualism. But the Anabaptists maintained that the only ones who have the Holy Spirit within, and thus are able to interpret correctly, are the pious, and the pious are equated exclusively with those who exhibit the fruit of the Spirit, who lead holy lives. Again the holy life is the normative and distinctive issue, the key to the right interpretation of the Word of God.[582]

There are at least four ascetically oriented facets in the development of the distinctively Anabaptist hermeneutic. The first is a limited kind of anti-intellectualism, including a simplicity of obedience without any admixture of or pollution by human inventions or philosophy.[583] This, too, is a mood which was strongly asserted within some branches of the ascetic tradition. It is a limited advocacy of "pious ignorance"; it does not deny some usefulness to intellectual tools, though asserting the inadequacy and danger of intellectualism without piety. They were usually highly skeptical of traditional "scholastic" scholarship.[584] Skepticism about scholarship's role and usefulness for biblical interpretation is not uniquely Anabaptist, though it is stronger among them than among the Magisterial Reformers, partly due to the early martyrdom of most of their more scholarly leaders. Rather, what makes the Anabaptist position different from the Magisterial (though similar to Erasmus) is their insistence that the one most necessary factor above and beyond academic skills is a pious faith; without that, Scripture cannot be rightly understood.[585]

Second, their dualism related to the baptisms of water and of the Spirit, or to mortification and spiritual regeneration, rather than Luther's law and promises; this takes on hermeneutical significance. It is most clearly enunciated in an early tract, perhaps by Sattler, entitled, "How the Scripture Is to be Discerningly Divided and Explained."[586] Three principles of interpretation are explicitly given: simple obedience to Scripture's "clear" commands, related to the Anabaptist's anti-intellectualism; getting repentance, faith, and baptism into the biblically correct order; and then there is also a long table of typically ascetic opposites, a dualistic key to clarify the correct thrust of scriptural teaching as it relates to the penitent life, death versus life, evil-good, flesh-spirit, external-internal, and so on. Similarly, the external baptism of water, it notes, is coupled with mortification on one side, whereas on the other, the internal baptism of the Spirit is aligned with the virtues of the new life.[587] But in this case, quoting John 3:5, both sides are made essential for entrance to the kingdom of God.[588]

Third, there is the Christocentric or "imitation of Christ" principle which also stresses the virtue of radical obedience to Christ. Hubmaier equates obedience to the Scriptures and the imitation of Christ.[589] The "Grüningen Eingabe" emphasizes that Christ is the ultimate key to a right understanding of the Old Testament; that He is its fulfiller and the end of the old law, but also the establisher of a new one which must be followed. Christ's teachings and sacrifice constitute the dominating interpretive norm for all the rest of the Scriptures.[590] Explicitly, the Swiss Brethren at the Bern Debate of 1538 denied both the charges of rejecting the Old Testament and of excessive literalism. But they also reasserted their conviction that Chris-

216 Anabaptism and Ascetitism

tians must obey in detail the clear demands of Christ and follow His example because of their belief that "what God did in Christ is His final Word to men, and therefore what Christ, who was perfectly obedient to the will of the Father, said and did, is simply God's demand."[591] Therefore, Christ Himself, and one's experience of Him and obedience to him and to His example, becomes the key to understanding the whole biblical revelation.[592] All the rest of Scripture must be subsidiary to this principle.

The fourth and perhaps the most distinctive facet in the Anabaptists' hermeneutic is the notion of a "non-flat" Bible, or, of the progressive nature of revelation within the inspired Scriptures.[593] It represents a significant variation on Luther's principle that Scripture interprets Scripture, a variation which evolves out of the other Anabaptist principles and for the same purpose. Its primary purpose is to defend and rationalize the dominance of a Christocentric, practical piety. Anabaptists usually expressed this progressive principle both in terms of the culmination of revelation in Christ and of the primacy of the New Testament over the Old, though the whole of Scripture is recognized also as divine and necessary.[594] For example, in his extensive writings, Menno Simons cites the New Testament 3 1/2 times more often than the Old, and 40 percent of the New Testament citations are from the Gospels.[595] Sattler defended his position on Christian conduct and life on the basis of the primacy of the Gospels: "I appeal to the Words of Christ."[596] Pilgram Marpeck later wrote the major apologetic for this principle;[597] but it is also found, in one germinal form or another, scattered through most of the early Anabaptist writings, in Grebel, Hubmaier, Sattler, Menno, Dirck Philips, and others.[598]

One must conclude that the Anabaptist movement from the beginning, with only minor variations,[599] had a common and unique hermeneutic which arose from their defense of an essentially ascetic and ethical conception of Christianity. Augsburger's conclusion from Sattler's writings that Anabaptists possessed an ascetic hermeneutic, which was not only Christological but ethical and practical, over against a soteriological hermeneutic centered on justification by faith in Luther, can now be extended justifiably to characterize all the major branches of Anabaptism. In place of the primacy of justification by faith is placed "the call to holiness, to sharing resurrection life," and to an explicit imitation of Christ.[600]

The Dominance of Asceticism 217

Asceticism clearly dominates the theology, soteriology, and sacramental teachings, ecclesiology, eschatology, and even the unique principles of biblical interpretation of Evangelical Anabaptism. Such domination requires the recognition of Anabaptism as a sixteenth-century expression of an ascetic theology of holiness which in one sense is "Protestant" but nevertheless makes questionable whether the Anabaptists can be considered part of "the great Protestant family" of the Magisterial Reformation.[601]

Theologically, Anabaptism's perspective and purpose is markedly medieval and ascetically oriented, with repentance, a discipleship of holiness, and a two-kingdom dualism functioning as pivotal issues. Institutionally, they insist on a brotherhood church which calls for a state of relative "perfection," similar to the way which that term is used of medieval Catholic religious communities, and in contrast to Luther's *Volkskirche*.[602] This includes the ideals of sharing and sometimes even the common life, the ethic of love in the brotherhood, and the necessary therapeutic functions of brotherly discipline. In practice also, the spirituality of the monastery is generally maintained;[603] that is, while the threefold ideals of chastity, poverty, and obedience are biblically adjusted and laicized, they are not abandoned. Accordingly, this chapter expands and verifies, theologically, Ritschl's contention that Anabaptism represents the laicization of monastic spirituality outside the Roman Catholic organization.

However, unlike the medieval Catholic religious, the holy life for Anabaptists was more than a superior way within the larger Christian schema; it became the sole and exclusive way to salvation. But even this variation also began within the ascetic tradition itself long before the Reformation.[604]

5 AGENCIES OF MEDIATION

Our investigation to this point demonstrates that Evangelical Anabaptism must be recognized as a Protestantized version of certain of the earlier reform trends evident within the highly complex, medieval, ascetic Weltanschauung. But the nature of the actual connections between Anabaptism and medieval asceticism needs further analysis. Therefore this chapter will proceed (1) to identify those specific aspects of the medieval ascetic tradtion sufficiently akin to Evangelical Anabaptism to justify assigning to them a precursory role, (2) to weigh the relative importance of these precursory agencies or agents, and (3) to indicate which agencies or persons are most immediately and directly responsible for the mediation of the ascetic ideas to formative Anabaptism.

The previous chapters have already suggested the most likely possibilities within medieval Catholic spirituality that may have functioned as precursors to that bundle of ideas and practices that are essentially Anabaptist and as actual agents of their mediation to Anabaptism. There were several references to a practical type of German mysticism derived largely from the *Theologie Deutsch* which seems to have influenced the South German Anabaptists especially.[1] Also, there was the direct impact of monasticism since several early Anabaptist leaders were previously monks;[2] for example, the ex-prior of St. Peter's,

Michael Sattler, was especially influential in the formative days.³ In addition, one must consider the many basic principles of the Franciscan "spirituals" and the laicized asceticism of the tertiaries to which Ritschl assigned a unique, pervasive, and formative influence on the whole Anabaptist movement, but especially on the South German branch.⁴ Finally, several recent historians have noted strong affinities by the founders of Anabaptism, the Swiss Brethren, and also by the Dutch Mennonites with Erasmian Christianity and, indirectly, with the *Devotio Moderna*.⁵

It is not possible or necessary to identify all of Anabaptism's essential characteristics with any one of these ascetic groups exclusively since in many ways they overlap and interconnect with each other (even, the some degree, with some "heretical" groups) in late medieval spirituality. Nevertheless one traditional group does seem to reflect a remarkably close ideological parallelism with Swiss Anabaptism as well as considerable actual contact with the first formative leaders of Anabaptism, that is, the "imitation of Christ" tradition through Erasmus. Consequently, what follows here is a synthesizing of recent scholarship about each of the other potential antecedents in order to indicate, tentatively, the extent of the specific contacts (institutional, literary, personal, or geographical) and the degree of ideological parallelism which would suggest possible dependency by Evangelical Anabaptism, but concluding with a more detailed evaluation of the relationship and significance of Erasmus to the Anabaptist synthesis.

German Mysticism

There seems to be little evidence of either strong direct contact with German mysticism, or essential ideological dependency on it, by the Swiss or Dutch Anabaptists during their early formative stages. Even the vocabulary of the moderate mysticism of the *Theologie Deutsch*, though this treatise was probably known to them, is not strongly or directly reflected in the Swiss or Dutch Anabaptists' literature. Nevertheless, there may have been some indirect mystical influence on them through the *Devotio Moderna* whose founder, Gerhard Groote, had some contacts with German mysticism and incorporated some of its more moderate motifs into the *Devotio Moderna*.⁶ Also, Lefèvre d'Étaple traveled into Germany and showed considerable interest in some of the mystical writings which he found there.⁷ Renaissance humanism also showed considerable affinity for the mystical or esoteric philosophy of Neoplatonism, especially of Augustine and Dionysius.

The theory of substantial, formative dependence by the early Swiss Brethren on the mystical, revolutionary teachings of Thomas Müntzer has been substantially discredited.[8] Though Hillerbrand reasserts the possibility of some minor ideological influence on the Swiss Anabaptists from Thomas Müntzer, he also notes the lack of evidence for extensive personal or ideological contacts.[9] Moreover, even the strongest of the few explicit motifs which, according to Hillerbrand, the Swiss Anabaptists and Müntzer held in comman and which he isolates as suggestive of dependence, namely, both their common concern for ethical weakening by a *sola fide* that becomes "easy believism" and their rejection of justification as forensic only, were common to the whole ascetically oriented, anti-Lutheran protest and reform movement, and were not unique to Thomas Müntzer. It seems more likely, as will be shown later, that these motifs, since they were also present there, were derived from the *Devotio Moderna* through Erasmianism, with which the Swiss Anabaptists had made contact at an earlier date. Similarly, Hillerbrand notes correctly that Müntzer's "Bund" is not really parallel to the Swiss Anabaptists' doctrine of the "church," except in the broadest sense that both recognized a separation of the elect from the godless. But when parallelism is reduced to such a broad generalization, while lacking parallelism in specific content, it is insignificant; especially when not only the same generalization but many of the specifics of the Anabaptist doctrine of the "church" were also expressed earlier by others who were closer to the Swiss Anabaptists than Thomas Müntzer.

Hillerbrand also admits that Thomas Müntzer failed to develop a theology of believer's baptism[10] and that Müntzer's mystical language is "conspicuously absent" in early Swiss Brethren writings.[11] It has not yet been convincingly demonstrated that Thomas Müntzer had any significant influence on the origins of Swiss Anabaptism. At best he contributed only a weak and, by the Swiss Anabaptists, a poorly understood supporting, encouraging, and substantiating voice for a few limited common motifs which were themselves not uniquely Müntzerian; the roots for Anabaptism of these common ideas can be found elsewhere. Moreover even the common motifs had been espoused by the Zürich Anabaptists before they read Müntzer's tracts — as Grebel's (undelivered) letter to Müntzer indicates.[12]

Jan Kiwiet, in his study on Denck, contends that a general resurgence of German mysticism during the early years of the Reformation, for example, in the Staupitz circle of Nuremberg, "created various opponents to the Lutheran Reformation,"[13] and that under the leadership of Hans Denck and Hans Hut, both of whom had contacts with this resurgence, early South German Anabaptism became the most mystical and chiliastic of the major groupings within Evangelical Anabaptism. Certainly South German Anabaptism exhibits the most mystical vocabulary of any branch; nevertheless, there may be a tendency to overdraw the significance of this more marked but still subsidiary mystical influence, and especially the notion that it too was derived from Thomas Müntzer.[14] For example, there has been a tendency to place great significance on Denck's brief personal contacts with Thomas Müntzer but to minimize his much more substantial contacts with the Swiss Anabaptists at St. Gall, with Hubmaier, and with numerous other Swiss Brethren ministers who were constantly coming and going. Swiss leaders, such as Jacob Gross, Gregor Maler, and Jacob Wideman, were present at the so-called "Martyrs' Synod" of South German Anabaptist leaders at Augsburg in 1527, and the strong Swiss influence is probably reflected in the strictures put on Hut's chiliastic preaching by this "Synod."[15]

The mystical elements even in South German Anabaptism were moderate, practical, and ascetic, closely akin to the *Theologie Deutsch,* which appears to have been its major source. This source was probably supplemented somewhat also by Tauler's sermons, by Thomas Müntzer, and by some Franciscan/Joachimite chiliasm. The mysticism of the *Theologie Deutsch* is sufficiently different from the Eckhartian type of speculative mysticism to cause Kiwiet to suggest that it is really an "anti-mystical" writing which stresses Christian discipleship and obedience in this life more than mystical, inner bliss.[16] Thus there is close kinship in purpose, though less in vocabulary and symbolism, in the *Theologie Deutsch* to the practical piety and moderate "mysticism" (or "devotionalism") of the *Devotio Moderna* but substantial contrast with the subjective, continuous revelationism of Thomas Müntzer and even with the purer spiritualism of Franck or Schwenckfeld.[17]

Apparently no single, thorough study has been undertaken yet on the relationship of Tauler and the *Theologie Deutsch* to Anabaptism and on their influence on Anabaptist doctrines and practices.[18] However, several scholars have noted casually numerous points of contact and of possible ideological dependency. From 1518 to 1523, Luther sponsored the publication and distribution of several editions of the *Theologie Deutsch*.[19] His support ended abruptly, coincident with the emergence of the ascetically oriented, anti-Lutheran reform movement. From 1525, the responsibility for its publication was taken over, almost exclusively, by Luther's opponents. A private edition was printed in 1526 by Silvan Othmar (with whom L. Haetzer had worked shortly before) in Augsburg, while Denck was there. Subsequently, two more private editions appeared in Nuremberg. Then, in 1528, some Anabaptists published it in Worms.[20]

The extent of Denck's involvement in these private, clandestine printings of the *Theologie Deutsch*, between 1525 and 1527, is uncertain but the Worms edition of 1528 contained also a pamphlet by Denck (*Etliche Hauptreden*) and most subsequent editions also included these *Hauptreden*.[21] Kiwiet asserts: "Because of Denck's influence the *Theologie Deutsch* received a place among the Anabaptists."[22]

Kiwiet also points out that Denck probably came into contact with the *Theologie Deutsch* and under its influence while at Nuremberg, in 1523-24 through a reform impetus begun earlier by the Staupitz circle. This circle encouraged a renewal of piety partly through a revival of the study of the *Theologie Deutsch*. Subsequently this pietistic circle also gained the support of a substantial group of Nuremberg humanists.[23] At first this pietistic and humanistic reform group supported Luther, but later (especially in 1523) became a source of disappointed dissent and protest on ascetic grounds. Some members were especially concerned about the moral laxity of Luther's reform.[24] This protest group of 1523 included Hans Denck.[25] Since this was a year before Thomas Müntzer's visit to Nuremberg, Kiwiet contends: "It is clear that the protest against Lutheranism was not evoked only by Müntzer and the Peasant's War as has been asserted often, but also by people of a real religious [ascetic] concern."[26] This ascetic concern seems to have arisen in part from the practical, ascetic mysticism of the *Theologie Deutsch* and independent of Müntzer.

Along with the *Theologie Deutsch*, but to a much lesser degree, some Anabaptists, mostly in the South German branch, also read some of Tauler's sermons.[27] These sermons also had formed a part of the original mystical stimulant to devotional and ascetic reform in the Staupitz circle at Nuremberg. Thus Tauler's thought also was transmitted to Hans Denck and probably through him, initially, to South German Anabaptism. However both Denck's and South German Anabaptism's theology and piety remained much closer to the mood and vocabulary of the *Theologie Deutsch* than to Tauler. Consequently, Christian Neff's brief article on Denck makes the sweeping assertion: "The real source of Denck's religious life and thought was in medieval mysticism as represented by *Deutsche Theologie* which Luther had reissued in 1518."[28]

A later article on Denck and Buenderlin by Charles Foster, Jr., attempts to strengthen this idea of major dependency by Denck on the *Theologie Deutsch* by drawing out several specific parallels between its teaching and the basic doctrinal system of Denck the Anabaptist.[29] Kiwiet adds his contention that Denck was not a spiritualist of the type of Sebastian Franck, Kaspar Schwenckfeld, or Thomas Müntzer, but rather a follower of the *Theologie Deutsch* "which opposed special experiences [Müntzerian direct revelations] and demands continual obedience by each individual."[30]

Neff, Foster, and Kiwiet concur on several points of close similarity between the teaching of Denck and the *Theologie Deutsch* which strengthens the probability of some direct dependency by him. But while the vocabulary and style of some aspects of these parallel motifs are often so close to the *Theologie Deutsch* that they suggest direct borrowing, the motifs themselves are not exclusive to the *Theologie Deutsch* nor are they always exactly parallel in meaning. In both Denck and South German Anabaptism they often undergo a uniquely Anabaptist transformation, and often are set into different and distinctively Anabaptist patterns. The following examples illustrate these points.

Certainly the "imitation of Christ" motif, strong in the *Theologie Deutsch*, also comes through strongly in the "Anabaptist" Denck. While Luther was stressing justification by faith, Denck's whole emphasis was put instead on discipleship to Jesus. Indeed his motto was: "No one may truly know Christ except one who follows Him in life"[31] and this statement by Denck is almost a direct quotation from the *Theologie Deutsch*.[32] But this same theme is emphasized by many others, by Erasmus, and by the Swiss Brethren too.[33] However Kiwiet observes that when the "imitation" motif comes close to "identification," that is, to Christoformity or *Vergottung*,[34] in Denck, this then is a more mystical aspect which is more prominent in the *Theologie Deutsch* than in Erasmus[35] or in the Swiss Anabaptists (though it is still present also in both).

The strong concern in Denck for a true faith that produces

practical piety is also closely related to the older, widespread "imitation of Christ" motif and to the ascetic insistence on human moral responsibility; both moral progress and responsibility seemed to require some measure of human free will. Thus Denck held that the eternal salvation of the soul and the imitation of Christ in life require active obedience to God in the sense of freely permitting God's will to exercise itself in one. While this conviction is also propounded clearly by the *Theologie Deutsch* (even in Eckhart),[36] it is equally in Hubmaier and in Erasmus.[37] Similarly, Denck is close to the *Theologie Deutsch*, and also to Erasmus, in asserting that God is not responsible for evil but evil is the product of man's disobedient will; disobedience is the root of all sin.[38] Thus, in order to preserve the justice of God and human responsibility for sin, Denck poses a kind of common grace or witness in all men. This inner witness becomes the agency of drawing men to salvation, but without compulsion. This type of drawing is not that of the *Theologie Deutsch* where it is "drawing" by the knowledge of "good" which may come from "a vision or ecstasy."[39]

Further, in spite of free will to respond or refuse, Denck insists in common with the *Theologie Deutsch* and most medieval piety that one cannot actually save oneself without divine aid or special grace; it is a cooperative enterprise.[40] However, Denck explains this synergism in an Erasmian fashion: that the will is free to surrender but unable to achieve anything.[41] Also, as in Erasmus, ascetic conduct is Denck's paramount desire; the gospel mediates power primarily to live the new life, and not just to provide the experience of inner union with God (of the mystics), nor just the forensic justification of Luther.[42] Kiwiet observes that "Denck regularly switches over from theological thinking to its practical issues. All his arguments against the doctrines of predestination and original sin [as defined by Luther] rise from his genuine concern for bringing the biblical message of repentance and conversion."[43]

A similar ethical concern is also present in the *Theologie Deutsch* but is not exclusive to it, nor even to Anabaptism. This concern for practical piety, for God's justice in relation to human sin and human responsibility related to some kind of common grace or remnant of free will, is common to the whole anti-Luther protest movement and thus, though common to the *Theologie Deutsch*, Denck, and Anabaptism, one cannot effectively verify any one source of influence.

Denck also describes conversion in "mystical terms," as a process over a lifetime,⁴⁴ which is quite compatible with the Swiss Anabaptists' concept of *Bussfertigkeit*. But what of his stress on the first free decision to begin the initial, complete surrender? Writes Denck: "The will of God is that we should die to sin before we can hear the gospel. This dying to sin, which must precede the new life, means a complete surrender of man himself and of all his desires."⁴⁵ In one sense, this initial surrender is also only a variation of Swiss Anabaptism which required full repentance before faith and regeneration; yet the terminology more closely reflects that of the *Theologie Deutsch* than of Swiss Anabaptism. While both place obedience and faith after repentance, the *Theologie Deutsch*, as also Denck, describes repentance more as a purification, as a descent into hell, as a strong sense of unworthiness and sinfulness, and as death to self-will.⁴⁶

Denck's contrasting of inner (spiritual) from that which is outer (objective, material, or physical), and his giving superiority to the former, is also found strongly in the *Theologie Deutsch*. Again, however, this concept is not unique; it is emphasized by Erasmus too, and is even in the Swiss Brethren to a degree. However, Denck tends to follow the *Theologie Deutsch*'s more distinctive application of this inner-outer contrast even to Christ's person and to the human soul.⁴⁷ The *Theologie Deutsch*'s assertion that when the true, spiritual awareness of truth comes, the external "imagery" of the church becomes unnecessary and outer works are transcended,⁴⁸ is combined by Denck with its warning against despising the "outer."⁴⁹ The latter becomes his means of reconciliation with Anabaptism. By using the principles of the superiority of the inner over the outer, and the ability to distinguish but not totally separate the two, Denck is able to contrast an inner witness to, and an illumination by the Holy Spirit on the Scriptures from (and places such above) the external Scriptures, rationally studied; but this distinction is understood in the same way as the *Theologie Deutsch*'s distinction between the divine Logos and the historic Jesus.⁵⁰ The historic Jesus is still uniquely the Son of God.

Thus Denck, in the spirit of the *Theologie Deutsch*, and harmonizing with Anabaptism, never discredits the "outer"; Scripture remains a valuable, necessary, and unique witness to, and clarification of, the prior inner Word.⁵¹ According to Kiwiet, this inner witness or Word in Denck is only a kind of inner spiritual or pious sensitivity or discernment; it never means continuous or subjective or independent revelation, and while it enhances, it too is limited by and cannot be divorced from its relationship to the "outer."[52]

On much the same principle, Denck approaches those sacraments retained by Protestantism. Here again, however, especially with baptism, the distinguishing of an inner spiritual baptism from the outer water baptism, with superiority to the former is yet without depreciating or eliminating the latter; this too is common to Erasmus and to the whole Anabaptist movement and is not necessarily derived directly from the *Theologie Deutsch* alone.[53] His insistence that the ordinances depend on the disposition of the receiver for effectiveness[54] is closer to Erasmus. In the Anabaptist Denck, the primary purpose of the "inner-outer" principle is to negate Luther's unconditional "election." In contrast to much of Christian mysticism, Denck does not intend to divinize nature nor any natural human instinct. The "inner" is combined always in Denck with a high respect for such "externals" as Scripture, the sacraments, the congregation, and brotherly discipline[55] — even in his last work, the so-called *Widerruf*.[56] Denck represents a very moderate, adapted mysticism and, according to Kiwiet, even less than the *Theologie Deutsch's* suggestions of God in man and of the Creator's close relationship to His creation. Kiwiet negates the parallelism on these points suggested by Foster.[57] Finally, Bender suggests that even though the title of one of Denck's works, *Ordnung Gottes*, was probably derived directly from the *Theologie Deutsch*, again the parallelism is superficial; Denck reinterpreted the content of this concept too.[58]

From the above, it is evident that Denck did have substantial exposure to the *Theologie Deutsch* type of mysticism and exhibited some sympathy for it. But it is also evident that the parallelism of ideas in Denck and the Anabaptists with the *Theologie Deutsch* is not exact, for there is usually a distinctively Anabaptistic twist which has its source elsewhere. Where close parallelism exists, it often relates to themes not at all unique to the *Theologie Deutsch* but equally, and sometimes even more closely, present in Erasmus too, and in much of lay, ascetic piety in general. As will be considered in detail later, Denck's associations with Christian humanism and directly with Erasmus were also extensive. Consequently, in spite of his contacts with the *Theologie Deutsch*, and considerable linguistic and some thematic parallelism, care must be taken not to overdraw the extent of Denck's and thus South German Anabaptism's dependency, even for semimystical ideas, on the *Theologie Deutsch*.

The case for direct contact with the mysticism of Tauler and the

Agencies of Mediation 227

Theologie Deutsch by the South German Anabaptists through Hans Hut is also weak, and mostly inferential. As a bookseller of popular Reformation (especially Lutheran) tracts[59] it is probable that he peddled the popular Luther edition (1518) of the *Theologie Deutsch* and had some knowledge of its contents. Such interest may well have been furthered by his close association with Hans Denck and his considerable intellectual and religious dependence on him, after 1524.[60]

To find specific examples of parallelism between the thought of Hans Hut, in his writings after his conversion to Anabaptism in May of 1526,[61] and the mysticism of Tauler and of the *Theologie Deutsch* is a more illusive task than one would expect in one who was a founding leader in the most mystical wing of Evangelical Anabaptism. Hut's basic pattern of theology, in 1526-27, except perhaps for his chiliastic eschatology (and that too seemed to be slowly changing in 1527 to conform to general Anabaptist interpretations), can be traced to three major Anabaptist sources of influence.

In common with the Swiss Brethren he emphasized: (a) the necessity of proper scriptural order for the right presentation of the gospel: preaching and teaching, repentance and faith, baptism; (b) strong congregationalism and brotherhood discipline; (c) an ascetic theology of the Lord's Supper and baptism; (d) anti-worldliness; and (e) the stewardship (not communism or even community) of goods. Hubmaier probably added the interpretations that conversion and baptism involve an entering into a covenant situation and that there are three baptisms: of spirit, of water, and of blood or suffering. Hans Denck (and perhaps Thomas Müntzer) probably contributed the most to his moderate mystical tendencies, especially the inner Word or logos as a kind of prevenient, common grace as distinguished from the outer Word or the Scriptures. Even the call to expect suffering, and the emphasis on its santicfying effects, is common in varying degrees to all Anabaptism.

Hut's explanations of the role of suffering, and much of his theological vocabulary, as with Denck and Müntzer, indicate a greater kinship with the mysticism of the *Theologie Deutsch* than is found in the Swiss Brethren writings. Similarly, in Hut as in Denck, there is greater stress than in the Swiss Brethren generally on a mystical union with Christ as the product of, or reward for, the cross-bearing, sanctification process.

Again, other slight variations from the Swiss Brethren which are more akin to the *Theologie Deutsch* include: the idea of *Gelassenheit* which, though involving repentance, emphasizes "resignation" more strongly; an "imitation of Christ" motif which is often associated with reliving Christ's passion within and without; an emphasis on presenting the "spiritual" Christ; and, at times, a characterizing of the brotherhood as almost a continuation of the incarnation of Christ. But as with Denck, these distinctively mystical elements are still secondary adjuncts and mostly variations in expression and vocabulary within a basically Anabaptist pattern.

The doctrinal patterns of Leonard Schiemer and Hans Schlaffer (two of the most notable converts of Hans Hut who were also important formative leaders in South German Anabaptism and who left significant writings), as outlined by Robert Friedmann,[62] are almost identical to that of Hans Hut. In Schlaffer's case especially, Friedmann notes substantial "verbatim borrowing" from Hans Hut[63] and that their substantial mystical motifs also bear strong similarities to and are influenced by Tauler and the *Theologie Deutsch*.

Again a thorough, detailed study is lacking and caution is necessary with reference to the extent and significance of such mystical influences, since, as in Hut, it seems that again the kinship of themes to the *Theologie Deutsch* and to Taulerian mysticism refers largely to the modes of expression in Schiemer and Schlaffer, not to the essential meaning and function in their theological patterns. Moreover, both men had extensive contacts also with other potentially significant influences, with Christian humanism, Denck, Franciscan spirituality, Hubmaier, and numerous Swiss Brethren preachers.[64]

The most obvious examples of ideological parallelism between Schiemer and Schlaffer and Tauler and the *Theologie Deutsch*, as given by Friedmann, are the same as already have been observed in Hut. There is the more mystical emphasis, within their expression of the theme of the "imitation of Christ," on the importance of association with Christ's sufferings and passions[65] and on suffering as part of the process of salvation (sanctification and justification are not disassociated).[66] Then, again, there appears the three kinds of baptism — spirit, water, and blood (or suffering) — which are also found in Hut and in Hubmaier[67] and are possibly derived from Tauler.[68] Finally, especially in Schlaffer, there appears the concepts of the primacy of the "spiritual Christ" and of the necessity for humility or utter lowliness (*Niedrigkeit*) to be saved.[69]

In at least one other area the *Theologie Deutsch* may have influenced Anabaptism. Bender reports that it was known and used by the sixteenth-century Hutterites.[70] It is quoted twice by name in Peter Walpot's tract "Concerning True Surrender and True Community of Goods" (cir. 1577).[71]

The above brief analysis confirms the need for a more detailed study of the influence of the German mysticism of Tauler and the *Theologie Deutsch* on Anabaptist thought. But most indications to the present strongly suggest that such influence, though present in varying degrees, was not dominant even in Denck, Hut, and South German branch; nor was it the originating source of the distinctively Anabaptist doctrinal motifs and priorities. While the impact of German mysticism seems to have been enough to give to much of early South German Anabaptism a distinctive character, making it a subdivision within Evangelical Anabaptism, it was inadequate to change most of the South German Anabaptists into "Spiritualists"[72] Its principal role seems not to have been fundamentally formative but rather to provide a vehicle of distinctive expression and explanation for the dominant Anabaptist motifs and convictions to which they were converted and which were derived from the earlier Swiss Brethren synthesis.

Traditional "Reformation" historiography concerning the Anabaptists, as expressed by Karl Holl,[73] presses the notion that Anabaptism in general took its rise from another mystical source, that is, from the mystical, spiritualistic revolutionaries of Zwickau, especially from Nicholas Storch and Thomas Müntzer. Bender's more recent study substantially refutes this theory and rejects any important ties between the Müntzer-Storch movement and Anabaptism's real founders at Zürich. He even questions though less convincingly, whether there was any significant influence by Müntzer on the early leaders (especially on Denck and the Hut circle) of the South German branch. Bender traces back the notion of Anabaptist's origins in Thomas Müntzer to Melanchthon's broad, ill-defined, and misinformed use of the name "Anabaptist" and, even more directly, to Bullinger's *Der Widertouffen Ursprung* (1560), where the assertion of Anabaptism's origins in Müntzer is made without adequate evidence, probably to remove the stigma of responsibility from Zwingli and Zürich.[74]

Bender, in the same article, and Robert Friedmann, later,[75] provide strong arguments to show that Thomas Müntzer and Nicholas Storch were neither Anabaptists nor even proto-Anabaptists, except in the very broad sense of being part of the general, anti-Lutheran (though still "Protestant"), reactionary movement.[76] Indirectly, Eric Gritsch supports the Bender-Friedmann position by advocating Thomas Müntzer as the father of Protestant Spiritualism rather than of Anabaptism.[77] Gritsch notes that though Thomas Müntzer also uses "the colorful language of German mysticism" and reflects somewhat the *Theologie Deutsch* and Tauler's sermons, Müntzer's ideology was also strongly influenced — so as to transform his mysticism into social and revolutionary activism — by the Joachimite historical schemata and by Taborite ideas through Storch and the Zwickau prophets.[78] Thomas Müntzer goes uniquely beyond Joachimism by making the elect people the agency of the great transformation by taking temporal power into their own hands.

This fundamental Müntzerite theme is completely foreign to the Anabaptist synthesis and spirit. Gritsch does not identify any source for this uniquely Müntzerite innovation.[79] Moreover, as Bender and Friedmann (and to a degree even Hillerbrand)[80] have observed, Müntzer lacked completely an Anabaptist sacramental theology (especially a positive theology of believer's baptism);[81] an Anabaptist theology of the separated, disciplined, believers' brotherhood;[82] an Anabaptist submission to the exclusive norms of scriptural revelation (accepted even by the South German branch);[83] and an Anabaptist concept of suffering which is rooted in the love ethic and including nonviolence.[84]

There are some points of similarity, especially the themes of "*Gelassenheit*" or resignation, suffering and cross bearing, free will and justification as more than imputation; but none of these is exclusive or unique to Thomas Müntzer. Kiwiet suggests that in these areas of similarity, both the Anabaptists and Thomas Müntzer probably drew from the common rootage of medieval mystical theology, especially the *Theologie Deutsch*.[85] Robert Friedmann insists that even in these "closest" areas of thematic similarity there were significant differences of interpretation and application.[86]

While the case for significant direct contact and ideological influence by Thomas Müntzer on the Swiss Brethren[87] and on Hans Denck of the South German branch[88] is readily shown to be weak, the significance and extent of Müntzer's influence on Hans Hut is still widely and inconclusively debated.[89] Certainly Hut had considerable direct contact with Thomas Müntzer and confessed to being, to some degree, briefly (1524-25) a follower of Thomas Müntzer.[90] However, Hut also asserts a major change at his conversion to Anabaptism[91] and Friedmann and Herbert Klassen demonstrate convincingly that thereafter important differences between Hut and Thomas Müntzer are observable, even in the "closest" motifs (that is, in Hut's chiliasm, in his conception of suffering, and in his spiritualistic tendencies).[92]

Though the sources for Hut's ideology during his Anabaptist phase are imprecise, even contradictory, therefore capable of widely varying interpretations,[93] it is evident that much of the data to indicate kinship to Thomas Müntzer comes from questionable testimony by his enemies and from confessions elicited under severe torture. Such evidence makes Hut appear to remain favorable to violent revolutionism, special revelations, and community of goods.[94] Herbert Klassen, however, shows that for the most part this evidence, if considered at all, must be relegated to application only to the period before his Anabaptist conversion.[95] From Hut's own writings it is clear that after May 1526 his ideological pattern is becoming more distinctly Anabaptist and less Müntzerite, and it becomes increasingly so. He becomes even more antisword (nonviolent) than Hubmaier, and the overthrow of the ungodly becomes strictly eschatological and not the function of the Christian before Christ's advent.[96] Repentance with the forsaking of sin becomes the dominant theme of his preaching.[97] Conversion and baptism are tied to a covenant concept which is predominately related to ethical conduct, discipline, and brotherly love.[98] Similarly, he strongly advocates and was a great founder of external, disciplined brotherhoods of baptized believers, which are quite different from Thomas Müntzer's "Bund," but are closer to the Swiss Brethren "church."[99] Neither is the Anabaptist Hut an advocate of community of goods, except in the Swiss Brethren sense of careful stewardship and generous sharing.[100]

Finally, Herbert Klassen notes even a weakening of Hut's chiliasm by the summer of 1527. He abandons date setting for the return of Christ, which makes a revolutionary program even less viable. The later Hut himself states (and all the testimony from his converts from his Austrian tour supports this) that "the date of the return of Christ is unknown."[101] Further, Hut confesses that he accepted the disciplinary restraints placed on his eschatological preaching by the brethren at Augsburg in 1527.[102] Most of Hut's teachings, after May 1526, incline toward the general Anabaptist pattern. While these teachings were expressed in much more mystical overtones than the Swiss Brethren, they tend to depart increasingly from the unique Müntzerian interpretations. For example, Herbert Klassen claims that Denck reflects little significant influence from Thomas Müntzer, but "the similarities in point of view between Denck and Hut are many."[103]

That Hut, though successfully abandoning the basic pattern of his earlier Müntzerite ideology, did not completely erase all of Müntzer's influence may be illustrated by his continued use of two distinctively and typically Müntzerite concepts: (1) the phrase, dated "at the cave of Elias"[104] and (2) the phrase, "the gospel of every creature,"[105] found in the tracts "Of the Mystery of Christian Baptism" (if Hut is the author — Rupp suggests that the real author is Thomas Müntzer[106]) and in Hut's "Ein Christlicher Underricht. . . ."[107] The former phrase seems to have no great significance in Hut's ideological pattern but the latter is more important. It propounds a unique kind of prevenient grace or extrabiblical, natural source of revelation. But it is primarily used by Hut only to illustrate the principle of suffering for righteousness' sake in the process of salvation.[108] While Thomas Müntzer apparently used it to discredit the Bible, as Rupp notes,[109] its use is much more limited by the South German Anabaptists. It becomes and is used only briefly as just another vehicle for illustrating and expressing typically Anabaptist motifs, but it does not seem to play, in itself, a significant role in the developing of the pattern of South German Anabaptist theology.

The foregoing considerations strongly indicate that the unique elements, doctrinal and social, in Müntzer's program, without major revisions, do not reflect the original Anabaptist thrust, that Thomas Müntzer was at best a minor agent for the mediation of some medieval mysticism to the Anabaptists, and that he had little significant, formative influence on the rise of Anabaptism even among the early leaders of the South German branch. His influence does appear stronger on the fringes of Anabaptism, such as the Münster episode, where main line leadership was lacking to check (as it did in Hut) any potential revolutionism.[110]

Franciscan Spirituality

Another suggested agency for the mediation to Anabaptism of ascetic spirituality, including some mystical and chiliastic ideas, is Franciscan piety. Albrecht Ritschl, the most notable advocate of this theory,[111] limited the possible connections primarily to the semiheretical "Spirituals" branch (which he equates, substantially, with the

Agencies of Mediation 233

late fifteenth-century Observants) and to the tertiaries as those who still retained and spread the original reform vision of Francis of Assisi.

The "Spirituals" branch, Ritschl maintains, retained through the fifteenth century some of its antipapal sentiment, some of its earlier affinity for Joachimite chiliasm, and a basic sympathy for reform.[112] Their reform program included a total restitution of true Christianity by a return to the teachings of Jesus; by reemphasizing the basic ascetic principle of renunciation, including poverty and simplicity of life and worship; by stressing the call, through preaching, to personal repentance; and by appealing to the norms of a gospel-oriented Biblicism.[113]

The Tertiaries also embodied and spread, fairly faithfully, the original Franciscan ideal of the "reestablishment of primitive Christianity" but extended the ideal explicitly to the laity by breaking down the notion that Christian society is divided into monasticism with a monoploy on perfectionism and a spiritually restricted and largely spiritually passive laity. With their lay-oriented, "imitation of Christ" piety, the tertiaries, claims Ritschl, prepared the soil for the rapid spread of Anabaptism, especially among the urban craftsmen.[114]

Accordingly, Ritschl portrays Anabaptism as quite distinct from Luther,[115] embodying and promoting instead that ascetic ideal of reform which was first clearly enunciated by Francis, then taken up also by others, including the Waldensians and Groote's *Devotio Moderna*. For all of these, a true reformation meant essentially the reestablishment of a correct relationship between the church and the world; these Reformers maintained that the present relationship was seriously distorted. They believed that a breakdown of the principle of separation, and the mixing of Christianity with the world, was at the root of Christianity's degeneration — both institutionally and individually.[116]

This study, thus far, corroborates substantially Ritschl's general position that this original Franciscan, ascetically oriented, reforming ideal was basic to Anabaptism at its beginning. There are five principles which Ritschl considers to be the major, core elements in the Anabaptist synthesis and which he singles out as being derived specifically from the medieval ascetic reform pattern. He contends that all five are variations and continuations of Francis' attempt to extend the possibility of "perfection," which until then was valid only for monasticism, to the whole church.[117] First, he centers on the Anabaptists' stress on amendment of life and on practical piety with reference to salvation, in contrast to Luther's forensic justification by faith. Then he notes their belief that Christians can perform the law of Christ as presented in the gospels. Third, there is the extension of monastic brotherly love, which included the ideal of "all things common," to the whole "true" church. In laicizing this ideal, however, most Anabaptists went no farther than recognizing an obligation to share and accepting a doctrine of the stewardship of goods.[118] Fourth, Ritschl points to the Anabaptists' separatism which is also in full accord with the medieval ascetic tradition, including their indifference to political involvement in the institutions of the worldly state and resistance to bearing arms and to the taking of the oath. Finally, as already noted, the original Franciscan ideal, which rejected the passivity of lay Christianity in favor of an ascetic commitment for all true Christians, comes to full fruition in Anabaptism. Ritschl notes also some additional subsidiary parallels such as the bearing of suffering, simplicity of dress and life, and rejection of worldly amusements.

Numerous subsequent studies both on Franciscan piety and on the distinctive character of Evangelical Anabaptism have supported and even extended, usually unwittingly, Ritschl's observation that Anabaptist piety was closely related to Franciscan spirituality.[119] Moorman's careful and detailed analysis of Franciscanism confirms that at the heart of original Franciscan spirituality and upheld by the "Spirituals" was the presentation of Christianity "above all things, as a personal experience."[120] He also reiterates that included among the most essential elements of Franciscanism are: devotion to the person of the incarnate Christ; inner identification with Christ, especially in His passion and sufferings; and the imitation of Christ's life as derived from a literal obedience to the gospels and involving renunciation, poverty, humility, and submission to the divine will. All of these with but slight variation not only occur in but are also at the very heart of Anabaptist piety.[121]

Again, as in Anabaptism, the main activity of the Franciscans, as originally conceived by Francis, was to be the preaching of repentance and of redemption through personal, ascetic conversions.[122] Moorman demonstrates that such preaching, highly reformatory and with a view to repentance and amendment of life, did continue strongly throughout the fifteenth century, especially among the Franciscan Observants[123] who were recognized by the Council of Constance in 1415.[124] Some of the most notable of these preachers even exalted the importance of preaching over participation in the mass. Their preaching stressed both the loving forgiveness of God and His righteousness. It emphasized that godly, ascetic conduct was the necessary fruit of faith.[125] Sermons often appealed to the penitents to burn their dice, playing cards, rouge, trinkets, and false hair, and they tried to curb extravagance, morally degrading pleasures and plays, and usury.[126] All of this is reflected also both in mood and detail in much of the earliest Anabaptist preaching.

Integrated with the emphasis on preaching was the Franciscan stress (as in Berthold of Regensberg, whom Moorman calls typical)[127] on simplicity of life and worship, the use of vernacular, and frequent reference to the Scriptures.[128] This accords with Francis himself who

> took each saying [of Scripture] in its natural sense and, putting aside every temptation to moralize or allegorize upon it he set himself to obey. His disciples were expected to treat the Bible the same way . . . as a handbook of marching orders.[129]

Moorman concludes that the friars promoted thereby "the importance of the natural and literal meaning of the words of Scripture."[130] For example, over one hundred editions of Nicholas of Lyra's (d. 1349) three-volume work *Postille literalis*, which insisted that any mystical interpretation must follow a mastery of the literal, were printed "from 1471 onwards" and over 1,200 manuscript copies are extant.[131] It strongly influenced Lefèvre d' Étaples and Erasmus and Martin Luther.[132] On the issues of *sola scriptura* and greater literalism in interpretation the Anabaptists held a position common to the Protestant Reformation movement as a whole.[133] With reference to interpreting the Bible with emphasis on the primacy of the New Testament, especially the Gospels, the Anabaptists were closer to Francis than to Luther. Francis made it clear from the beginning that the real "Rule" was simply the precepts of the Gospels.[134]

There is confirmation of Ritschl also in regards to several less significant details such as: the bearing of persecution and suffering, voluntarily, humbly, and patiently;[135] a positive attitude to secular work and the continuing of one's trade, if it is honest and not contrary to the good of the soul[136]; and some suspicion of learning which, though the Franciscans produced many noted scholars, was also derived from Francis himself.[137] Blaurock's use of the symbolic expression "rose-red blood [*rossenfarbentn blutt*]," in reference to the wine

236 Anabaptism and Asceticism

of the Holy Communion[138] may be derived from Bonaventura's imagery of the red rose at the foot of the cross to symbolize love and the shedding of sacrificial blood.[139]

Also, there is additional evidence to indicate that Ritschl was basically correct in seeing the Franciscan reform movement as greatly stimulating a laicization of asceticism, and for suggesting that many of the Franciscan ideals, which in a general way parallel sixteenth-century Anabaptism, come even closer when institutionalized in the Franciscan Tertiaries.[140] Ritschl put it this way: "The morality and aim of the Anabaptists coincide with parts of the rule of the Franciscan Tertiaries and with parts of the first rule of St. Francis to such a degree that one cannot fail to recognize a generic relationship here."[141] According to Ritschl, the Third Order (Tertiaries) or Brotherhood of Penitence was intended by Francis to guide the laity to heaven; it was a program for the salvation of all men everywhere involving a diligent following of the gospel ideals to the degree permitted while remaining in the world, working, and using posessions.[142]

Again, Moorman confirms that the earliest known "Rule" simply sets "a standard of life, devout, simple, and disciplined."[143] The "rule" approved by Pope Honorius III (1221) has many similarities to the "Rule" approved by Innocent III in 1201 for the "Humiliates" brotherhoods in Lombardy. Both stress humility, penance, obedience, patience, bearing of suffering, moderation and self-control, abstention from certain morally questionable and frivolous amusements, prayers, charity, plain dress, peacefulness, opposition to the carrying of the deadly weapons, and the rejection of oath-taking.[144] Moorman also suggests that the Rule of the Tertiaries of Perugia (circ. 1392) is probably typical of attitudes in the fourteenth century. It also stressed living a "godly, righteous, and sober life, abstention from worldly pleasures and from some worldly occupations, doing deeds of mercy, and loyalty to the common will of the community."[145]

The Tertiaries formed fraternal communities of various kinds, originally with government vested in themselves (local autonomy) and with only limited ties to the First Order and very limited episcopal control. The extent of outside control varied, subsequently, from time to time and in various places, in succeeding centuries.[146] Through the fourteenth century, in accordance with the assumptions of the Rule of 1289, most Tertiaries lived in their own houses, followed their callings, and met periodically for worship and devotional and charitable activity. A growing number, toward the end of the fourteenth century, often in the same industry, formed communities of common life and went out daily to work; some even became fully enclosed, like monks, with added rules.[147] Similar variations occur also in Anabaptism, for example, the formation of the Hutterite communities.

Also, significant to this whole pattern of parallelism is Pope Honorius III's original exemption of the Third Order from the obligation to bear arms, to take oaths, and to fulfill feudal military service, as an aid to their pursuit of perfection. Later popes allowed a moderation of these points, under pressure from civil authorities; though Pope Gregory IX still decreed that the Tertiaries were not obliged to accept public office. As close to the Reformation era as 1514, Pope Leo X initially confirmed these same immunities, though in 1516, he too had to partially retract them, especially the exemption from office holding.[148] But the pattern and precedent for Anabaptism are there.

In addition to Ritschl's general thesis that Franciscan piety and reform ideals are the progenitors of Anabaptist reform sentiment, he proposes also the sub-thesis that the Franciscan Spirituals and the Franciscan Tertiaries are also most probably the direct mediators of these ideals to Anabaptism.[149] On this issue subsequent study has raised serious difficulties and has indicated that substantial limitations must be imposed. Ritschl made a strong point of an inherent anti-papalism within the Franciscan tradition which continued to be spread to a significant degree by them up to the sixteenth-century Reformation in spite of the institutional recognition of the Observants.[150]

The degree of continuation of this sentiment in organized Franciscanism remains highly conjectural and the evidence is inadequate and even contradictory. For example, while the stand of the fourteenth century Spirituals certainly implied a challenge to and even defiance of the authority of the Papacy,[151] in the fifteenth century there was a strong trend toward institutionalization and closer papal ties, manifest in the triumph of the Observants both with Council and with papal support, and manifest within the Tertiaries by the approval by popes of an increasing trend to Third Order "Regulars," resulting in the loss of their local independence.[152] Also, the Observants who absorbed much of the earlier Spiritual movement were generally opposed to the heretical and schismatic "Spiritual" Franciscans, called Fraticelli.

The rise of the Observants actually led to a decrease in Fraticelli numbers and influence after the mid-fifteenth century.[153] Similarly, the reform preacher, John of Capistrano, who favored the Observants, was at the same time a strong supporter of the authority of the Holy See, and also strongly opposed to the Fraticelli.[154] In spite of Erasmus' opinion to the contrary, and of some slight initial support for Luther's resistance to the papacy,[155] the Franciscans do not appear to have been significantly more disloyal to the papacy or more readily won over to Protestantism than many others.

Since Ritschl's picture of Anabaptism is largely drawn from Bullinger,[156] there is also a tendency to exaggerate the importance of Joachimite, chiliastic, and mystical motifs which are found extensively and mutually only in parts of Anabaptism and in parts of Franciscanism. The latter believed Joachim of Fiore's "everlasting gospel" predicted the coming of an era of the Holy Spirit when a true Christianity which did not need authoritative institutions would emerge, aided by Orders living in apostolic poverty and willing to suffer for the gospel.[157] Joachimism encouraged an interpretation of history which saw primitive Christianity as normative and the church as "fallen" and awaiting some eschatological restitution.[158]

John of Parma was elected Minister-General of the Franciscans in 1247. He was not only a "Spirituals" sympathizer but an advocate of Joachimite teachings, and this encouraged its further spread among the "Spirituals." Though they were severly persecuted by several popes, especially Boniface VIII and John XXII, both for their ideal of poverty and their promotion of Joachimite theory, and forced to carry on secretly, this Spiritual branch grew in the fourteenth century and encouraged the fusion of Joachimite-Franciscan reform ideals and of negative attitudes to the papacy.[159] The combination of Joachimite historical interpretations and Franciscan rejection of worldly institutions is often given credit as the ideological progenitor of the rise of the "free church" concept.[160] Ritschl notes that these "Spirituals" also revised Joachim to the extent of leaving to an unknown future the time for the collapse of the corrupt institutional church and for the restitution of an apostolic church free of secular involvements, and the time when the eternal gospel of the Spirit would become effective. They often related this future hope to apocalyptic elements in the New Testament Book of the Revelation.[161]

However, as noted previously, contrary to this sub-thesis, after the mid-fifteenth century, the "Spirituals" were mostly absorbed into the newer "Observant" movement which was neither anti-institutional nor antipapal. Rather it was recognized and encouraged by both popes and councils. Also while it moderately sustained the ideals of the "Spirituals," the main concern was for the rigorous restoration of the observance of the "Rule" within the institutional structures. It was not strongly Joachimist, as is reflected in their often vigorous anti-Fraticelli attitude (the Conventuals were also anti-Fraticelli); the Fraticelli declined in the fifteenth century.[162] There was a brief revival and proliferation of pure, original "Spiritual" Franciscanism toward the end of the century (mostly in Italy — for example, the Clareni)[163] but this revival was relatively insignificant and these groups also were eventually absorbed into the Observants.[164] Some semi-Joachimite apocalypticism was revived in Spain during the reign of Ferdinand and Isabella and continued into the sixteenth century, where it is reflected in Geronimo Mendieta's writings, and entered into Franciscan policy on the evangelization of the Indians in Mexico.[165]

Thus while there was some limited revival of Joachimite concepts, in modified form, Joachimism does not seem to have been extensive or influential in Germany or Switzerland in the early sixteenth century. The actual strength of Joachimite ideas in Franciscanism among the Observants at the end of the fifteenth century is hard to assess and requires additional specialized study, but it seems quite limited.

In the fourteenth century, some of the Tertiaries were also closely allied in belief with the "Joachimite-Spirituals." In some areas, such as southern France, they were persecuted and martyred, but in other areas they were highly respected and had civic approval.[166] Whether they remained a *significant vehicle* for communication of the ideals of the "Spirituals" and of Joachimite theory into the sixteenth century is also highly conjectural.

Ritschl's rather strong accent on the Joachimite and mystical content in basic Anabaptist theology also needs modification in the light of more recent studies. Admittedly, some specifically mystical and eschatological elements, possibly Joachimite and probably derived from Thomas Müntzer and the Zwickau prophets, were present initially in Hans Hut.[167] But, contrary to Ritschl, these chiliastic aspects of Hut, and the mystical norms of authority of Thomas Müntzer, do not play a dominant role in Evangelical Anabaptism as a whole. Even in Hut, these aspects, as already noted, were undergoing modification and suppression through the influence of the other Anabaptist leaders.[168] Little trace of Joachimism can be found in the writings of Grebel,

Manz, Hubmaier, Sattler, or other formative leaders.[169]

The Swiss Anabaptists and Evangelical Anabaptism as a whole, however, did espouse an interpretation of history that saw the medieval ecclesiastical institutions as fallen, and as instruments of Antichrist, needing to be totally repudiated. Also the only true "reformation" was for the Holy Spirit to work, through the gospel which was now available, a "restitution" of the true apostolic church.[170] But neither of these interpretations is exclusively or strictly Joachimite. In two letters, Grebel mentions this "restitution" in somewhat eschatological terms; but they are incidental remarks and there is no specific evidence in his writings of distinctively Joachimite terminology or influence.[171] To a slight degree, some Joachimite overtones may underlie both the phenomenon of the solemn parade of the Zollikon "prophets"[172] and the often-repeated assertion in the writings and preaching of many of the pioneer Swiss Anabaptists that "the axe is laid to the root of the tree,"[173] But, contrary to the Ritschl,[174] neither Joachimite chiliasm, nor mystical idealism which puts "the value of morally good behavior . . . far beneath the ecstatic union with God,"[175] nor the validity of ecstatic revelations can be considered "leading motifs" in Evangelical Anabaptism, not even in the South German branch. Since Joachimism and mysticism are not "leading motifs" in Anabaptism, and probably even less than Ritschl thought in sixteenth-century Franciscanism, Ritschl's attempt to use it as a major factor in tying together Anabaptism and Franciscanism is seriously weakened.[176]

Though one part of his sub-thesis is questionable, Ritschl's other and more general contention, that Franciscan influence on the religious and reform expectations and ideals of early sixteenth-century European society was pervasive, has been strengthened by subsequent research. The Observants gained in popular support through the fifteenth century, especially in France, Germany, and Spain; most of the new houses established in the fifteenth century were Observants and their membership reached about 22,400 by 1493.[177] Largely due to the rise of the reformed "Observants" and the number of outstanding fifteenth-century Franciscan preachers, who preached in the vernacular, often in the open air, on reformatory, moralistic, and biblical themes, the Friars continued to be held in high esteem by the laity, for the most part. The sermon became an event of great importance in city life.[178] John of Capistrano followed the practice of giving "letters of affiliation" to large numbers of lay people, to all those who showed signs of repentance in response to his preaching.[179] One should note however that a number of Dominican revivalist preachers (such as Vincent Ferrer and Jerome Savonarola) also became popular in the fifteenth century and similarly preached on the themes of repentance and piety.[180]

Some Franciscans wrote books on the Christian life and holy living which became quite popular. For example, Dietrich Coelde of Münster, an Observant, wrote *Christenspiegel*, in German, and there were twenty-six editions in his lifetime. Angelo Carletti of Chivasso wrote an aid to confessions and Christian living for the people, called *Summa Conscientiae*, more frequently known as the *Summa Angelica*. Though it was "bitterly condemned by Luther," it was popular among the faithful. Henry Herp, an Observant, wrote a three-part *Theologica Mystica* in which part two, called *Speculum Perfectionis*, accents complete self-renunciation and self-abasement. This work also had wide circulation until put on the Index as too Protestant and too individualistic.[181]

Also significant for evaluating the pervasiveness of Franciscan ideals of Christian piety and reform was the size and popularity of the third order, or the Tertiaries. In the mid-fifteenth century, the third order seculars were weak in England and France but strong in Germanic areas and in Italy, especially in the cities. John of Capistrano estimated the number in Italy alone, in 1451, at 600,000.[182] Also, the Tertiary movement, which had been closely allied to "Spirituals" ideals in the fourteenth century,[183] experienced much interaction and fusion with various other religious and semireligious groups. Reinmann notes that in many places, especially in Germany and the Netherlands, various communities, such as Beghuines and guilds of workingmen, joined the Tertiaries in order to acquire both legal status and the spiritual privileges and immunities. Thus in 1289, many groups of Beghard weavers in the Netherlands adopted the rule of the Tertiaries and later formed a federation of such communities. In 1346, delegates from seventeen houses of Beghards passed a resolution that none but Tertiaries be admitted to membership in their weaving organization. This fusion with similar type organizations spread widely through the fourteenth and fifteenth centuries.[184]

A similar extension of influence, and of cross-fertilization of both ideals and even institutions, took place also between Franciscanism, especially the Tertiaries, and the Brethren of the Common Life, who were at the heart of the reform movement called the *Devotio*

Moderna. Many of the Brethren of the Common Life also became Franciscan Tertiaries.[185] As previously mentioned, Henry Herp of the Brethren of the Common Life later even joined the Observants (1450) and authored the influential *Theologia Mystica.*[186]

There are also some serious negative findings with reference to Ritschl's thesis of the pervasiveness of Franciscan piety and its ties to Anabaptist reform. At the end of the fifteenth century, the Tertiaries were undergoing major changes of a sort and in a direction quite other than toward Anabaptism. The trend toward the "seculars" becoming "regulars" was strong and the Tertiaries, with the three basic vows added, began to approximate the first or second orders.[187] With this trend there entered greater hierarchical connections and a loss of autonomy for individual houses.[188] There was a corresponding trend, derived in part from the ideals of Bonaventura and David of Augsburg's *Directory*, toward ascetic rigorism and methodical penitential and devotional exercises, as expressed in the fifteenth-century appearance of the *Exercitatoria* or collections of prayer-exercises laid down for every day of the week.[189] Again, both the early Spirituals and the later Observants tended to favor a semi-hermit ideal, quite contrary to the strong Anabaptist congregationalism.[190] It is not insignificant that even with such leaders as John of Capistrano, the friars, who acted as the chief agents of the Papacy for arousing Europe to a crusade against the threatening Turks, had very little success.[191]

Finally, and most important, the evidence for direct contact between the Franciscans and the first, formative group of Anabaptists is inadequate to support Ritschl's thesis fully. Therefore, while subsequent research has substantiated that the initial appeal of both the Swiss and South German Anabaptists was strongest among the urban artisans and craftsmen, where the Tertiary movement was also concentrated and that Anabaptism was not at first primarily a peasant movement,[192] yet there is little concrete evidence of specific ties between the Anabaptists and these Tertiaries, or of the latter's aid in Anabaptism's success. Moreover, under persecution, Anabaptism soon switched largely to the peasantry with, apparently, equally widespread appeal and success.

Ritschl's assumption of direct contacts was based mostly on Bullinger's generalized, exaggerated, and unspecific statement that among the Anabaptists were "numerous barefooters" (Observants).[193] Admittedly South German Anabaptism did derive some

Agencies of Mediation 243

supportive leadership from the Franciscans, including Sigmund Salminger, the first Anabaptist pastor at Augsburg and Leonard Schiemer of the Hut circle,[194] but none are known to have been directly involved in the initial, Swiss formation of the Anabaptist synthesis. A few Franciscans appear on the fringe of the Swiss Anabaptist circle of leadership but are not ideologically significant.[195] There is in the *Hutterite Chronicle* a sympathetic mention of the work of Petrus Olivi (d. 1298), a Franciscan leader who wrote a *Postil* on the apocalypse favoring Joachimite ideas.[196] Also Dirk Philips, an ex-Observant, plays an important supportive, anti-Münsterite role in the later rise of "Evangelical" Dutch Anabaptism.[197] Among the earliest Anabaptist apologists, Hubmaier, the preacher, may have become familiar during his time at Regensberg with Franciscan ideals through the lingering reputation of the great Franciscan preacher, Berthold of Regensberg. The main thrust of Berthold's ministry seems to approximate much in Hubmaier, the Anabaptist.[198] Also Sattler's wife, a former Beguine, may have had some ties with the Tertiaries. But most of this is purely conjecture. Grebel expressed deep disdain for the institutionalized friars.[199] One must conclude that there is no known evidence of significant, direct ties between the earliest, formative, Swiss Anabaptist leadership and the Franciscans.

Consequently, while substantial ideological and conductural parallelism tends to substantiate Ritschl's claim that the Franciscan concept of Christianity and of reform played a significant role, perhaps even the most significant role, as preparatory both for the development of another type of Protestant reform which was in essence and aims quite distinct from Luther's, and for the existence of a popular predisposition toward a specifically Anabaptist presentation, yet its lack of direct contact with the initial, formative Anabaptist leadership has made Franciscanism doubtful as the primary, immediate progenitor or most direct agency of mediation of medieval ascetic, reforming piety to Anabaptism. Ritschl himself suggests an alternate, and closely related, channel of mediation, the movement known as the *Devotio Moderna*.[200]

The Devotio Moderna

A recent, comprehensive monograph by R. R. Post[201] seeks to revise and moderate some previously widely accepted notions concerning both the functions and concepts of the *Devotio Moderna*. When the designation *Devotio Moderna* is restricted to its narrowest, institutional dimensions, to the actual members of the brothers and sisters of the Common Life and to the Windesheimer congregation, as it is by Post, and when he analyzes the sources, thus restricted, then Post can effectively demonstrate that the *Devotio Moderna* cannot be assigned a significant role in instigating and fostering fifteenth-century pedagogical innovations, the northern humanist movement, concepts of religious liberty and toleration, and the essential elements of the Magisterial Reformation's theology and practice.[202] Rather, Post contends that the *Devotio Moderna* (as strictly, institutionally, defined) was almost exclusively concerned for a rather typical though reforming brand of medieval piety. Even in its outreach by the brother houses or cloisters, since it did not have the capacity or talent to do otherwise, it limited its activities mostly to fostering its own kind of spiritual reform by functioning as chaplains, spiritual advisers, and promoters of pious literature. Its many hostels for students, a few actual schools which it started late in the fifteenth century, its copying and publishing activities, and ultimately its presses were largely subsidiary to its single, religious concern. Its members rarely functioned as teachers themselves, and very rarely did any of its number take university training.[203]

Post also demonstrates that even the thesis that the "Brethren of the Common Life" was primarily a unique lay organization needs modification; rather, it was a mixture of clergy and laity. Most of its "houses" became training schools for the priestly office.[204]

Significantly, while trying to demonstrate the essential incompatibility of the *Devotio Moderna* with the (Magisterial) Reformation and to show instead its Catholic orthodoxy, its lack of uniqueness and originality, and its strong and essential adherence to medieval ascetic values in doctrine and practice, Post, apparently quite unwittingly, actually strengthens Ritschl's thesis of the possibility of a relationship instead to the Anabaptists and the Radical Reformation. Both Post and Ritschl tie the *Devotio Moderna* closely to that larger, ascetic, pre-Reformation reform movement which, as previous chapters have indicated, provided the framework for the emergence of Anabaptism. This larger movement includes several closely related groups, such as the Franciscan Spirituals and their Tertiaries, the orthodox branch of the Beghard and Beghuine movement, and much of an even larger tradition of affective, practical mysticism or spirituality related to Bernard, Francis, Jean Gerson, and the *Theologie Deutsch*[205] (though, strangely and without explanation, Post denies that there is much in common between *Devotio Moderna* piety and the piety of the *Theologie Deutsch*).[206]

There is much evidence of extensive cross-fertilization of ideas and even of institutional connections among these medieval, ascetic, and reformatory groups. Gerhard Groote expressed sympathy with the "reformed" Franciscans.[207] Radewijns and Zerbolt

> were deeply interested in a mystical treatise by the Franciscan friar, David of Augsburg, entitled *Profectus Religiosorum*. Radewijns strongly urged his disciples to read that inspiring book, and it is mentioned in the introduction to the original constitution of the brethren house at Deventer. The two famous works by Zerbolt contain large sections copied almost verbally from this treatise. In the *Treatise of Spiritual Exercises* by Radewijns numerous quotations have also been found.[208]

It is also significant that according to Erasmus the friars, especially the Franciscans and Dominicans, recruited many of their novices from pupils associated with the Brethren of the Common Life.[209] In 1471, the famous Franciscan preacher, John Brugman, praised the educational work of the Brethren.[210] Post substantiates in considerable detail the interrelationships between both the Brethren and the Sisters and the Franciscan Tertiaries. For example, as early as 1399, part of the Brethren house of Amersfoert went over to the Franciscan Tertiaries.[211] Shortly after, several more houses of both Brethren and Sisters, especially in the Utrecht area, followed suit. By 1470, about eighty-two houses are known to have had some association with the Franciscan Tertiaries.[212] Henricus Wilhelmi and Werembold de Boscoop promoted among the Brethren and Sisters both the Franciscan Tertiary movement and the reformatory, observantism of the Augustinian Rule of the Windesheimers.[213] Many of the Brethren and Sisters of the Common Life after initially taking the Rule of the Franciscan Tertiaries went on to become monastic regulars — usually Windesheimers.

With such cross-fertilization, it would be astonishing if many of the same religious motifs were not common to the *Devotio Moderna* and to the Franciscan Tertiary movement. As noted earlier, the Franciscans, seeking to intensify and internalize personal spirituality and inspired by both Bonaventura and by David of Augsburg's *Directory*, encouraged the development of affective piety through methodical prayer in meditation. About the mid-fifteenth century, there appeared the *Exercitatoria* or collections of prayer-exercises laid down for every day of the week.[214]

Groote, Radewijns, and Zerbolt similarly encouraged private meditation for spiritual growth. Among the Brethren, this meditation was at first a kind of mental rumination to go along with the performing of other mundane tasks but, similar to the Franciscans, by the mid-fifteenth century it had developed to the place where Wessel Gansfort could formulate a method or ladder for meditation for the Windesheim congregation. His work became popular, was taken over by the Brethren Houses also, and became a part of the whole reform program of the *Devotio Moderna*.[215] Thus, as Post acknowledges, and in agreement with Ritschl, the *Devotio Moderna* again emerges as very much a part of the larger religious, ascetic reform movement and as closely related both organizationally and thematically to the Franciscan Tertiaries.[216]

Both Post[217] and Ritschl[218] contrast these and similar medieval ascetic reform motifs, which are common to the essence of both the Franciscan Tertiaries and the *Devotio Moderna*, with the aims and ideals of the Magisterial Reformation. But these same motifs also form the basis for Ritschl's contention that there is a remarkable parallelism between the original Franciscan "Rule," the Franciscan Tertiary organization, and the original Franciscan reform aims on the one hand, and the Anabaptist ideals and objectives on the other[219] — a thesis which originally failed primarily because of a lack of adequate supporting evidence of direct ideological and institutional connections between Franciscanism and Anabaptism. However, the evidence for extensive cross-fertilization makes a reevaluation of Ritschl's thesis necessary. Instead of the Franciscan Tertiaries, the *Devotio Moderna* must be considered as possibly functioning as the primary agency for the mediation of many of these ascetic ideals, motifs, and practices to Anabaptism.

Several writers in, or closely associated with, the *Devotio Moderna* movement asserted the primacy of the religious authority of the Bible, the subjective internality of true spirituality, and the necessity of faith for salvation. If one centers attention exclusively or primarily on these themes, it is possible to portray the *Devotio Moderna* as a precursor to several quite distinct segments of sixteenth-century "Reformation" fervor: Erasmian Christian humanism, Magisterial Protestantism, and Anabaptism. But when several necessary qualifications are added, especially that some in the *Devotio Moderna* also granted the early Fathers considerable authority, that they did not completely eliminate the use of external rites or the sacraments (though, in varying degrees, their interpretation weakened the *ex opere operato* validity of the sacraments),[220] and that some synergism, or human cooperation, for salvation was always retained, direct connections with the "Magisterial" expression of the Reformation are weakened.

When one also adds the *Devotio Moderna's* much stronger and constantly present emphases on the essentiality for any valid reform of ascetic, conductual idealism and its conviction that such, without the requirement of the traditional monastic vows, is necessary for, and must be extended to the laity, the ordinary person who remains in the world, the swing away from ties with Magisterial Protestantism is even further; but even with the additional qualifications, the *Devotio Moderna* remains substantially compatible with both Erasmian Christian humanism and Anabaptism.

In a paper delivered at the Goshen Biblical Seminary in 1965, Albert Hyma has drawn attention in tentative and general terms to numerous ideological similarities on fundamental issues between the *Devotio Moderna* and the Swiss founders of Anabaptism.[221] Since much recent historical scholarship now supports Ritschl's contention of a fundamentally different, even antithetic, approach to reformation between the Magisterial Reformers and the Anabaptists,[222] Hyma's redirection of the *Devotio Moderna's* influence on and relationship to the Reformation from the Magisterial Reformation toward Anabaptism becomes most significant.

Similar to Ritschl's methodology, Hyma first draws attention to the parallelism between the Anabaptists and the *Devotio Moderna* regarding the importance and ascetic nature of Christian conduct; both groups make it essential for all Christians. The rest of Hyma's argument is based mostly on an ideological comparison of the *Imitation of Christ* (as the primary *Devotio Moderna* source) with those basic elements of Anabaptist ideology delineated by Harold S. Bender's article on Anabaptism.[223] Hyma accents specifically the common espousal of nonconformity to the world through a common emphasis on renunciation, of holiness of life through full and literal obedience to Christ, especially to His teachings in the Sermon on the Mount, and of the imitation or idealization of the primitive church.[224]

Hyma also draws attention to their mutual concern that true spirituality be understood as firstly and fundamentally personal and internal. Again the evidence is drawn mostly from *The Imitation*. At the same time, both the Anabaptists and the Brethren of the Common Life upheld the ideal of the universal necessity for a practical and ascetic manifestation of this inner spirituality, especially in terms of a repudiation of material values, including their common espousal of the wearing of simple garments.[225] To prove the commonality of *Devotio Moderna* and Anabaptist views regarding mutual aid and community of goods, Hyma quotes from article 6 of the defense of Zerbolt, an early leader of the Brethren of the Common Life, that "Christ lived the common life and whatever He had, He had in common with His disciples"; in article 7 also, Zerbolt praises the common life as practiced by the apostles.[226]

However, Hyma fails to note the variety of interpretations of community of goods among the Anabaptists; that the Hutterite communitarianism most akin to the Brethren communes was always a minority view among Anabaptists and one which developed later. Little evidence is given by him for any concrete or detailed parallelism between the more important Anabaptist concept of the brotherhood church and the brotherhoods of Brethren of the Common Life. Also Hyma makes no comment on how Bender's first point on the nature of Anabaptism, that the Anabaptist brotherhood was a voluntary church of believers only, with initiation by baptism on personal confession of faith and personal commitment to discipleship, would relate to the *Devotio Moderna*. But, as discussed in the previous chapter, even for this seemingly very unique aspect of Anabaptism, there is a parallel within the ascetic, cloister ideal.[227]

Hyma's further claim of parallelism between the Anabaptists and the *Devotio Moderna*, especially the Brethren, as mutual advocates of religious toleration, and separation of church and state, is based largely on a dissertation by William Spoelhof[228]; a thesis which is strongly but not too successfully contested by Post.[229] Hyma sees the Anabaptist's love ethic, in terms of nonresistance and rejection of force and warfare, as emerging out of the ideal of tolerance found in the *Devotio Moderna*. But this is not an adequate comparison since the essence of the Anabaptists' love ethic and pacifism according to their own writings is not derived primarily from the tolerance motif.

Post's objection to Hyma's and Spoelhof's advocacy of the "Brethren" as precursors of religious tolerance and nonconformity is

Agencies of Mediation   249

based largely on his own very narrow and institutional definition of the *Devotio Moderna* by which he can minimize some of Spoelhof's major sources as either outside of the movement (for example, Gansfort) or as at least outside the Brethren expression of it (for example, H. Mande, G. Peters, and T. à Kempis), and thus make their testimony irrelevant.[230] He also requires Spoelhof's witnesses to take absolute positions, such as rejecting pilgrimages "completely," or he rejects the validity of their support for Spoelhof's thesis.[231]

These highly technical procedures by Post are themselves suspect and unconvincing. From its beginning the *Devotio Moderna* had as its objective the total regeneration of the church in terms of a revival of apostolic primitivism which included the notions of a revitalized conductual piety, a radical separation of the church from the world, and an active, personal devotion to Christ.[232] Its fulfillment was never intended to be contained strictly within its own institutions; rather, it readily encouraged the transference of its methods and goals to others. That the movement was intended to transcend its own institutions is apparent from the methods chosen for its promotion. Both the reforming activities of the monastic Windesheimers and the practical, educational interests of the Brethren were deliberate vehicles, in place of preaching which was forbidden to them, to extend their influence and ideals and thus create a reform movement much larger than their own specific organizations.

These factors make necessary a much larger definition for the *Devotio Moderna*, as an intellectual movement, than Post allows. Gansfort, Erasmus, and others cannot be as readily dismissed from the movement as Post desires simply because they functioned outside its membership per se and because they fused some of its ideals with other contemporary currents of thought. Many northern humanists who received their initial education in schools under Brethren spiritual guidance continued in later life to reflect the spiritual outlook of the *Devotio Moderna*. This kind of extension of the movement is completely consistent with its original objectives.

When the *Devotio Moderna* is given its larger, less institutional definition, then several recent, specialized studies strengthen the preliminary indications in Hyma's essay of substantial *Devotio Moderna* and Anabaptist parallelism and perhaps dependency. The significance of that parallelism becomes even more striking by making a comparative analysis utilizing the same categories used in the previous chapter for structuring the Anabaptist movement. Such an analysis follows. It does not imply that the two are identical but only that a body of ideology and practice existed of sufficient similarity to indicate that the Anabaptists probably derived much from it.

This work has already demonstrated extensively the general concord, with reference to primitivistic and pietistic reform ideals, among the *Devotio Moderna*, the Franciscans, the late fourteenth-century Prague Reformers, the orthodox Beghards, and others.[233] Furthermore, Post and Hyma concur that one of the strongest elements within the general reform objectives of the *Devotio Moderna*, from Groote on, was to restore the church to holy living by renunciation of this world, by upholding the efficacy of inner repentance and love, and by tying salvation to the pursuit of perfection by all.[234] Such a program was not unique or heretical but quite orthodox and fully consistent with the larger body of moderately ascetic, practical, and reform mysticism.[235] This program also suggests a potential role as a precursor of Anabaptism.

The Brethren leader, Radewijns, states that the objective of the *Devotio Moderna* was to show men the way of eternal salvation.[236] Then he essentially equates this goal with the pursuit of perfection since he describes identically the means to both; that is, by becoming aware of one's imperfections, by becoming "humble inwardly" (repentance), by acquiescence or obedience to God's will through self-surrender, and by the practical imitation of Christ and of the primitive church.[237] Landeen demonstrates a substantial continuation of these ideals in the movement's expansion into Germany during the fifteenth century. The constant repetition of such terminology in the sources there, with reference to the movement's objectives, as: "amendment" of life, the persuading of all men to "despise this world," perfection, purity, and piety[238] verifies the persistence of these basic concerns.

Though the very existence of Brethren brotherhoods implied a rejection of monasticism as the only, or necessary, or perhaps even as the best road to saving holiness and perfection, they do not negate the validity of the underlying ascetic ideals. Therefore a Brethren leader in Germany, Peter Dieburg, asserts: "We are not monks but we aim and desire to live piously in the world." Similarly he praises the principles of the renunciation of the world and simplicity of dress, while resisting the necessity of the imposition of a monastic "rule" and of "heavy burdens" at the expense of liberty.[239] It is not surprising therefore that the Brethren in Germany were sometimes denounced as Lollbrothers (Lollards) and that those at Magdeburg were accused of dressing like Bohemian heretics.[240]

Thus the testimony concerning reform aims of the *Devotio Moderna*, especially of the Brethren, both from the sources and by most of those researching the movement, overwhelmingly indicates that the primary reform thrust of the *Devotio Moderna* does not parallel that of the Lutheran Reformation but rather, in both spirit and terminology, is remarkably close to that of the Anabaptists; whose concept of reform was also ascetic, conductual, lay-oriented, primitivistic, and perfectionistic, with the way of salvation itself closely tied to the pursuit of an ascetically conceived holiness.

Post points out, from the Doesburg annalist, that in spite of some initial sympathy for Luther and commitment to a scripturally based reform, many of the "Brethren" in the early sixteenth century rejected both the apparent evil "fruits" of Luther's emphasis on election and Christian liberty, and also his apparent spirit of violence and lack of concern for submission and humility.[241] This kind of reaction also strongly resembles the expressed basis for the Anabaptist protest and rejection of Luther.

The remarkable parallelism, already observable, between the *Devotio Moderna* ideals and the Anabaptists extends beyond the general reform aims and purposes to a large number of unique and significant sub-issues. Again, Hyma has drawn the attention of scholars initially to the distinctiveness of much of the *Devotio Moderna's* anthropology. His initial observation was that Groote and Zerbolt, with reference to the "fall" and the extent of the subsequent depravity and helplessness, were much closer to the position of total depravity of Luther than to the dominant scholastic traditions which, in varying degrees, upheld much more limited effects from the "fall."[242] Consequently, and partly because Luther himself intimated the same, he suggested that in this also the *Devotio Moderna* was perhaps a significant precursor to, and influence on, the development of Luther's view of depravity. Actually, though many spokesmen of the *Devotio Moderna* allowed for only a smidgen of free will, even by such allowance its view was still fundamentally different from Luther's total bondage of the will. Hyma's more recent works indicate his awareness of that difference,[243] and also an awareness that it resembles much more closely the anthropology of Anabaptist Protestantism.[244]

Hyma's basic presentation of the nature of this somewhat distinctive anthropological/soteriological pattern found in many representatives of the *Devotio Moderna*, that is, their concepts of grace, free will, repentance, and the powers of man, remains relatively unchallenged.

The most unique and therefore significant aspect of this emphasis was the retention of a very limited free activity of the will in salvation in conjunction with a strong stress on the effects of the "fall"; the "fall" produced a universal situation of bondage to sin and a state of depravity which can be described as "total," but which is still not identical to Luther's absolute use of the term. That is, it is total in that it involves not only the corruption of the flesh but affects the intellect and the will to the point of total inability of man to save himself or in any way actually merit or earn salvation by good works. Groote writes: "From all evil satisfaction with ourselves and our good works free us. From thinking that we have anything good in ourselves free us."[245] Though close, this still falls short of the total inertia of the absolute depravity of Luther; there is not the complete extinction of all prelapsarian, human, moral powers.

What remains? Only the minutest element of free will; sufficient only to reject or respond to grace, and thus to give men moral responsibility for their fate. There is also, therefore, a kind of *sola gratia*. The provision of salvation is all of grace, through Christ, a gift, and the initiative is also of grace; but, the necessity of God's gracious initiative, through the gospel, must not be made a coercive act. Man remains a responsible moral creature. He is not passive in salvation but must do what little he can.[246] The *Devotio Moderna's* concern for reform of life, its biblical Sermon-on-the-Mount orientation, its relationship to the practical, preachers-of-repentance tradition, some influence of nominalism, but even more the influence of the Old Franciscan school upon its more learned spokesmen appear to be the principal factors in the development of this rather unique emphasis.[247]

The same paradoxical combination of depravity, redemptive helplessness, and salvation by grace on one hand, and the retention of a minute but responsible element of human free will on the other, is closely paralleled in Anabaptist literature[248]; not in Luther's. Also, in both the *Devotio Moderna* and the Anabaptists, the objective behind the insistence on some freedom is piety, to provide a motivation and some justification for moral responsibility. This kind of emphasis on freedom is not aimed directly at enhancing the dignity or autonomy of man, as in more secular humanism, but is quite compatible with a

Agencies of Mediation 253

Christianized version of it. Thus, even the same combination of ingredients appears to underlie both the *Devotio Moderna* and the Anabaptist positions: piety, repentance, and Sermon-on-the-Mount biblicism combined with elements of nominalism, Franciscanism, and Christian humanism.[249]

Clearly the *Devotio Moderna*, in general, in spite of its Augustinian connections, did not espouse a strong predestinarianism with its corollaries of double election and limited atonement.[250] By quoting a passage, inserted in Book IV of the *Imitation of Christ*, from the Nijmegen manuscript (not Thomas à Kempis'), Hyma illustrates that at least the branch of the *Devotio Moderna* represented by this manuscript version held to a universal offer of saving grace. It says:

> Be joyful and glad to go [into my dining place] at my expense; so you go freely; and not you alone but come all, the spiritually inclined and the worldly, good and bad, poor and rich. Whoever you are, come in the same way.[251]

Again the parallelism with the Anabaptists is striking. The earliest leaders of the Swiss Brethren, the South German Anabaptists, and the Dutch Mennonites specifically upheld the universal nature of the atonement and of the offer of grace. The universal atonement was generally held to be immediately and forensically applicable to all infants, and potentially applicable to, and available for, all who would repent.[252]

Repentance emerges as one of the most vital factors in the soteriology of the *Devotio Moderna*. This stress on repentance, its definition, and its operation or functioning is also remarkably close to the Anabaptist position. Again, note the Nijmegen manuscript of the *Imitation*:

> Come unto Me all that labor with penitence. . . .
>
> Be converted and come with all your heart unto Me. . . .
>
> Forsake the world; leave behind you everything in the world. Give up your old sinful life and join Me, that you may entrust Me with your faith, consolation, and love.[253]

Not only is repentance the prerequisite for forgiveness but it must be sincere and must include a resolution to amend one's evil ways.[254] Even this wording bears a remarkable similarity to any number of Anabaptist writers; for example, Menno Simons wrote:

> He will not save you nor forgive your sins nor show you His mercy and grace except according to His Word; namely, if you repent . . . if you do what He has commanded and walk as He walks. . . . But if you wish to be saved . . . first all of your earthly, carnal, ungodly life must be reformed.[233]

Hyma notes two fifteenth-century manuscript variations of Groote's translation of Psalm 32 which suggest a change in emphasis. One (N. van Wijk) reads, "Blessed are those who have earned that their sins be forgiven"; but the other (Hyma) reads, "Blessed are those whose sins have been forgiven on condition of repentance [rouwe]."[256] Both renderings are fifteenth-century variants of Groote but the nature of the variation in the latter again suggests the existence within the *Devotio Moderna* of a significant antecedent to the sixteenth-century Anabaptist theology of repentance.

The same concern, that true contrition before confession is the real agency of forgiveness, occurs also in Wessel Gansfort.[257] Landeen finds the same emphasis among the Brethren in Germany. Peter Dieburg, Rector of Hildesheim on the eve of the Reformation (1477-94), clearly maintained both the possibility and sufficiency of contrition, and to some degree this even occurs in Gabriel Biel.[258] One finds the same emphasis, on repentance and amendment of life, in the sermons of Standonck, in France.[259] The comparative picture is again one of remarkable parallelism with reference to the emphasis on the necessity of repentance in the soteriology of both the Anabaptists and much of the *Devotio Moderna*.

Incidentally, Melchior Hofmann's and Menno Simons' unique view of the incarnation, that Jesus was sinless because He was born "out of" the Virgin Mary but did not receive his human nature from her, was widespread among the Dutch Anabaptists and, significantly, Verheyden claims that here too they were "following in this point the spokesmen of the *Devotio Moderna*."[260]

Another point of considerable importance when considering the possible relationship of the *Devotio Moderna* to various elements of the Reformation is the *Devotio's* insistence on the necessity of conscious, willing, human cooperation in the process of sanctification or of maturing in holiness and an insistence on eternal salvation as not totally separated from this process; as it is separated in Luther. Radewijns made clear that the Brethren believed that if one is to find eternal salvation, the initial conversion and amendment of life must be

Agencies of Mediation   255

followed by a continuous, daily striving to conquer sin and subdue the sinful self and the flesh, based on a conscious, willing imitation of the life of Christ and on obedience to the principles of the Sermon on the Mount especially.[261] Gansfort and Biel similarly insisted on free human cooperation as a condition for grace aiding the will in developing faith. Gansfort saw the source of even this capacity as a kind of prevenient grace, the breath of God still present from creation.[262] Post agrees that this matter of cooperation is an essential element in *Devotio Moderna* piety[263] and that this confirms the typically medieval character of the *Devotio Moderna*.

Yet there is a somewhat unique element in that many of the *Devotio Moderna*, including in varying degrees Wessel Gansfort, John Pupper, and even the *Imitation*, maintain that in contrast to nominalism or even Thomas Aquinas' provision for some meritorious involvement, man's ability to exercise a limited freedom of will, and the necessity for his cooperation with God, is nevertheless without any "merit" because it is totally occasioned by grace; grace is enhanced as the decisive factor.[264] Pupper, Gansfort, and Biel also all had strong elements of Ockhamist nominalism mixed into their theological formulations, especially the Ockhamist principle that man must do what he can as a condition for grace: *facere quod in se est*.[265] Nevertheless, as Gansfort notes, though working is necessary, it not only is "in vain" without divine aid and mercy to the humble, but also "it counts for nothing," ever, with reference to merit.[266] What could be more Anabaptistic and less like Luther? For example, not only does Menno Simons insist that salvation requires continuous repentance, doing as Christ commands and walking as He walked, but at the same time he insists "that we do not believe nor teach that we are saved by our merits and works."[267]

Hubmaier similarly rejects the view of Thomas, and even of the Old Franciscans, that good works performed in the state of grace are meritorious *de condigno*, and rejects even more the nominalist contention that grace is the reward of meritorious moral activity from the exercise of one's own natural powers. For him, unlike Luther and close to Gansfort, the good works of a Christian man are only but still meritorious *de congruo*, and are retained in the schema of salvation.[268]

In much of the *Devotio Moderna* the emphasis is on love for God emerging from contrition through the Holy Spirit, more than on faith and intellectual belief.[269] Gansfort probably theologizes this emphasis more than any other *Devotio Moderna* writer. For Gansfort, "Faith is not the cause of our justification, but its proof. . . . When indeed faith works through love, it is firm and the beginning of our confidence is firm."[270] Love rooted in the Holy Spirit (grace) strengthens and nourishes faith. Mande and Gansfort both see such love as the ground of eternal life and the motivation for "good" works. As late as the last quarter of the fifteenth century, this love ethic was still being manifested in practical ways by the Brethren. The Brethren in Germany were called "golden priests" by the people for bringing help and consolation to the poor and the sick.[271] Love diffused by the Holy Spirit, when related to the fellowship, is even equated by Gansfort with the Petrine keys.[272] Here again one is reminded of the powerful love ethic, the loving, brotherly discipline of the fellowship, and the insistence on true faith as a loving, working faith, and as preceded by repentance, in most Anabaptist writings.

While the Anabaptist brotherhood or believers' church, even the Hutterian community, is not in every point identical to the Brethren community, yet the number of common motifs are significant and the rationale for them sound much alike. The church, asserts Hyma and Spoelhof, was conceived by some of the Brethren of the Common Life as a brotherhood of believers[273] with a democratic structure, local autonomy, and separation from the world while living piously in the world and working, not begging[274]; as a fellowship of love, praticing mutual aid and community of goods and opposing any use of physical force with reference to faith[275]; and as a reforming and missionary agency. All of these are motifs much more akin to Anabaptism than to the Magisterial Reformation.[276] Post's criticisms of this portrait of the Brethren by Spoelhof are only partially convincing, and Post seems totally unaware of the research on the Brethren in Germany by Landeen, which complements and supports Spoelhof on many points.[277]

For the most part, the *Devotio Moderna* does not question the maintenance of the external sacraments in the traditional church but it does change the focal point by elevating the subjective, spiritual involvement of the recipient to primary importance. This change, when coupled with its repentance theology, results in several writers explicitly departing from an *ex opere operato* interpretation of the sacraments, especially of the Lord's Supper and penance.[278]

Post maintains that such radical ideas, found in Gansfort, "diverge

Agencies of Mediation 257

completely" from the Brethren of Common Life.[279] This is demonstrably a gross overstatement. Peter Dieburg, rector of the Hildesheim brotherhood, asserts virtually the same ideas as Gansfort on the sacraments. There is no evidence to suggest that Dieburg was consciously voicing new or revolutionary ideas, nor was he in any way disciplined or even challenged for his statements by fellow Brethren. Dieburg clearly stresses that the right attitude and piety of the believer is of greater significance than the visible and external forms of the Eucharist; inner devotion is the essential element for effective participation in the sacraments. He even repeats Gansfort that the total inability to partake of the external rites due to an "interdict" situation represents no real spiritual loss, one can still spiritually and thus adequately commune with Christ. Dieburg does not advocate by this the discarding of the external sacrament or disrespect for proper church discipline, but rather that Christ alone is the Mediator, and all sacraments are but useful symbols.[280]

These radical concepts, clearly articulated in Gansfort and Dieburg, appear to be a consistent theological extension of similar intimations in Groote, the founder, and even in the *Imitation of Christ*. Though Groote does not repudiate priestly absolution if properly performed, for example, he does warn concerning actual contemporary practices: "You are making mock of the keys of the church and the sacraments. Take care! If you receive absolution and communion and have not a firm purpose of improvement . . . absolution and communion will not help you."[281] Similarly, the *Imitation* implies that spiritual success is ultimately inner, personal, and direct; bypassing, if necessary, the ecclesiastical externalities. It warns: "The wearing of a religious habit, and the shaving of the crown, do little profit, but change of manners and perfect mortification of passions make a true religious man."[282] It adds that even pilgrimages are insignificant if "little fruit of amendment is carried home."[283] Most pertinent, the *Imitation* suggests that spiritual communion with Christ, which is given the highest spiritual value, "is in the power of any devout person every day and every hour"[284]; it is not dependent solely on the sacramental Eucharist.

Hyma also has drawn attention to connections both through Gansfort to Erasmus and thus to the Swiss Reformers, and through Henin Rode's conveyance of Cornelius Hoen's treatise on the Eucharist (based on Gansfort) to Oecolampad, Bucer, and Zwingli, and thus to the Anabaptists. Especially important were the matters of the interpretation of "is," in "This is my body," as "signifies" and the stress on the memorial aspects.[285] Hoen was the rector of the brother house in Utrecht. Post claims that there is no evidence to suggest that Rode's treatise was generally supported by the Brethren[286] but the evidence for the existence of a considerable sacramentarian movement in the area,[287] the testimony of both Gansfort and Dieburg (about the latter Post says little), and also Hoen's connections with Rode cannot be so easily discarded.

Though there seems to be some general relationship between the sacramental theology of the Anabaptists and the *Devotio Moderna*, a significant correlation with the most distinctively Anabaptist aspects, such as the practice of believer's baptism, is lacking, generally — though Gansfort does suggest one very Anabaptistic notion, that in the sacrament of the Eucharist, Christians are signifying their willingness to share in Christ's sacrifice by helping bear His cross.[288]

The final point of comparison relates to the place of the Scriptures and especially to the hermeneutical pattern in each. There is substantial scholarly consensus that the *Devotio Moderna* gave priority to the Holy Scriptures as the basis for religious authority and for reform. Gansfort was most definite on this point.[289] Even at the time of Luther, the Brethren express considerable sympathy for this aspect of the Reformation.[290] The espousal of biblical authority is closely tied to primitivistic and imitation-of-Christ ideals of reform. However, ecclesiastical authorities were not totally without value also, especially the early fathers. Also, in spite of a general coolness to some aspects of secular learning, even the classics could be useful, though "only to the extent they stress spiritual values."[291] Groote took some interest in the moral philosophy of the classics and Radewijn also saw some value in it if it related to "amending one's life."[292]

Though stressing the primacy of the authority of Scripture, the representatives of the *Devotio Moderna* generally conceded to the church some power of interpretation.[293] How this power functioned institutionally, and who exercised it, was somewhat nebulous; but according to the *Devotio Moderna*, the exercise of this power must be in accord with certain other, definite, and firmly held, hermeneutical principles.

The most vital of these additional hermeneutical principles were as follows: Gansfort upholds the hermeneutical power of the theologians over that of the pope; if there is consensus and they are "true,"

Agencies of Mediation   259

that is, pious, theologians.²⁹⁴ Repeatedly *Devotio Moderna* writers insist that if Scripture is to be rightly understood by anyone, there must be a devotional approach to it, not purely an academic one. In addition to learning, and to a considerable degree apart from learning, the keys which are essential to unlock Scripture's real treasures are humility and piety. The *Imitation* requires approaching the Scriptures "meekly, simply, and truly, not desiring to have a name of knowledge."²⁹⁵ In addition, within the scriptural revelation, the gospel of Christ is made supremely definitive. The Holy Scriptures are defended as the foundation of truth and learning because "therein is the life of Christ."²⁹⁶

Zijl has made a list of Groote's reading and study habits and his use of traditional Christian literature, with significant results. Groote's order of preference emerges as follows: (1) the Gospels, with the life of Christ as the highest ideal, (2) early Christian councils and the lives of the church fathers, (3) the rest of the New Testament, especially the Epistles, (4) books of devotion, (5) lives of saints, (6) moral instructions from the church fathers, and (7) the Old Testament.²⁹⁷ As a result of this stress by the *Devotio Moderna* on the Gospels and concern for the imitation of Christ, there developed a kind of practical literalism about its imitation of and obedience to Christ and correspondingly to much of its interpretation of the New Testament.²⁹⁸

Lastly, their emphasis on preaching and teaching from Scriptures, when coupled with their copying and translating Scriptures and hymns into the vernacular so that the common people might read and use them for themselves,²⁹⁹ implies and encourages a belief in some ability by the individual to interpret for himself. Gansfort actually insists on the interpretive responsibility of the individual, thus: "I believe the gospel more than [I believe] any human multitude and, what is more, I ought to believe it even if I thought everyone else disbelieved it."³⁰⁰ This aspect of individual responsibility does not contradict his other statements on the importance for correct interpretation of consensus by the "whole church" or again on interpretation by the "wise men" (theologians).³⁰¹ It seems that Gansfort expected a common consensus was possible, aided by the true theologians, through a common piety and guidance by the Holy Spirit, if and when Scripture was accepted by all as final authority. But the individual remains at all times ultimately responsible.

Verheyden comments:

The activity of the Brethren of the Common Life in bringing the Bible to the people in the vernacular, which released the individual from conformist thinking and enabled him to express his religious views freely, penetrated into the broadest areas of contemporary Flemish society.[302]

It may well have gone farther abroad, since three of these four hermeneutical principles, which go beyond just the Reformation principle of asserting biblical authority, are remarkably close to some vital and distinctively Anabaptist hermeneutical emphases. The formative Swiss Anabaptists, especially, emphasized piety as a prerequisite to interpretive insight, progressive revelation with an interpretive primacy within Scripture granted to the New Testament, and literalism, especially in regards to obedience to the laws of Christ.

The preceding broad comparison of the *Devotio Moderna* to Anabaptism is not intended to imply *exact* identity between the two, not even between those specific doctrines and practices which seem closest. Exact identity is not necessary, though some exists. What is necessary and indicated in the *Devotio Moderna* is a compatible body of belief and spirituality within which concepts are growing and being expressed which could provide most of the basic materials for the later Anabaptist snythesis.

But the existence of significant ideological parallelism is not in itself an adequate basis for assuming actual dependence. Several additional questions arise. Were the founding Anabaptist leaders in actual contact with representatives of the *Devotio Moderna?* Did they read *Devotio Moderna* literature? Was there any geographical correlation between the two movements?

In spite of remarkable ideological parallelism at vital points, there are practically no direct, institutional connections between the founding Anabaptists and the *Devotio Moderna*. The *Devotio Moderna* institutions (monasteries, brotherhoods, and schools) spread widely by the late fifteenth century into Germany and to a lesser degree into France, but not significantly into the founding area of Anabaptism, North Switzerland.[303] There were no brotherhoods or schools established in Switzerland, but the Windesheim Canons Regular founded St. Martin in 1471 near Zürich, which was their most distant house, and St. Leonard shortly after at Basel.[304] Both appear to have been very small. Erasmus reported that St. Martin's had already disappeared when St. Leonard, which then had only six inmates, was secularized in 1525.[305] There is no evidence that these two monasteries were

Agencies of Mediation   261

significantly involved in either the Magisterial or Anabaptist reform movements in either place, though they may have made some *Devotio Moderna* literature available through their libraries.

Direct literary connections are also somewhat tenuous. Hyma stresses the widespread dissemination of *Devotio Moderna* literature, especially the *Imitation*,[306] and asserts that the Anabaptists were familiar with the *Imitation*.[307] This assertion is doubtlessly valid with reference to the later Dutch Anabaptists, but is less certain with reference to the Swiss founders; he gives no evidence. The works of Zerbolt were still being published at the end of the fifteenth century,[308] but are not referred to specifically by the Anabaptist founders. The libraries of the Windesheim monasteries, including Meaux where reform broke out early in the sixteenth century, and especially the library of Montaigu at the University of Paris made *Devotio Moderna* literature accessible to some who became formative Anabaptist leaders; but whether any of them actually used these libraries is largely conjecture.

Pourrat analyzes some anonymous collections of books, published in 1498, which are remarkably akin to the *Imitation of Christ*.[309] This suggests that by the end of the fifteenth century, *Devotio Moderna* ideas were fairly widespread and not confined strictly to its own institutions and writers. Post supports this idea by suggesting that the *Devotio Moderna* "may indeed have propagated the *contemptus Mundi* over too wide a field, permeating religious life with a pessimism against which the optimism of the Renaissance and the Evangelical freedom of the Reformation came as a reaction."[310]

According to Seguy, the theme of at least one passage in Menno Simons is exactly the same as the first paragraph of the *Imitation*.[311] But since Menno does not represent the initial Anabaptism, this contact does not indicate formative influence. Similarly, even if Melchior Hofmann derived his unique incarnation doctrine from the Brethren, this too only represents a later and subsidiary addition to the established Anabaptist synthesis.[312]

Hyma suggests that though Anabaptism was born in Zürich, it expanded rapidly and endured in the Netherlands. He asserts that "before the year 1566, the majority of Protestants in the Low Countries were Anabaptists," and the reason he gives is "that the Dutch people had been strongly affected by the Brethren of the Common Life."[313] Kühler also maintains that the Brethren of the Common Life prepared the soil for Anabaptism in Holland.[314] Nevertheless, the

German Mennonite historian, Christian Neff, admits that institutionally there is "no evidence of any connection with the Anabaptist brotherhood."[315] Some early Dutch Anabaptist leaders apparently came out of the pre-Reformation "Chambers of Rhetoric" but these local, lay, and sometimes reform groups are not institutionally and directly related to the *Devotio Moderna* either.[316] Moreover, as noted before, even if there was some direct contact between the *Devotio Moderna* and the Dutch Anabaptists, this represents influence only on a later variation of the original Swiss Anabaptism.

Though direct connection by the institutions and literature of the *Devotio Moderna* with the founders of Evangelical Anabaptism seem negligible, there are some other most significant, though more indirect, channels of influence. One of the more tentative and indirect possibilities is between Gabriel Biel, the "Brethren" professor and preacher of the University of Tübingen (1484-92), and Balthasar Hubmaier, a founding theologian of the Anabaptists who also spent some time on the faculty at the University of Tübingen. The influence of Biel at Tübingen was substantial and enduring, having established near the university a Brethren dormitory in which Wendel Steinbach, a disciple of Biel, became the subsequent adviser and editor of Biel's lectures.[317] Even so, any suggestion of a relationship between Biel's piety and Hubmaier is at best circumstantial. Biel was also a nominalist theologian; Hubmaier had a similar educational background. Both Biel and Hubmaier found their piety and theology compatible with the new humanism.[318] Biel had been a famous pulpit orator and cathedral preacher; so also was Hubmaier.

It is difficult to assume, in such an environment and with such theological affinity, that the earlier pulpit master with his "Brethren" piety did not have some influence on Hubmaier's religious development. However, Hubmaier himself limits this influence. Biel, the nominalist, would seem to be included to some degree in Hubmaier's criticism of his education at Tübingen. Hubmaier refers later to Thomas Aquinas, Scotus, and Occam, as "pretentious wits" and propagators of "chaff and bran" in that "they did not recognize decrees, decretals, and legends as false substitutes for the authority of pure Scripture."[319]

While Post has challenged any notion that the *Devotio Moderna*, per se, was directly involved in the emergence toward the end of the fifteenth century of northern humanism, he is not able to erase the fact of considerable affinity. *Devotio Moderna* piety found itself sufficiently compatible with numerous aspects of humanism as a scholarly technique that many whose religious understanding was framed by the *Devotio Moderna* also became reform-oriented, Christian humanists.[320] The evidence still seems to indicate that this was a major factor in creating a distinctive and somewhat homogeneous group, which is often designated as Christian humanism, within northern humanism. That the same combination is also found among many of the founding leaders of Anabaptism, many of whom, such as Grebel, Manz, Reublin, Hubmaier, Denck, and others, had some humanist training or showed considerable affinity with Christian "humanism," is also well documented.[321]

Of particular importance is the influence of the *Devotio Moderna* on the development of Fabrian Christian humanism (or Fabrian Evangelicalism) in Paris and Meaux, and through it to the Anabaptist founder Conrad Grebel and perhaps to Felix Manz. Louise Salley observes that Lefèvre d'Étaples headed a biblical reform movement, first at Paris, then at Meaux, "which bore close resemblance to the one which had its origins in Deventer and Windesheim."[322] She goes on to enumerate many connections: the tie between Lefèvre and Nicolas of Cusa and the Brethren; Lefèvre's contacts with, and spiritual dependency on, the Windesheim Reformers, Mombaier and Standonck; Lefèvre's sojourn at the Brethren of the Common Life house at Cologne in 1509; his reading and publishing of *Devotio Moderna* literature; and his involvement in the Windesheim reform which came to the Abbey St. Germain-de-Près in 1513 (the year after Lefèvre published his notable and evangelical *Commentaries on the Epistles of St. Paul*) through a number of his young disciples who came to live there, including "Vatable, Budé, Roussel, Farel, Clichtove, D'Arande, Cop, Poncher and Petit."[323]

With extensive documentation, Salley demonstrates that the Fabrian evangelical reform movement in France was closer to the *Devotio Moderna* than to Lutheran Protestantism. But, as with so many historians, she ignores the possibility of parallelism with Anabaptist Protestantism. Again, one observes, that many of the very points of difference from Luther, and of closeness to the *Devotio Moderna*, parallel closely Anabaptist perspectives and concerns. For example, Salley develops six areas at the core of Fabrianism which have close affinity with *Devotio Moderna* and are somewhat different from Luther. Each of these areas can be shown readily to be very close to the Anabaptist pattern.

In common with the whole Reformation there is Lefèvre's strong emphasis on biblical authority, on the gospel as the essential core of faith, on reform according to the gospel, and therefore the necessity of Scriptures for the people in the vernacular. But Lefèvre's additional contentions, that the gospel is the "rule of Christ" and that the Scriptures must be interpreted by the humble, penitent, spiritual heart, are distinctly both *Devotio Moderna* and Anabaptist concepts.[324]

Salley also claims that basic to the whole body of Lefèvre's teaching is the general Reformation doctrine of justification by grace through repentance and inner, personal faith. But again, uniquely common to the *Devotio Moderna* and the Anabaptists, Lefèvre accents repentance and also insists that faith must lead to, and be evidenced and sustained by Christlike conduct and good works. Justification is not separated completely from an ongoing sanctification, nor faith from works. Also, in Anabaptist, not Lutheran, terms Lefèvre insists that God "desires that all be saved," that grace is potentially a universal free gift, but He does not force His grace on those who resist. He gives it only to those who indicate that they are "ready to receive His teachings." It is because response is free that few are actually saved; the number of the elect remains small.[325]

The "imitation of Christ" motif is strong in Lefèvre, as in the *Devotio Moderna* and the Anabaptists. While works done in imitation of Christ do not justify, they are part of a necessary, willing cooperation with the Holy Spirit which is essential to the ongoing of justification. Truly pious and Christian works are done out of love for Christ and from the inner desire to imitate Him. The "imitation" motif includes sharing in Christ's suffering and the mortification of fleshly affections.[326]

Accordingly, Lefèvre, as found in the *Devotio Moderna* and the Anabaptists, stressed separation from the world but not complete withdrawal. Concerning secular learning, as a Christian "humanist" he writes: "It is better for you to go into eternal life ignorant than gifted in doctrine and learning, to be sent to eternal damnation." Again, he adds: "Follow Christian teachings, not those of Plato."[327] The true Christian was also expected to develop a deep inner contempt and disdain for the world and its pleasures, for its riches and its honors.[328]

Even Lefèvre's mystical elements, including the ascent of the soul to God through purification from sin, illumination by the Word, and perfection through the Holy Spirit, have some Anabaptist equivalents. His emphasis on ultimate perfection as a mystical union with God is close to some writers in the *Devotio Moderna* but is somewhat stronger than in others; similarly it is close to the South German branch of Anabaptism but stronger than in the Swiss Anabaptists.[329]

Finally, there is in Lefèvre, and in the *Devotio Moderna* and the Anabaptists, a common distaste for nonbiblical religious externalities and empty formalism. Lefèvre warns against confusing the doctrines of Christ, from the Word, with "human traditions." His intention was to return to a simpler, purer form of worship based on a more literal interpretation of the Scriptures.[330]

Even the theological grounds on which Lefèvre, and Bishop Briconnet, initially rejected Luther sound very Anabaptist; that is, Luther's exaggeration of divine sovereignty or election and of Christian liberty. Lefèvre believed that both of these weakened human responsibility and led to immorality.[331]

Lefèvre's reform Evangelicalism derived in part from the *Devotio Moderna* appears to have influenced many young, humanist-trained scholars and thus also must be considered a significant contributor to the development of that larger movement which has been designated northern "Christian humanism." Lefèvre and Erasmus were on intimate terms, except for one brief interlude of coolness, due to a difference of opinion on a minor issue. Their two circles of influence overlapped constantly. Lefèvre dedicated a work to Gilles of Delft, a pupil of Erasmus; he designated Jacques Fabri who was editor of the poetry of Alexander Hegius and Henri Glarean, both friends of Erasmus, as his close friends also; and he carried on friendly correspondence with Erasmus' associates, Henri Agrippa, Hummelberg, Wolfgang Capito, and Beatus Rhenanus. Erasmus approved of Lefèvre's *Commentaries* by writing, on August 22, 1516: "Our friend Jacques Lefèvre d'Étaples has done quite recently for St. Paul what I have done for the entire New Testament." When Lefèvre came under attack by the theologians of the Sorbonne, Erasmus came to his defense.[332] Thus Fabrian Evangelicalism with its roots in the *Devotio Moderna*, through its close alliance with Erasmian Christian humanism which is turn encompassed many early Anabaptist leaders, becomes indirectly an agency for mediating the ascetic-reform tradition of the *Devotio Moderna* to the Anabaptists.

In one important instance, this mediation by the Lefèvre circle becomes direct. Conrad Grebel, a founding father of Anabaptism, had direct contact with the Lefèvre circle while he was studying in Paris.[333] That this initial contact with the *Devotio Moderna* through Fabrianism by Grebel was probably prior to his religious (ascetic) "conversion," and that his surviving correspondence reveals accordingly no immediate effect or influence, does not nullify its potential when religious concerns were awakened later. There is even something of a common pattern of religious development and awakening in the lives of Lefèvre, Erasmus, and Grebel. All three were exposed, though in varying ways, to the piety and reform aspirations of the *Devotio Moderna*; all three went through an early stage of devotion, almost exclusively, to secular or classical humanism; in all three it was followed by a religious "conversion" to such a degree that all else, even humanist interests, became subordinate to Christian pursuits, Christian reform, and the advancement of piety. Humanism becomes a tool only. Christian discipleship is the desired goal. In each, the resultant concept of Christianity and reform has much in common with the *Devotio Moderna*.

Erasmianism

Finally, the most likely and strongest agent for the mediation of the *Devotio Moderna* type, ascetic tradition to Anabaptism is none other than Erasmus himself. Such a suggestion raises a problem which, for detailed investigation, is beyond the immediate scope of this work; namely, the degree to which Erasmian Christianity is rooted in the *Devotio Moderna*. It must suffice to note that the weight of contemporary scholarly opinion seems to support such a relationship, but the issue is complicated and awaits more thorough analysis.

There is no question of Erasmus' early association and some schooling with the Brethren, followed by a sojourn in the Windesheim reformed monastery at Steyn. By residing at the College of Montaigu, even his university studies at Paris continued that association.[334] But a division of opinion arises over the degree to which Erasmus turned away from the ideals of the *Devotio Moderna* when he chose not to be academically or physically bound within the institutions of the *Devotio Moderna*.[335] Salley presents convincing evidence that in spite of his reaction against corrupt monasticism and initial displeasure with the intellectual limitations of the schooling and teachers of the *Devotio Moderna*, Erasmus maintained a positive attitude toward the religious reforming goals and efforts of the *Devotio Moderna*; for example, his fostering of the reforms in France of Mombaier and his sympathy and support for the reform circle of Lefèvre.[336]

Critics of Erasmus' Catholic orthodoxy have usually tended to portray Erasmus as primarily a moralistic humanitarian and a rational secularist whose concerns and motivations were largely divorced from orthodox Christianity, as a classicist more than a Christian. Concomitantly, these historians usually weaken Erasmus' dependency on the *Devotio Moderna* and strengthen his dependency on Neoplatonic influences to account for his religious perspective.[237]

Others go further by not only accepting the stress on Erasmus as the humanist but also by intensifying the contrast by an extreme emphasis on the conservativism and orthodoxy of the *Devotio Moderna*. Consequently, these historians generally mantain also that Erasmus abandoned the *Devotio Moderna* and also seek other sources of inspiration for his religious works, especially for his *Enchiridion* (the *Handbook of the Christian Soldier*). For example, Meissinger's biography suggests that the Erasmus of 1503 repudiated the influence of the *Devotio Moderna*, and ascribes instead the source of Erasmus' inspiration for the *Enchiridon* (1503) to John Vitrier, the guardian of the Franciscan monastery at St. Omar.[338]

In rebuttal, Hyma comments that Meissinger was not sufficiently familiar with the *Devotio Moderna* to make such a judgment.[339] Also, Meissinger apparently was not aware of the ties between the Franciscans and the *Devotio Moderna*. Telle similarly portrays Erasmus as a rebel against the principles of the *Devotio Moderna* — due to Erasmus' seeming rejection and criticism of monasticism subsequently.[340] But on closer analysis Erasmus' attitude is not inconsistent with the *Devotio Moderna*. It too was ambivalent on the subject, encouraging monastic observantism as one kind of reform while also both criticizing monastic abuses and, through the Brethren, maintaining that the highest Christian piety was possible apart from monastic institutions. Thus Erasmus could comment both that:

> Bertha was beautiful and rich and devout. Why didn't she enter a convent? It would have been more prudent, I admit, but in my opinion it is far more meritorious to lead a pure and innocent life amidst the seductions of vice, to pass her existence in tranquillity in the midst of the turmoil of the world.[341]

268   Anabaptism and Asceticism

and, in a letter to the nuns of a covent near Canterbury, that "you who have departed from the worldly life have already here upon earth a heavenly life, as you withdraw yourselves with Christ your Bridegroom." In his *Catechism* he wrote: "The chaste married life is something dignified, but far more dignified is continuous chastity, if spontaneous and freely undertaken."[342] None of this indicates any real abandonment of *Devotio Moderna* principles.

Post has written one of the most recent criticisms of Erasmus as an exponent of the piety of the *Devotio Moderna*.[343] He bases his first objection on the technicality that though Erasmus received his early education at St. Lebwin's at Deventer, the school was not actually run by the Brethren of the Common Life at that time. However, Post cannot deny the presence of some influence by the Brethren of the Common Life, especially through Alexander Hegius and through the pastoral guidance of the Brethren "chaplains."

Second, *De Contemptu Mundi* (1488), the product of Erasmus' monastery years, has a similar style, admits Post, to the *Imitation of Christ*; but, he contends, since there was available much non-*Devotio Moderna* literature of the same style and theme, this does not prove dependence on or influence from the *Devotio Moderna* — a rather weak evasion when one remembers both that Erasmus was then part of a monastic brotherhood espousing *Devotio Moderna* reforms and that he maintained a close friendship afterward with the Windesheimer, Cornelius Aurelius, and continued interest in the Windesheim reforms in Paris.

Third, Post argues that, in part, the *De Contemptu Mundi* advocates the monastic life for typically humanist reasons, more for its peace, liberty, pleasure, and eternal assurances than as a means of service for Christ. This can be expected, however, since Erasmus was still in the early flush of his humanist pursuits and he had not yet experienced his own "conversion," only after which, according to his own testimony, he gave the cause of Christ and the service and imitation of Christ priority over humanist pursuits and motivations, as found in the *Enchiridion* of 1503. The wonder is that he retained as much of the ascetic idealism as he did during his "worldly" stage (1493-1499). Furthermore, the last chapter of *De Contemptu Mundi*, added in 1523, clearly reasserts the validity of the ascetic principles though espousing the "Brethren" type expression of them, that is, ascetic virtues practiced "in the world."

Finally, Post seems to support Huizinga's view that Erasmus'

"Philosophy of Christ," developed after *De Contemptu Mundi* of 1488, also owed little to the *Devotio Moderna* but was rather the product of the addition, after his trip to England in 1499-1500, of Ficino's philosophy and Colet's piety to his own basic humanist interests.³⁴⁴ Again Erasmus remains primarily the humanist and only secondarily the Christian. But this runs counter both to Erasmus' own evaluation of his change of interest, and to similar changes induced by Erasmus in others who through contact with him were influenced toward Christian reform.

There is little to indicate that Erasmus took on a whole new pattern of religious ideas from Colet. Rather, it seems that he was influenced toward a religious reawakening which reactivated a faith latent within him. The change was largely a matter of priorities, a transfer of primacy of interest from secular to religious pursuits by making his humanist philological techniques and interests serve the Christian ideals and principles which were well rooted already in Erasmus, and more akin to the *Devotio Moderna* than to Ficino. Of course, there were several points, such as the inwardness and personalness of religious experience and the priority of Christian antiquity, which Erasmus, Ficino, and the *Devotio Moderna* held in common; the difference was a matter of degree and overall pattern. One must also note that Post's attack on Paul Mestwerdt, for supporting a relationship between the *Devotio Moderna* and Erasmian humanism, shows no knowledge of Kohl's subsequent treatment of the subject, which carries forward and confirms much of Mestwerdt.³⁴⁵

In contrast to those who minimize *Devotio Moderna*'s influence on Erasmus, a large and growing number of scholars, including C. Thompson, J. Dolan, L. Bouyer, J. Etienne, A. Auer, and K. Oelrich, assert both affinity with the *Devotio Moderna* and a basic Christian orthodoxy for Erasmus.³⁴⁶ For example, Thompson asserts: "In basic conceptions of Christianity there is a significant affinity between his habitual outlook and that of the Brethren of the Common Life."³⁴⁷ He contends that even Erasmus' so-called humanist views on virtuous pagans were carefully framed so as not to depart from earlier, accepted medieval Christian judgments; they were not peculiarly "Renaissance."³⁴⁸ In addition, Dolan maintains that Erasmus' religious perspective was not only indebted to the "Brethren" directly but also, and through their influence, to the early fathers, and thus Dolan also questions the viewpoint that Erasmus was primarily motivated by humanistic classicism. Moreover, claims Dolan, it was more the combined influence of the Brethren and the fathers than humanism that caused him to develop a reform-oriented program which was in reaction against sixteenth century, institutional Catholicism but not against orthodox Christianity as defined biblically, patristically, and by the great creeds.[349]

Thus, the combination of Erasmus' initial contacts within the *Devotio Moderna*, evidence of his continuing sympathy toward those espousing its ideals, and the contents of his own religious writings represents a body of strong and harmonious evidence affirming Erasmus' retention of the ideals of the *Devotio Moderna*. Many scholars affirm that after his "conversion," the faith that reasserts itself in Erasmus clearly accords with and contains the main principles of the *Devotio Moderna*, especially of the "Brethren." Even his moments of reaction against asceticism, especially before his own interests in religion became ascendant in his life, were directed primarily against monastic legalism and its intellectual mediocrity and constrictions. Accordingly, the assertion by the Anabaptist scholar, von Muralt, that "through Erasmus has been transmitted to the Anabaptist leaders the fundamentals of an older movement of piety, the *Devotio Moderna*,"[350] becomes both plausible and most significant.

In recent years, there has been developing a growing body of historical literature relating Erasmus to the emergence of Anabaptism. Von Muralt, as quoted in the previous paragraph, and others,[351] strongly assert, while Bender tries to minimize, Erasmian origins for Anabaptism. This difference relates directly to the previous problem of Erasmus and the *Devotio Moderna* and to the variations of interpretation regarding the nature of Erasmian Christian "humanism," not to disagreement over the nature of Anabaptism. As a specialist in Anabaptist studies, Bender simply cannot conceive of a secular humanistic basis, which he assumes to be dominant in Erasmus, for the birth of Anabaptism. Kreider also, though not as much as Bender, concludes that Anabaptism and humanism are quite distinct. Several of the major Anabaptist leaders, including Pilgram Marpeck, Menno Simons, and even Conrad Grebel, Kreider demonstrates, were not humanists nor even profoundly influenced by humanism; the major exception being Hans Denck.[352] But again in this analysis Kreider fails to distinguish adequately between those elements in the Christian "humanism" of Erasmus which are rooted in the *Devotio Moderna*, making his "humanism" somewhat unique, and humanism in general. Therefore he fails to see adequately the possibilities for Erasmus'

Agencies of Mediation   271

influence on formative Anabaptism, even though Anabaptism and secular humanism are quite distinct.

More recently, now treating Erasmus as a Christian reformer in his own right, based on his religious writings, and not just as a more or less variant representative of northern humanism, the trend of historical scholarship is much stronger in favor of a substantial, significant, and formative relationship between Erasmus and the Anabaptists. George Williams recognizes Erasmus as the "patron" of the Radical Reformation; though, he suggests, more directly related to the "Evangelical Rationalist" (the Unitarian) branch than to Anabaptism. This latter point Dolan would doubtlessly reject.[353] An article by Thor Hall emphasizes the influence of Erasmus on Denck and Hubmaier — especially on the questions of grace and free will.[354] He shows that Erasmus' criticism of Luther was based on biblical and thoroughly Christian concerns, not humanistic.[355] Heinhold Fast maintains that the first Anabaptists were largely dependent on Luther, Zwingli, and Erasmus.[356] However, the points of similarity with Luther which he uses are from the very early writings of Luther (1517-21), and are all found also, and even earlier, in Erasmus; that is, the Anabaptists seem to incorporate those aspects of early Luther and Zwingli which are Erasmian! Fast, because he accepts Bender's theory of little direct influence by Erasmianism on Grebel, makes Zwingli almost the exclusive mediator of Erasmian ideas to those who later formed Anabaptism. He also makes the early Zwingli somewhat more consistently Erasmian, and thus more Anabaptist than he was, and provides no basis to account for why only one part of Zwingli's circle consistently (mis)interpreted him and his reform in exclusively Erasmian terms.

Hillerbrand also finds considerable Luther-Zwingli influence in the initial formulations of Anabaptism; but, as with Fast, the points in common which he enumerates are those in Luther or Zwingli which were not uniquely Lutheran or Reformed but largely and previously presented by Erasmianism too, such as, the necessity of grace in justification, a personalism that led to the priesthood of all believers, the preeminence of Scripture, no music in worship, and a necessary relationship between the inner faith of the recipient and the sacraments. However Hillerbrand correctly observes that in those areas most unique to Anabaptism, such as their concepts of church, baptism, free will, faith evidenced by conduct, and pacifism, where Luther and Zwingli's positions were different than Erasmus', their influence is not strong at all. Therefore the background for these vital and unique matters must be "attributed to additional influences."[357]

Hillerbrand suggests that these additional influences came mostly from Carlstadt, Thomas Müntzer, and Erasmus. However, again those specific influences which he then attributes to Carlstadt and Müntzer either do not involve directly the most vital motifs of Anabaptist ideology, or are compared only in broad, indecisive terms; for example, Müntzer's "Bund" and the Swiss Brethren "Brotherhood-Church" are really quite different, unless the comparison avoids details and is limited to broad generalities.

Neither does Hillerbrand prove that the influences ascribed to Carlstadt and Müntzer came to the Anabaptists either first or exclusively from Carlstadt and Müntzer. Almost every one of the motifs which Hillerbrand isolates as paralleling Carlstadt and Müntzer were also implicit (and often explicit) in Erasmus much earlier. Hillerbrand admits that, with one or two minor exceptions, Müntzer's language is "conspicuously absent" from formative Swiss Anabaptist works.[358] At best Müntzer, it seems, only confirmed and encouraged patterns and concepts to which the Anabaptists were already predisposed, as Grebel's letter to Thomas Müntzer strongly indicates. The strongest influence again seems to be Erasmianism. Hillerbrand recognizes it as "most prominent" and "striking," and especially strong in the most distinctive areas of Anabaptist ideology.[359]

In his published, inaugural address at the University of Amsterdam, upon his acceptance of the professorship in Anabaptist history, Irvin B. Horst promises a program of further investigation into this whole subject of Anabaptist-Erasmian relationships.[360] While acknowledging some areas of disparity between Erasmus and the Anabaptists, Horst maintains that "in regard to religious life there was a door between them that was open much further than between the Anabaptists and the Reformers."[361] The uniqueness of this door was not their common awareness of the *need* of reform in the church, this they had in common with Luther and Zwingli and others, but rather "the Anabaptists had much more in common with Erasmus as to *how* this was to be done. . . ."[362] The Catholic scholar, John P. Dolan, in his review of Horst's booklet, goes even further than Horst on several points. He suggests that the Anabaptists more than any other group reflect and promote Erasmus' most essential ideals, and that the Anabaptists' development of religious liberty, free church membership, and even separation of church and state "germinated in no small way in the spiritualism of Erasmus."[363]

Thus, as with the problem of Erasmus' relationship to the *Devotio Moderna*, so with Erasmus and the Anabaptists there is need for a separate, major, detailed study. What follows here is only a preliminary analysis and reevaluation of his contacts with the Anabaptists and then, a comparison of his views from his pre-1525 religious writings with those concepts already delineated as the most crucial in the Anabaptist synthesis.

There are numerous points of direct contact and numerous indirect avenues of influence between Erasmianism and Anabaptism; several have been mentioned previously in this work. Though some of these contacts are controversial, especially in reference to Grebel, the cumulative evidence is most impressive.

It is known that Conrad Grebel, at about sixteen years of age, attended the University of Basel (the philosophy faculty) for about five months, 1514-15. Here, primarily through the private tutor, Glarean, in whose residence Grebel lived, his interest in humanism developed. Erasmus, already famous, was also in Basel from August 1514 to March 1515 as a guest of the publisher, Froben (Beatus Rhenanus was also present as an associate of Froben), and from that time Glarean became an increasingly close friend and follower of Erasmus. Subsequently Erasmus refers approvingly to Glarean's scholarship and piety.[364] As Ludwig Bauer, a professor at the university, had been led earlier to biblical studies in Paris by Erasmus, so Glarean also testified that "you [Erasmus] taught me to know Christ and not only to know Him but to imitate Him, to honor Him, and to love Him."[365] Erasmus' personal influence was apparently strong — and toward the primacy of a commitment to a personal, reformed, biblical, Christocentric piety. In 1516, Glarean is clearly a convinced Erasmian.[366]

Similarly, the humanistically trained scholar and later also a close friend of Grebel, Oswald Myconius, was also present, teaching school in Basel at this same time; he too became a strong Erasmian sympathizer for several years. Bender notes that "all these men felt themselves engaged in a labor that was to mean a renaissance of Christianity," a "moral reform of Christendom" through the impact of "the gospel sources."[367]

Though some direct contact by Grebel at Glarean's residence with Erasmus and his works seems certain, Grebel's youthfulness, his apparent religious indifference, the shortness of his time at Basel, and the fact that this represents only the beginnings of even Glarean's Erasmianism are used by Bender to argue against significant Erasmian influence on Grebel at this time. Nevertheless, these were formative and impressionable years for Grebel, Erasmus' fame was great, and the negative argument regarding religious influence is largely based on the silence of the few sources. The fact of contact warrants the assumption of at least some latent predisposition in Grebel toward Erasmus and the Erasmian brand of Christianity.

From September 1515 to June 1518, Grebel studied at the University of Vienna, largely under Vadian (Joachim von Watt of St. Gall), professor of rhetoric. In general, the Viennese circle of humanists was largely oriented toward classicism and secular studies and added little to Grebel's religious development, except negatively. Though Grebel developed great respect for and friendship with Vadian, he expressed disappointment in Vienna in comparison to his brief time with Glarean at Basel. Consequently, in 1518 both Vadian and Grebel left Vienna and returned to Switzerland.[368]

Meanwhile, Glarean had taken up teaching at Paris, again as a private tutor with his own residence. Grebel rejoined him and continued his studies in Paris, from October 1518 to June 1520. Lefèvre d'Étaples was also in Paris to the end of 1519, was "esteemed very highly" by Glarean, and often visited at Glarean's residence.[369] Moreover, many of the leading Parisian humanists of 1519-20, such as Glarean, Budé, Lefèvre and Badius, were friends of Erasmus also, and in all of them too, Christian reform of an Erasmian type had become their dominant life-concern.[370] After only three months in Glarean's residence, a personal (not ideological) misunderstanding arose and Grebel left the residence not to return until January 1, 1520, a year later. Since Glarean left Paris in April 1520, only about six months of Grebel's time in Paris was actually in direct contact with him at the residence, and only about three months were spent at the residence while Lefèvre was personally visiting there. Nevertheless, even this limited time would be adequate to reintroduce Grebel to the Erasmian-Glarean-Lefèvre circle of Christian humanists, especially since Grebel's departure from the residence did not mean a break with his former student-friends. Again, Erasmian Christianity seems to be the primary factor in Grebel's religious background.

Even though Erasmian Christianity was probably not yet in a dominant position in Grebel's life, there is some evidence of a growing religious-moral interest during this period. Grebel's student-friend,

Peter Tschudi, mentions the group's interest in some of Luther's writings, which were reaching Paris in 1519.[371] One letter from Paris by Grebel to Vadian, dated January 14, 1520, does suggest a developing religious faith and moral sensitivity. In it, he expresses both moral concern about accepting financial aid from the French king whose income he felt was raised by oppressive taxation of the poor, and his assurance of readiness "to meet Christ" in case of his own death.[372] In 1520, Grebel also read with enthusiasm the Erasmian-type pacifist manuscript, *Philirenum*, written by Myconius.[373]

Though Bender refuses to admit that Grebel's letter indicates a growing Erasmian religious influence, no other alternative is given to account for Grebel's expressed sentiments. As with the earlier contacts at Basel, Bender rejects again the possibility of significant Parisian influence on Grebel's faith on rather subjective grounds, that is, the lack of *specific* allusions to it in Grebel's few letters, and the rather turbulent conditions surrounding Grebel's sojourn in Paris. Actually, Grebel's letters say little about any of his studies; they are much too full of personal matters. The real basis for Bender's de-emphasis on Erasmian influence, in both Basel and Paris, is his suspicion of the quality of Erasmian Christianity and his desire to accent the more Protestant and Zwinglian influences in Grebel which came later.

There is little doubt that, after Grebel's return to Zürich from Paris in 1521, Zwingli personally played a major role in Grebel's religious development. Bender is probably correct that the direct agent of Grebel's "awakening," or conversion, was Zwingli, not Erasmus. Nevertheless, since Zwingli himself was still quite strongly under Erasmian influence, it seems probable that Grebel saw no distinction at that time and that his conversion was to the Erasmianism to which he had been previously predisposed.

Bender designates Zwingli as an Erasmian up to 1522. In 1521 Zwingli invited Erasmus to settle permanently in Zürich, and translated Erasmus' *Querela Pacis* for publication in Zürich; also Dolan claims that Zwingli's first reforming work, *Auswahl und Freiheit der Speisen* shows strong Erasmian influence.[374] However, after Luther's excommunication, Zwingli, also strongly committed to reform, appears to have begun to favor Luther over Erasmus[375] — but the transition was quite slow. In several letters, 1521-22, Grebel referred to Erasmus' visit to Basel and his own and Zwingli's desire and plans to go to him there.[376] Similarly, Grebel's considerable interest in the

276   Anabaptism and Asceticism

church fathers, indicated in several of his letters to Vadian in 1521, is a typically Erasmian type of scholarly interest.

That Grebel only gradually (1521-23) became aware of a possible tension between Luther and Erasmus and that he also resisted such an idea is evident from his letter to Vadian along with which he sent a work (Luther's *Urtayl*) containing Luther's opinions against Erasmus. In the letter he comments that the work was "not published by the desire or consent of Luther."[377] Grebel apparently continued to favor Erasmus over Luther. In September 6, 1523, he sent Vadian a copy of Erasmus' *Spongia*, and in May 1525, in a letter to Andreas Castelberger, he referred to Erasmus' *Annotations on the New Testament* as in his possession, and also to having had some personal contact with Erasmus.[378]

Thus, when Zwingli moved away from Erasmus, under the pressures of Luther's excommunication and teachings, and of local political and religious conditions, Grebel continued to maintain a more Erasmian perspective, though it developed into a more radical Erasmianism; that is, it became more Protestantized. This Protestantization was due primarily to his involvement in Zürich's religious break with Rome which freed the Grebel group from the major institutional limitations of pure Erasmianism and due to an increasing dependence on private, independent Bible studies carried on by him and by his closest associates. The result was an increasing polarization within the Zwinglian reform, and led to the development of a distinct movement within the "Protestant" Reformation: Anabaptism.[379]

Grebel was, of course, not the sole originator of Anabaptism at Zürich. There is evidence that Erasmianism was perhaps also a major factor in the common religious predisposition of some of the other leaders who constituted the Grebel circle. Both Stumpf and Manz, appear to have had a humanistic training in an Erasmian context, in part through Zwingli himself. Reublin also had humanistic training, which was related to Erasmianism, at the University of Freiburg im Breisgau and at Basel. Heinold Fast remarks on the closeness of Castelberger's teachings, as early as 1522, to the *Enchiridion* of Erasmus.[380] Part of the reason for the widespread interest in the Bible among the Swiss people was due to Leo Jud's (a colleague of Zwingli) publication of *Propagandaschriften der Reformation*, which was his translation of Erasmus' *Paraphrases on the New Testament*.[381] Jud also translated and published Erasmus' *Enchiridion* (*Handbook of the Christian Soldier*).[382]

Erasmian influence on other founding Anabaptist leaders (1525-27), outside of Zürich and the Grebel group, is also significant. Balthasar Hubmaier, as discussed earlier, was also educated at the University of Freiburg im Breisgau where Erasmianism was strong. He thought of Erasmus as one of his friends and actually visited him at Basel at least once for advice at a critical point in his religious evolution to Anabaptism.[383] Hans Denck, the South German leader probably baptized by Hubmaier, is presented by Kreider as "thoroughly matured in humanism" and was perhaps even a student of Erasmus while he (Denck) studied at Basel in 1522.[384]

Both Denck's and Hubmaier's important Anabaptist writings on free will (1526 and 1527 respectively) are close to and heavily dependent on Erasmus' *Diatribe*, published in September 1524.[385] Dirk Philips, Menno Simons, and Bernhard Rothman, seminal leaders of Dutch and North German Anabaptism, considered Erasmus as "the great originator of the new order and the restoration of the true church. To Menno Simons, he is 'the very wise and learned Erasmus of Rotterdam,' and the annotations of the Erasmian *Novum Testamentum* along with the paraphrases of the gospels, the Epistles of Paul, and other books are accepted both for erudition and authority and even to throw light on the problem of believer's baptism."[386] The Anabaptists never attacked Erasmus as they did Luther, Zwingli, and Calvin.

Erasmus was not only esteemed by the Anabaptists but, as is evident from his writings, he was also fairly well informed about them. Though requested by Johann Cochlaeus, in January 1528, to write against them,[387] he was one of the few reforming leaders who never did. Rather, as Horst has pointed out, the following year, writing to Archbishop Alfonso Fonseca at Toledo, he includes some commendatory remarks about them.[388] He refers only to the revolutionary kind of "Anabaptism," of Münster (1534-35), in tones of disappointment and disillusionment.[389] As Dolan comments, "It is little wonder that Erasmus was accused of being an Anabaptist."[390]

The following theological comparison, based on Erasmus' religious writings before 1525,[391] is not intended to show simply some rather close parallels between Anabaptism and Erasmus on several random topics. Such would not be significant since one can draw out some similarities between Erasmus and any one of the Reformers. Rather, the topics selected for analysis and comparison are the same as those shown previously to be the most essential to the es-

278   Anabaptism and Asceticism

sence of Anabaptism, and to be the issues that most account for the Anabaptists separating from Luther and Zwingli. They also relate to one another in a single, meaningful pattern. There is no intention of claiming, or demonstrating, exact identification or exact parallelism with Erasmus in every detail, or of reconstructing a full Erasmian theology — rather, only to show that the seeds for most of the Anabaptist distinctives are contained in pre-1525 Erasmus and through him were available to the Anabaptists.

In the introduction to his translation of the *Enchiridion (The Handbook of the Militant Christian)*, Dolan contends that the "grand design" of reform in Erasmus, "to restore all things in Christ," with its strong stress on moral, conductual, and lay-oriented renewal, had a biblical, a redemptive, and an ascetic set of norms underlying it; it cannot be reduced to "basically an ethical humanitarianism."[392] Erasmus is quite clear that his optimism about human powers over evil comes ultimately only through the triumph of Christ, through "participation" in the divine life; all must "be applied and referred to Christ." The goal is more than moralism; it is holiness in Christ without which all are "outside the pale."[393] If Erasmus' objective is thus understood — and this seems to have been the way his Christian associates and friends personally understood him — it is in complete harmony with the reform traditions of Francis and the *Devotio Moderna*. This same "design," for a general renaissance of the church to a purer Christianity with practical applications and on a redemptive basis, appears also to have been part of the goal of the early Zwinglian and of the whole Swiss Evangelical reform movement, at first.[394] And when "church" is given a more ascetic and a less geographic, institutional, and political definition, its realization becomes the very essence of the reform drive of the Swiss Brethren, the Anabaptists.

Also in terms of the nature of the reform, both Erasmus and the Anabaptists agree that while it is built essentially on a vital, inward, and personal faith, nevertheless the inner reality must and will produce an outward expression, or conduct, of a particular kind — an ascetically oriented kind. In both Erasmus and the Anabaptists, as reflections of true inner devotion, the repudiation of such externals as wealth and usury, luxury, ostentatious clothing, intemperance, gaming, dancing, and so on is essentially the same. Erasmus' criticisms of and concern over the lack of moral reform, or the lack of moral fruitage, in much of early Protestantism[395] closely parallel similar protestations by the Anabaptists. The same concern, as discussed earlier, constituted a major factor in the emergence of Anabaptism.

Much of the basic pattern of Anabaptist anthropology and soteriology, which contrasts markedly with the Magisterial Reformers, can be found in Erasmus. He subscribes to the biblical doctrine of the fall and sinfulness of man. But, while recognizing as a result of the fall the lostness, helplessness, sickness, and need of salvation of all mankind, for Erasmus, as in Hubmaier, it is primarily a total fall of the flesh, encompassing the soul, but not of the soul and spirit per se, not a total fall of the "directive faculty [reason]."[396] Right reason is warped and "obscured" by sin but "not extinguished."[397] The will too has lost its prelapsarian freedom and is "worsened . . . so that it could not improve itself by its own natural means" and has become "unproductive of virtuous deeds."[398] Yet the will's freedom is described as only paralyzed, not completely extinct, and some limited capacity for moral responsibility and choice is left, in relation to natural law; but no capacity remains apart from special grace with reference to salvation.[399] Though the Anabaptists did not all express these ideas identically, the basic motifs and concerns are the same. Erasmus' will is not really a "free will" in a classical humanistic sense but rather it is only a morally responsible will and not able to respond to grace until liberated by Christ. As with the Anabaptists, this doctrine is held by Erasmus for the sake of other thoroughly Christian concerns, namely for preserving human motivation for virtue and moral effort and for upholding the justice and holiness of God.[400]

Erasmus' doctrine of grace is also very close to the Anabaptists' especially to Hubmaier's. Salvation requires "special" (or "second" or "extraordinary") grace which is both a forgiving and an aiding or sanctifying grace. Special grace provides both forgiveness of sins and a freeing of the will so as to permit perservance in righteousness even though one's "inherited propensity" to sin is not extirpated; this is not just imputed sanctification nor the advocacy of an absolute actual perfectionism.[401] Such special grace is a necessary, divine gift. It cannot be earned by natural merits, and is available to all, but is not forced on the individual; each must choose to receive it willingly and each one can so choose, and also can refuse.[402] Erasmus states his approval of a theological position that ascribes much to grace and "hardly anything to the free will, though not completely abolishing it."[403] Most of the founding Anabaptists also consistently follow this pattern of grace and freedom, even to the same use of Erasmus' scriptural texts for support.[404]

Erasmus' distinguishing of four varieties of grace, but also recognizing that the last three are essentially only different functionings of the same grace, is also close to the Anabaptists. First there is natural grace or common grace which is corrupted but not extinguished by the Fall, which cannot effect salvation, but which perhaps (Erasmus is indefinite) "can prepare for the reception of grace and can move God to be merciful." Then comes extraordinary or special grace by which "God through mercy moves the undeserving sinner to contrition." Cooperative or sanctifying grace follows and is distinguished as that which "promotes that which is begun." Ultimate or perfecting grace is that which leads "to the final goal" of eternal perfection.[405] He aligns this pattern, later, with the notion that salvation has a beginning, a continuation, and an end and suggests that grace is everything at the beginning of salvation; but he means apparently only that grace "is the first to excite our spirit," since in other statements some cooperation is required at this stage also. Then grace cooperates with human will in a more balanced way for salvation's continuation, and the end is all of grace.

Erasmus, as also the Anabaptists, is somewhat more concerned about the necessity of cooperation with grace — of moral effort after special grace or justification — than he is about free will before, though he insists on nonpassivity in repentance too.[406] He concludes that since "grace" is the "principal cause and will a secondary, since the will is impotent without the principle cause, while grace has sufficient strength by itself . . . man must ascribe his total salvation to divine grace. . . ."[407]

Does the emphasis on repentance in Anabaptism also find rootage in Erasmus? Most assuredly. He writes that repentance, in the sense of personal contrition, must precede the gift of special grace or at least be involved in initiating its saving effectiveness.[408] He describes repentance as a kind of "self-submission" or, using the "baptism" figure in Romans chapter six, as related to a dying to sins; while grace effects the resulting resurrection to newness of life.[409] This does not mean that man has the capacity to repent entirely on his own. Rather, "God through mercy moves the sinner to contrition."[410] Expounding John 6:44, Erasmus comments that even the Father's "drawing" us to Himself (to repentance) is not a forced "drawing"; the cause or "doing" may be all of grace but the "willing" is thus "both grace and human will."[411] The will is not passive; the sinner must repent, at least in the minimal sense of a positive response to grace, or of allowing himself to be led to repentance by grace. Thus, though the will is not capable of full repentance by itself without grace, neither is it compelled.[412]

Faith for Erasmus as for the Anabaptists must be a "heart," not just a "calculated" faith. It comes essentially from the Scriptures and represents the penitent turning in his need, trustingly, completely, and solely to the right source of help, Jesus Christ the Savior.[413] Erasmus understood and explicitly asserts his acceptance of Luther's justification by faith.[414] But he is also quite clear that true faith results in more than a forensic imputation of righteousness; it must also produce active discipleship: including willing obedience, mortification of the flesh, the triumph of the spiritual, and perseverance in the path to a perfection which includes being "crucified to this world."[415] Thus faith is given a broader definition than in Luther, exactly as by the Anabaptists, and produces the same required fruitage; justification can be distinguished but not separated from Christian life and its sanctification.

The concept of regeneration, which is most important to the Anabaptist synthesis,[416] is also found in and is vital to Erasmus. So Dolan comments that the spirit of optimism both in Erasmus and the Swiss Anabaptists is not in human nature but in the possibility of its regeneration through Christ. The purpose of Christ's work is such that men do not have to remain bound and diseased and dominated by evil. Therefore Erasmus wrote: ". . . for what else is this doctrine of Christ, which He called a new regeneration, but a restoring or repairing of our nature which in His first creation was good."[417] It is quite clear from rules four and six in the *Handbook* that, for Erasmus, Christ as the Example first depends on Christ as the Redeemer by whom man is reborn. Therefore, in contrast to classical humanism, the only true nobility consists in being reborn in Christ, in being engrafted into His body, in being made one with God.[418]

Regeneration's beginning seems to correlate with initial justification by faith, but there is also an element of process in it, akin to what is found in Anabaptism. Regeneration effects not only a freeing of the will but a change of nature so that one no longer loves sin.[419] Accordingly, in marked contrast to Luther, but wholly compatible with the Anabaptists, Erasmus writes that "we do not assume that even a justified man is capable of nothing but sin, especially because Christ speaks of rebirth and Paul of a new creation."[420] Regeneration is what removes the invincibility of original sin so that the Christian can keep the divine precepts.[421] Regeneration makes justification actual in outward conduct: a thoroughly and distinctively Anabaptistic contention.

Though Bender has objected to the notion of a close relationship between Anabaptist piety and Erasmianism, yet numerous elements, distinctive to the Anabaptist understanding of the Christian life and piety, can be found in it. Only a few key examples follow:

There is the same overarching concern for personal progress toward divine perfection.[422]

There is the same relationship between faith and works. True faith is a working faith and true faith must evidence itself by godliness of life. Therefore Erasmus writes: "Faith without morals worthy of faith only serves to assure men of damnation,"[423] but he is also clear that works "do not make the Christian."[424]

There is the same definition of the nature of Christian piety and of the expected fruitage of faith. The pattern and example is Jesus Himself; here Erasmus and the Anabaptists are both fully in the "imitation of Christ" tradition.[425] Erasmus maintains the validity of the law of Christ for all true disciples, especially as prescribed in the Sermon on the Mount, and that such is literally observable by them. "Thus," comments Hillerbrand, "he follows the literal injunction against swearing, insisting that Jesus meant to forbid all swearing since He wanted His disciples to be perfect."[426] Not only is the nature of Christian piety defined in terms of the imitation-of-Christ and Sermon-on-the-Mount ethics, but also in terms of a mild asceticism. Erasmus maintains: "There are only two paths open to you. The one, through gratification of the passions, leads to perdition; the other, through mortification of the flesh, leads to life."[427] His mildly ascetic, lay piety includes also a strong emphasis on cross-Christianity and suffering. He declares that "the coat of arms of this [God's] family is the cross, which should be the insignia of all Christians"; he is referring here not to a symbol but to the cross-life.[428]

There is also in Erasmus the same means to, or agencies for, sanctification and piety as in Anabaptism. Cooperation is the key. From the divine or "grace" side, the agencies in Erasmus are primarily the Holy Spirit, "without whose help no man attains salvation" and by whom there is an internalization and spiritualization of values, and the Word, or "divine wisdom," the "inner penetration" of which produces holy life.[429] He writes that the wisdom of God

Agencies of Mediation 283

leads to gentleness and modesty and "gentleness enables you to receive the divine Spirit, for the Spirit rejoices to rest upon a gentle and humble person."[430]

The human ingredients in this synergistic counteraction of evil and progress in sanctification — and he flatly states that "this victory will not come without your own effort and diligence . . ."[431] — include obedience to knowledge, especially from Scripture,[432] prayer,[433] works of piety,[434] a mildly ascetic mortification,[435] self-examination,[436] and striving.[437] The close parallelism with the Anabaptist pattern is unmistakable.

The church is an additional and important element in this synergistic enterprise. It too is redemptive. Both repentance (*poenitentia*) and works of charity (*misericordiae*) are ineffective apart from it. The "keys," in Erasmus' understanding, belong to the church — but by church he does not mean the hierarchy or even the Catholic institution, exclusively, but true Christians "gathered by the Spirit of Christ."[438]

There is the same optimism by both Erasmus and the Anabaptists about the possibility of the success of this synergistic enterprise in this life. Erasmus maintains that in the Christians, "bad inclinations can be overcome and that they do not necessitate sinning."[439] The evil one is a defeated foe, "overthrown" by Christ and so our "ever-present" and "all powerful auxiliary," Christ, "will unquestionably subdue him again in us."[440] He adds:

> Anyone who has failed in this struggle was simply lacking in a will to conquer. . . . If you but listen to His call and do your part you shall be assured of victory for not only will He fight alongside you but His very liberality will be imputed to you as merit.[441]

Later, he concludes that "to say it [godly living] is beyond our capacities is ridiculous . . . Christ has trodden this same path."[442]

Many other examples of parallelism could be added to this section on sanctification and synergism, especially where Erasmus reflects his *Devotio Moderna* heritage. The whole of Rule 2 in his *Handbook* should be read. If it were quoted here, in full, without naming the author, it would probably be misunderstood as an Anabaptist writing; especially such ideas as believing in Christ with one's whole heart, fleeing the world and the flesh pots of Egypt, being crucified to this world to live for Christ, suffering with Christ, dying to sin as the only

284 Anabaptism and Asceticism

way of salvation, and comments such as: "All of us must aim for this goal with all our efforts. The honest decision to become a Christian implies that one has already chosen the better part of Christianity [that is, the ascetic way]." He flatly asserts that "if you are in the world you are not in Christ"; if you are absorbed in ambition, pleasure, and lust, "then I doubt if you are even a Christian. Christ spoke indifferently [indiscriminately] to all men, that whoever would not take up His cross and follow Him would not and could not be His disciple."[443]

Does Erasmus significantly foreshadow or contribute to the development of the Anabaptist doctrine of the believers' church? If the real issue in the Grebel-Zwingli breach relates to purging the membership of the church, and to the belief that contemporary, baptized society was made up partially of non-Christians who took offense at obedience to the Word, not primarily to the speed of the reform and to the role of the magistracy,[444] then one must inquire whether the predominance given to this concern by the Grebel circle also has roots in Erasmus. There is substantial affirmative evidence.

In Erasmus there is a strong ethical dualism between the church and the world, similar to the two-kingdom concept so central to Anabaptism.[445] Erasmus' high and visible conductual standards required of the true Christian make discernible a clear distinction between the members of each "kingdom."[446] That is, the true church should be made up of cross-bearing, obedient disciples, who are distinguishable by their separation from the world and worldly conduct, and by their personal, voluntary belief. He writes that the true church is composed of those "who agree in the faith of the gospel, who worship one God the Father, who put their whole confidence in the Son, who are guided by the same Spirit of Him; from whose fellowship He is cut off that commits a deadly sin."[447]

He also makes most clear his position that "if you are in the world you are not in Christ," and adds, of one indulging in worldly conduct, "I doubt if you are even a Christian."[448] He reiterates, "Unless I see the fruits of the Spirit I shall not believe that you are in the Spirit."[449] He describes the world as composed of those who are "enemies of the faith and of the cross of the Christ. It is from this world that Christ separated not only His apostles but all who would be worthy of Him."[450] Thus it is a body of true believers or true Christians discernible from the world by conduct and spirit that constitutes the true church in Erasmus.[451] — At least he could be understood to mean this. He also describes this church as "gathered by the Spirit of Christ."[452] More Anabaptistic-sounding statements are hard to imagine!

For Erasmus, the true church operates also as a distinguishable fellowship or brotherhood under the "rule" or discipline of the gospel.[453] Accordingly he advocates that the authentic church is typified by brotherly peace and charity.[454] The two best known pamphlets by Erasmus against carnal warfare and violence were published in German in Switzerland: *Dulce bellum inexpertis* in 1519 in Basel, and *Querela Pacis* in 1521 in Zürich, and were doubtlessly well known to the Zürich Anabaptists. Fast suggests that on the point of pacifism or nonviolence "there is greater agreement between the Anabaptists and Erasmus than on any other. For here Erasmus' thought is derived from the Bible and is Christocentric. . . ."[455] While Erasmus is not always sure whether his principle of pacifism is absolute, in all circumstances,[456] neither is the absolutism of Grebel and Sattler unanimously accepted among all the earliest Anabaptists, and it is also tempered in practice in Hubmaier.[457] Certainly, in accord with all Evangelical Anabaptists, Erasmus rejected all violence and force in reference to religion; the Christian way he asserts is to persuade.[458] Also, as with the Anabaptists, Erasmian Christan nonviolence is based on the combination of taking the Sermon on the Mount seriously, the concept of the suffering church, and the belief that peace is necessary for piety.[459]

Just as the authentic church in Erasmus upholds nonviolence, so it also practices brotherly concern and the stewardship of possessions. In typically Anabaptistic fashion he asserts that the Christian has no private possessions, and is obliged by love to share that which he has:

> You believe that only to monks was property forbidden and poverty imposed? You have erred, for it pertains to all Christians. The law punishes you if you take unto yourself what belongs to another. It does not punish you if you take your possessions away from a needy brother. Yet, even so, Christ will punish you.[460]

Again, "Christian charity recognizes no [private] property."[461] The advocacy of stewardship and the rejection of lust for wealth and things, shown by sharing and the absence of avarice, represents in Erasmus a kind of spiritualization of the virtue, or vow, of poverty; the persons' heart is thus possessed by poverty.[462] He also makes

286 Anabaptism and Asceticism

the stewardship and sharing of possessions necessary for the right understanding of, and spiritual participation in, the sacrifice of the mass. The stewardship of goods becomes a vital part of his concept of the nature of the fellowship of the church.[463]

Erasmus is hesitant in his approval of Christians accepting governmental office, and again, as with pacifism, the Anabaptist position is correspondingly divided. Erasmus approves only if one gives prior accountability for all actions to Christ and still conforms oneself to Him in all things, "even to the loss of your life."[464] His conditions, which are the primary consideration, almost negate (and for some Anabaptist interpreters, it did) his original approval of holding offices, in the worldly, political kingdom.

The true church in Erasmus is not only distinguishable in that it functions as a brotherhood on kingdom principles, but it also has a necessary, external, corporate identity. This identity, the one Catholic church, is manifest as many "churches" and is not equated with the Roman Catholic Church alone.[465] Erasmus is clear that the keys have not been entrusted to the Papacy but to the church of believers.[466] As with the earliest Anabaptists, especially the Swiss, where much is made of it, Erasmus asserts in a lengthy exposition the importance of the practice of discipline according to Matthew 18, and is clearly referring to "church" in its local, congregational aspect.[467] Bainton concludes that in Erasmus' exposition of Matthew 18 on discipline, Erasmus calls "for a complete separation of church and state. Caesar has nothing to do with the case. The ban is the only penalty and it is to be imposed or remitted solely by the congregation."[468]

Finally, and again in thoroughly Anabaptistic fashion, Erasmus maintains that the true church is small. In the *Enchiridion* (the *Handbook*), he reminds his readers that the path of life is one "upon which few men walk" and again, later, he reiterates that "the number of those whose hearts are possessed by Christian simplicity, poverty, and truth will always be small . . . and to them alone belongs the kingdom of God."[469]

Erasmus' views on the sacraments are rather ambiguous; much is not Anabaptistic, but some vital points are. In general, his emphasis is on the internal and spiritual aspects over the external, without completely abandoning the usefulness of the latter as a starting point, and on a biblical understanding and spiritual reception of them.[470] Therefore images, singing, and even the sacraments are not objectively conveyers of grace.[471] He also distinguishes biblically-based sacraments from those founded on church tradition, such as the confessional, without actually abandoning the latter.[472] While these points may be semi-Protestant, they are not uniquely Anabaptist. However, some other of his pre-1525 interpretations of baptism and the Lord's Supper are significantly close to distinctively Anabaptist doctrines.

Hillerbrand notes that the implications of Erasmus' insistence that, to be valid, baptism must be accompanied by true discipleship helped prepare the way for the Anabaptist position.[473] There are several other important facets of Anabaptist baptism also found in Erasmus, particularly the ascetic element in his understanding of its meaning. He refers to true Christians as those who died once and for all to this world and who "through baptism have been buried with Christ, and after the mortification of the flesh live henceforth with the Spirit of Jesus into whose body they have been ingrafted, through faith."[474]

The ascetic factor combines also with the idea of baptism as covenant; again an Anabaptist pattern. For Erasmus, as with the Swiss Anabaptists, baptism is a pledge to serve, "to take up arms in this struggle against vice." Any peace treaty with evil "violates the agreement made with God in baptism."[475] Note also how Erasmus relates this baptismal pledge to the monastic vow:

> I will grant that to die to sin is a difficult accomplishment. Even few monks ever actually achieve this [Yet] . . . when you were baptized you took an oath to do just that . . . there is no vow . . . more religious and sacred than this.[476]

As with the Anabaptists, Erasmus in his comments on Romans 6 also ties repentance and forgiveness of sins closely to baptism, but scornfully asks "do you really think that the ceremony of itself makes you a Christian?" Nothing happens "unless you cleanse the inner filth of your mind."[477]

Bainton refers to Erasmus as "radical" for his advocacy of a second baptism. Since, unlike the Anabaptists, Erasmus never totally repudiated the external rite of infant baptism, his stress on personal involvement and spiritual participation if any external rite is to be effective forces him to advocate a rebaptism or second baptism in such cases. His second baptism then becomes very close in meaning to Anabaptist baptism. At the age of puberty, he suggests, the rite of baptism should be solemnly, personally, and publically reenacted, after thorough instruction relative to the meaning of the baptismal vow. He writes:

> We actually put on plays in our churches, showing the resurrection, the ascension, the descent of the Spirit and these performances I do not wholly discountenance, but how much more glorious a spectacle to hear the voices of so many youths dedicating themselves to Christ, so many initiates pronouncing their vows, renouncing the world, abjuring Satan; to see new Christians bearing the mark of the Lord of their foreheads, to behold the great crowd of candidates coming up from the sacred laver, to hear the voices of the multitude acclaiming the beginners in Christ! . . . If this were done, we should not have so many at the age of fifty who do not know what was vowed in baptism. . . . And what is worse, there are among us priests who have never given any serious thought to what Christianity is all about. . . .[478]

Finally, in reference to Erasmian influence on Anabaptist baptism, Hubmaier actually refers to Erasmus as anticipating his views; quoting Erasmus, on Matthew 28, thus:
After you have taught the nations these things

> [the articles of faith], and they have believed what you have taught them, and repented of their former life, and are ready henceforth to change their life according to gospel teaching, then dip them in the water in the name of the Father and of the Son and of the Holy Spirit.[479]

In reference to the Lord's Supper, Hillerbrand claims that the views of Erasmus and the Anabaptist Hans Denck are "virtually identical," but he gives no details to support the claim.[480] One significant parallel with Anabaptism, is Erasmus' ascetic interpretation of the Mass. That is, he writes that the death of Christ, "there represented" (at the mass), must also "take place in their [the recipients'] souls" and should render them "dead to the world."[481] Also, part of the right spiritual understanding of the nature of the sacrifice of Christ in the mass is the relating of it to the sharing of the sacrificial life of the church, to the love ethic and brotherhood, and to the cross life in action.[482] Similarly, he describes the Eucharist as signifying the concord of peace and fellowship.[483]

Whether Erasmus also advocated an understanding of the Eucharist as essentially, though not exclusively, a memorial is still controversial. Spitz declares that "Renaudet's assertion that Erasmus wanted the Eucharist returned to a simple commemoration is simply mistaken."[484] But Etienne has reasserted that in Erasmus the rite of the Eucharist "is reduced to the role of pure symbol, thus constituting an inferior level of reality. For Erasmus, the rite is not the means by which and in which I encounter God really and continually; it is but the figuration of this encounter, which I must realize by other means."[485] Dolan adds that in this Erasmus was expressing the *Devotio Moderna* reaction against scholasticism.[486]

Certainly Erasmus made several comments that lend themselves to such an Anabaptist interpretation, as some of his contemporary critics pointed out. For example, in his paraphrase on Matthew's account of the Lord's Supper, he writes: "Jesus instituted this sacred symbol of His death as a perpetual memorial of His immense love."[487] And, as Bainton has pointed out, the text in John's Gospel (John 6:63) that "the flesh profiteth nothing, the spirit gives life," was "particularly congenial to the mind of Erasmus who caused Christ to elaborate, saying, 'My flesh and blood I call My teaching and if this be taken up into your very marrow, you will be one with Me. As a mystical symbol of this union I have left you my flesh and blood, of which none can partake save in the Spirit.' "[488]

Some of the ambiguities and seeming contradictions in Erasmus' views of the sacraments can be reconciled by his principle of the accommodation of the weak — a principle to which Hubmaier also subscribed, briefly. Erasmus grants to the externals, per se, and, to a degree, to traditional interpretations of them a preliminary usefulness for weak, baby Christians; that is, useful if they become steps "that lead to more appropriate means of salvation."[489] Perhaps in the same way that examples from the classics were considered useful by him as conducive to right living.

Lastly, the acceptance of the superiority of biblical norms for religious authority is neither uniquely Erasmian nor Anabaptist; but there are several supplementary facets in Erasmus' hermeneutics which are more distinctive and are also found in Anabaptism. Erasmus notes both this general agreement with the Reformation and also the hermeneutical difference when he comments: "I admit that it is right that the sole authority of Holy Scripture surpasses the voices of all mortals," and then adds: "Our battle concerns the sense of Scripture."[490]

The predominance of the ascetic element comes through repeatedly in Erasmus' hermeneutics — as in Anabaptism. Though Scripture is authoritative, yet it cannot be understood correctly or be effective unless studied with "a heart purified by reverence."[491] While he recognizes paradoxes (not contradictions) in "inspired" Scripture and also its unsystematic nature, that it is not bound by systematic theology or logic, yet he insists that the data on piety, on the "precepts for a morally good life," are clear.[492] Since, in Erasmus, truth and piety are inseparable and since passionate argumentation hinders and destroys piety (ascetically understood), argumentation as a means to understand truth or the Scriptures is rejected by Erasmus.[493] Hubmaier expressed the same idea.

At times, as with the Anabaptists who held to the principle of the necessity of spiritual, almost ascetic, discernment in close relationship to the grammatical sense, Erasmus is willing to depart from a strict, cold literalism in favor of a spiritualized understanding of some passages; and primarily because he thinks such is necessary in order for these passages to contribute to piety;[494] also because he holds to the necessity of spiritual discernment since "the Spirit has His own manner of speaking and His own figures of speech."[495]

Belief in the superiority of the devotional over the intellectual (especially scholastic) approach to Scriptures, though the latter is not without some positive value in combination with the former, is also common to both Erasmus and the Anabaptists.[496] The application of the best scholarly techniques to obtain the best text upon which to base interpretation is important, but interpretation itself is something further. The practical issue of who is the most likely to be a correct interpreter of Scripture is decided by Erasmus on pietistic, not institutional or even theological grounds; that is, he gives priority to those, like the apostles with miraculous powers for good and to those with the "sincerity and simplicity of the apostolic life" — both of which, he claims, in Anabaptistic tones, is lacking in the Lutheran Reformation.[497]

Closely related to the "ascetic" and devotional principle is his application of "Rule 5" in the *Enchiridion*, his longest rule, on the superiority of the internal, invisible, and spiritual over the external, visible, and physical, not only to rites and sacraments but also, to some degree, to Scripture — somewhat akin to Denck's inner and outer Word. Therefore he stresses the "inner penetration of the Word of God" and the prime necessity of "understanding the spiritual worth

Agencies of Mediation 291

it contains" in contrast to the "scholastic method."[498]

The principle of the "non-flat" Bible, or progressive revelation (that the Old Testament must be understood only in subservience to the New Testament), a principle most vital to the Anabaptist synthesis, is also found in Erasmus and in much of the "imitation of Christ" tradition. His rejection, in *Querela Pacis*, of the use of the Old Testament to support vengeance, bloodshed, violence, and war is identical to numerous similar Anabaptist arguments.[499] All must "be applied and referred to Christ."[500]

An interesting and significant point, which is strongly reflected in Anabaptist hermeneutics, especially during its Zürich beginnings (for example, in Grebel's "Letter to Müntzer"), is Erasmus' insistence that "Christ's teaching shall not be mingled with human teaching. The learned give uncertain counsel, for the light of faith does not shine in them."[501]

Even Erasmus' statement that he is willing to submit his own personal interpretations, but not Scripture per se, to the church,[502] is more akin to Anabaptism than the initial impression might indicate, since "church" in Erasmus is not always equatable simply with the Roman hierarchy. If church is interpreted as a brotherhood of believers, his statement is quite compatible with the Anabaptists. Also his way of resolving conflicts in interpretation in the church, especially when occurring among the pious (which he seems to imply actually occurs only rarely with reference to essentials), is by respecting what the Holy Spirit "seemed" to teach the majority of the best (of the fathers) over the centuries, *if* such is also consistent with "the Spirit of the gospels."[503] In the last analysis, the decision seems to be the individual's.

The foregoing section is not intended to be a balanced or integrated summary of all of Erasmus' theology, nor to imply that Erasmus was a secret Anabaptist (though some accused him of it), nor that Anabaptist theology and piety were an exact copy or extension of Erasmus'; there are many differences. Erasmus' adiaphora (suspensive judgment on minor issues) and his willingness to accommodate to human weakness and to the system is in sharp contrast to the dogmatism on minutia and to the strict and exclusive biblicism of the Grebel (Swiss) Anabaptists.

Similarly, Erasmus was less concerned than the Swiss Anabaptists about the externalities of the sacraments. He retains infant baptism though seeming to have destroyed its meaningfulness. His advocacy of an ascetic separation preserved by the use of the ban, locally, was not fully developed and was perhaps an unresolved contradiction with his abhorence of institutional schism. Erasmus' presentation is from within the context of the Roman Church and much of it antedates the Reformation; the Anabaptists' is forged within the Zwinglian Reformation and assumes schism. Erasmus seemed also to integrate into his system more humanistic optimism relative to the powers of human nature apart from special grace (though not redemptively), to take a broader attitude to the heathen, and to allow more value to human learning.

These and other differences increase after 1525 and the elucidation of their subtleties is beyond the scope of this work. What emerges clearly is that almost the whole essential and distinctive core of the Anabaptist synthesis is contained in Erasmus' pre-1525 religious writings and to a much greater degree than in Luther, Zwingli, Carlstadt, or Thomas Müntzer. Furthermore, Erasmus had copious direct and indirect contact with many of the founding leaders of Anabaptism. All of which strongly supports the thesis that the Anabaptists can best be understood as, apart from their own creativity, a radicalization and Protestantization not of the Magisterial Reformation but of the lay-oriented, ascetic reformation of which Erasmus is the principle mediator.

6 SUMMARY AND CONCLUSIONS

Reform Expectations

The Christian ascetic tradition was still profoundly influential in the religious thinking and aspirations of many in Europe at the beginning of the sixteenth century. As a reforming impulse it moved mainly in two directions during the fifteenth century: toward monastic reform by a return to a more faithful and rigorous keeping of the "Rule" of the Order, and toward an internalization and spiritualization of the monastic ideals and their extension to lay society. The latter trend received its principle impetus much earlier from Francis of Assisi (1182-1226), but was maintained in varying degrees by the Tertiaries and in the Brethren of the Common Life, one of laicized asceticism's most influential expressions in the fifteenth century.

None of these lay, ascetic movements, though reformatory, were consciously revolutionary or heretical; but some pre-Protestant principles were inherent or latent in their ideals of reform. Also, there did develop among some notable individual Reformers of the late fifteenth century some indications that their reform expectations were now beginning to involve, even require, more revolutionary characteristics. They anticipated a total reorganization of the whole church before the necessary separation from worldly involvements could be achieved and before the ascetic ideals could be transmitted to, and come to characterize, the whole new and purified church.

294 Anabaptism and Asceticism

A widespread reforming explosion was triggered by Martin Luther in 1517. Most of the existent reforming elements in early sixteenth-century society gave it initial support as an abuse-correcting movement, morally and institutionally, with biblically based norms as the positive corrective, now stimulated by the widespread distribution of the printed Scriptures.

The first major break in the overall movement came about 1520-21 when, under Luther's leadership and writings, the movement took a definitely Protestant stance, that is, a revolutionary or schismatic position. At this point substantial support was lost; a Catholic," nonschismatic reform began to separate itself or become distinct from "Protestant" reform.

Anabaptists as Protestants

Anabaptism did not arise directly out of the medieval Catholic Church, but from within the Reformation movement after 1520-21. This means that Anabaptism was initially allied with those Reformers who were prepared to share in the more revolutionary aspects of a "Protestant" Reformation, including the break with papal primacy, traditional ecclesiastical authority, and the scholastically defined sacramental-sacerdotal system. Even in the years 1521-23, this "Protestant" reform movement of Luther, Zwingli, et al., though now more clearly distinct from those Reformers still loyal to the old church, was still theologically vague on many points. It assumed a general but undefined unity within itself based on common involvements in the basic break with Rome, and especially on the assertion of the alternative primacy of biblical authority. But the years 1523-25 witnessed the disintegration of this assumed unity and the emergence of Anabaptism.

Anabaptism as Distinct from the Magisterial Reformation

Within the "Protestant" Reformation, especially after 1523 when the implications of Luther's strong advocacy of Augustinian-predestinarian theology and of forensic justification and sanctification became clearer, a substantial body of dissent arose. These dissenters held a definition of reformation which in essence was fundamentally different from that of the Magisterial Reformers; it was ascetically oriented and demanded, as the essential fruit of a true reformation, a moral and spiritual purification of the church, a separation of the church from the world. It was an extension of the ideals of the ascetic reform tradition into the "Protestant" camp. Anabaptism arose from within this "Protestant" but dissenting context.

Accordingly, as Ritschl noted, one must not assume that because the earliest Anabaptist leaders, 1523-26, moved from medieval Catholicism to the Reformation of Luther and Zwingli first, and after that to Anabaptism, therefore Anabaptism was a radicalized extension of the genus of the Magisterial Reformation, since the reform aims and theology which are distinctively "Magisterial" only began to clarify in 1523-24. While these potential Anabaptists became reforming "Protestants" first, they were never "Magisterial" Protestants as their futile debates with Zwingli reveal. Though willing to share in the break with Rome and in the promotion of the supremacy of biblical authority (even some Catholic Reformers could agree on the latter), they were committed to a different set of religious assumptions and expectations. The Anabaptist break with Zwingli, and thus with Luther and the whole of Magisterial Protestantism, and their creation of a distinctive and alternative synthesis was relatively complete by January 1525.

Anabaptism as Distinct from Medieval Heresy

There is no evidence to support the notion of significant ties between the formative leadership of Anabaptism and the medieval underground church or heretical sects. Direct contacts are almost totally absent. There is little or no evidence in initial Anabaptist literature to indicate either awareness of or dependency upon any heretical antecedent groups. The attempt to tie the formation of Bernese Anabaptism to the Waldensians has failed, according to Heinold Fast, and significant ties between Moravian Anabaptism and the Bohemian Brethren have been shown by J. K. Zeman to be absent. It is possible that previous heretical tendencies and teachings may have predisposed some areas toward an acceptance of Anabaptism, but such had little influence on the original formation and structuring of the movement.

Almost every distinctive aspect (especially from the Magisterial Reformation) of Anabaptist theology and practice, for which heretical antecedents have been claimed, can equally and more readily be found in the previous medieval, Catholic ascetic tradition.

Anabaptism and the Ascetic Tradition

Most of the issues and the predisposing climate of opinion, which gave rise to Anabaptism and provoked their separation from Magisterial Protestantism are, even in details, closely parallel to some aspects of the medieval ascetic tradition. The central factor in the emergence of Anabaptism is demonstrated as the ascetic concern that the church, visibily and practically, should manifest moral righteousness and holiness of conduct and life, patterned on the imitation of Christ motif, guided by the "Rule of Christ," and explicitly obedient to the law of Christ in the New Testament. An ascetic factor, namely, the pursuit of holiness, also emerges as the fundamental principle in the formulation and structuring of Anabaptism's distinctive theology and in much of its related practices and institutionalization. What results from the total combination of ingredients is a unique movement, a Protestantized, biblical, and ascetic movement, which is a logical continuation into the "Protestant" Reformation of the trend to laicization and internalization of ascetic principles which had already begun within the highly adaptable, Christian ascetic tradition.

Furthermore, the evidence is conclusive that most of the earliest formative Anabaptist leaders were sympathetically acquainted with these laicizing and internalizing elements in the medieval ascetic tradition and that they had considerable direct and indirect contact with them. Several of the early significant Anabaptist leaders were ex-monks, some even ex-Franciscans. But the most influential leaders (Michael Sattler excepted), such as Grebel, Manz, Reublin, Denck, and Hubmaier, were demonstrably and strongly influenced by those aspects of Christian Erasmianism which mediated specifically the basic, lay, ascetic reform principles of the *Devotio Moderna*. To a lesser degree, a moderate, practical, activistic, ascetic tradition was also mediated to Anabaptism through the influence of the *Theologica Germanica* and indirectly (perhaps even directly in Anabaptism's initial urban thrust) through the Franciscan Tertiary movement.

Anabaptism and Interpreting the Reformation

The repeated assertion that early Anabaptism was socially revolutionary and violent and that 1535 (the fiasco of Münster) was the turning point in the history of its doctrinal development, after which Menno Simons led it to a simple, pietistic, and quietistic Christian faith, is completely erroneous since Anabaptism was from its inception related to the advocacy and reemphasis of ascetic, not revolutionary, motifs.

If, as Donald Durnbaugh suggests, a growing body of historical opinion now advocates sixteenth-century Anabaptism as the direct fountainhead of the free church movement, then this study indicates that the whole free church tradition also derives its basic ideals and original impulse from the Christian ascetic tradition and relates more to this branch of the medieval Catholic Church than to the tradition of medieval heresy.

This study also necessitates a reinterpretation and realignment of the principal groups in the Reformation as a whole. It suggests that the main, distinctive religious movements of the era include two extremes in conflict, both highly structured theologically and to a degree institutionally, and both retaining the inclusivistic, sacralist position, the state-church alliance. On one hand there was the scholastic sacramental-sacerdotal system of Roman Catholicism, reasserted and reformed at Trent, on the other, the Protestantized, Augustinian theology of Luther and Calvin. But between these two, and quite distinctive, existed a third genre, an internalizing, personalizing, devotional, laicized, ascetic, and biblical reform movement related to the ideals of Franciscanism and the *Devotio Moderna*. This third movement expressed itself largely through two distinct, but closely related, reforming forces: a moderately ascetic, Catholic reformation, associated largely with Erasmianism, and an ascetic Protestantized version of the same, expressed primarily by Anabaptism. Thus, Anabaptism emerges as a unique, independent Reformation movement, a Protestant adaption of a Christian ascetic tradition, more akin to Erasmus than to Luther, more right-wing than left, more conservative than radical, unless the last term is used with reference to a radical Erasmianism. Whereas, in one sense, Luther's and Calvin's Reformation may be considered a Protestantization of Augustine of Hippo, so Anabaptism is a Protestantization of Francis of Assisi, Gerhard Groote, and, perhaps even more, a Protestantization of Erasmus.

NOTES

1. Introduction

1. They were given other derogatory labels also, such as: fanatics, communists, sectarians, Donatists, and so on. Cf. Leonard Verduin, *The Reformers and Their Stepchildren* (Grand Rapids: Eerdmans, 1964), p. 9.
2. *The Mennonite Encyclopedia* (4 vols.; Scottdale, Pa.: Mennonite Publishing House, 1955-1959). Henceforth referred to as *ME*. Cf., *ME*, II, 752.
3. *ME*, II, 752.
4. *Ibid.*
5. Gottfried Arnold, *Unparteyische Kirchen-und Ketzer-Historie* (1699; 3rd ed.; Schaffhausen, 1740-1742), was probably the first major exception but it had little effect.
6. C. A. Cornelius, *Geschichte des Münsterischen Aufruhrs* (Leipzig, 1855-1860).
7. *ME*, II, 752 (from A. Harnack, *Lehrbuch der Dogmengeschichte*, III [1910], 772).
8. Note especially the publication by the Verein für Reformationsgeschichte of the series, *Quellen zur Geschichte der Täufer*, henceforth designated *QGT*. Cf. *ME*, II, 756, for a list and for references to other similar projects.
9. Ernst Troeltsch, *The Social Teachings of the Christian Churches*, II, trans. O. Wyon (New York: Harper Torch, 1960, German ed., 1911), p. 461.
10. Roland Bainton, *Studies on the Reformation* (New York: Hodder & Stoughton, 1963), pp. 122-126, suggests the following broad, common characteristics: (1) intense ethical concern, (2) separation of church and state, (3) radical primitivism, and (4) to a lesser degree, heightened eschatological consciousness and anti-intellectualism. But not one of these traits, unless very generalized, actually applies *in the same way* to all groups in the Left Wing (for example, separatism [political] falls before Waldshut, Nicolsberg, and Münster; and primitivism for some went back to Jesus but for others, to Abraham, and so on).
11. *Ibid.*
12. George H. Williams, *The Radical Reformation* (Philadelphia: Westminster Press, 1962), p. xxiv.
13. *Ibid.*
14. J. C. Wenger, *Die dritte Reformation* (Kassel: Oncken, 1963). In English, *Even unto Death* (Richmond: John Knox, 1961).
15. Leonard Verduin, *op. cit.*, pp. 11-12.
16. Though H. J. Hillerbrand calls Portestant radicalism "an heterogeneous phenomenon," he still suggests that there were also some "common lines." Cf. Hillerbrand, *The Reformation* (New York: Harper & Row, 1964), p. 214.
17. Also concurring with R. Bainton and G. Williams, for a threefold subdivision, is Robert Friedmann, *Mennonite Piety Through the Centuries* (Goshen, 1949), p. 3. For a historiographical survey of Spiritualism, see *ME*, IV, 597 f.; for Anabaptism see *ME*, II, 751 f.; for Socinianism and Evangelical Rationalism, see *ME*, IV, 565 f.
18. J. C. Wenger, *Even unto Death* (Richmond: John Knox Press), p. 57, maintains Anabaptism's closeness, on doctrinal fundamentals, to Zwingli and to Protestant theology.
19. These include L. von Muralt, E. Troeltsch, F. Blanke, O. Vasella, R. Bainton, H. S. Bender, F. Littell, R. Friedmann, G. H. Williams, and many others, especially most Mennonite historians. In opposition, see Karl Holl, *Gesammelte Aufsätze* (Tübingen, 1932), pp. 420-467; Heinrich Böhmer, *Urkunden zur Geschichte*

der Bauerkriegs und der Wiedertäufer (Bonn, 1910), 35 pp.; and more recently Alexander Rempel's address delivered at Tübingen (unpublished ms. at the Mennonite Historical Library, Goshen); and Delbert Gratz, *Bernese Anabaptists and their American Descendants* (Scottdale, 1953), 219 pp., who suggests that while urban Bernese Anabaptism may have been derived from Zürich, rural Bernese Anabaptism may have developed independently.

20. Cf., Hans Hillerbrand, "The Remarkable Interdependencies Between Certain Anabaptist Doctrinal Writings," *The Mennonite Quarterly Review* (Jan., 1959), pp. 73-76. Also Delbert Gratz, "Bernese Anabaptists in the Sixteenth Century," *MQR*, XXV (July, 1951), refers to the quick adoption of the Schleitheim Articles. Numerous reflections and even copies of it were found among Bernese Anabaptists shortly after its composition. Myron Augsburger, "Michael Sattler" (unpublished DTh thesis, Richmond: Union Theological Seminary, 1964), p. 216, gives priority to the Schleitheim Articles as a unifying factor in the whole Anabaptist movement.

21. Torsten Bergsten, *Balthasar Hubmaier* (Kassel, 1961), p. 25, recognizes considerable ideological cohesion among the Swiss Brethren, the Mennonites, and the Hutterites, but considers the South German branch as more detached. N. van der Zijpp, "The Early Dutch Anabaptists," also saw a marked relationship between the congregational life of the Dutch Anabaptists and the Swiss "Schleitheim" position and also a similarity between Sattler's and Menno's theology, in G. F. Hershberger (ed.), *The Recovery of the Anabaptist Vision* (Scottdale: Herald Press, 1957), pp. 71-82.

22. Although there were numerous anti infant-baptism protesters on the Reformation scene before the organization of the Swiss Brethren in January 1525, there is not evidence for a prior, positive, practical theology of believer's baptism, including the "rebaptism."

23. Bergsten, *op. cit.*, pp. 26, 16.

24. *Ibid.*, p. 16. See also Hershberger, *op. cit.*, pp. 171, 176.

25. F. Littell. *The Origins of Sectarian Protestantism* [also titled *The Anabaptist View of the Church*] (New York: Macmillian Co., 1952), pp. 14, 79 ff.; and L. Verduin, *op. cit.* Bergsten takes both radical biblicism and the gathered church as distinguishing features of the Swiss Brethren (Bergsten, *op. cit.*, p. 16).

26. H. S. Bender, "The Anabaptist Vision" in Hershberger, *op. cit.*, pp. 42-43. Note also his "Anabaptist Theology of Discipleship," *MQR* (Jan., 1950), 25-32.

27. R. Friedmann, "The Essence of Anabaptist Faith: An Essay in Interpretation," *MQR*, XLI (Jan., 1967), 5-24.

28. A. Beachy, "The Concept of Grace in the Radical Reformation" (unpublished DTh thesis, Harvard Divinity School, 1960), pp. 325-334.

29. Since the major opposition to Anabaptism came from the Magisterial Reformation and Roman Catholicism rather than from other elements in the Radical Reformation, Anabaptist characteristics tend to be articulated in reference to the former, primarily. An exception is the controversy between Marpeck and Schwenckfeld.

30. For example, though the South German branch tended toward mystical subjectivism and stress on the Spirit over the letter, the essence of *sola scriptura* remains intact, in contrast with Müntzer.

31. Both H. S. Bender, "The Zwickau Prophets and the Anabaptists," *MQR* (Jan., 1953), 3-16; and R. Friedmann, "Thomas Müntzer's Relation to Anabaptism," *MQR* (Apr., 1957), 75-87, strongly reject the idea of Anabaptist relationships with Müntzer, or with the revolutionary ideology — as espoused by Karl Holl, *Gesammelte Aufsätze* (Tübingen, 1932), pp. 420-467.

32. Both the Schleitheim Confession (1527) and the "Martyrs' Snyod" (1527) are representative of early efforts at *order, restraint, and unity*, with some effectiveness.

33. The theological outlook on sin, free will, and grace, and the concern for moral

300 Anabaptism and Asceticism

reform are also somewhat applicable to the Spiritualists but, as noted by Bergsten, *op. cit.*, p. 25, the importance of believer's baptism and the essentialness of the disciplined fellowship do not apply to Storch, Müntzer, Carlstadt, and Schwenckfeld.

34. Bainton, *op. cit.*, pp. 125-126, maintains that both eschatological expectation and a doctrine of the suffering church are essentially "incompatible" with a program of revolution; also "a new birth theology and mysticism" do not "lie any too well together."

35. Friedmann, *Mennonite Piety*, p. 3, believes that the Swiss Brethren, Dutch Mennonites, and Moravian Hutterites only after the first half of the sixteenth century "went rather different ways, losing to a certain extent their original parallelism."

36. The South German group requires a full study too extensive to be included in depth in this project. The degree of uniqueness of South German Anabaptism in essential characteristics is still debatable and depends largely on the considerably varied interpretations relating to Hut and Denck. Also Wenger, *Even unto Death*, p. 31, comments that "recent research suggests that Marpeck's Anabaptist followers may not have been one group with the Swiss Brethren, although any differences were trivial."

37. Heinold Fast, "The Dependence of the First Anabaptists on Luther, Erasmus and Zwingli," *MQR* (Apr., 1956), 115.

38. Fritz Blanke, *Brothers in Christ* (Scottdale: Mennonite Publishing House, 1961), p. 10.

39. *Ibid.*, p. 39.

40. H. S. Bender, *Conrad Grebel* (Scottdale: Herald Press, 1950), p. 214.

41. H. Bornkamm, "Besprechung von F. Blanke, *Brüder in Christo* (1955)," in *Historische Zeitschrift* (München, 1956), pp. 387 f.

42. W. Köhler, "Besprechung von G. Below, *Die Ursachen der Reformation*" in *Historische Zeitschrift*, 121 (München, 1920), 322. He also asserts that "the profound spiritual father of the Anabaptists was Erasmus" in "Wiedertäufer," *Die Religion in Geschichte und Gegenwart*, V (2 Aufl., Tubingen, 1931), pp. 1918, 1931.

43. Bender, *Conrad Grebel*, pp. 65 ff., 201 ff.

44. Robert Kreider, "Anabaptism and Humanism," *MQR*, XXVI (Jan., 1952), 123-141.

45. Leonhard von Muralt, *Glaube und Lehre der Schweizerischen Wiedertäufer in der Reformationszeit* (Zürich, 1938), pp. 4, 6-7.

46. Hans Hillerbrand, "The Origins of Anabaptism: Another Look," *Archiv für Reformationsgeschichte*, LIII (1962), 152-180.

47. *Ibid.*, p. 179.

48. A. J. F. Zieglschmid (ed.), *Die älteste Chronik der Hutterischen Brüder* (Ithaca: The Cayuga Press, 1943).

49. Ludwig Keller, *Ein Apostel der Wiedertäufer* (Leipzig: S. Hirzell, 1882), pp. v, 30, 13; and also see L. Keller, *Die Reformation und die älteren Reformparteien* (Leipzig, 1885), p. 372; and *ME*, III, 162 ff.

50. See "Historiography I: Anabaptism" in *ME*, II, 754.

51. H. C. Vedder, *Balthasar Hubmaier* (New York: G. P. Putnam's Sons, 1905), p. 13. Also note H. Wamble, "Landmarkism," *Church History* (December, 1964), pp. 439 ff.

52. Gratz, "Bernese Anabaptists in the Sixteenth Century," pp. 172-174.

53. Heinold Fast, "On the Beginnings of Bernese Anabaptism," *MQR*, XXXI (Oct., 1957), 292-293, shows that Bullinger's letter referring to Anabaptists in Berne was not written in 1524 but in the fall of 1525.

54. H. S. Bender, "Again on the Beginnings of Bernese Anabaptism," *MQR*, XXXI (Oct., 1957), 295.

55. An address delivered at Tübingen in 1953; copy is at the Mennonite Historical Library, Goshen, Ind. Also, E. G. Rupp, "Thomas Müntzer, Hans Hut, and the 'Gospel

of All Creatures,' " *Bulletin of the John Rylands Library*, XLIII (1961), 492-519, reaffirms Hut's dependence on Müntzer.

56. Verduin, *op. cit.*, pp. 5, 16, 17, 25-30, 59-62.

57. John Oyer, "Review of *The Stepchildren of the Reformation*," *MQR* (Oct., 1965), 320. Similarly, Fast in his "The Dependence of the First Anabaptists," p. 115, rejects the idea that the essential element in the Magisterial Reformation was union with the political powers of the state and that such was the most critical issue in Anabaptist separatism.

58. Albrecht Ritschl, *Geschichte der Pietismus*, I (Bonn: Adolph Marcus, 1880), pp. 1-37.

59. Muralt, *op cit.*, p. 7.

60. N. van der Zijpp, *Geschiednis der Doopsgezinden in Nederland* (Arnhem, 1952), p. 28. Also note an unpublished address delivered at Goshen Biblical Seminary by Albert Hyma, 1966 (manuscript at the Mennonite Historical Library, Goshen).

61. Bainton, *op. cit.*, p. 123.

62. Bergsten, *op. cit.*, p. 24 (my own translation).

63. Friedmann, *Mennonite Piety*, pp. 11-12.

64. J. J. Kiwiet, "The Theology of Hans Denck," *MQR*, XXXII (Jan., 1958), 3-27. Friedmann urges caution, however, since though some of the vocabulary is obviously common, even in South German Anabaptism its meaning, for example, *Gelassenheit*, often took on a different emphasis; see Friedmann, "The Essence of Anabaptist Faith," p. 12.

65. R. Friedmann, "Anabaptism and Protestantism," *MQR*, XXIV (Jan., 1950), 20.

66. Friedmann, *Mennonite Piety*, pp. 3-4.

67. Wilhelm Pauck, "Historiography of the German Reformation During the Past Twenty Years," *Church History* (1940), 339.

68. Bornkamm, *op. cit.*, pp. 387 f.

69. Fast, "The Dependence of the First Anabaptists," p. 115.

70. Protestantized in the sense of rejecting the medieval hierarchy, the sacramental system, and institutional monasticism.

71. For example, Francis of Sales. An investigation of this relationship is planned as a future work.

72. Krebs, TA: *Elsass*, I, 82, on Capito. See also, on Zwingli, W. Wiswedel, *Bilder und Führergestalten aus dem Täufertum* (Kassel: J. G. Onchen Verlag, 1952), pp. 11-12.

73. Heiko A. Oberman, *Forerunners of the Reformation* (New York: Holt, Rinehart & Winston, 1966), p. 32 f., suggests that it is not as much the task of the historian of ideas to establish causal connections as to show illuminating parallels.

74. Strange myths arose to account for this appeal, for example, Wenger, *Even unto Death*, p. 93, reports: "One curious explanation of the rapid spread of Anabaptism in the early years of the movement was that missioners carried little flasks with them, and whoever drank from their flask was bewitched and charmed into uniting with the church of the hedgepreachers."

75. For example, one is largely limited for biographical material to brief and often incidental references, letters, confessions, and trial reports scattered throughout a vast variety of records in various cities, especially Zürich, St. Gall, Bern, Basel, Freiburg, and so on. Also, there are scanty allusions to their spiritual pilgrimage in the works of those few Anabaptists who left writings, especially the Grebel group, Balthasar Hubmaier, Michael Sattler, and a few others. Finally, there are allusions and references in some of the writings of the major Reformers, especially Zwingli.

76. Hubmaier is included with the Swiss Brethren because he was converted by them, instructed by them, was considered one of them initially; and these ties were never officially repudiated though some estrangement developed over the "sword" and

302   Anabaptism and Asceticism

the "magistracy."

77. For example, G. D. Davidson's translation of the writings of Balthasar Hubmaier (an unpublished typescript at William Jewell College, Mo., 1939), though a valuable aid, must be used with caution because the translator lacked familiarity with the theological nuances of its contents and therefore made numerous errors in judgment.

2. The Christian Ascetic Tradition
Before the Reformation

1. M. Viller (ed.), *Dictionaire de Spiritualité, Ascétique et Mystique, Doctrine et Histoire*, Vol. I (Paris: G. Beauchesne et fils, 1937), pp. 937-938.

2. *The Catholic Encyclopedia*, I (New York: Appleton Co., 1907), p. 766; also, *The New Schaff-Herzog Encyclopedia of Religious Knowledge*, I, 309.

3. The article comments, concerning the negative stress: "Qui se rencontre le plus habituellement chez les auteurs protestants, et non-catholiques en générale." Viller, *op. cit.*, p. 938. H. B. Workman, *The Evolution of the Monastic Ideal* (London: Epworth Press, 1927), p. 5, makes "renunciation" the fundamental principle.

4. Viller, *op. cit.*, p. 936.

5. For example, St. Jerome: "It [mortification of the body] . . . is only a help . . . for the attainment of true perfection," *The Catholic Encyclopedia*, I, 768.

6. Jean Séguy, "L'ascèse dans les sectes d'origine protestante," *Archives de Sociologie des Religions* (July, 1964), p. 56. Cf. also Max Weber, *Wirtschaft und Gesellschaft* (Tübingen: Mohr, 1956), I, 328.

7. Troeltsch, *op. cit.*, pp. 102 f.

8. cf. also, Séguy, *op. cit.*, p. 57.

9. *The Catholic Encyclopedia*, I, p. 768.

10. *Ibid.*

11. *Ibid.*, p. 769: "The motives and manner . . . are laid down in the Gospel, which is the basis taken by the ascetic writers for their instructions."

12. For example, in the Old Testament ritual legislation, including fasting (Jer. 36:9; Ezek. 8:23), abstinence and vows (for example, anti-wine. Numb. 6:2, Judg. 13:4) and in Israel as a separate holy nation — but also there are prohibitions against self-mutilation, Lev. 19; Deut. 23; 1 Kings 18:28f. and encouragements to marriage and procreation.

13. Mk. 18:34, one is to "deny [or renounce] self" and "take up his cross" (also Mt. 10:38; 16:24; Jn. 13:13).

14. ". . . cast off the old man" (Eph. 4:22-25; Col. 3:8-10) and "crucify the old man" (Rom. 6:6).

15. Mt. 6:16; 9:15; Acts 13:2; 14:23; 2 Cor. 11:27.

16. 1 Cor. 7:1, 8, 25, 26, 29.

17. Mt. 6:19; 19:21; Acts 2:44, 45; 4:32; 5:4.

18. Gal. 5:24; Rom. 13:14; Col. 3:5.

19. "Be ye perfect even as your father in heaven is perfect" (Mt. 5:48, KJV); also 1 Pet. 2:21, "follow in his steps."

20. *The Catholic Encyclopedia*, I, 768. Cf. also Jas. 5:12, 2 Pet. 3:14, 1 Cor. 13:1, 1 Jn. 3:16.

21. For a "Sermon on the Mount" definition of *ascèse*, see Louis Bouyer, *Dictionaire Theologique* (Desclee et Co., 1963), p. 80.

22. Patrice Cousin, *Précis d'Histoire Monastique* (Belgium: Bloud et Gay, 1956), p. 28, says of Christian monasticism that its origin is the imitation of Christ in response to the appeal of Mt., "Be ye perfect. . . ."

23. Workman, *op. cit.*, pp. 37-54, 76.

24. *Ibid.*, pp. 6-11; also, Cousin, *op. cit.*, p. 29, on the enhancement of ascetic martyrdom.

25. *Ibid.*, pp. 27-31, asserts the origin of Christian asceticism in the gospel and especially in the example of the Jerusalem Christians, Acts 2:42-46.

26. Villers, *op. cit.*, p. 963, says that the spiritual combat "demanded even corporal penitence, both interior and exterior mortification (1 Cor. 9:25, 1 Cor. 6:13, Col. 3:5)."

27. The influence of Origen on the development of monasticism has been traced by W. Seaton, *Revue d'Histoire des Religions* (Paris: Presses Universitaires de France, 1933), pp. 197-215.

28. *The Catholic Encyclopedia*, I, p. 769. Cf. 1 Cor. 9:27, Mt. 10:38, Lk. 9:22, Rom. 8:17, Jn. 18:36, Mt. 19:16-28, 1 Jn. 2:15-17, Lk. 14:26, Mt. 19:12.

29. Cousin, *op. cit.*, p. 29; and Villers, *op. cit.*, pp. 967-968.

30. Workman, *op. cit.*, p. 63, is especially severe; also Hastings, *Encyclopedia of Religion and Ethics*, II, 67, claims that the flight of Paul of Thebes to the desert meant that Gnosticism "had really conquered" and "forced upon the church the dualistic conception of life."

31. Viller, *op. cit.*, p. 965, quotes Origen as relating ascetic spiritual combat with martyrdom. Cf. also, R. P. Viller, "Martyre et Ascèse," *Revue d'Ascétique et de Mystique* (1925), pp. 105 f.

32. Cousin, *op. cit.*, p. 30.

33. *Ibid.*; also Workman, *op. cit.*, p. 10, says: "The hermit fled not so much from the world as from the world in the church." Cf. also Viller, *Dictionaire*, p. 969.

34. Cf. the *Vita Antonii*, discussed in Cousin, *op. cit.*, pp. 44-45; also H. Waddell, *The Desert Fathers* (Ann Arbor: University of Michigan Press, 1957).

35. Cf. Armand Boon, *Pachomiana latina* (ed. par Th. Lefort, Louvain, 1932), discussed in Cousin, *op. cit.*, pp. 56-61; see also H. Bacht, "L'importance de l'idéal monastique chez saint Pachôme pour l'histoire du monachisme chrétiens," *Revue d'Ascétique et de Mystique* (1950), pp. 308-326.

36. Cousin, *op. cit.*, p. 41. G. M. Columbàs, "The Ancient Concept of the Monastic Life," *Monastic Studies* (1964), p. 74, notes that St. Athanasius' biography of St. Anthony sets up four stages of Anthony's spiritual maturation which coincide with four stages of withdrawal from human society.

37. Waddell, *op. cit.*, p. 5, gives a contemporary description of the monks of the desert at Scete as: "Here abide men perfect in holiness. . . ." Similarly she quotes St. Anthony as saying, concerning prospective monks: ". . . they ought to set nothing of this world before love towards Christ" (*Ibid.*, p. 23). Concerning St. Anthony, his biographer comments: "He was never agitated, his soul being in a deep calm." (*Ibid.*) Cf. also *Dictionaire de Spiritualité*, p. 969, and Waddell, *op. cit.*, p. 22.

38. Waddell, *op. cit.*, p. 22.

39. *Ibid.*, p. 18.

40. Columbàs, *op. cit.*, pp. 87-88, describes it as "dialogue with God." Again, "Scriptural sources inspire all of St. Anthony's thinking; Scripture is the principle and norm of all his actions." Columbàs adds that the primitive monks recognized "no law other than the Bible in general and the New Testament in particular" (pp. 95-96).

41. Cousin, *op. cit.*, pp. 41-42. (There are some notorious exceptions, for example, Simeon Stylites.)

42. *Dictionaire de Spiritualité*, p. 969.

43. Cousin, *op. cit.*, p. 42.

44. *Ibid.*, p. 53. (Cf. also Workman, *op. cit.*, pp. 70-73.)

45. Cousin, *op. cit.*, p. 53.

46. *Ibid.*, pp. 53-54.

47. *Ibid.*, p. 54.

48. *Ibid.* In Waddell, *op. cit.*, p. 27, F. Sheed notes that the monks of Arsinol sometimes hired themselves out to work and gave their earnings to the poor.
49. *Dictionaire de Spiritualite,* p. 970.
50. *Ibid.*
51. Waddell, *op. cit.*, p. 5.
52. Workman, *op. cit.*, pp. 54-55. Workman adds that the renunciation of sex also included family relationships in general; for example, Anthony considered the remembrance of one's relatives to be a temptation of the devil. (*Ibid.*, p. 59).
53. Cousin, *op. cit.*, p. 57, suggests that the figure is somewhat excessive.
54. Workman, *op. cit.*, p. 11.
55. See *Ibid.*, pp. 15-17 for illustrations.
56. *Ibid.*, p. 14.
57. *Ibid.*, p. 13. Monks were regarded strictly as laymen until the end of the fifth century. Late in the sixth century, Pope Gregory decreed still that no one could have the "cure of souls" and be a monk at the same time (although this was not consistently applied), p. 11.
58. *Ibid.*, pp. 20-21.
59. *Dictionaire de Spiritualite,* p. 970.
60. Colombàs, *op. cit.*, p. 70. (In Jerome and Augustine, the eremetic remained valid for an elite few.)
61. *Ibid.*
62. *A Catholic Dictionary of Theology,* I (New York: T. Nelson & Sons, 1962), p. 167. Cf. also *Dictionaire de Spiritualite,* p. 974.
63. *Ibid.*
64. *Ibid.*, p. 975.
65. *Ibid.*, "Chez Cassian, chez Saint Augustin la doctrine ascétique chrétienne trouve sa parfaite expression."
66. Columbàs, *op. cit.*, pp. 71-94, gives an expanded account based on Cassian's writings.
67. *Ibid.*, p. 72. (Cassian titles Book IV of his *Institutes* as *De institutes renuntiantium*.)
68. *Ibid.*
69. *Ibid.*, p. 74. (Jerome notes that cenobitics lived like anchorites "internally." Again, a Coptic cenobite is quoted: "We are men who have withdrawn from the world and have come together in the name of the Lord." This sounds very much like the Anabaptist "pure" church.)
70. *Ibid.*, p. 75.
71. *Ibid.*, p. 77.
72. *Ibid.*, pp. 81-82.
73. This is often equated with the giving up of personal liberty by attachment to a monastery (for example, Jerome), *ibid.*, p. 80.
74. *Ibid.*, p. 82.
75. *Ibid.*, p. 83.
76. *Ibid.*, p. 86.
77. *Ibid.*
78. *Ibid.*, p. 88.
79. *Ibid.*, p. 89.
80. *Ibid.*, p. 90.
81. *Ibid.*, p. 91.
82. *Ibid.*, p. 106.
83. *Ibid.*, p. 107 (from *Con.* XVIII, 5).
84. M. W. Baldwin, *The Medieval Church* (New York: Cornell University Press, 1953), pp. 26-27.

85. *Ibid.*, pp. 24-25.
86. *A Catholic Dictionary of Theology*, I, 256. (The second book of Gregory's *Dialogues* is devoted to Benedict.)
87. Cf. E. C. Butler, *Benedictine Monachism* (Cambridge, 1961).
88. Concerning the use of wine, formerly consistently forbidden, he writes: "Let us agree to use it temperately." *A Catholic Dictionary of Theology*, I, 256.
89. Cousin, *op. cit.*, pp. 238-239. Also, according to Baldwin, *op. cit.*, p. 35, "By the 12th C. the abbot of Cluny was recognized as the titular head of over 300 houses. This was a distinct break with the Benedictine system of autonomous abbeys."
90. *The Catholic Encyclopedia*, X, 306-307, notes that the Templars followed the Cistercian Reform and the Hospitallers, the Rule of St. Augustine.
91. *Ibid.*, p. 307.
92. Workman, *op. cit.*, p. 266.
93. *Ibid.*, p. 271.
94. Cf. *A Catholic Dictionary of Theology*, p. 168. Also, the *Dictionaire de Spiritualité*, p. 979, notes that Pope Alexander IV affirmed the legitimacy of voluntary begging, as a way of perfection.
95. Workman, *op. cit.*, p. 272, "The most ecstatic joy of the Umbrian saint was when he heard the voice of God 'that it behoved him by preaching to convert much people. Thus saith the Lord: "Say unto brother Francis that God has not called him to this estate for himself alone, but to the end that he may gain fruit of souls, and that many through him may be saved" ' (Little Flowers, c. 16)."
96. G. G. Coulton, *Ten Medieval Studies* (Cambridge: The University Press, 1930), pp. 48, 56, 64, describes second-generation Franciscanism as anti-laughter, for strong, personal discipline, anti-oaths, for seriousness of speech and tears in prayers, anti-secular airs, for modesty of dress. Also, "no village tabernacle was ever plainer than the first Franciscan churches" (p. 56) and there was "a definite dislike for church music" (p. 64).
97. *Ibid.*, pp. 295-296.
98. *Dictionaire de Spiritualité*, p. 980.
99. Coulton, *op. cit.*, pp. 40-57.
100. Hastings, *Encyclopedia of Religion and Ethics*, II, 78.
101. *Dictionaire de Spiritualité*, pp. 980-981 ("avec le *Rosetum* de Mauburnus [Mombaier]").
102. G. G. Coulton, *Five Centuries of Religion*, Vol. IV (Cambridge: The University Press, 1950), pp. 182-183.
103. A. Hyma, *The Brethren of the Common Life* (Grand Rapids: Eerdman's, 1950), pp. 32-33.
104. *Ibid.*
105. *Ibid.*, p. 78 (from Chapter 8 of G. Zerbolt's "Treatise on the Common Life").
106. *Ibid.*, p. 114.
107. *Ibid.*, p. 115.
108. *Ibid.*, p. 44. (He quotes numerous passages, supporting internalization, from G. Groote's *Epistolae* [ed. W. Mulder], p. 53).
109. Based primarily on Mt. 5:48, "Be ye perfect. . . ."
110. Cenobitism places more emphasis on the social virtues than anchoritism does, for example, on Gal. 5:22.
111. Based on repeated reference to such passages as 1 Jn. 2:15-17.
112. Gal. 2:20 is emphasized.
113. Hyma, *op. cit.*, p. 60.
114. Concerning mortification, poverty (or unworldliness), and chastity (or family detachment), *The Catholic Encyclopedia*, I, 769, says that these three facets may be accomplished through internal disposition or readiness, though God may not actually

306 Anabaptism and Asceticism

require them in every case.

115. C. Peifer, "Feature Review," *Monastic Studies* (1964), p. 163.

116. Workman, *op. cit.*, ends his book on monastic development with the rise and decline in the twelfth to thirteenth centuries of the Mendicants.

117. David Knowles, *Christian Monasticism* (New York: McGraw-Hill, 1969), pp. 113-118, and *The Religious Orders in England* (Cambridge University Press, 1959), III, 458-460. Cousin, *op. cit.*, entitles Chapter XVIII "Apogée, Stagnation et Décadence de l'Ordre Monastique du 12e Siecle au Début du 14e Siècle," but suggests that the fifteenth century saw the beginning of attempts to "check the general decadence," (p. 393).

118. Knowles, *Religious Orders*, II, 114, 218; III, 60-61.

119. Knowles, *Christian Monasticism*, pp. 141-142. Cf. also Daniel-Rops, *op. cit.*, pp. 182, 363. For a brief overview of the history of *commendam*, see Cousin, *op. cit.*, pp. 389-391.

120. H. v. d. Hardt, *Magnum Concilium Constantiense*, I, viii, 409 ff., and H. Fincke, *Acta Concilii Constanciensis*, II, 394 (both cited in G. G. Coulton, *Five Centuries*, IV, 48 f.).

121. *Ibid.*, p. 80.

122. Hyma, *op. cit.*, pp. 53 f.

123. J. Busch, *Chronicon Windeshemense und Liber de Reformatione Monasteriorum*, ed. K. Grube (*Geschichtesquellen der Provinz Sachsen*, XIX, Halle, 1886).

124. Hyma, *Christian Renaissance*, pp. 138-139.

125. Busch, *op. cit.*, pp. 490-491; cf. also J. G. R. Acquoy, *Hit klooster te Windesheim en Zijn invloed* (Utrecht, 1880), II, 193-203, 284-286, 291-294, 311-313, 333-335, (cited in G. G. Coulton, *Five Centuries*, IV, 158-162), and A. Hyma, *The Brethren of the Common Life*, pp. 109-115, 140-144.

126. Acquoy, *op. cit.*, p. 299.

127. Though Busch used wine moderately and feasted heartily on occasion (Busch, *op. cit.*, p. 745).

128. Daniel-Rops, *op. cit.*, I, 200. He also maintains a connection between the origins of the *Devotio Moderna* and the Beghards and Beguines (p. 201).

129. H. Oberman, *The Harvest of Medieval Theology* (Cambridge: Harvard University Press, 1963), pp. 344-345.

130. *Ibid.*, pp. 201, 203; for example, the writings of Gerard of Zutphen, *The Spiritual Ascents*; Gerlac Peters, *Soliloquy*; Thomas à Kempis, *The Imitation of Christ*.

131. Busch, *op. cit.*, (in the Epilogue of his *Chronicon*).

132. A. Hyma, *The Christian Renaissance* (2d ed.; Hampden: Archon Books, 1965), p. 134. (There were 1,200 pupils at Deventer and 1,500 at Emmerich late in the fifteenth century.) Cf. also J. Henkel, "An Historical Study of the Educational Contributions of the Brethren of the Common Life" (unpublished PhD thesis, University of Pittsburgh, 1962).

133. Cousin, *op. cit.*, p. 396.

134. *Ibid.*, p. 397.

135. *Ibid*.

136. Hyma, *Christian Renaissance*, pp. 144-145.

137. J. Busch, *op. cit.*, pp. 518 f., and Trithemius, *Annales Hirsaugienses*, II (1690), 346 f.

138. As papal legate, Nicholas came to Germany in 1451 with a special commission for monastic reform and empowered to enlist the secular arm, if necessary.

139. His seven orations, between 1490-1500 are in *Joannis Tritemii ad Monachos Dehortations* (Romae, typis Vaticanis, 1890).

140. E. Vansteenberghe, *Le Cardinal Nicolas de Cues* (1920), pp. 118, 121, 143; Trithemius, *Annales*, II, 423-450 and *Dehortationes*, p. 267.

141. Trithemius, *Dehortationes*, 2nd Oration. 1492 (cited in Coulton, IV, 178).
142. For a fuller description see A. Renaudet, *Préréforme et Humanisme à Paris* (2d ed.; Paris, 1953).
143. Daniel-Rops, *op. cit.*, I, 194.
144. For more details on Chezal-Benoit see Pierre Imbart de la Tour, *Les Origines de la reforme*, II (Paris, 1909).
145. Jouenneaux, Abbot Guy, *Reformationes Monastice Vindicie*, 1503 (trans. G. Coulton, *Medieval Studies*, XI, Cambridge, n.d.), pp. 6-7.
146. Renaudet, *op. cit.*, p. 174 f.
147. Georges Goyeaux, in Hanotaux, *Histoire de la Nation Francaise*, VI, 320.
148. Knowles, *Christian Monasticism*, p. 117. Moorman, *op. cit.*, p. 349, agrees that "invective against the friars was at its height" but also notes that to a large section of the community the friars "were still popular."
149. R. W. Emery, *The Friars in Medieval France* (New York: Columbia University Press, 1962), p. 3, notes that 136 new mendicant houses were established in France, 1451-1550 (almost all before 1517). Of these, 88 were Franciscan, which is more than were founded in the previous 175 years. The Minims accounted for 13 more.
150. Daniel-Rops, *op. cit.*, I, 200.
151. *Ibid.*, pp. 157-158.
152. D. Hay, *Europe in the 14th and 15th Centuries* (New York: Holt, Rinehart, 1966), p. 321.
153. *Ibid.* (From a sermon of St. Bernardine, 1427: "And if of these two things you can do only one — either hear the Mass or hear the sermon — you should let the Mass go rather than the sermon. . . . There is less peril for your soul in not hearing Mass than in not hearing the sermon.")
154. Daniel-Rops, *cop. cit.*, I, 159.
155. *Ibid.*
156. Moorman, *op. cit.*, pp. 526, 535, 543, (also Coulton, *Five Centuries*, IV, 363, 370).
157. L. Dacheux, *Un Réformateur Catholique à la fin du XVe siècle, Jean Geiler de Kaysersberg* (Paris: C. Delagrave, 1876), pp. 496-497. Also, M. Gilmore, *The World of Humanism* (New York: Harper & Bros., 1952), p. 179, notes a similar pattern in Savonarola.
158. See Chapter V.
159. Bainton, *op. cit.*, p. 112.
160. D. Erasmus, *Ten Colloquies*, trans. C. Thompson (New York: The Liberal Arts Press, 1957), p. 160 (selections of his *Colloquia Familiaria*, translated from the *Erasmi Opera Omnia*, Basel, 1540).
161. *Ibid.*, p. xi.
162. D. Erasmus, "The Enchiridion," in *Advocates of Reform*, ed. M. Spinka (Philadelphia: Westminster Press, 1953). Part I portrays perfection and holiness in terms of the centrality of love and conformity to the precepts of Christ.
163. For example, Erasmus, *Ten Colloquies*, pp. 56-91 ("A Pilgrimage for Religion's Sake").
164. Lewis Spitz, *The Religious Renaissance of the German Humanists* (Cambridge: Harvard University Press, 1963), p. 268.
165. *Ibid.*, p. 273.
166. Coulton, *Five Centuries* IV, 41-44, describes Rolewinck's book, *Fasciculus Temporum*, and notes its strong sense of impending tragedy.
167. Daniel-Rops, *op. cit.*, I, 156; Hyma, *Brethren*, p. 74.
168. Hay, *op. cit.*, p. 357, notes 99 printings by the year 1500. As of the present, over 6,000 printings have appeared in over fifty languages.
169. Spitz, *op. cit.*, p. 269. Also Daniel-Rops, *op. cit.*, I, 368-370, notes that

308   Anabaptism and Asceticism

"the period abounds in saints" to an unusual degree, typifying the vitality of the ascetic ideal of holiness. Knowles, *Christian Monasticism*, p. 141, notes that in France the use of *commendam* by the monarchy made attempts at reform "come to nothing."

170. Hardt, *Magnum Concilium Constantiense*, I, X, XII (Coll 616-722), cited in Coulton, IV, 55.

171. Spitz, *op. cit.*, p. 274.

172. Oberman, *Forerunners*, p. 11 (cf. "Apocalypticism and Despair," pp. 9-14). Cf. also Hay, *op. cit.*, p. 342, which tells of Jean Gerson giving his own sister "the Huss-like advice not to enter a nunnery if she wished to lead a life of piety." See also, Oberman, *op. cit.*, introductory chapter; and Daniel-Rops, *op. cit.*, I, 373, who notes the appearance of the Blessed Virgin (1491) warning that "the wrath of God was about to descend like a hailstorm."

173. Daniel-Rops, *op. cit.*, I, 372.

3. Ascetic Factors in the Emergence of Anabaptism

1. Hillerbrand, *op. cit.*, p. 217.
2. Otto A. Brandt, *Thomas Müntzer* (Jena, 1933), pp. 38-39.
3. *ME*, II, 33.
4. *Ibid.*
5. J. J. Kiwiet, "The Theology of Hans Denck," *MQR*, XXXVI (1958), 10-15. Cf. also *TA: Denck*.
6. The first organized congregation of Anabaptists, at Zollikon, called themselves "Swiss Brethren" (*TA: VMS*, No. 48, pp. 58-59).
7. Zwingli to Myconius, August 26, 1522, *ZSW*, VII, 568.
8. E. Krajewski, *Leben und Sterben des Zürcher Täuferführers Felix Manz* (Kassel: J. G. Oncken Verlag, 1957), p. 21.
9. Bender, *Conrad Grebel*, p. 87.
10. Bender's heading for the Foreword to his book, *Conrad Grebel*, is "Conrad Grebel, the Acknowledged Leader of the First Swiss Brethren."
11. *Ibid.*, p. 87; confirmed also by Krajewski, *op. cit.*, pp. 22-27.
12. The theory by Bullinger that Grebel and some associates broke with Zwingli when he failed to give them teacher's appointments in the new theological school (H. Bullinger, *Reformationsgeschichte*, I, 237-238) is rejected by Krajewski, *op. cit.*, pp. 33-36, and by Bender, *Conrad Grebel*, pp. 251-252, as inconsistent with the sources and other statements by Bullinger.
13. *ZSW*, II, 783-784 (Council did not permit the abolition of the mass until Easter 1525).
14. Zwingli's original position is stated in his letter to Myconius, July 25, 1520, *ZSW*, VII, 341 ff. Again, in the "disputation" of January 1523, Zwingli asserted: "In worldly things and actions . . . I would be very glad to accept my lords of Zürich as judges. But in matters concerning divine wisdom and truth, I would accept no one as witness and judge except the living Scriptures and the Spirit of God which speaks out of the Scriptures" (*ZSW*, I, 557-558).
15. J. H. Yoder, "The Turning Point in the Zwinglian Reformation," *MQR* (1958), pp. 128-140.
16. Drei Zeugenaussagen Zwinglis in Täuferprozess, *ZSW*, IV, 168-175. (Also in *TA:VMS*, Nos. 87, 120, 121, 122, 124, 198, 200.) The three accounts in: 1. *Von dem Tauf, vom Widertauf und vom Kindertauf*, May 1525 (*ZSW*, II, 206-209, 257, 286). 2. The answer to Hubmaier's *Tauchbüchlein* (*ZSW*, IV, 590-592). 3. *Catabaptistarum Strophus Elenchus* (*ZSW*, VI, 32-42).
17. *TA:VMS*, p. 121.

18. *Ibid.*, p. 122.
19. *Ibid.*, p. 127.
20. *Ibid.*, p. 214. Zwingli says that "the opinion of the Anabaptists had always been . . . to set up a special church of their own to which no one should go but those who know themselves without sin."
21. G. M. Jackson (ed.), *Select Works of Huldreich Zwingli* (Philadelphia: University of Pennsylvania, 1901), p. 132.
22. *Ibid.*, p. 133.
23. *Ibid.* Zwingli had, however, advocated the baptism of catechumens rather than infants as early as 1523.
24. *Ibid.*, p. 172. Doctrine, as a basis for Zwingli's accusations, was added only later when he begins to deal with the Schleitheim Confession (1527); see p. 179.
25. *Ibid.*, p. 134.
26. Edward Yoder (ed. and trans.), *Epistolae Grebelianae, 1517-1525* (unpublished manuscript, Goshen College: The Mennonite Historical Library), n.p. (letter to Vadian, January 30, 1522).
27. Cf., *New E.R.K.*, XI, 305, 307; also TA:VMS, p. 18; and C. Krahn, *Menno Simons* (Karlsruhe, 1736), p. 42.
28. Yoder, *Epistolae Grebelianae*, December 1, 1922.
29. G. M. Jackson (ed.), *The Latin Works of Huldreich Zwingli* (New York: Putnam's Sons, 1912), I, 292 (from *ZSW*, I, 256-327).
30. Yoder, *Epistolae Grebelianae*, December 29, 1522.
31. *Ibid.*, July 21, 1925.
32. *Ibid.*, December 15, 1524.
33. *TA:VMS*, No. 16 (English translation by E. Correll, *Goshen College Record Review Supplement*, 1926). This tract was first assigned to Conrad Grebel but more recently to Felix Mantz; see the study by W. Schmid in *Zwingliana*, IX, 139.
34. *TA:VMS*, No. 16, p. 24.
35. *Ibid.* (italics mine).
36. *Ibid.*
37. Hillerbrand, *Reformation*, p. 228 (translated from H. Bullinger, *Reformationsgeschichte*, I, 237-239) (italics mine).
38. *Hutterite Chronicle* (New York: Cayuga Press, 1943), pp. 46-47 (italics mine).
39. *TA:VMS*, p. 218 (Felix Manz an seine Mitbrüder, cir. Januar 6, 1527).
40. *Ibid.*, p. 219.
41. *Ibid.*
42. *Ibid.*
43. Krajewski, *op. cit.*, p. 32.
44. *TA:VMS*, pp. 13-21 (English translation by W. Rauschenbusch, *The American Journal of Theology* [1905], pp. 91-99). For a photographic reproduction of the original letter and a fresh English translation, see *Conrad Grebel's Programmatic Letters of 1524* . . . transcribed and translated by J. C. Wenger (Scottdale, Pa.: Herald Press, 1970).
45. Krajewski, *op. cit.*, pp. 48-59, examines Müntzer's influence on the founding Swiss Brethren and concludes that it was insignificant. Hillerbrand suggests "phony faith" as a translation of *getlichten Glauben*.
46. *TA:VMS*, p. 17.
47. *Ibid.*, pp. 17-18 (italics mine).
48. A certified typescript copy is at the Mennonite Historical Library, Goshen College — taken from the Stadtbibliothek St. Gallen, Ms. 31, 222 (8 pages).
49. Cf. Bender, *Conrad Grebel*, p. 121.
50. Jackson, *Select Works*, pp. 153-154; cf. also pp. 128-129, 150-151.
51. Hegenwald, *op. cit.*

52. See Chapter IV for details of the ascetic nature of their expectations.

53. Most Anabaptists held to a fellowship of sharing and the stewardship of possessions, not to a communism of consumption (cf. P. Klassen, *The Economics of Anabaptism*, 1525-1560 [London: Mouton & Co., 1964]). F. Manz explained this distinction to the Zürich council, April 1525, Wenger, *op. cit.*, p. 22.

54. ZSW, IV, pp. 404-405 (*Von dem Predigtamt*) suggests that the Grebel group offered Zwingli 100 guilders yearly in free, voluntary support, if he would give up his benefice.

55. ZSW, VI, 33 (*Elenchus*). Bender maintains that "their hope was to replace this council after the pious had secured a majority in the city . . . the brethren had originally (1523-24) proposed to establish a 'Christian' government" (Bender, *Conrad Grebel*, p. 255, footnote 31).

56. *TA:VMS*, p. 123, reports Manz as testifying on trial (Nov. 1525) that "no Christian could be a magistrate, nor could he use the sword to punish or kill anyone, for he had no Scripture for such a thing."

57. *TA:VMS*, p. 14 (Letter to Müntzer).

58. Bender, *Conrad Grebel*, p. 105.

59. *Ibid.*, p. 125. There is no indication that Grebel's second child, born in August 1523, was not baptized. The subject does not arise in the 1524 conferences.

60. Zwingli preached that unbaptized infants "will not be damned" and admits he questioned the legitimacy (biblically) of infant baptism (Bender, *Conrad Grebel*, pp. 126, 260; and ZSW, IV, 228). In 1524, fines for evasion were light and the practice was temporarily made optional in Strassburg in 1524 (Bender, *Conrad Grebel*, p. 127).

61. ZSW, IV (Taufbüchlein), 207 (italics mine).

62. ZSW, III, 368-372; and *TA:VMS*, No. 16, p. 23 f.

63. A description of the meeting is given in the *Hutterite Chronicle*, p. 47.

64. Bender, *Conrad Grebel*, p. 138.

65. *TA:VMS*, pp. 103-104.

66. E. Egli, *Aktensammlung zur Geschichte der Züricher Reformation in den Jahren 1519-1533* (Zürich, 1879), No. 792, p. 372 (henceforth designated Egli, *Akten*).

67. L. von Muralt, "Jorg Berger," *Zwingliana*, V, 115-116.

68. *Ibid.* (italics mine).

69. *The Hutterite Chronicle*, p. 47, correctly comments that when the Swiss Brethren began, January 21, 1525, "therewith was the separation from the world and its evil works begun."

70. ZSW, IV, 228.

71. ZSW, I, 142-154 (English translation in Jackson, *Zwingli's Latin Works*, I, 113-129).

72. Jackson, *Zwingli's Latin Works*, I, 121-122 (italics mine).

73. *Ibid.*, p. 128. This is also his opening premise in the Zürich Disputation (January 1523) and he insists that even the General Council's decrees must be in accord with the "gospels." Cf. Jackson, *Selected Works*, pp. 48, 84.

74. Jackson, *Zwingli's Latin Works*, I, 122.

75. *Ibid.*, p. 123.

76. *Ibid.*, p. 126.

77. *Ibid.*, pp. 136, 138-139 (ZSW, I, 165-168).

78. *Ibid.*, p. 141.

79. *Ibid.*, p. 135.

80. *Ibid.*, pp. 150-165 (ZSW, I, 197-209).

81. *Ibid.*, p. 154.

82. *Ibid.*, p. 160.

83. *Ibid.*, pp. 197-292 (ZSW, I, 256-327).

84. *Ibid.*, pp. 203-204.

85. *Ibid.*, p. 224.
86. *Ibid.*, p. 230.
87. *Ibid.*, p. 283.
88. *Ibid.*, pp. 284-285.
89. *Ibid.*, p. 239.
90. *Ibid.*, p. 263.
91. *TA:VMS*, p. 20.
92. Jackson, *Zwingli's Latin Works*, I, 267 (Archetelas).
93. *Ibid.*, p. 240.
94. *Ibid.*, p. 256.
95. *Ibid.*, p. 240.
96. *Ibid.*, p. 282.
97. Jackson, *Select Works*, pp. 40-117. The "67 articles" are in pp. 111-117.
98. *Ibid.*, pp. 85-86. Cf. also a much earlier reference to the true church as experiencing persecution, ZSW, VII, 341.
99. Jackson, *Select Works*, pp. 102-103.
100. *Ibid.*, p. 106.
101. Blanke, *op. cit.*, p. 39, claims that Swiss Anabaptist theology was "not middle ages, neither the Roman nor the Waldensian, but Zwingli's reformed preaching." Also, that even in its distinctive features, Anabaptism "was a daughter, self-willed to be sure, of the Reformation" (p. 40). Cf. also, Bender, *Conrad Grebel*, p. 74.
102. Krajewski, *op. cit.*, p. 27.
103. See Chapter 5 for an examination of possible contacts.
104. *TA:VMS*, p. 14.
105. Blaurock became one of the most successful proselytizers and the Swiss Brethren spoke of "the three shepherds, Grebel, Manz, and Blaurock" (Bender, *Conrad Grebel*, p. 135).
106. *ME*, I, 354, and O. Vasella, "Anfange der Täuferbewegung in Graubünden," *Zeitschrift für Schweizerische Geschichte*, XIX, Heft II (1939), 172, 180.
107. *ME*, I, 356; also J. A. Moore, *Der Starke Jorg* (Kassel: J. G. Oncken Verlag, 1955), pp. 22, 47.
108. Negated by Moore, *ibid.*, p. 47 (n. 1), and by Vasella, *op. cit.*,
109. *TA:VMS*, No. 65, p. 74.
110. Blanke, *op. cit.*, p. 136.
111. Moore, *op. cit.*, pp. 46, 22.
112. *The Hutterite Chronicle*, p. 46.
113. Moore, *op. cit.*, p. 12.
114. *The Hutterite Chronicle*, p. 46.
115. Stanza 6 of Blaurock's hymn, *"Gott führt ein recht gericht"* (in Moore, *op. cit.*, p. 36) repeats the same ideology: *"Sein wort lässter hie zeygen an, der Mensch sol sich bekehren, Glauben dem Wort und taufen lahn, und folgen seiner Lehren."*
116. *TA:VMS*, p. 43.
117. *Ibid.*, p. 40.
118. Blanke, *op. cit.*, p. 35.
119. Bender, *Conrad Grebel*, pp. 86-87 (Egli, Akten., No. 252, p. 85).
120. *TA:VMS*, p. 36; cf. also Cornelius, *op. cit.*, p. 17.
121. Blanke, *op. cit.*, p. 21.
122. *TA:VMS*, pp. 41-42.
123. *ME*, I, 439.
124. T. J. van Braght, *The Martyrs Mirror* (trans. from the Dutch edition of 1660 by J. F. Sohm) (Scottdale, Pa.: Mennonite Publishing House, 1951), p. 427 (hereinafter referred to as *MM*).
125. *TA:VMS*, p. 54, suggests the first letter was written shortly after February

5, 1525. The first letter mentions this date as his first Sunday preaching at Hallau. The second letter states that it was written fourteen days after the first one, but now mentions four public preachings as major accomplishments. This suggests that the second letter was probably sent near the end of February.

126. *Ibid.*, p. 45.

127. D. E. Staehelin, *Das Buch der Basler Reformation* (Basel: Helbing & Lichtenhaln, 1929), p. 137 ("*Das ist das recht heiltum, das andere sind Totenbeine*").

128. *ME*, IV, 304.

129. Egli, *Akten*, No. 285.

130. *Ibid.*, No. 552 (b).

131. *Ibid.*, No. 378.

132. *TA:VMS*, p. 10.

133. Reublin's letter to P. Marpeck, January 31, 1531, translated by J. C. Wenger (cf. *MQR* [1949], pp. 67-75), indicates a moderate theology and practice akin to Hubmaier.

134. *ME*, II, 622. Cf. also G. F. Goeter's *Ludwig Haetzer, 1500-1529, eine Randfigur der frühen Täuferbewegung* (Gütersloh, 1957).

135. Cf. the extensive biography by T. Bergsten, *Balthasar Hubmaier, Seine Stellung zur Reformation und Täufertun* (Kassel: J. C. Oncken, 1961), and the *Hubmaier Schriften* (*QGT*, IX, 1962).

136. Vedder, *op. cit.*, pp. 33-34, 36.

137. *Ibid.*, pp. 41-43, 49-50 (even at Freiburg, he testifies to have objected to a superfluity of feast days).

138. Bergsten, *op. cit.*, pp. 92-93.

139. F. L. Weiss, *The Life and Teachings of Ludwig Haetzer* (Dorchester, Mass.: Underhill Press, 1930), pp. 26-27, notes that "from 1505-1515, humanistic and biblical studies flourished under Ulrich Zasius, Jacob Wimfeling, Joseph Breisgauer, and the young tutors Johann Eck, Matthew Zell, Jacob Sturm, and Wolfgang Capito.... Breisgauer brought new inspiration ... from the pages of the mystic Johann Tauler while Zell ... from his explanations of the excellent sermons of Geiler of Kayserberg."

140. Bergsten, *op. cit.*, p. 102.

141. *Ibid.*, p. 98.

142. *Ibid.*, pp. 97-98.

143. *Ibid.*, pp. 99-100; and *TA:Elsass*, I, 41.

144. Bergsten, *op. cit.*, p. 101.

145. From Hubmaier's testimony at Zürich (October 1523): "Scripture alone ... ought to be our judge on the throne" (Vedder, *op. cit.*, p. 59).

146. Bergsten, *op. cit.*, p. 105, reports that during his brief return to Regensberg (December 1522-March 1523) he preached expository sermons on the Evangelical reform pattern (and left again when unable to support the Maria pilgrimages at all).

147. At Regensberg (Vedder, *op. cit.*, p. 56); at Waldshut (p. 57); at Zürich (pp. 62-63).

148. Bergsten, *op. cit.*, p. 103.

149. *Ibid.*

150. Thor Hall, "Possibilities of Erasmian Influence on Denck and Hubmaier in their Views on the Freedom of the Will," *MQR*, XXXV (1961), 149-170.

151. Vedder, *op. cit.*, pp. 62, 64; and *TA:HS*, pp. 79, 83.

152. Within one month after his return to Waldshut from Regensberg (March 1, 1523), Hubmaier was in contact with the Zürich Reformers. He visited St. Gall and Zürich both that spring and in the fall (Vedder, *op. cit.*, p. 57).

153. Bergsten, *op. cit.*, pp. 211-212.

154. In his *18 Theses* (1524 *TA:HS*, p. 72), the wording "faith alone makes us pious before God [*macht uns frumm*]," followed by "this faith cannot remain dead

but must manifest itself," seems to anticipate the divergence.
  155. Bergsten, *op. cit.*, p. 141.
  156. Vedder, *op. cit.*, pp. 105 f.
  157. *TA:HS*, p. 73.
  158. *Ibid.*, pp. 97, 99.
  159. *TA:VMS*, No. 36, p. 45.
  160. Grebel wrote to Vadian, January 14, 1525, that Hubmaier was "against Zwingli as far as baptism is concerned," *TA:VMS*, pp. 33 f.
  161. *TA:VMS*, pp. 194, 195; *TA:HS*, pp. 186, 234 f; *ZSW*, IV, 602 and VIII, 254.
  162. *TA:HS*, p. 232 f.
  163. Vedder, *op. cit.*, p. 93.
  164. Translated by Vedder, *op. cit.*, pp. 108-109 (also in Hubmaier Briefe No. 15, Ock. Br., I, 342 f).
  165. Vedder, *op. cit.*, p. 108.
  166. Bergsten, *op. cit.*, p. 214, suggests that by October 1524, Hubmaier had taken the position on baptism of the Zürich radicals but that is an oversimplification.
  167. The debate appears not to have taken place publicly but a letter from Waldshut to Strassburg, 1528, indicates that there was a small conference about this time. (*TA: Baden*, No. 383, p. 391.)
  168. *TA:HS*, p. 102, presents strong "imitation of Christ" sentiments and obedience to Scripture is equated with a correct *Christo Nachudgt*.
  169. *Ibid.*, p. 104.
  170. Cf. Bergsten, *op. cit.*, p. 254; and TA:VMS, p. 391, for details of Reublin's visit of late January 1525; also the testimony of Jacob Gross (TA: *Elsass*, I, 64) and of Johannes Kessler, *Sabbata* (St. Gallen, 1902), p. 144, for a pre-Easter visit by Grebel.
  171. *TA:VMS*, pp. 391 f.
  172. Vedder, *op. cit.*, p. 112, reports that Reublin baptized Hubmaier and sixty others (on Saturday), then, on Easter and Sunday, Hubmaier baptized 300, and 60-70 more the following week. For the Saturday and Sunday count, see *TA:VMS*, pp. 391, 392; for the following week see Bergsten, *op. cit.*, p. 306. Waldshut's total population was about 1,000.
  173. *TA:VMS*, pp. 113, 161, 194, 196-197. Bergsten, *op. cit.*, p. 320; and Bender, *Conrad Grebel*, p. 147, place this visit in early June.
  174. *TA:HS*, pp. 111, 123-127.
  175. *Ibid.*, p. 145.
  176. *Ibid.*, p. 110.
  177. *Ibid.*, p. 111.
  178. *Ibid.*, p. 135.
  179. *Ibid.*, p. 111.
  180. *Ibid.*, p. 123 (the opening paragraph of *Von der Taufe* is almost identical to Manz's *Protestation*).
  181. *Ibid.*, p. 111.
  182. *Ibid.*, p. 145.
  183. *Ibid.*, p. 112.
  184. *Ibid.*, p. 219.
  185. *ZSW*, IV, No. 68, 577 f.
  186. *TA:HS*, p. 110; *ME*, III, 791, 794; cf. also *TA:VMS*, pp. 14-15.
  187. *ME*, II, 826; also, J. H. Yoder, "Balthasar Hubmaier and the Beginnings of Swiss Anabaptism," *MQR*, XXXIII (1959), 8.
  188. *TA:VMS*, p. 108; and *TA: Elsass*, I, 63.
  189. Bergsten, *op. cit.*, p. 205. (Note, however, the strong pacifist consensus of the Grebel circle in the 1524 Letter to Müntzer.)
  190. Vasella, *op. cit.*, p. 166.

314 Anabaptism and Asceticism

191. *Ibid.*, pp. 168-171; though Vasella notes that St. Luzi did not play as central a role as E. Egli thought (in E. Egli, *Quellen zur Schweizerischen Reformationsgeschichte* [Zürich, 1910], pp. 140, 325) since Zwingli's friend. Jakob Salzmann, was not schoolmaster at St. Luzi but at the cathedral; also Blaurock was a secular priest and never a monk at St. Luzi.

192. Cf. *Vadianische Briefsammlung*, No. 297, p. 142.

193. Vasella, *op. cit.*, p. 168.

194. The term "monk" is used here to refer to all "religious" orders, including canons regular and even friars.

195. E. Dürr and P. Roth (eds.), *Aktensammlung zur Geschichte der Basler Reformation in den Jahren, 1519-1534*, II (Basel, 1921-), 483. Actually, at his trial in Basel in 1527 he refers loosely to the date of his baptism as "three years ago."

196. *Ibid.*; also P. Peachy, *Die soziale Herkunft der Schweizer Täufer in der Reformationszeit* (Karlsruhe, 1954), p. 25.

197. Dürr and Roth, *op. cit.*, II, 483.

198. *Ibid.*, pp. 484-485.

199. *Zwingliana*, VIII, 66 (from the St. Galler Ratsbuch, June 16, 1525).

200. Peachy, *op. cit.*, p. 109 (and *Zwingliana*, VIII, 66 ff., notes that Krüsi was also called Hans Nagel of Klingau).

201. *ME*, III, 250; Kessler, *op. cit.*, I, 270 ff.

202. *Zwingliana*, VIII, 69; cf. also E. Egli, *St. Galler Täufer* (Zürich, 1887), p. 42, n. 6.

203. Kessler, *op. cit.*, p. 197.

204. *Zwingliana*, VIII, 69.

205. *TA:Württemberg*, pp. 962-963, 972, 980.

206. *Zwingliana*, I, 367; IV, 58.

207. *Ibid.*, VIII, 69.

208. *Ibid.*

209. *Ibid.*, p. 68.

210. *Ibid.*, pp. 67-69.

211. *TA:VMS*, p. 194.

212. Egli, *St. Galler Täufer*, p. 42.

213. Peachy, *op. cit.*, pp. 26, 109.

214. Vasella, *op. cit.*, p. 167.

215. *ME*, II, 771; Dürr and Roth, *op. cit.*, II, 33; *ME*, IV, 787.

216. Kessler, *op. cit.*, I, 143-144; also Dürr and Roth, *op. cit.*, II, 33, 367.

217. *Ibid.*, pp. 262-263 (and *ME*, IV, 787).

218. *ME*, IV, 787.

219. *Ibid.*, p. 788.

220. *Ibid.*

221. *TA:VMS*, p. 118 (and Egli, *St. Galler Täufer*, p. 19).

222. Dürr and Roth, *op. cit.*, II, 484; III, 151, 152.

223. *The Hutterite Chronicle*, p. 48 (and also *MM*, p. 427).

224. Peachy, *op. cit.*, pp. 25, 60 ff. (from Bern, Stattarchiv, Unnütze Papiere, Bd. 80, Stk. 1). Also see R. Steck and G. Tobler (eds.), *Aktensammlung Geschichte der Berner Reformation, 1521-1532* (Bern, 1923), pp. 763, 1180.

225. Yoder, "Balthasar Hubmaier," p. 11 ff.

226. *TA:VMS*, pp. 117-120.

227. *Ibid.*, p. 118.

228. Augsburger, *op. cit.*, pp. 6-7, 177-184.

229. G. Bossert, Jr., "Michael Sattler's Trial and Martyrdom in 1527," *MQR* (1951), p. 201.

230. Valerius Anshelm, *Bernischen Chronik*, V. (Bern, 1896), 185. (Anshelm's

wife was also from Staufen.) Sattler's role as prior is substantiated by references at his trial (see *MM*, p. 418).

231. *The Hutterian Chronicle*, pp. 54-55.

232. At his trial he conversed in Latin and offered to defend his position from the Bible in its original languages (see *MM*, p. 417).

233. Bossert, Jr., *op. cit.*, p. 201, notes that though his name does not appear on the University matriculation lists (Freiburg), as a monk at St. Peter's he may have been in attendance anyway.

234. Weis, *op. cit.*, pp. 26-27 (and Chapter 5).

235. Peter Albert, *Die Reformatorische Bewegung zu Freiburg bis zum Jahre, 1525* (in *Freiburger Diocezan Archiv*, 1919), p. 26.

236. *Ibid.*, p. 35.

237. *Ibid.*, p. 38.

238. *MM*, p. 417.

239. John Horsch, *Mennonites in Europe* (Scottdale, Pa.: Mennonite Press, 1942), p. 70. (He gives no source verification.)

240. *MM*, p. 417.

241. Anshelm, *op. cit.*, p. 186.

242. E. W. McDonnell, *The Beguines and Beghards in Medieval Culture* (New Jersey: Rutger's University Press, 1954), pp. 3-5, 141.

243. *Ibid.*, pp. 128, 155.

244. *Ibid.*, p. 320.

245. Cf., the Mandate in Anshelm, *op. cit.*, pp. 2-5.

246. Bossert, Jr., *op. cit.*, p. 202.

247. Augsburger, *op. cit.*, p. 6.

248. *TA:VMS*, pp. 250-253.

249. Bossert, Jr., *op. cit.*, p. 202, says he was not present at the January 1525 and March 1525 disputations at Zürich; he was only at the November 1525 one, but see *TA:VMS*, pp. 73-75. (He is referred to as Brother Michael and designated as a "foreigner.")

250. *TA:VMS*, pp. 270-273.

251. *Ibid.*, p. 136 (Brenwald also joined them at Hinwil; *Ibid.*, pp. 109-110).

252. *Ibid.*, p. 136.

253. Augsburger, *op. cit.*, p. 24.

254. For a fuller treatment see *ibid.*, Chapter 5, and *TA:Elsass*, I, 68-91.

255. *TA:Elsass*, I, 58-62; Bossert, Jr., *op. cit.*, pp. 202-203; exaggerates the differences doctrinally (for example, Denck may not have been teaching actual universalism, only potential. See J. Kiwiet, "The Theology of Hans Denck," *MQR* [1958], pp. 3-27). There is clearly a more mystical emphasis, however, even in his Anabaptist writings.

256. For a listing of the "20 Articles" see *ME*, IV, 428.

257. *ME*, I, 447.

258. Walter Koehler, *Brüderlich Vereinigung etzlicher kinder Gottes sieben Artikel betreffend* (Leipzig, 1908), pp. 19-20.

259. *TA:Elsass*, I, 68-70, 98-102.

260. *ME*, I, 456 (from M. Bucer, *Getreue Warnung der Prediger des Evangelii zu Strassburg über die Artikel* [July 1527]).

261. *TA:Elsass*, I, 68-69 (though Sattler addresses the Strassburg Reformers as "beloved brethren in God," or similar terms, six times).

262. *ME*, IV, 433; cf. also J. W. Baum, *Capito und Butzer, Strassburger Reformation* (Elberfeld, 1860), p. 373.

263. Cf. *Hutterite Chronicle*, p. 54; and B. Jenny, *Das Schleitheimer Täuferbekenntnis, 1527* (Thayngen: Karl Augustin Verlag, 1951), p. 7. Zwingli's *Elenchus* is a

reply to the Schleitheim Articles, ZSW, VI.

264. J. J. Kiwiet, *Pilgram Marbeck* (Kassel: J. G. Oncken, 1957), pp. 25-26.
265. *TA:VMS*, p. 136.
266. *Ibid.*
267. *ME*, II, 350-351.
268. Peachy, *op. cit.*, p. 115.
269. *Handlung oder Acta der Disputation gehalten zu Zoffingen* (Zürich: Froschauer, 1532); cf. also J. H. Yoder, *Täufertum und Reformation in der Schweiz*, I (Karlsruhe, 1962), 138-143.
270. *TA:VMS*, p. 366.
271. *ME*, III, 351; also, S. Geiser, *Die Taufgesinnten-Gemeinden* (Karlsruhe, 1931), p. 179.
272. J. C. Wenger (ed. and trans.), "Martin Weninger's Vindication of Anabaptism, 1535," *MQR*, XXII (1948), 180-187 (in J. J. Spleiss, *Akten aur Geschichte der Reformation in Schaffhausen*, Bd. II [Ms., Stadtarchiv, Schaffhausen], 106-112).
273. Wenger' "Weninger's Vindication," pp. 182-183.
274. *Ibid.*, p. 186.
275. *Ibid.*, p. 185.
276. *Ibid.*
277. Even Bullinger admitted: "There is no doubt that people in general sin very grievously . . . yea the preachers themselves" (Geiser, *op. cit.*, p. 179); Capito likewise wrote: "He [Sattler] saw a lack in our preachers . . . especially in the outward life of the congregation. . . ." (*TA:Elsass*, I, 81).
278. Wenger, *Even Unto Death*, p. 34.
279. *MM*, p. 432 (Blaurock's "Admonition").
280. *TA:VMS*, pp. 42-43.
281. *Ibid.*, pp. 183-184.
282. Blanke, *op. cit.*, p. 33.
283. Oddly enough, Grebel never quotes the Sermon on the Mount in his writings (Bender, 179).
284. *MM*, p. 432.
285. *TA:VMS*, p. 24 (Mantz); p. 118 (Guldi); *TA:HS*, p. 163 (Hubmaier).
286. J. C. Wenger (ed. and trans.), "Two Early Anabaptist Tracts," *MQR*, XXII (1948), 34-42.
287. *Ibid.*, p. 36.
288. *Ibid.*, p. 37.
289. *Ibid.*
290. *Ibid.*, p. 39.
291. *Ibid.*
292. *TA:VMS*, p. 13.
293. *Ibid.*, p. 124, No. 122.
294. *TA:VMS*, p. 218.
295. *TA:HS*, pp. 340, 341 (italics mine).
296. *Ibid.*, p. 308.
297. Cf. Sattler's letter to Capito and Bucer (*TA:Elsass*, I, No. 70); also the two tracts *The Hearing of False Prophets* and *Concerning Evil Overseers*, translated from the *Sammelband* by J. C. Wenger, "Three Swiss Brethren Tracts," MQR, XXI (1947), 274-281.
298. *TA:Elsass*, I, 81-83 ("Since he saw a lack in our preachers and . . . in the outward life of the congregation, he perhaps paid less attention to our admonition," wrote Capito).
299. Wenger, "Weninger's Vindication," pp. 186, 182-183.
300. Verduin, *op. cit.*, p. 106 (from *Acta des Gespräch* Bern, [1538]).

301. *TA:Hesse*, p. 238 ff.
302. F. H. Littell, "What Butzer Debated with the Anabaptists at Marburg; a Document of 1538," *MQR*, XXXVI (1962), 256-276.
303. *TA:Hesse*, pp. 202 ff.
304. *The Hutterite Chronicle*, p. 44.
305. Wenger, "Weninger's Vindication," p. 185, says: "They do not preach the doctrine of Christ and consent not to the saving words of the doctrine of godliness."
306. J. C. Wenger (ed. and trans.), "Concerning the Satisfaction of Christ," *MQR*, XX (1946), 252 (italics mine).
307. *Ibid.*, p. 247.
308. *TA:HS*, pp. 381, 339-340.
309. Verduin, *op. cit.*, p. 106 (from *Acta des Gespräch, 1538*); cf. also Wenger, "Weninger's Vindication," p. 183; and *CWMS*, p. 631 for the complaint that the Magisterial Reformers preached grace and forgiveness without "demand for repentance."
310. *TA:VMS*, pp. 15, 17 (Letter to Müntzer); cf. also Verduin, *op. cit.*, p. 121.
311. Wenger, "Weninger's Vindication," pp. 184-185.
312. Littell, "What Butzer Debated," p. 260.
313. *Ibid*, pp. 259, 263.
314. Erhart Hegenwald, "Hegenwald and Konrad Grebel, January 1, 1525" (Staatbibliothek St. Gallen, Ms. 31, 222, 8 pages; a certified typescript copy is at the Mennonite Historical Library, Goshen College, and in the *Epistolae Grebelianae*); cf. also *ME*, IV, 1090.
315. Cf. Hegenwald's letter to Grebel (in *Epistolae Grebelianae*). Also Wenger, *Even Unto Death*, p. 57, quotes from the Zofingen Debate (1532) the Reformed opinion that the differences were concerned primarily with "external things."
316. *TA:VMS*, pp. 21-22. 127.
317. Jackson, *Selected Works*, pp. 181-182, 187, 190 f., 197.
318. *Ibid.*, p. 187.
319. *Ibid.*, p. 190.
320. *Ibid.*, pp. 197-198.
321. *TA:HS*, p. 465.
322. *Ibid.*, p. 195 (and in *ZSW*, IV, 245).
323. *TA:HS*, p. 217.
324. *TA:Elsass*, I, 82.
325. Kessler, *op. cit.*, p. 48.
326. J. Pelikan and H. Lehman (eds.), *Lectures on Galatians*, in *Luther's Works*, XXVII (Phila.: Fortress Press, 1964), 149. Cf. also XXI (*The Sermon on the Mount*, 1956), 259: "Until recently they were called monks, now they are the Anabaptists, the new monks"; also, XXI, 5 and LIV (*Table Talk*, 1967), 140.
327. Beachy, *op. cit.*, p. 34 (from Calvin's *Institutes*, I, 651); cf. also Augsburger, *op. cit.*, pp. 83-88 (analyzing Calvin's *Short Instruction, 1541*, against the Anabaptists).
328. Wenger, *Even Unto Death*, pp. 57-59; and Blanke, *op. cit.*, p. 40.
329. Beachy, *op. cit.*, pp. 7-8, 85 ff, 124-131.
330. Williams, *op. cit.*, p. 228.
331. See Friedmann, *The Theology of Anabaptism: An Interpretation*, 1973.
332. *ME*, IV, 415 (on "Sanctification").
333. See Chapter IV.

4. The Dominance of Asceticism in the Structuring of Anabaptist Theology

1. Cf. R. Friedmann, "Recent Interpretations of Anabaptism," in *Hutterite Studies*

(Goshen: Mennonite Historical Society, 1961), pp. 22-40.

2. E. Stauffer, "The Anabaptist Theology of Martyrdom," *MQR* (1945), pp. 179-214.

3. H. S. Bender, "The Anabaptist Theology of Discipleship," *MQR* (1950), pp. 25-32.

4. In Hershberger, *op. cit.*, pp. 105-118. More recently his posthumous *Theology of Anabaptism: An Interpretation* (Scottdale, Pa.: Herald Press) appeared.

5. Augsburger, *op. cit.*, p. 232.

6. Garrigou-Lagrange, *Christian Perfection and Contemplation*, trans. M. T. Doyle (St. Louis: B. Herder Co., 1951), p. 13.

7. Matthew 5:48 (KJV).

8. Garrigou-Lagrange, *op. cit.*, p. 14.

9. Beachy, *op. cit.*, p. 8, notes that Calvin had a stronger doctrine of regeneration than Luther.

10. Cf. article 22 of "The 67 Articles" in Zwingli, *Selected Works*, p. 113.

11. G. Williams, "Sanctification in the Testimony of Several So-Called Schwärmer," *MQR* (1968), pp. 5-6.

12. Cf., Chapter V, pp. 473 ff.; also Chapter II.

13. Garrigou-Lagrange, *op. cit.*, p. 15.

14. *Ibid.*, p. 16.

15. *Ibid.*, p. 28, notes that for those distinguishing the ascetic way from the mystical, "the mystical union no longer appears . . . as the culminating point. . . ."

16. *Ibid.*, pp. 16, 23-24 (he follows Thomas Aquinas on this point [p. 25]; cf. *Summa*, q. 182, 2-3).

17. *Ibid.*, p. 10.

18. *Ibid.*, pp. 27-28. The mystical way is considered valid but is relegated to the extraordinary, for a few rare souls.

19. Guibert, Joseph de, *The Theology of the Spiritual Life*, trans. P. Barrett (New York: Sheed and Ward, 1953), pp. 10-11.

20. Garrigou-Lagrange, *op. cit.*, p. 10.

21. Ritschl, *op. cit.*, p. 23.

22. Williams, "Sanctification in the Schwärmer," p. 22. Cf. also Karl Holl, *The Cultural Significance of the Reformation* (new York: Meridian Books, 1959), pp. 33-35.

23. Based especially on passages such as Colossians 3:5, 10; Romans 6:4-6; Galatians 5:24; 2 Corinthians 4:10. Cf. also, Garrigou-Lagrange, *op. cit.*, p. 9.

24. "The Conferences of Cassian" in O. Chadwick (ed.), *Western Asceticism* (Philadelphia: Westiminster Press, 1958), p. 252, records Cassian thus: "This last text 'he cannot sin' [1 John] must only be understood of deadly sin, not of all sin . . . no holy man can prevent himself falling into the little sins, sins of speech and thought, of ignorance and forgetfulness, sins which we do not will. . . ."

25. *TA:HS*, pp. 338-339, refers to "the goal which is eternal life, a gift of God." Also, see Manz's testimony, *MM*, p. 415.

26. Cf. one of Sattler's hymns (stanza 4) in Augsburger, *op. cit.*, pp. 273-275, which refers to "living in righteousness whereby one can attain to eternal blessedness [*Seligkeit*]."

27. *TA:HS*, pp. 338-339.

28. Wenger, "The Satisfaction of Christ," pp. 247, 252.

29. J. C. Wenger (ed. and trans.), "Two Kinds of Obedience," *MQR* (1947), p. 20. Cf. also Wenger, *Weninger's Vindication*, p. 183.

30. *TA:Elsass*, I, No. 70, 69-70.

31. *TA:HS*, p. 157, describes Christ as the only Savior and Healer "who has come into this world to make righteous and sanctify [*gerecht und fromb zumachen*] sinners." Cf. also on Luther, Williams, "Sanctification Among the Schwärmer," p. 6,

n. 1 and 2.

32. Wenger, "The Satisfaction of Christ," p. 247.

33. There are repeated references to Isaiah 53 and to Christ as the Physician and Healer: *MM*, p. 432 (Blaurock); *TA:HS*, pp. 157, 275; "The Satisfaction of Christ" (Sattler), p. 252.

34. Wenger, "Weninger's Vindication," p. 186.

35. *TA:VMS*, p. 382.

36. TA: *Elsass*, I, 70 (Article 18). Similarly, Sattler asserts that filial obedience "strives for and attains perfection." Wenger, "Two Kinds of Obedience," p. 20.

37. Augsburger, *op. cit.*, pp. 140-148.

38. *Ibid.*, p. 144.

39. Wenger, "Weninger's Vindication," p. 185.

40. Beachy, *op. cit.*, pp. 131-132, suggests that divinization was intended to make man God. He goes too far; rather, it was only a limited, creaturely godlikeness; for example, Blaurock, in Egli, *Akten*, p. 288, says: "Christ came to bring again what was lost through the fall of Adam," and Hubmaier adds, "As in Paradise, save for the flesh" (*TA:HS*, pp. 394, 390).

41. *Handlung oder Acta (1532)*, p. 30; also *CWMS*, pp. 409-410.

42. *TA:VMS*, pp. 42-43; also *CWMS*, p. 93, asserts that regeneration causes one "to live no longer after the old corrupted nature of the first earthly Adam but after the new upright nature of the new and heavenly Adam, Jesus Christ."

43. *TA:VMS*, p. 219 (Felix Manz) writes that Christ's true servants "follow Christ . . . on the way on which He preceded them." Hubmaier, *TA:HS*, p. 413, asserts: "The plain and simple will of God is that we model [*furbilden*] ourselves after His dear Son, Jesus Christ, and follow His life and teachings. Thereon hang all the law and the prophets." Cf. also *TA:Esass*, I, No. 70 (Article 7); *CWMS*, pp. 93, 101, 798; J. C. Wenger, "The Schleitheim Confession," *MQR* (1945), p. 251.

44. Wenger, "Weninger's Vindication," p. 186; P. Rideman, *Account of Our Religion, Doctrine and Faith*, trans. K. E. Hasenberg (London: Hodder & Stoughton, 1950), pp. 37-38.

45. *MM*, p. 415 (Manz).

46. *TA:HS*, pp. 338-339. Also, Manz (*MM*, p. 415) observes: "It is love alone that is pleasing to God"; also "He who does not demonstrate Christian love finds no acceptance with God," and "The sheep of Christ seek the praise of Christ; this is their choice." Cf., also *CWMS*, p. 558.

47. Blaurock's "Admonition," (*MM*, p. 432): "This is what God requires: that the whole human race shall love and fear Him, that they should follow His son, Jesus Christ, and observe His divine doctrine."

48. R. Duerkson, "Doctrinal Implications in 16th-Century Anabaptist Hymnody," *MQR* (1961), p. 40.

49. *MM*, p. 20 (Sattler).

50. *TA:HS*, pp. 217, 460.

51. Sattler urged, *MM*, p. 419: "Forget not charity without which it is not possible for you to be a Christian flock."

52. *TA:HS*, pp. 174, 185.

53. *MM*, p. 432 (Blaurock). Grebel (from "Hegenwald's Letter"): "Whoever really believes will obey. . . ." *TA:HS*, pp. 338-339, says true Christians "are devoted servants of righteousness in obedience." (Cf., also, *TA:HS*, p. 370; *MM*, p. 420.)

54. Wenger, "Two Kinds of Obedience" (Sattler), p. 20.

55. *TA:HS*, pp. 460, 287.

56. Walter Klassen, "Some Anabaptist Views on the Doctrine of the Holy Spirit," *MQR* (1961), p. 130, notes the strong agreement among all branches of Evangelical Anabaptism on the work of the Holy Spirit in producing the Christian life.

57. Cf., Grüninger Eingabe, TA:VMS, pp. 236-237, on the required "fruit of the Spirit."

58. Hubmaier describes Christian character and conduct in terms of the Beatitudes (Matthew 5); TA:HS, p. 328. For a "Sermon on the Mount" definition of asceticism, see Bouyer, Dictionaire Theologique, p. 80.

59. MM, p. 432 (Blaurock's "Admonition"); also TA:HS p. 413.

60. Grebel stated that whoever is covetous, a usurer, a gambler, or in other ways is guilty of vice should "in no case be considered a Christian" (TA:VMS, p. 124). Cf., also TA:VMS, p. 382.

61. Bender, Conrad Grebel, pp. 206-207; cf., also TA:HS, p. 313.

62. TA:VMS, p. 17 (Letter to Müntzer); cf. also, Wenger, "Schleitheim Confession" (article 6).

63. Bender, Conrad Grebel, p. 146; cf. also TA:VMS, p. 124; and Manz, "The sheep of Christ do not suffer themselves to be hindered either by possessions or by temporal goods" (MM, p. 415).

64. TA:VMS, p. 17; and TA:HS, p. 377.

65. Note, however, P. Marpeck's fear of legalism (ME, III, 500, 501).

66. Cf. M. Ebersole, "The Anabaptist View of the Church and the Therapeutic Community," MQR (1961), pp. 218-237.

67. Anabaptists maintained, according to Friedmann, that "one cannot find salvation without caring for the brother. . . ." in R. Friedmann, "On Mennonite Historiography and on Individualism and Brotherhood," MQR (1944), p. 121.

68. TA:HS, p. 318.

69. R. Friedmann, "The Doctrine of the Two Worlds," in Hershberger, op. cit., pp. 105-108.

70. Ibid., and cf. also Friedmann, "The Essence of the Anabaptist Faith," p. 9.

71. TA:VMS, pp. 236-237.

72. J. C. Wenger (ed. and trans.), "An Early Anabaptist Tract on Hermeneutics" ("How Scripture Is to Be Rightly Explained and Divided, by M.S."), MQR (1968), pp. 42-43.

73. TA:Elsass, I, No. 70; Articles 7-20 expound an ethical dichotomy and end with, "Christ and Belial have no fellowship (2 Cor. 6:15)."

74. Augsburger, op. cit., p. 55, describes "separation" as the central and unifying theme of the Schleitheim Confession.

75. Jackson, Selected Works of Zwingli, pp. 188-189, 203.

76. Acta des Gesprächs (1538), Article VI on the State, records that the Anabaptists insist on a great gap between Christians and the world; the former live by the standards of the Sermon on the Mount, the latter is governed by Satan. Also, Article VII, the Ban, divides the world into two parts: believers and unbelievers (or not yet believers). Believers are in the world but not of the world; believers are in light while the world is in darkness.

77. R. E. Wingart, "The Meaning of Sin in the Theology of Menno Simons," MQR (1967), pp. 26, 28; also CWMS, pp. 93, 554.

78. Wenger, "Schleitheim Confession," p. 249.

79. Ibid., p. 246; Augsburger, op. cit., p. 50.

80. Friedmann, "Two Worlds," in Hershberger, op. cit., pp. 105-118. Cf. also TA:Elsass, I, No. 70; TA:HS, pp. 259-260, 222-223, 122.

81. Moore, op. cit., p. 38.

82. Cf. Chapter III.

83. TA:HS, p. 275.

84. Hubmaier, TA:HS, p. 217, refers to the last judgment and the coming of Christ as the time when finally "our carnal, sinful, godless life will have an end. Then will every man receive the reward of his works."

85. Manz, *MM*, p. 415, refers to it as "eternal joy with Him and pure love for Him and all His righteousness. . . ." Also Hubmaier, *TA:HS*, p. 217, describes glorification as "a certain, clear, joyful, rich vision of Thy divine face."
86. *TA:VMS*, p. 235; *TA:Elsass*, I, 69; Wenger, "Schleitheim Confession," p. 247.
87. *TA:HS*, pp. 260-261.
88. *MM*, p. 420.
89. *TA:VMS*, p. 17 (Letter to Müntzer); *TA:VMS*, pp. 236-237; *TA:HS*, pp. 222-223; Wenger, "Schleitheim Confession," p. 248.
90. *TA:VMS*, pp. 42-43; also Hans Marquart's statement in *Vadians Deutsche Historische Schriften*, ed. E. Goetzinger (St. Gallen, 1879), III, 466.
91. Augsburger, *op. cit.*, p. 142.
92. Wenger, "The Satisfaction of Christ," pp. 248-249.
93. *TA:VMS*, p. 216.
94. *TA:HS*, p. 185.
95. *MM*, p. 418 (Sattler urges group separation and corporate holiness).
96. Beachy, *op. cit.*, pp. 85-86.
97. *TA:HS*, pp. 380-397; 400-431.
98. Cf. R. Friedmann, "The Doctrine of Originial Sin as Held by the Anabaptists of the 16th Century," *MQR* (1959), pp. 206-214; Hall, *op. cit.*,; Fast, "The Dependence of the First Anabaptists"; Kreider, *op. cit.*
99. *TA:HS*, pp. 405-410, 417.
100. Blaurock's "Admonition" (in *MM*, p. 432) records: "Oh, how awful it will be with the sinner who now refuses help." Again, "All those who use diligence to do Thy will, Thou acceptest as Thy children."
101. Wenger, "The Satisfaction of Christ," p. 251; and *TA:HS*, pp. 415, 416; and (p. 414) "This child [of God] relationship is offered to all men equally."
102. Cf. William Klassen, "Was H. Denck a Universalist?" *MQR* (1965), pp. 152-154.
103. *TA:HS*, pp. 416, 468.
104. *Ibid.*, pp. 405-410; and Langenmantel's sermon in Wenger, "Two Anabaptist Tracts," p. 37.
105. Wenger, "The Satisfaction of Christ," p. 250.
106. *TA:HS*, p. 467.
107. *MM*, p. 432; *TA:HS*, p. 414 (that is, any commission or omission contrary to the will of God).
108. In *MM*, p. 415, Manz refers to the "Fall" as Adam's becoming, "disobedient to God."
109. *TA:HS*, p. 311.
110. *Ibid.*, p. 389; Friedmann, "The Doctrine of Original Sin," pp. 206-214.
111. Augsburger, *op. cit.*, p. 106.
112. Beachy, *op. cit.*, pp. 67-68.
113. Free choice is implicit in Manz, "Protestation," *TA:VMS*, p. 24.
114. The testimony of Peter Tesch, at the Marburg Disputation, comes closest to eliminating this initial free choice and making freedom only "after" regeneration. But this is an isolated case, a defense against charges of Pelagianism, and it is rather ambiguous (*TA:Hesse*, p. 247 f.).
115. *TA:HS*, pp. 382-386.
116. Beachy, *op. cit.*, pp. 331-332.
117. *Ibid.*
118. *TA:HS*, p. 385.
119. *Ibid.*
120. *Ibid.*, p. 389.

322 Anabaptism and Asceticism

121. *Ibid.*, p. 390.
122. *Ibid.*
123. *Ibid.*, p. 394 (italics mine).
124. *Ibid.*, p. 397.
125. *Ibid.*, p. 418. Cf. also the Sermon on Jeremiah (Wenger, "Two Early Anabaptist Tracts," p. 39) which refers to the work of the Word in preparing the heart for greater grace but then cries out, "Would to God that people would hearken, believe on Him, and follow Him."
126. Cf. the *Devotio Moderna* in Chapter V. Erasmus also wrote on the subject before Anabaptism began (*Concerning Free Will*, 1524).
127. The "attainment" of salvation is stressed over "election" in Anabaptist vocabulary: for example, *TA:HS*, pp. 324-325; *MM*, p. 415; Wenger, "Two Kinds of Obedience," p. 20.
128. H. Lüdemann, *Reformation and Täufertum in ihren Verhältnis zum Christlichen Prinzep* (1890), p. 86.
129. Wenger, *Even Unto Death*, pp. 31-32; and Bender, *Conrad Grebel*, p. 204, align the Anabaptists with Reformation theology too readily. The necessity, even priority of grace is present in some medieval theology too.
130. *TA:HS*, pp. 323, 325.
131. Note Hubmaier's use of Blaurock's terminology on the Lord's Supper, the "rose-red blood" (*TA:HS*, p. 162), and his references to John the Baptist, from Manz, "Protestation" (*TA:HS*, p. 123).
132. Beachy, *op. cit.*, pp. 124-125; R. Friedmann, "Peter Rideman on Original Sin and the Way to Redemption," *MQR* (1952), pp. 210-215.
133. *TA:HS*, pp. 386-387, 390, 217, 313.
134. *Ibid.*, p. 403; also Muralt, *op. cit.*, p. 34.
135. *TA:HS*, p. 322, records Hubmaier: "If one says there is nothing good in man, he has said too much . . . for the likeness of God has not yet been entirely wiped out in us."
136. *Ibid.*, pp. 390-391, 394, 411, 418.
137. Beachy, *op. cit.*, pp. 124-125, 141-144.
138. *TA:HS*, pp. 390-391, states: "God created you without your aid but He will not save you without your aid."
139. *Ibid.*, p. 389, that is, the soul is "awakened by the Word of God." Also, *Ibid.*, pp. 390-391: "First God speaks . . . now man through the power of the Word can help himself or willfully neglect to do so."
140. *Ibid.*, pp. 390, 312-313.
141. *Ibid.*, pp. 387, 322.
142. *Ibid.*, pp. 123, 127.
143. *Ibid.*, p. 384.
144. *Ibid.*, p. 390 (that is, "comes to know again what is good and what is evil").
145. *Ibid.*, pp. 390-393.
146. *Ibid.*, p. 216 (Article 3); also p. 321 (that is, human nature after the Fall, and then after regeneration "must be carefully distinguished"); pp. 162-163, 127 (on comfort in pardon); and pp. 394-395 (in the power of the gospel one "can will and do all things that he is bidden").
147. *Ibid.*, pp. 383-384, 387.
148. *Ibid.*, p. 322.
149. *Ibid.*, pp. 167, 323.
150. *Ibid.*, pp. 121, 216-217.
151. *Ibid.*, p. 313.
152. *Ibid.*, p. 395.
153. *Ibid.*

154. *Ibid.*, p. 265.
155. *Ibid.*, p. 383 ("He helps our spirits, witnesses to them, strengthens them"). Also, before baptism (outer), there must be both the effective work of the Word on the individual *plus* "the purpose by *God's aid* to change his life...." (*Ibid.*, p. 123.) Cf. also *ibid.*, p. 477.
156. *Ibid.*, p. 311.
157. *Ibid.*, p. 322.
158. *Ibid.*, p. 312.
159. *Ibid.*, p. 157 ("*Nicht mehr tun ist die beste Busse*").
160. *Ibid.*, p. 110.
161. *Ibid.*, p. 477.
162. *Ibid.*, pp. 469-470.
163. *Ibid.*, p. 476.
164. *Ibid.*, p. 312.
165. *Ibid.*, p. 219.
166. *Ibid.*, p. 470.
167. Wenger, *Even Unto Death*, p. 94.
168. *TA:HS*, p. 110 (italics mine).
169. *Ibid.*
170. *Ibid.*, p. 111 (italics mine).
171. *Ibid.*
172. *Ibid.* (italics mine).
173. *Ibid.* (this passage is taken from Hubmaier's publication of July 1525 when he was in closest cooperation with the Grebel group).
174. *Ibid.*, p. 222 (Hubmaier prays for the Holy Spirit to "actuate in us a true faith, a constant hope, an ardent love by which we make our wills in all things submissive to your Fatherly will").
175. *Ibid.*, p. 461.
176. *Ibid.*, p. 313.
177. *Ibid.*, p. 174.
178. *Ibid.*, pp. 183, 185.
179. *Ibid.*, p. 316.
180. *Ibid.*, p. 313.
181. *Ibid.*, p. 324.
182. Beachy, *op. cit.*, pp. 87-99.
183. *TA:VMS*, pp. 236-237.
184. *MM*, pp. 415, 431 (Manz): Wenger, "Satisfaction of Christ," p. 251, notes that Christ takes the sin of the world "insofar as the world surrenders to Him in faith."
185. For the divine activity, see von Muralt, *op. cit.*, pp. 33-34; John Horsch, "The Faith of the Swiss Brethren," *MQR* (1931), pp. 128-129. Also, in *MM*, pp. 415, 431, Manz writes that salvation is through "pure grace," in the sense of being purchased by the shedding of Christ's blood and because there is otherwise no hope.
186. Cf. Grebel's assertion of the need for renunciation before baptism, *TA:VMS*, No. 98; Bender, *Conrad Grebel*, pp. 205-208 (Manz "Protestation"); Wenger, "How Scripture Is to Be Explained," p. 42 (Sattler); and "The Schleitheim Confession," p. 248, refers to true Christians as those "who have learned repentance."
187. Cf. Mantz, "Protestation," (*TA:VMS*, No. 16) says that faith is false without continuous fruitage of holiness; also, in reference to the power of the Holy Spirit, he adds: "Whoever receives and uses it, grows and is made perfect" (*MM*, p. 415).
188. *MM*, p. 431; Bender, *Conrad Grebel*, pp. 206-208.
189. *TA:VMS*, p. 25.
190. Cf. *TA:VMS*, p. 24 (Manz); *MM*, p. 432 (Blaurock); Wenger, "The Satisfaction

of Christ," p. 246.
191. *Ibid.*, pp. 243-254.
192. Augsburger, *op. cit.*, p. 137, notes that justification as forgiveness is only part of a justification conceived by the Anabaptists as a transforming relationship.
193. Wenger, "The Satisfaction of Christ," pp. 251-252 (n. 37).
194. *Ibid.*
195. *Ibid.*, p. 253.
196. *Ibid.*, pp. 248-249; cf. also Wenger, "The Schleitheim Confession," pp. 247-248, for the same antithesis between true faith and the "self-indulgence of the flesh."
197. Wenger, "The Satisfaction of Christ," p. 251.
198. *Ibid.*
199. *Ibid.*, pp. 251, 252, 249; (cf. also Wenger, *Even Unto Death*, p. 32).
200. Wenger, "The Satisfaction of Christ," p. 250 (italics mine).
201. Wenger, "The Schleitheim Confession," (Article 4) insists on the absolute necessity for the true Christian to walk "in the obedience of faith" and to "*want* to do God's will."
202. Wenger, "The Satisfaction of Christ," p. 250.
203. *Ibid.*, p. 246.
204. *Ibid.*, p. 251.
205. *Ibid.*, p. 252.
206. *Ibid.* ("will" here may refer to the freeing by regeneration and not to Hubmaier's initial free choice).
207. *Ibid.*, p. 250.
208. *Ibid.*, p. 252.
209. Augsburger, *op. cit.*, pp. 246, 112.
210. *TA:Elsass*, I, 110.
211. The atonement is conceived of as universal, potentially, but actuated only through a voluntary "surrender" to Christ by faith and by the obedient performance of His commandments. (Wenger, "The Satisfaction of Christ," p. 251.)
212. *Ibid.*, pp. 248-249, 251-252.
213. Wenger, "The Schleitheim Confession," pp. 243-244.
214. Augsburger, *op. cit.*, p. 50. Cf. also, R. Friedmann, "The Schleitheim Confession (1527) and Other Doctrinal Writings," *MQR* (1942), pp. 86 f.
215. Gratz, *op. cit.*, pp. 25 ff.
216. Augsburger, *op. cit.*, pp. 48-50; Friedmann, *Mennonite Piety*, p. 160; Wenger, "Schleitheim Confession," pp. 244-246.
217. J. C. Wenger, "Grace and Discipleship in Anabaptism," *MQR* (1961), p. 50 (n. 1, n. 1a).
218. *Acta des Gesprächs*, f. 59-60.
219. Von Muralt, *op. cit.*, pp. 32-33.
220. *Acta des Gesprächs*, f. 86-87.
221. Wenger, "Grace and Discipleship," p. 52.
222. *Acta des Gesprächs*, f. 179.
223. *Ibid.*, f. 180.
224. *Ibid.*, f. 191.
225. Wenger, "Weninger's Vindication," pp. 183-184, 186. Weninger also calls for a renunciation of the lusts of the flesh (p. 184) and maintains that those who fail to do so have a "spurious faith" (p. 186).
226. *TA:Hesse*, p. 247 f.
227. *Ibid.*
228. Beachy, *op. cit.*, pp. 30-35 (on repentance before regeneration, in Menno Simons and in D. Philips). Cf. also William Keeney, "The Development of Dutch Anabaptist Thought" (PhD thesis, Hartford, 1959), pp. 53-54, 92-107; and Bender (ed.),

Hutterite Studies, pp. 87-90.
229. *TA:VMS*, pp. 17 f. (italics mine). Similarly, Hubmaier, *TA:HS*, p. 316, writes that though faith alone makes one *fromm* (in the potential, regenerate sense) yet it alone does not lead to salvation; there must also be the confession by baptism, works of faith, and so on. So also, Menno Simons combines "the spiritual birth and sanctification without which no one shall see the Lord" (*CWMS*, p. 54).
230. *TA:HS*, p. 275.
231. *TA:VMS*, pp. 23-24. Cf. also Wenger (ed.), "The Schleitheim Confession," p. 248 (Article 1); and *TA:HS*, pp. 123, 142.
232. Wenger, *Even Unto Death*, pp. 94-95.
233. *TA:VMS*, p. 24; and *MM*, p. 415.
234. *TA:HS*, p. 377. Cf. also Hotz' comment, in *Acta des Gespräch* (1538), f. 115-116: "But whoever falls away from faith and does evil, must repent [*bus thün*], have sorrow [*Ruw*] and suffering [*leid*] over his sins, or he has no salvation."
235. *TA:HS*, p. 426 (Article 13) (italics mine).
236. Augsburger, *op. cit.*, pp. 273-274, stanza 4.
237. *Handlung oder Acta* (1532), f. 450; (see Horsch, *op. cit.*, p. 137).
238. *Acta des Gespräch* (1538), f. 30, 41, 49, 65, 86-87, 98, 269.
239. *Ibid.*, f. 30.
240. *Ibid.*, f. 41.
241. *Ibid.*, f. 86-87.
242. *Ibid.*, f. 98.
243. Cited in Wenger, "Grace and Discipleship," p. 52.
244. B. Poschmann, *Penance and the Anointing of the Sick*, trans. F. Courtney (New York: Herder & Herder, 1964), pp. 20-24.
245. *Ibid.*, p. 113.
246. *Ibid.*, pp. 124-125.
247. *Ibid.*, p. 128.
248. *Ibid.*, p. 132.
249. *Ibid.*, p. 145.
250. See H. A. Oberman, *The Harvest of Medieval Theology* (Cambridge: Harvard University Press, 1963), pp. 460-464.
251. Poschmann, *op. cit.*, pp. 184-185.
252. *Ibid*.
253. *Ibid.*, pp. 191-192.
254. *Ibid.*, p. 196.
255. *ME*, II, 448-449 (*Gelassenheit*).
256. *TA:VMS*, pp. 17-18 (resistance makes the ban necessary and a dying to self must precede faith). Wenger (ed.), "The Satisfaction of Christ," p. 251, refers to the need to "surrender to Christ in faith." Cf. also, *TA:HS*, pp. 111, 136, 145, 160, 487.
257. *Ibid.*, p. 467. (He also ties it to John the Baptist and repentance, p. 110 f.)
258. *Ibid.*, pp. 338-339; *ME*, II, 448-449.
259. Friedmann, "The Essence of the Anabaptist Faith," p. 12, contends with some warrant that the Anabaptists used the term *Gelassenheit* with a different meaning than the contemplative mystics, that is, with practical, ascitivistic implications.
260. *TA:VMS*, p. 18; *TA:HS*, p. 136, says that true faith includes a "surrendering of oneself to God. . . ." Cf. also Kiwiet, *op. cit.*, pp. 74-77.
261. *TA:HS*, p. 487.
262. Kiwiet, *op. cit.*, p. 74.
263. *Ibid.*, p. 80 (from Denck's *Ordnung*).
264. *TA:HS*, p. 159 (italics mine).
265. *Ibid.*, p. 167. Cf. also p. 139 ("You may grow in faith"); and *MM*, p. 415.
266. *Vadians Deutsche Historische Schriften*, III, 466.

326 Anabaptism and Asceticism

267. *Ibid.*, cf. also Wenger (ed.), "The Schleitheim Confession," article 4.
268. *TA:HS*, p. 272.
269. Walter Klaassen, *op. cit.*, pp. 130-139. Cf. also *Acta des Gespräch* (1958), pp. 228-229; Rideman, *An Account of Our Religion*, p. 38; and *LCC:SAW*, pp. 190, 199-201 (Hubmaier).
270. *Handlung oder Acta* (1532), f. 30, as cited in H. S. Bender, "Walking in the Resurrection: The Anabaptist Doctrine of Regeneration and Discipleship," *MQR* (1961), p. 96.
271. *TA:HS*, p. 189.
272. Wenger (ed.), "The Schleitheim Confession," p. 248, Article 1.
273. *TA:HS*, pp. 383 f.
274. *Ibid.*, pp. 383-384, 390-391, 405.
275. *Ibid.*, pp. 383-384.
276. *MM*, p. 415 (italics mine).
277. Friedmann, "The Essence of the Anabaptist Faith," p. 12.
278. Bender, *Conrad Grebel*, p. 207.
279. *Ibid.*, p. 206.
280. Wenger (ed.), "Two Kinds of Obedience," p. 20.
281. *TA:HS*, p. 189.
282. *Ibid.*, p. 160.
283. R. Friedmann, "Concerning the True Soldiers of Christ," in Hershberger (ed.), *op. cit.*, says that *Gelassenheit* is described in this Hutterite tract primarily as a true mortification of the flesh, as a rejection of the world and the fallen creatureliness (pp. 248-249), and these are given redemptive values (p. 252). It becomes one of the four weapons of the Christian soldier, along with faith, hope, and love" (p. 245).
284. Wenger (ed.), "Weninger's Vindication," p. 183.
285. Friedmann, "Concerning the True Soldiers of Christ," pp. 248-249.
286. *TA:HS*, p. 391.
287. *Ibid.*, pp. 390 f.
288. *Ibid.*, pp. 383-394 (italics mine), also p. 425.
289. *Ibid.*, p. 392.
290. *CWMS*, pp. 600-601, 93, 99.
291. *TA:HS*, p. 223.
292. *TA:VMS*, p. 17.
293. Wenger (ed.), "The Schleitheim Confession," p. 248.
294. *TA:HS*, p. 161.
295. *Ibid.* (italics mine).
296. *Ibid.*, p. 360 (italics mine); cf. also similar references to the penitent life as a crucifying, suppressing, and taming of the flesh and its lusts, in *CWMS*, pp. 93, 99.
297. *TA:HS*, p. 477.
298. *Ibid.*, p. 274.
299. *Ibid.*, p. 317 (re: "grievous" sins), 477 (re: "mortal" sins).
300. *Ibid.*, p. 355.
301. *Ibid.*, p. 477.
302. *Ibid.*, p. 355.
303. *Ibid.*, pp. 356, 161.
304. *Ibid.*, p. 318.
305. *Ibid.*, p. 355.
306. Wenger (ed.), "The Schleitheim Confession," p. 252.
307. *TA:HS*, p. 361.
308. *Ibid.*, pp. 159, 321.
309. *Ibid.*, p. 324.

310. G. J. Reinmann, *The Third Order Secular of St. Francis* (Washington: The Catholic University of America, 1928), pp. 29 ff.
311. *TA:HS*, p. 476.
312. *Ibid.*, pp. 273-274, 318; cf. also Reinmann, *op. cit.*, p. 29.
313. *TA:HS*, p. 357.
314. *Ibid.*, pp. 338-339 (italics mine). Almost identical wording is found in the "Grüninger Eingabe," *TA:VMS*, pp. 236 f.
315. *TA:HS*, pp. 324-325.
316. *Ibid.*, p. 360.
317. *Ibid.*, pp. 161, 162-3.
318. For a fuller description of the "imitation" or *Nachfolge* tradition in Anabaptism, see H. Bender, "The Anabaptist Vision," in Hershberger (ed.), *op. cit.*, pp. 42-43; also J. Burkholder, "The Anabaptist Vision of Discipleship," in Hershberger, *op. cit.*, pp. 135-151; and Augsburger, *op. cit.*, p. 137.
319. Wenger (ed.), "The Satisfaction of Christ," pp. 251, 247.
320. *MM*, p. 420.
321. *TA:VMS*, p. 26.
322. *Ibid.*, pp. 25, 94; *TA:HS*, p. 111; *CWMS*, pp. 558, 598, and Wenger (ed.), "Weninger's Vindication," p. 187.
323. Beachy, *op. cit.*, p. 134.
324. *MM*, p. 915.
325. *TA:HS*, pp. 111, 287, 467, 161-162, 395.
326. Wenger (ed.), "The Satisfaction of Christ," p. 250.
327. *TA:HS*, p. 413.
328. Wenger, "A Letter from Reublin," p. 74.
329. Stauffer, *op. cit.*, pp. 179-214.
330. *Ibid.*, pp. 180 f. Cf. also the suffering remnant and "little flock" idea in Grebel (*TA:VMS*, pp. 15-17); *TA:Elsass*, I, No. 70 (article 9); *CWMS*, pp. 579-622.
331. Cf. Chapter II.
332. Verduin, *op. cit.*, pp. 257-258.
333. Stauffer, *op. cit.*, pp. 182-183.
334. *TA:HS*, pp. 313-314.
335. *Ibid.*, p. 275; also Poschmann, *op. cit.*, p. 123.
336. *MM*, pp. 984-985.
337. *TA:HS*, p. 275.
338. *TA:VMS*, p. 17.
339. *MM*, p. 419.
340. *TA:HS*, p. 490.
341. Wenger (ed.), "The Satisfaction of Christ," pp. 248-249.
342. Wenger (ed.), "The Schleitheim Confession," p. 251. Sattler describes his passive acceptance of prison and torture as part of the "divine warfare" (*MM*, p. 419).
343. Hubmaier still upheld the principle of bearing of persecution patiently and passively (*TA:HS*, pp. 167, 310, 325); he even questions the right to defend oneself from attackers, unless for the sake of others (*TA:HS*, p. 272).
344. Friedmann, "Doctrine of the Two Worlds," in Hershberger, *op. cit.*, p. 114.
345. *TA:HS*, p. 487.
346. *MM*, p. 419.
347. *TA:HS*, p. 310.
348. *Ibid.*, p. 325.
349. Moore, *op. cit.*, p. 38 (stanza 17).
350. Wenger (ed.), "A Letter from Reublin," p. 75. (This letter illustrates Moravian, Pilgramite, and Swiss Brethren connections.)
351. *TA:VMS*, p. 20.

352. Wenger (ed.), "The Satisfaction of Christ," p. 249.
353. *Ibid.*, p. 250.
354. *TA:HS*, p. 360.
355. *Ibid.*, pp. 272-273.
356. *ME*, IV, 433. Cf. also *MM*, pp. 420-422 (Leonard Keyser and Thomas Herman).
357. Friedmann, "The Essence of the Anabaptist Faith," p. 21, says that "work was for the Anabaptists always testimony, *Bezeugung des Glaubens* . . . and never an act of self-redemption or purchase of merits."
358. *TA:HS*, p. 381.
359. *Ibid.*, p. 476.
360. Rideman, *Account of our Religion*, p. 36. Cf. also *TA:HS*, pp. 325 f. and *TA:Hesse*, pp. 202 f., which emphasizes final judgment according to "deeds," not "imagined faith" and ". . . eternal life to him who . . . in well doing seeks after eternal life."
361. *TA:VMS*, p. 25; Wenger (ed.), "The Satisfaction of Christ," p. 252; cf. also, Wenger, "Weninger's Vindication," p. 187; and *TA:HS*, p. 320.
362. Augsburger, *op. cit.*, p. 112; *TA:VMS*, p. 219 (Manz); *TA:HS*, pp. 323, 412, 418; *MM*, p. 432.
363. *TA:HS*, p. 323; and Wenger (ed.), "The Satsifaction of Christ," p. 250.
364. *Ibid.*, pp. 252-253.
365. *TA:VMS*, p. 217.
366. P. Marpeck, *Vermanung* (in *Gedenkschrift zum 400 jährigen Jubiläum der Mennoniten oder Taufgesinnten: 1525-1925* [1925]), p. 291.
367. *TA:HS*, pp. 403, 410.
368. Friedmann, "Doctrine of Two Worlds," in Hershberger, *op. cit.*, pp. 112-113; and *TA:HS*, p. 171 (where Hubmaier refers to the brotherhood-church "outside of which there is no salvation").
369. *Ibid.*, p. 185.
370. Friedmann, "The Essence of the Anabaptist Faith," p. 13.
371. *Ibid.*
372. *TA:HS*, p. 339.
373. *Ibid.*, pp. 139, 145.
374. *MM*, p. 418.
375. Hubmaier (*TA:HS*, p. 145), notes the close tie between baptism and the acceptance of discipline: "Whence comes this power [disciplinary] except only from the obligation of baptism?"
376. *Ibid.*, p. 308.
377. *Ibid.*, p. 136.
378. Cf. Grebel in *TA:VMS*, pp. 15, 17, 20; Sattler in Wenger (ed.), "The Schleitheim Confession," p. 248 and "The Satisfaction of Christ," p. 254; and Hubmaier *TA:HS*, pp. 111-112 ("lead a new life according to the rule and teaching of Christ"); similarly *TA:HS*, pp. 339, 136, 139, 145, 308.
379. *TA:HS*, p. 219 (Article 10) ascribes the power of the "keys" to the church universal but *TA:HS*, pp. 315, 478, to the local brotherhood.
380. *Ibid.*, pp. 316, 339 (Hubmaier applies the power of the "keys" specifically to cases of discord in the brotherhood and public and "grievous" sins).
381. *Ibid.*, p. 339; also *TA:VMS*, p. 17.
382. *TA:HS*, p. 339.
383. *Ibid.*, p. 377.
384. *Ibid.*, p. 356.
385. *Ibid.*, p. 190.
386. Wenger (ed.). "The Schleitheim Confession," p. 250.

387. *TA:HS*, p. 356.
388. *Ibid.*, p. 355. Sattler also refers to united prayer "in our meeting, for all our shortcomings" (Wenger [ed.], "The Schleitheim Confession," p. 252).
389. *TA:HS*, p. 357.
390. Friedmann, "Essence of the Anabaptist Faith," p. 10.
391. Augsburger, *op. cit.*, pp. 142-143, 125.
392. *TA:VMS*, pp. 17-18.
393. Moore, *op. cit.*, p. 38, quotes Blaurock's hymn, stanza 33: "Hold fast if you would receive the crown." Cf. also Wenger (ed.), "Weninger's Vindication," p. 186; *TA:VMS*, p. 238, stressing "abiding in the teachings of Christ"; and *Handlung oder Acta*, 1532, p. 30.
394. *Ibid.*
395. Wenger (ed.), "The Schleitheim Confession," p. 252.
396. *TA:HS*, p. 465 (Article 5).
397. Moore, *op. cit.*, p. 38 (stanza 33). Cf. also, *MM*, p. 432 (Blaurock) and *Vadians Deutsche Historische Schriften*, III, p. 466 (Hans Marquart).
398. *MM*, p. 432 (italics mine).
399. Moore, *op. cit.*, p. 38 (stanza 3 of "Gott führt ein recht Gericht").
400. *MM*, pp. 401-2; Vadians Deutsche Schriften, p. 466 (Marquart).
401. *TA:HS*, pp. 316f.; and Wenger (ed), Schleitheim Confession," pp. 248, 402.
402. Wenger (ed), "Vindication," p. 186.
403. Bender, "Walking in Resurrection," p. 109; Friedmann, "Essence of Anabaptist Faith," pp. 17 ff.; and von Muralt, *op. cit.*, pp. 36 f.
404. *ME*, IV, 1115 (Perfectionism). Cf. also, Friedmann, "Essence," pp. 17-18.
405. Verduin, *op. cit.*, pp. 102 ff.; Horsch, "The Faith of the Swiss Anabaptists," Part IV, pp. 133, 137.
406. Friedmann, "Essence," p. 18; and *TA:HS*, pp. 175-187.
407. For example, J. C. Wenger admits what he calls a seemingly "naive perfectionism," strongly expressed in Weninger's "Vindication"; but he writes it off without reconciliation, simply quoting Weninger's rejection of "sinlessness" at Zofingen (*Even Unto Death*, p. 34).
408. *TA:HS*, pp. 454, 456, 361.
409. *Handlung oder Acta*, 1532, f. 121 (cited by Wenger, *Even Unto Death*, p. 34). Cf. also *TA:HS*, pp. 390, 391.
410. Wenger, *Even Unto Death*, p. 34; and *TA:HS*, p. 391.
411. *TA:HS*, p. 390.
412. *MM*, pp. 418-419.
413. Pourrat, *op. cit.*, II, 134-135 (cf. also Chapter II).
414. Wenger (ed.), "Schleitheim Confession," p. 248 (Article 2); *TA:HS*, p. 361; and *CWMS*, p. 95.
415. Egli, *Akten*, p. 384. Cf. also *Acta des Gespräch*, 1538, f. 91, 101, 94.
416. Friedmann, "Essence of Anabaptist Faith," p. 15; and *TA:HS*, p. 111.
417. Wenger (ed.), "The Satisfaction of Christ," pp. 251-252.
418. *Acta des Gespräch*, 1538, f. 87.
419. Hubmaier notes that the prerequisite for participation in the Lord's Supper is to be "mindful and willing," not absolutely perfect in understanding or deed (*TA:HS*, p. 359).
420. *Ibid.*, p. 361 (italics mine), and p. 122.
421. *Ibid.*, pp. 162-163.
422. Wenger, *Even Unto Death*, p. 34 (from Zofingen, 1532).
423. Wenger (ed.), "Weninger's Vindication," pp. 183 f. (italics mine).
424. Bender, *Conrad Grebel*, p. 206.
425. *TA:HS*, pp. 394, 395 (italcs mine).

426. For example, the followers of the "Prophet" and the libertines of Hans Krug (see John Oyer, "Anabaptism in Central Germany," *MQR* [1961], pp. 11-12).
427. Bender, "Walking in Resurrection," p. 101.
428. ZSW, IV, 171-173. Sebastian Hofmeister's testimony is essentially the same, that is, that Manz taught that "the baptized should live without sinning" (*TA: VMS*, p. 123).
429. *TA:VMS*, No. 201, p. 202; *TA:HS*, p. 185.
430. Friedmann, "Essence of Anabaptist Faith," p. 13.
431. Friedmann, "On Mennonite Historiography," p. 121.
432. Wenger (ed.), "Weninger's Vindication," p. 184.
433. Wenger (ed.), "Schleitheim Confession," p. 250.
434. Friedmann, "Doctrine of the Two Worlds," in Hershberger, *op. cit.*, pp. 116-117.
435. Williams, "Sanctification Among the Schwärmer," p. 24.
436. *Ibid.*
437. *TA:VMS*, p. 15 (point 4).
438. *Ibid.*, pp. 16-17.
439. *Ibid.*
440. *TA:HS*, pp. 142-143, 265.
441. *Ibid.*, p. 160. Reublin criticized some who overlooked the priority of the internal (Wenger [ed.], "A Letter from Reublin," p. 73).
442. *TA:VMS*, p. 25.
443. Wenger (ed.), "The Satisfaction of Christ," p. 250.
444. Wenger (ed.), "Two Kinds of Obedience," pp. 18-22.
445. Friedmann, "Essence of Anabaptist Faith," pp. 19-20, acknowledges the later development of some formalism and sterile legalism.
446. *TA:HS*, p. 478.
447. Bender (ed.), *Hutterite Studies*, pp. 82 f.
448. Wenger (ed.), "Weninger's Vindication," p. 184.
449. Wenger, *Even Unto Death*, p. 34. Cf. also *TA:VMS*, p. 17 (Letter to Müntzer), which insists that those who reject the church of obedient disciples, under the rule of Christ, were to be regarded as "heathen and publicans."
450. Wenger (ed.), "Schleitheim Confession," p. 249; *TA:HS*, p. 360; *CWMS*, p. 54.
451. *TA:HS*, pp. 142-143, 145, 171, 183.
452. *Ibid.*, p. 171.
453. *Ibid.*, p. 340. Cf. also M. Gingerich, "Change and Uniformity," *MQR* (1966), p. 249.
454. The "Schleitheim Confession" summarizes all these areas of separation.
455. *TA:Bayern*, II, 34; and Beachy, *op. cit.*, p. 232.
456. For such an appeal, see Verduin, *op. cit.*, p. 239.
457. Beachy, *op. cit.*, p. 237.
458. Wenger (ed.), "Schleitheim Confession," p. 249.
459. *TA:VMS*, p. 16; and Bender, *Conrad Grebel*, p. 313.
460. J. C. Wenger (ed. and trans.), "Concerning Divorce," *MQR* (1947), pp. 118-119.
461. *Ibid.*, p. 116.
462. *Ibid.*, p. 117.
463. *TA:HS*, p. 479 (Article 18): "Whoever keeps his virginity has a precious jewel that then excels marriage and widowhood, however both are pleasing, honorable, and good to God."
464. Reinmann, *op. cit.*, pp. 70 f., 218, 296.
465. *Epistolae Grebelianae* (Grebel's letter to Vadian, July 13, 1523, commends Jacob Strauss for his anti-wealth and anti-usury stance). Cf. also Beachy, *op.cit.*, p. 13.

466. P. Klassen, op. cit., p. 136.
467. TA:HS, p. 178.
468. Verduin, op. cit., p. 226. Cf. also Castelberger's pre-Anabaptist protest (Egli, Akten, No. 623).
469. Vedder, op. cit., pp. 108-110.
470. TA:HS, pp. 345, 487.
471. TA:Bayern, I, 125 f.; Verduin, op. cit., p. 240.
472. Reinmann, op. cit., pp. 20, 29 f. 58, 60; and John Moorman, A History of the Franciscan Order, to 1517 (Oxford University Press, 1968), p. 216.
473. Wenger (ed.), "Schleitheim Confession" (Articles 6 and 7); TA:VMS, pp. 17, 128, 216.
474. Beachy, op. cit., pp. 337-338; and Bender, Conrad Grebel, pp. 200-202.
475. Verduin, op. cit., p. 271, says of the Anabaptists' pacifism that in this too they were "heirs to... the legacy of the heretic."
476. For less extreme positions, note Jacob Gross (TA:Elsass, I, 64; TA:VMS, p. 109); and Henri Aberli (ME, I); and cf. Beachy, op. cit., pp. 304-306, 314, 316.
477. Wenger (ed.), "Schleitheim Confession," p. 250.
478. Beachy, op. cit., pp. 310, 311.
479. TA:HS, pp. 437, 441, 442-444, 446.
480. Kessler, op. cit., pp. 147-148.
481. Verduin, op. cit., p. 225.
482. TA:HS, pp. 480-481; CWMS, p. 373.
483. Wenger (ed.), "Two Kinds of Obedience," p. 21.
484. TA:HS, pp. 480-481.
485. TA:VMS, p. 14; and TA:HS, p. 110.
486. TA:VMS, pp. 109-110, 388-389; and Moore, op. cit., appendix.
487. Bender (ed.), Hutterite Studies, pp. 82-84.
488. TA:HS, p. 468.
489. Norman F. Cantor, Medieval History (New York: Macmillan Co., 1963), p. 182.
490. Augsburger, op. cit., pp. 93-94, 232.
491. TA:HS, pp. 380-397, 400-435, 468 (Article 7).
492. Wenger (ed.), "Schleitheim Confession," pp. 247-253.
493. Wenger (ed.), "Weninger's Vindication," p. 186.
494. TA:VMS, No. 390, p. 382.
495. Beachy, op. cit., p. 2.
496. Wenger (ed.), "Vindication," pp. 183-185.
497. Wenger (ed.), "The Satisfaction of Christ," p. 247, Cf. also CWMS, p. 337; and Bender, "Walking in Resurrection," p. 101.
498. Blanke, op. cit., pp. 35-36, refers to the distinctive and "new" doctrine of repentance as "the theological motive of the movement."
499. Wenger, Even Unto Death, p. 98; and Hans Hillerbrand, "Anabaptism and the Reformation: Another Look," Church History (1960), pp. 404-423.
500. Beachy, op. cit., p. 33; and Wenger (ed.), "The Satisfaction of Christ," pp. 247-248, 252.
501. Augsburger, op. cit., p. 121; Jackson, Latin Works, II, 23; Beachy, op. cit., p. 189.
502. Ibid., pp. 189-190; and R. S. Armour, Anabaptist Baptism (Scottdale: Herald Press, 1966), p. 140.
503. TA:VMS, pp. 23-28.
504. Ibid., p. 23.
505. Ibid., p. 25.
506. Ibid., pp. 25-26.

507. *Ibid.*, p. 26.
508. *Ibid.*, p. 41. Cf. Blanke, *op. cit.*, pp. 33-34.
509. *Acta des Gespräch, 1538*, p. 179.
510. *TA:VMS*, pp. 236-238.
511. *Ibid.*, pp. 234-235.
512. *Ibid.*, p. 236.
513. *Ibid.*
514. *TA:HS*, pp. 487, 338-339.
515. *Ibid.*, p. 160 (italics mine).
516. Beachy, *op. cit.*, p. 139; Armour, *op. cit.*, pp. 40-44, 138-139, Covenant terminology is strong in the South German branch (for example, Scharnschlager, *ME*, IV, 398).
517. *TA:HS*, p. 145; and Grebel: "Even an adult person is not to be baptized without Christ's rule of binding and loosing" (*TA:VMS*, p. 17).
518. *Ibid.*; and *MM*, pp. 190, 198.
519. Stauffer, *op. cit.*, pp. 206-207.
520. *TA:Bayern*, I, 254.
521. A. L. Verheyden, *Anabaptism in Flanders, 1530-1650* (Scottdale: Herald Press, 1961), pp. 4-5.
522. Wenger (ed.), "Schleitheim Confession," p. 248.
523. Bender (ed.), *Hutterite Studies*, p. 38 (italics mine).
524. Michael Novak, "The Free Churches and the Roman Church," *Journal of Ecumenical Studies*, II (1963), 433, 436.
525. *Ibid.*, p. 438.
526. Friedmann, "Ecumenical Dialogue Between Anabaptists and Catholics," *MQR* (1966), pp. 261, 264-265.
527. *Ibid.*, p. 265.
528. Poschmann, *op. cit.*, p. 20.
529. Pourrat, *op. cit.*, III, 67 n.
530. *TA:HS*, p. 487.
531. *Ibid.*, pp. 188, 274.
532. *ZSW*, IV, 231, 245; and *TA:HS*, p. 195.
533. Armour, *op. cit.*, p. 41, Cf. also D. Erasmus, "Enchiridion" in *LCC: Reform*, p. 298.
534. *TA:VMS*, p. 15 (letter to Müntzer).
535. Wenger, (ed.), "The Satisfaction of Christ," p. 249.
536. *TA:HS*, p. 358.
537. Wenger (ed.), "Schleitheim Confession," pp. 248-249.
538. *Acta des Gespräch*, p. 180.
539. *TA:HS*, p. 358 (article 5).
540. Melchior Hoffmann, "The Oridnance of God," *LCC:SAW*, pp. 189-190.
541. For a more extended treatment, see Beachy, *op. cit.*, pp. 200 f.
542. *ME*, II, 347-348 (foot washing); cf. also, Clarence Hiebert, "The History of the Ordinance of Foot Washing in the Mennonite Churches" (unpublished S.T.B. thesis, Biblical Seminary, New York, 1952).
543. The Benedictine Rule prescribes both hospitality and foot washing for humility (*ME*, II, 348).
544. *Ibid.*
545. Wenger (ed.), "Weninger's Vindication," pp. 184-185; Muralt, *op. cit.*, p. 15; Bender, *Conrad Grebel*, pp. 203-208; and *TA:VMS*, pp. 234, 236-237. Bender recognized the Anabaptist's concept of the church as a "derivative idea" from their understanding of the nature of the true Christian life (Bender, "Anabaptist Theology of Discipleship," p. 26).

546. ZSW, VI, 21 f.
547. Wenger (ed.), "Vindication," p. 185; TA:Hesse, pp. 288 f. (Hans Kuchenbacher's testimony).
548. Wenger (ed.), "Vindication," pp. 184-185.
549. TA:Hesse, p. 288.
550. Von Muralt, op. cit., p. 16 (from Zwingli's sermon, "Von der göttlichen und menschlichen Gerechtigkeit").
551. Beachy, op. cit., pp. 221, 229.
552. The parable of the wheat and the tares was sometimes applied by the Anabaptists to society at large, but not to the church (TA:HS, p. 309).
553. Augsburger, op. cit., p. 134.
554. TA:HS, p. 345.
555. Ibid., pp. 367, 373. Also, the "Grüninger Eingabe" (TA:VMS, p. 236) assigns the power of binding and loosing only to those believers "who have died to the will of the flesh and now walk in the will of the Spirit."
556. Beachy, op. cit., p. 223 (Hubmaier's testimony), p. 229 (Marpeck's), and p. 224 (Denck's).
557. An anonymous tract, "Christian Baptism," MQR (1947), p. 283.
558. TA:Hesse, pp. 288 f.
559. Augsburger, op. cit., pp. 144, 93-94.
560. W. Wiswedel, Bilder und Führergestalten aus dem Täufertum (Kassel: J. G. Oncken, 1952), pp. 11-12.
561. Wenger, Even Unto Death, pp. 81, 86. Cf. also J. D. Graber, "Anabaptism Expressed in Mission and Social Service," in Hershberger (ed.), op. cit., pp. 152-166.
562. F. Littell, "The Discipline of Discipleship in the Free Church Tradition," MQR (1961), p. 111.
563. Friedmann, "The Oldest Church Discipline of the Anabaptists," MQR (1955), pp. 141-161.
564. Friedmann, "Hutterite Worship and Preaching," MQR (1966), p. 7; and A. Beachy, "The Theology and Practice of Anabaptist Worship," MQR (1966), pp. 169, 175-176.
565. Friedmann, "Hutterite Worship," p. 6.
566. Ibid., and Beachy, "Anabaptist Worship," pp. 173-174.
567. TA:HS, pp. 341-342, 373, 375.
568. Cf. the appendix in Heinrich Bullinger, Der Widertoufferenn Ursprung (Zürich, 1561).
569. Beachy, "Anabaptist Worship," pp. 166-167.
570. Novak, op. cit., p. 437.
571. TA:HS, pp. 217, 222; also ME, II, 247-248.
572. Stauffer, op. cit., pp. 197-198.
573. Cf. R. Friedmann, "Concerning the True Soldier of Jesus Christ, A Hutterite Tract," MQR (1931), pp. 87-99.
574. MM, p. 420 (Sattler).
575. Ibid.
576. The exclusive authority of the Word, even the external Word, is repeatedly asserted: TA:VMS, pp. 23-28 (Manz): MM, p. 420 (Sattler); CWMS, p. 213; Wenger, Even Unto Death, p. 60.
577. Beachy, The Concept of Grace, p. 240; and TA:VMS, pp. 16-17 (stresses the internal, except for Scripture).
578. Beachy, The Concept of Grace, p. 246.
579. Von Muralt, op. cit., p. 27.
580. Beachy, The concept of Grace, p. 246.
581. Augsburger, op. cit., p. 203.

334 Anabaptism and Asceticism

582. Von Muralt, op. cit., p. 27; and TA:HS, p. 79.
583. TA:VMS, pp. 15, 18, 20; and Wenger (ed.), "How Scripture Is to Be Explained," p. 28.
584. TA:HS, p. 309. Cf. also Walter Klaassen, "Speaking in Simplicity: Balthasar Hubmaier," MQR (1966), p. 143.
585. Bender, Conrad Grebel, pp. 203-205; (cf. Grebel's letter to Vadian, December 15, 1524, Epistolae Grebelianae).
586. Wenger (ed.), "How Scripture Is to Be Explained, by M.S.," pp. 26-44.
587. Ibid., pp. 42-43.
588. Ibid., p. 30.
589. TA:HS, p. 104.
590. TA:VMS, pp. 237-238.
591. Acta des Gespräch, pp. 290-291; and Walter Klaassen, "The Bern Debate of 1538," MQR (1966), pp. 148-156.
592. CWMS, pp. 343, 220 (Menno accents that according to conformity to the "example of Christ," all must be judged).
593. Wenger, Even Unto Death, p. 67; and Augsburger, op. cit., pp. 192-193.
594. TA:HS, p. 210.
595. Keeney, op. cit., p. 47 (and footnotes).
596. MM, p. 420.
597. Marpeck's Testamentserläuterung (c. 1544) is his major work (over 800 pages). It compares and contrasts the two Testaments, giving priority to the New; cf. J. C. Wenger, "The Theology of Pilgram Marpeck," MQR (1938), pp. 207-210.
598. Augsburger, op. cit., pp. 193-195, 199; Beachy, Concept of Grace, p. 246; Muralt, op. cit., p. 30; Wenger (ed.), "Two Kinds of Obedience," p. 21; TA:HS, pp. 153, 157, 110; and Keeney, op. cit., p. 47.
599. Beachy, Concept of Grace, pp. 245-246. Cf. also William Klassen, "Anabaptist Hermeneutics: The Letter and the Spirit," MQR (1966), pp. 87-88, 90 f.
600. Augsburger, op. cit., p. 191.
601. Bender (ed.), Hutterite Studies, p. 32.
602. Novak, op. cit., p. 434.
603. Das Kunstbuch, ed. G. Maler. (A sixteenth-century manuscript collection of Anabaptist tracts and letters at the Bürgerbibliothek in Bern, Switzerland, fol. 220 b.) A typescript copy is at the Mennonite Historical Library, Goshen College.
604. Reinmann, op. cit., pp. 10-18.

5. Agencies of Mediation

1. Cf. Hillerbrand, "Origins of Anabaptism," pp. 152-180; H. Klassen, "The Life and Teachings of Hans Hut," MQR (1959), pp. 171-205, 267-304; Bender, "The Zwickau Prophets," pp. 3-16, regarding Thomas Müntzer and Anabaptism. Cf. C. R. Foster, "Hans Denck and Johannes Buenderlin: A Comparative Study," MQR (1965), pp. 115-124; J. J. Kiwiet, "Hans Denck and His Teaching, 1500-1527" (unpublished BD thesis, typescript at the Mennonite Historical Library, Goshen College); and G. H. Williams, "Popularized German Mysticism as a Factor in the Rise of Anabaptist Communism," Glaube, Geist und Geschichte Festschrift für Ernst Benz, ed. G. Müller and W. Zeller (Leiden, 1967), pp. 290-312, evaluate the influence of German mysticism on

South German Anabaptism, especially through Denck.
  2. See Chapter III, pp. 146 ff.
  3. *ME*, IV, 427 ff.
  4. Ritschl, *op. cit.*, pp. 31 ff.
  5. Hillerbrand, "Origins of Anabaptism," pp. 157-161, discusses Erasmus and Anabaptism. Cf. also Hall, *op. cit.*, pp. 149-168, on Erasmus' influence on Denck and Hubmaier; Fast, *op. cit.*, pp. 104-117; Kreider, *op. cit.*, pp. 123-141; and Bender, *Conrad Grebel*, pp. 10-73.
  6. R. R. Post, *The New Devotion* (Leiden: E. J. Brill, 1968), pp. 106, 120.
  7. L. Salley, "Jacques Lefèvre de' Étaples," in *The Dawn of Modern Civilization*, ed. K. Strand (Ann Arbor: Ann Arbor Publishers, 1962), p. 95.
  8. Bender, "The Zwickau Prophets," pp. 3-16.
  9. Hillerbrand, "Origins of Anabaptism," p. 177.
  10. *Ibid.*, p. 176.
  11. *Ibid.*, p. 172.
  12. *TA:VMS*, No. 14, pp. 13 ff.
  13. Kiwiet, *Hans Denck*, pp. 15, 17-18, 20.
  14. Kiwiet, "Theology of Denck," pp. 22, 25.
  15. H. Klassen, "Life of Hans Hut," p. 303.
  16. *ME*, IV, 704.
  17. Kiwiet, "Theology of Denck," p. 8.
  18. *ME*, IV, 704; cf. also S. E. Ozment, *Mysticism and Dissent*, New Haven: Yale University Press, 1973.
  19. Cf. F. Pheiffer, *Theologie Deutsch* (Stuttgart, 1885), pp. xiv-xv.
  20. Kiwiet, "Theology of Denck," p. 23.
  21. *ME*, II, 43.
  22. Kiwiet, "Theology of Denck," p. 23.
  23. Kiwiet, *Hans Denck*, pp. 15-18. Cf. also T. E. Philoon, "Hans Greiffenberger and the Reformation in Nuernberg," *MQR* (1962), p. 70.
  24. Kiwiet, *Hans Denck*, p. 20; and Philoon, *op. cit.*, pp. 66-67; Griffenberger stresses that "man must turn from the ways of the world, the flesh, and the devil" (p. 66), and the title of one tract is "The World Says That It Sees Little Improvement in Those Who Call Themselves Lutherans" (p. 67).
  25. Kiwiet, *Hans Denck*, p. 23; also, L. Keller, *Von Staupitz und Anfänge der Reformation* (Leipzig, 1888), p. 206.
  26. Kiwiet, *Hans Denck*, p. 20.
  27. *ME*, IV, 687.
  28. *ME*, II, 33.
  29. Foster, "Denck and Buenderlin," pp. 115-124.
  30. Kiwiet, "The Theology of Denck," p. 8.
  31. *ME*, II, 33.
  32. "Theologica Germanica," in *LCC:Mysticism*,Chapters IX, XLV.
  33. D. Erasmus, "Handbook of the Militant Soldier," *The Essential Erasmus*, ed. and trans. J. P. Dolan (New York: New American Library, 1964), pp. 124, 144.
  34. Kiwiet, "Theology of Denck," p. 18; "Theologica Germanica," in *LCC: Mysticism*, Chapter XVI.
  35. Dolan (ed.), "Handbook," p. 123.
  36. "Theologica Germanica," in *LCC:Mysticism*, Chapters XLIV, LI.
  37. Foster, *op. cit.*, pp. 119-120; *TA:Denck*, II ("Was Geredt sei"), 32, 34, 37; F. Heer (ed.), *Meister Eckhardt, Predigten und Schriften* (Frankurt, 1956), p. 31.
  38. Foster, *op. cit.*, pp. 118-120.
  39. "Theologica Germanica," *LCC:Mysticism*, Chapter LIII.
  40. Foster, *op. cit.*, p. 121.

41. Kiwiet, "Theology of Denck," p. 15.
42. *Ibid.*, p. 11.
43. *Ibid.*, p. 15.
44. *Ibid.*, p. 12.
45. *Ibid.*, p. 11.
46. "Theologica Germanica," in *LCC:Mysticism*, Chapter XI.
47. *Ibid.*, Chapter VII.
48. *Ibid.*, Chapter XIII.
49. *Ibid.*, Chapters XXVI, XXX, XXXIX, XLIII.
50. *ME*, II, 33; Foster, *op. cit.*, p. 122; Kiwiet, "Theology of Denck," p. 8.
51. *Ibid.*, p. 8; Foster, *op. cit.*, pp. 122-123.
52. Kiwiet, "Theology of Denck," p. 6.
53. *ME*, II, 33.
54. Kiwiet, "Theology of Denck," p. 21.
55. *Ibid.*, pp. 6, 8.
56. *Ibid.*, p. 20.
57. Foster, *op. cit.*, p. 118.
58. *ME*, IV, 704.
59. *ME*, II, 846.
60. Herbert Klassen, "Life of Hut," p. 282.
61. The following summary of Hut's theology is taken from *Ibid.*, pp. 189-203.
62. R. Friedmann, "Leonard Schiemer and Hans Schlaffer, Two Tyrolean Anabaptist Martyr-Apostles of 1528," *MQR* (1959), pp. 31-41.
63. *Ibid.*, p. 40.
64. *Ibid.*, pp. 31, 38.
65. *TA:Glaubenzeugnisse*, I, 53.
66. *Ibid.*, pp. 74-77.
67. *TA:HS*, pp. 383, 385.
68. Williams, "Sanctification Among the Schwärmer," p. 17.
69. Friedmann, "Schiemer and Schlaffer," pp. 40-41; cf. also *TA:Gl.*, I, 96.
70. *ME*, IV, 704.
71. In *MQR* (1957), pp. 59, 62.
72. See G. Williams classifications in *LCC:SAW*, pp. 22 ff.
73. Cf. K. Holl, "Luther und die Schwärmer," *Gesammelte Aufsätze*, I, (Tübingen, 1923).
74. Bender, "The Zwickau Prophets," p. 14.
75. Friedmann, "Müntzer's Relation to Anabaptism," pp. 75-87.
76. *Ibid.*, pp. 80-84; also Bender, "Zwickau Prophets," pp. 5-8.
77. E. W. Gritsch, "Thomas Muentzer and the Origins of Protestant Spiritualism," *MQR* (1963), pp. 147-172.
78. *Ibid.*, pp. 181, 182, 184.
79. *Ibid.*, pp. 190-191.
80. Hillerbrand, "Origins of Anabaptism," p. 176.
81. *Ibid.*, Friedmann, "Müntzer's Relation to Anabaptism," p. 80; and Bender, "Zwickau Prophets," pp. 5-7.
82. *Ibid.*, p. 6; and Hillerbrand, "Origins of Anabaptism," pp. 172-173.
83. Bender, "Zwickau Prophets," p. 15; and Friedmann, "Muentzer's Relation to Anabaptism," p. 82.
84. Hillerbrand, "Origins of Anabaptism," p. 173.
85. *ME*, IV, 704; and Kiwiet, *Hans Denck*, p. 22.
86. Friedmann, "Muentzer's Relation to Anabaptism," p. 82.
87. Cf. Krajewski, *op. cit.*, pp. 48-59.
88. Kiwiet, *Hans Denck*, pp. 21-22.

89. Affirming significant dependence by Hut on Müntzer are: Rupp, *op. cit.*, pp. 492-519; Walter Klaassen, "Hans Hut and Thomas Müntzer," *The Baptist Quarterly* (1962), pp. 209-227.
90. Klaassen, *op. cit.*, p. 178.
91. J. M. Stayer, "Hans Hut's Doctrine of the Sword: An Attempted Solution," *MQR* (1965), p. 182, notes that Hut asserted that since his conversion to Anabaptism "he had changed his mind, and been told and taught other things."
92. Friedmann, "Muentzer's Relation to Anabaptism," pp. 82-83; and Klaassen, *op. cit.*, pp. 180, 190, 197-198.
93. *Ibid.*, p. 177.
94. *Ibid.*, pp. 175-176.
95. *Ibid.*, pp. 179-184.
96. *Ibid.*, pp. 180, 183, 198-200 (though there are some conflicting reports from Hut's early converts, p. 181, and also Stayer, *op. cit.*, p. 190).
97. Klaassen, *op. cit.*, pp. 181-183.
98. *Ibid.*, p. 182.
99. *Ibid.*, pp. 187, 189; also Hillerbrand, "Origins," p. 173.
100. Klaassen, *op. cit.*, p. 191.
101. *Ibid.*, p. 185.
102. Stayer, *op. cit.*, p. 187.
103. Klaassen, *op. cit.*, p. 282.
104. *ME*, II, 849.
105. Rupp, *op. cit.*, p. 516 (a concept taught by Müntzer in 1523).
106. *Ibid.*, pp. 501, 503.
107. *TA:G1*, I, 28 ff; also found in Schiemer and Schlaffer (Rupp, *op. cit.*, pp. 516-517).
108. *Ibid.*, p. 504.
109. *Ibid.*, p. 516.
110. Stayer, *op. cit.*, pp. 190-191.
111. Ritschl, *op. cit.*, I, 7-36.
112. *Ibid.*, pp. 18, 34.
113. *Ibid.*, p. 13.
114. *Ibid.*, pp. 14-15.
115. *Ibid.*, pp. 22-23.
116. *Ibid.*, pp. 18-20.
117. *Ibid.*, pp. 23-25.
118. Similarly, in their debate with Pope John XXII, the Franciscans defined Christ's example as approving the simple use of possessions for Christians, but not dominion over them; that is, not proprietors as Pope John demanded, but stewardship only (Moorman, *op. cit.*, pp. 315-316).
119. Cf. Moorman, *op. cit.*; and Reinmann, *op. cit.*
120. Moorman, *op. cit.*, p. 261.
121. *Ibid.*, pp. 3, 256, 259.
122. *Ibid.*, pp. 17, 122; and Pourrat, *op. cit.*, II, 163.
123. Moorman, *op. cit.*, pp. 459, 461, 519, 525-526 (for example, John of Capistrano, James of the March, Bernardino of Feltre, John Gritsch, John Burgman, and even a "Conventual," Thomas Murner).
124. *Ibid.*, pp. 383, 459.
125. *Ibid.*, pp. 517, 528.
126. *Ibid.*, pp. 463, 527-529 (for example, John of Capistrano's tract *De Cupiditate* was printed in Cologne in 1480).
127. *Ibid.*, pp. 275-276 f. (Moorman lists collections of material related to Franciscan preaching).

338 Anabaptism and Asceticism

128. *Ibid.*, pp. 272, 277.
129. *Ibid.*, p. 393.
130. *Ibid.*, pp. 393-396, gives numerous fourteenth-century illustrations.
131. *Ibid.*, p. 395 (cf. H. Labrosse, "Sources de la biographie de Nicholas de Lyre," *Études Franciscaines*, XVI, XVII, XIX [1906-8]).
132. *Ibid.*, p. 396, and Oberman, *Forerunner*, pp. 286 f., 305, 311 f.
133. Wenger, *Even Unto Death*, pp. 59-67.
134. Moorman, *op. cit.*, p. 78.
135. *Ibid.*, pp. 13, 400; Pourrat, *op. cit.*, II, 163.
136. Moorman, *op. cit.*, p. 17 (begging was intended only as a secondary expedient, an emergency measure, since there was to be no accumulation — begging was not prescribed for the Tertiaries, p. 78).
137. *Ibid.*, p. 54.
138. *TA:VMS*, No. 32, p. 43.
139. Pourrat, op. cit., II, 184.
140. Ritschl, *op. cit.*, p. 32.
141. *Ibid.*, p. 31.
142. Pourrat, *op. cit.*, II, 167; and Moorman, *op. cit.*, pp. 40-42.
143. *Ibid.*, p. 42.
144. Reinmann, *op. cit.*, pp. 19-20. For a detailed analysis of the Rule of 1221 see pp. 28 ff.
145. Moorman, *op. cit.*, p. 418.
146. Reinmann, *op. cit.*, p. 37 (also Moorman, *op. cit.*, pp. 218 f).
147. Moorman, *op. cit.*, pp. 416-417, 419, 500-562. By the fifteenth century the Tertiaries were divided into "Seculars," those living at home, and "Regulars," those cloistered; the trend toward becoming "Regulars" was strong.
148. Reinmann, *op. cit.*, pp. 58-62.
149. Ritschl, *op. cit.;* p. 30.
150. *Ibid.*, pp. 17-18.
151. Moorman, *op. cit.*, pp. 188-215, 331, 370.
152. *Ibid.*, pp. 563-566, 580, 383.
153. *Ibid.*, pp. 455-456.
154. *Ibid.*, pp. 470-471.
155. Ritschl, *op. cit.*, p. 34.
156. *Ibid.*, p. 24.
157. Moorman, *op. cit.*, p. 115; Littell, *The Anabaptist View of the Church*, p. 53.
158. *Ibid.*, pp. 52-55, 77-78.
159. Moorman, *op. cit.*, pp. 331-370.
160. Littell, *The Anabaptist View*, p. 77.
161. Ritsch, *op. cit.*, p. 17.
162. Moorman, *op. cit.*, pp. 456, 470-471.
163. *Ibid.*, p. 496.
164. *Ibid.*, pp. 499-500.
165. J. L. Phelan, *The Millennial Kingdom of the Franciscans in the New World* (Berkeley: University of California Press, 1956), pp. 15, 43-45.
166. Moorman, *op. cit.*, pp. 424-427.
167. Gritsch, *op. cit.*, pp. 188-189.
168. Cf. Chapter V, 419, n. 7; and *ME*, III, 530-531.
169. Littell, *Anabaptist View of the Church*, p. 54.
170. *Ibid.*, pp. 76-78.
171. Blanke, *op. cit.*, p. 64.
172. *Ibid.*, p. 62.

173. *Ibid.*, p. 63; *TA:VMS*, p. 24.
174. Contrary to Ritschl, *op. cit.*, p. 33, most Anabaptists were not chiliasts, but expected a spiritual kingdom (*ME*, II, 847, 247-248).
175. Ritschl, *op. cit.*, pp. 27, 29.
176. *Ibid.*, p. 35.
177. Moorman, pp. 442, 489-490, 581.
178. *Ibid.*, 517 f. Moorman says preaching is now "on a new basis."
179. *Ibid.*, pp. 514-515; (cf. also Pourrat, *op. cit.*, II, 185-188).
180. Pourrat, *op. cit.*, II, 200 f.
181. Moorman, *op. cit.*, pp. 539 f.
182. *Ibid.*, p. 560.
183. *Ibid.*, pp. 424-425.
184. *Ibid.*, pp. 219-220; Reinmann, *op. cit.*, pp. 70-72.
185. Moorman, *op. cit.*, p. 542.
186. *Ibid.*
187. *Ibid.*, pp. 420, 562-566.
188. *Ibid.*
189. *Ibid.*, pp. 505 f.; Pourrat, *op. cit.*, II, 260, III, 13.
190. Moorman, *op. cit.*, pp. 378, 458.
191. *Ibid.*, p. 519.
192. Peachy, *op. cit.*, p. 35.
193. Ritschl, *op. cit.*, p. 32.
194. *ME*, IV, 408, 452; and Paul Dedic, "The Social Background of the Austrian Anabaptists," *MQR* (1939), p. 12.
195. See Chapter III, pp. 172 ff.
196. *ME*, IV, 1113.
197. *Ibid.*, II, 65-66.
198. Moorman, *op. cit.*, p. 275.
199. Grebel's letter to Vadian, June 17, 1523, *Epistolae Grebelianae*.
200. Ritschl, *op. cit.*, p. 20.
201. Post, *op. cit.*, 694 pp.
202. *Ibid.*, pp. 16-24, 257.
203. *Ibid.*, pp. 14-15, 244, 256-258, 445.
204. *Ibid.*, pp. 348-349, 364.
205. Pourrat, *op. cit.*, II, 20 f., 132 f., 271 f.
206. Post, *op. cit.*, p. 12.
207. *Ibid.*, pp. 192-193, 310-311.
208. Hyma, *The Christian Renaissance*, p. 544.
209. Post, *op. cit.*, p. 254; cf. *Opus Epistolarum Erasmi*, Allen, II, 215.
210. Post, *op. cit.*, p. 253.
211. *Ibid.*, p. 211.
212. *Ibid.*, pp. 195, 212, 270-271.
213. *Ibid.*, pp. 300, 312.
214. Pourrat, *op. cit.*, II, 185-187; III, 13.
215. *Ibid.*, III, 14; (cf. also Post, *op. cit.*, pp. 537, 546).
216. Post, *op. cit.*, pp. 300, 301-311; (cf. also Ritschl, *op. cit.*, pp. 20, 21).
217. Post, *op. cit.*, p. 655. Post suggests that the Magisterial Reformation may even have been a reaction against the renewed *contemptus mundi* of the Franciscans and the *Devotio Moderna* (p. 680).
218. Ritschl, *op. cit.*, pp. 20-21.
219. *Ibid.*, pp. 22-37.
220. For the ties between the *Devotio Moderna* and the Dutch Sacramentarians see Williams, *The Radical Reformation*, pp. 27-37.

340 Anabaptism and Asceticism

221. A. Hyma, "The Theology and Anthropology of the Brethren of the Common Life and the Anabaptists" (an unpublished paper, delivered at the Goshen Biblical Seminary, Fall, 1965).
222. For example, the title of Wenger's monograph, *Die Dritte Reformation*.
223. L. A. Loetscher (ed.), *Twentieth-Century Encyclopedia of Religious Knowledge* (Grand Rapids: Baker, 1955), I, 37.
224. Hyma, "The Theology of the Brethren and Anabaptists," pp. 2-4; and Hyma, *Christian Renaissance*, pp. 266, 573, on Christian primitivism in the Brethren.
225. *Ibid.*, p. 334.
226. Hyma, "Theology of the Brethren and the Anabaptists," p. 10.
227. Chapter IV, pp. 364 ff.
228. Cf., W. Spoelhof, "Concepts of Religious Non-Conformity and Religious Toleration as Developed by the Brethren of the Common Life in the Netherlands, 1374-1489" (unpublished PhD thesis, University of Michigan, 1946).
229. Post, *op. cit.*, pp. 17 ff.
230. *Ibid.*, pp. 10, 19-21. (Post questions whether Mande, Peters, and Thomas à Kempis were valid representatives of the "Brethren" before they became Windesheimers. With the same technical procedures he eliminates John Cele, Alexander Hegius, and even, to a degree, Erasmus from representing the movement.)
231. *Ibid.*, p. 39.
232. Hyma, *Christian Renaissance*, p. 512.
233. Post, *op. cit.*, pp. 13, 278, 225-228, 320.
234. *Ibid.*, pp. 82, 87, 315, 318, 374; Hyma, *Christian Renaissance*, pp. 512 ff. (Post shows no knowledge of the added chapters in Hyma's second edition.)
235. Post, *op. cit.*, pp. 232, 234; Spoelhof, *op. cit.*, pp. 4, 33.
236. W. M. Landeen, "The Devotio Moderna in Germany in the 15th Century" (unpublished PhD thesis, University of Michigan, 1939), p. 22.
237. Hyma, *Christian Renaissance*, pp. 535-536, 572-573.
238. Landeen, *op. cit.*, pp. 23, 121, 128, 143-147, 181, includes extensive quotations from "Brethren" such as Godfrey of Hildesheim, Peter Dieberg, and from the Wessel "Memory Book."
239. *Ibid.*, pp. 128, 143 (from R. Doebner [ed.], *Annalen und Akten der Brüder des gemeinsamen Lebens im Luchtenhofe zu Hildesheim* [Leipzig, 1903], p. 113).
240. Landeen, *op. cit.*, p. 157 (cf. Doebner, *op. cit.*, p. 191; and Johann Busch, *Chronicon*, p. 115).
241. Post, *op. cit.*, p. 586.
242. G. P. Fisher, *History of the Christian Church* (London: Hodder & Stoughton, 1913), p. 220, and David Steinmetz, "Scholasticism and Radical Reform: Nominalist Motifs in the Theology of Balthasar Hubmaier" (a paper delivered at the American Historical Association, December 1969), pp. 5 f.
243. Hyma, *Christian Renaissance*, pp. 519, 570, 591, 599. Cf. also on the emphasis on will rather than intellect, Spoelhof, *op. cit.*, p. 94.
244. Hyma, "Theology of the Brethren and Anabaptists."
245. Hyma, *Christian Renaissance*, p. 600 (from Groote's Book of Litanies).
246. For evidence, Hyma draws heavily upon Groote, Zerbolt, Gansfort, and the *Imitation of Christ* (Hyma, *Christian Renaissance*, pp. 519, 538, 540, 594-595, 597). Even the *Imitation* (Bk. III, Chapter 55) says that man without grace is but a piece of wood, lifeless, impotent; cf. also Sally, "Jacques Lefèvre" in Strand, *op. cit.*, pp. 79 f.
247. Spoelhof, *op. cit.*, p. 94. Spoelhof attributes it only to nominalism but this is too limited; cf. also Steinmetz, *op. cit.*, pp. 10-11, 22 f. For a brief exposition of the doctrine of grace in Old Franciscan theology, see Friedrich Loofs, *Leitfaden zum Studium der Dogmengeschichte*, rev. ed. by Kurt Aland (Tübingen, 1959), pp. 447-451.

248. Wenger, *Even Unto Death*, p. 94.
249. For example, this combination appears in both Gansfort and Hubmaier. Cf. Steinmetz, *op. cit.*, pp. 1-33; note also that Reuchlin urged Melanchthon to study Gansfort's writings, and Stupperich ascribes several Anabaptist characteristics to Melanchthon in R. Stupperich,*Der Unbekannte Melanchthon*(Stuttgart: W. Kohlhammer, 1961), pp. 19, 26-30.
250. Hyma, *Christian Renaissance*, p. 579.
251. *Ibid.*, p. 577.
252. Beachy, *op. cit.*, pp. 70, 77-78, 177 f. Beachy suggests Dutch sacramentarian derivation for this doctrine.
253. Hyma, *Christian Renaissance*, p. 577.
254. Hyma, *The Brethren of the Common Life*, p. 36 (from G. Groote, *Epistolae*, ed. W. Mulder, p. 147).
255. *CWMS*, p. 92.
256. Hyma, *Christian Renaissance*, p. 600.
257. Post, *op. cit.*, p. 484.
258. Landeen, *op. cit.*, pp. 147, 290, also Post, *op. cit.*, p. 488, on the efficaciousness of contrition.
259. Salley, "Jacques Lefèvre" in Strand, *op. cit.*, p. 84.
260. Verheyden, *op. cit.*, p. 7 (unfortunately he gives no source reference). Keeney, *op. cit.*, pp. 145-147, refers it back to a suggestion by W. J. Kühler in *Geschiednis der Nederlandeche Doopsgezinden in de Zestunde Eeuw* (Haarlem, 1932), pp. 56 f. It is also close to the church father, Hilary of Poitiers, says Keeney.
261. Landeen, *op. cit.*, pp. 22-23 (from *Vita Domini Florentii*, Chapter XXIII, 2).
262. Hyma, *Christian Renaissance*, p. 538; Landeen, *op. cit.*, pp. 288-289.
263. Post, *op. cit.*, p. 382.
264. *Ibid.*, pp. 476, 482-483, 538. Cf. also the anti-Pelagian doctrine of unmerited love in Biel (Oberman, *Harvest of Medieval Theology*, p. 349).
265. *Ibid.*, pp. 341-342.
266. E. Miller and J. Scudder, *Wessel Gansfort* (New York, 1917), II, 83.
267. *CWMS*, pp. 92, 506.
268. Steinmetz, *op. cit.*, pp. 22 f.
269. Post, *op. cit.*, pp. 45, 40-41.
270. Hyma, *Christian Renaissance*, p. 539.
271. Landeen, *op. cit.*, pp. 200, 249.
272. Hyma, *Christian Renaissance*, p. 540.
273. Landeen, *op. cit.*, p. 145.
274. *Ibid.*, pp. 120, 127, 141, 143 (concerning Godfrey, founder of Hildesheim, 1439, the *Annalen* reports that he sought "that just men would be separated from the false, according to the Word of the Lord"; also at the Münster Colloquium 1477, Rector Peter Dieburg comments: "It had no authority over our house, except that of love," Doebner, *op. cit.*, pp. 17, 267.
275. Landeen, *op. cit.*, pp. 43, 144, 273, 279 (Henry von Ahaus expressed the ideal that "according to the example of the primitive church they should live the common life in purity and unity of hearts . . . and should serve God in all humility and voluntary poverty, in patience, reverence, and fear" [from the Wessel *Memory Book*, fol. 39a]. Also, Dieburg refers to Charlemagne's conversion of the Saxons, commenting that they indeed came in but not in wedding garments [Mt. 22:11, 12], Doebner, *op. cit.*, p. 114).
276. Landeen, *op. cit.*, p. 129.
277. Post, *op. cit.*, pp. 28 ff. (Post's attempt to minimize Spoelhof's witnesses borders on nit-picking and his contention that the *Devotio Moderna* is far short of

342 Anabaptism and Asceticism

being fully Protestant does not eliminate the developing tendencies noted by Spoelhof. Post wants too much from a "precursor").

278. Miller and Scudder, *op. cit.*, I, 65 f.; II, 320, Cf. also Peter Dieburg's letter to the rector at Münster, 1490, in Doebner, *op. cit.*, pp. 113-115.

279. Post, *op. cit.*, pp. 486, 538.

280. Landeen, *op. cit.*, pp. 146-147; Doebner, *op. cit.*, pp. 144-146, 150.

281. Post, *op. cit.*, pp. 113-114.

282. Landeen, *op. cit.*, p. 27 (*The Imitation of Christ*, Bk. I, Chapter 17).

283. *Ibid.*, Bk. IV, Chapter 1.

284. *Ibid.*, Bk. IV, Chapter 10.

285. Hyma, *Christian Renaissance*, pp. 218-219, 276, 285.

286. Post, *op. cit.*, p. 575.

287. Williams, *The Radical Reformation*, pp. 27-37.

288. Post, *op. cit.*, p. 540.

289. *Ibid.*, p. 484 (Gansfort: "Do you wish to place the authority of the Pope above the Holy Scriptures? The will of the Pope and the authority of Scripture have not been placed on an equal footing . . ." [Miller and Scudder, *op. cit.*, II, 305, 166]).

290. Post, *op. cit.*, p. 586.

291. Landeen, *op. cit.*, p. 10 (from T. à Kempis, *Vita Gerardi Magni*, Chapter VIII, pp. 6-7).

292. *Ibid.*, p. 23 (from *Vita Domini Florentii*, Chapter XXIV, pp. 6, 9, 11). Cf. also K. Strand, "The Brethren of the Common Life and 15th-Century Printing," in *op. cit.*, pp. 344-345. (Strand notes that the Brethren presses at Zwolle and Deventer alone put out over 600 editions in the 15th century, of both religious and classical works, more editions of classics than either England or Paris.)

293. Landeen, *op. cit.*, p. 288 (on Biel).

294. W. Gansfort, *Opera M. Wesseli Gansfortii Groningensis* (1614 ed. Albert Hardenberg. Nieuwkoop: B. deGraaf, 1966), pp. 766-777.

295. T. à Kempis, *The Imitation of Christ* (Modern Library ed.; New York: Random House, 1943), Bk. I, Chapter 5, p. 136. Cf. also Landeen, *op. cit.*, p. 10.

296. *Ibid.*, p. 10 (from T. à Kempis, *Vita Gerardi Magni*, Chapter VIII, pp. 6-7).

297. T. P. Van Zijl, *G. Groote, Ascetic and Reformer, 1340-1384* (Washington: Catholic University Press, 1963), p. 107.

298. Landeen, *op. cit.*, p. 11.

299. Hyma, *Christian Renaissance*, p. 17.

300. W. Gansfort, *Opera*, p. 893.

301. *Ibid.*, pp. 766-767.

302. Verheyden, *op. cit.*, p. 13.

303. See charts, Post, *op. cit.*, pp. 695, 597.

304. *Ibid.*, p. 510.

305. *Ibid.*, p. 641.

306. Hyma, *Christian Renaissance*, pp. 152-156. Over 80 editions of the *Imitation* were printed, 1450-1500, according to P. Fitzgerald, *The World's Own Book of Treasury of à Kempis: An Account of the Chief Editions* (London, 1895), p. 5.

307. Hyma, "The Theology of the Brethren and Anabaptists."

308. Hyma, *Christian Renaissance*, p. 596; and Salley, "Jacques Lefèvre," in Strand, *op. cit.*, p. 81.

309. Pourrat, *op. cit.*, pp. 22 ff.

310. Post, *op. cit.*, p. 680.

311. J. Séguy, "Problèmes historiques et sociologiques actuals de l'Anabaptisme," *Archives de Sociologie des Religions* (1959), p. 109.

312. Williams traces the origin of the doctrine in part to Ruysbroeck, in Williams,

Radical Reformation, p. 330.
  313. Hyma, "The Theology of the Brethren and Anabaptists," pp. 10, 13.
  314. *Mennonitisches Lexikon*, I, 279 (cf. Kuhler, *op. cit.*, I, 24-32).
  315. *ME*, I, 426. (For the most complete attempt to relate the Brethren of the Common Life to the Dutch Anabaptists, cf., G. E. Frerichs, "Menno's Taal," *Doopsgezinde Bijdragen* [1905], pp. 81-83.)
  316. L. Verduin, "The Chambers of Rhetoric and Anabaptist Origins in the Low Countries," *MQR* (1960), pp. 192-196.
  317. Landeen, *op. cit.*, pp. 259-260.
  318. Cf. Chapter III; and Oberman, *Harvest*, pp. 19-20.
  319. *TA:HS*, p. 309.
  320. Without doubt there was some relationship between the *Devotio Moderna* and such leading humanists as R. Agricola, J. Wimpheling, A. Hegius, J. Reuchlin, P. Melanchthon, J. Badius, B. Rhenanus, G. Budé, G. Farel, Lefèvre d'Étaples, and D. Erasmus (Hyma, *Christian Renaissance*, pp. 329-331; Salley, "Jacques Lefèvre" in Strand, *op. cit.*, pp. 82, 94-95).
  321. Kreider, *op. cit.*, pp. 123-141; T. Hall, *op. cit.*, pp. 149-170.
  322. Salley, *op. cit.*, pp. 90, 86.
  323. *Ibid.*, p. 96; also pp. 90-91, 95.
  324. *Ibid.*, pp. 94, 96, 104, 123 (footnotes 194-196).
  325. *Ibid.*, pp. 105-106.
  326. *Ibid.*, pp. 108-109.
  327. *Ibid.*, pp. 109, 114-115.
  328. *Ibid.*, pp. 110-111.
  329. *Ibid.*, pp. 112-113.
  330. *Ibid.*, p. 113.
  331. *Ibid.*, p. 102.
  332. *Ibid.*, pp. 92, 96-98.
  333. Bender, *Conrad Grebel*, pp. 9-16, 32-75.
  334. A. Hyma, *The Youth of Erasmus* (Ann Arbor, 1930), pp. 92-98.
  335. A. Hyma, "Erasmus and the Sacrament of Marriage," *ARG* (1957), pp. 145-164.
  336. Salley, *op. cit.*, pp. 88-89, 92 f. Cf. also Post, *op. cit.*, pp. 635, 671, 674; Allen, *Opus Epistolarum*, I, 200, n. 73; P. Debognie, *Jean Mombaier* (Louvain, 1928), p. 90.
  337. R. Bainton, *The Reformation of the 16th Century* (Boston: Beacon Press, 1956), pp. 69-70; E. Harbison, *The Christian Scholar in the Age of the Reformation* (New York: Scribner's Sons, 1956), p. 72; P. Smith, *Erasmus* (New York: Harper & Bros., 1923), p. 441. Others, who question Erasmus' Catholic orthodoxy still acknowledge substantial dependence by Erasmus on and faithfulness to the *Devotio Moderna*, for example, A. Renaudet, *Erasme, sa Pensée Religieuse* (Paris, 1926), p. 8; A. Renaudet, *Études Erasmienne* (Paris, 1939), p. 126; and A. Hyma, "Erasmus and the Northern Renaissance," *Medievalia et Humanistica*, VIII, 9-11.
  338. K. Meissinger, *Erasmus von Rotterdam* (Berlin, 1948), pp. 70-73.
  339. A. Hyma, "Erasmus and Marriage," p. 157.
  340. E. V. Telle, *Erasme de Rotterdam et le Septième Sacrament* (Geneva, 1954), pp. 29, 81, 441.
  341. Hyma, "Erasmus and Marriage," p. 147.
  342. *Ibid.*, p. 159.
  343. Post, *op. cit.*, pp. 658 f.
  344. J. Huizinga, Erasmus (Harper Torch, 1957), pp. 29-54.
  345. Post, *op. cit.*, pp. 1-8. Cf. also P. Mestwerdt, *Die Anfänge des Erasmus* (Leipzig, 1917); and E. Kohls, *Die Theologie des Erasmus* (Basel, 1966).

344 Anabaptism and Asceticism

346. Cf. J. P. Dolan's "Introduction" in *The Essential Erasmus, op. cit.*, pp. 11-13; and J. P. Dolan (ed.), *The Handbook of the Militant Christian* (Notre Dame, 1962), pp. 12-55.

347. D. Erasmus, *Ten Colloquies*, ed. C. R. Thompson (New York: Bobbs Merrill, 1957), p. xi.

348. C. R. Thompson (ed.), *Inquisitio de Fide: A Colloquy by D. Erasmus Roterdamus, 1524* (New Haven: Yale University Press, 1950), pp. 111, 113, 117, 120.

349. J. P. Dolan (ed.), *The Essential Erasmus*, pp. 11-13.

350. Von Muralt, *op. cit.*, p. 7.

351. Cf. also Kühler, *op. cit.*, pp. 40-42; and W. Köhler, "Wiedertaufer," *Die Religion in Geschichte und Gegenwart* (2nd ed.; Tübingen, 1931).

352. Kreider, *op. cit.*, pp. 121-141.

353. *LCC:SAW*, pp. 23-24.

354. T. Hall, *op. cit.*, pp. 149-150, 168.

355. *Ibid.*, pp. 152-153.

356. Fast, "The Dependence of the First Anabaptists," pp. 104-119.

357. Hillerbrand, "Origin of 16th-Century Anabaptism," p. 157.

358. *Ibid.*, p. 172.

359. *Ibid.*

360. I. B. Horst, *Erasmus, The Anabaptists and the Problem of Religious Unity* (Haarlem, 1967), p. 7.

361. *Ibid.*, p. 11.

362. *Ibid.*, p. 13.

363. J. P. Dolan's review of Horst, *op. cit.*, in *MQR* (1969), pp. 343-344.

364. Bender, *Conrad Grebel*, pp. 11, 15.

365. *Ibid.*, p. 14 (from a book published by Glarean in 1516, exhorting young men to espouse a higher morality and to pursue virtue).

366. *Ibid.*, p. 15.

367. *Ibid.*, p. 16.

368. *Ibid.*, p. 23.

369. *Ibid.*, p. 34.

370. *Ibid.*, p. 49.

371. *Ibid.*, p. 50. Cf. Peter Tschudi's letter to Beatus Rhenanus, May 17, 1519, in *Briefwechsl des Beatus Rhenanus* (Leipzig, 1886), p. 157.

372. *Epistolae Grebelianae* (Grebel to Vadian, January 14, 1520).

373. Kreider, *op. cit.*, p. 128.

374. Bender, *Conrad Grebel*, p. 73; and J. P. Dolan's "Review," *MQR* (October 1969), p. 343.

375. *ME*, IV, 1052 (Zwingli).

376. *Epistolae Grebelianae* (to Vadian, Decmeber 18, 1521; January 12, 1522; February 6, 1522).

377. *Ibid.* (to Vadian, July 13, 1523).

378. *Ibid.* (to Castelberger, May 1, 1525).

379. Additional distinctive elements in the Swiss Brethren may be from Grebel's strong personality (for example, in the Hegenwald letter), his youthfulness, the brevity of his and his associate's careers, and the monastic dogmatism of Sattler, the ex-prior.

380. Fast, "The Dependence of the First Anabaptists," p. 111 (footnotes 37-38), Cf. also *TA:VMS*, pp. 386-387.

381. Von Muralt, *op. cit.*, p. 9.

382. Fast, "Dependence of the First Anabaptists," p. 109.

383. Allen, *Opus Epistolarum des Erasmii*, V, 76.

384. Kreider, *op. cit.*, p. 134.

385. T. Hall, *op. cit.*, pp. 154, 163.
386. Horst, *op. cit.*, pp. 10-11 (cf. also *CWMS*, pp. 138, 248, 270, 521; also Keeney, *op. cit.*, pp. 24-25). For a complete list of citations from Erasmus in Menno Simons, see Krahn, *op. cit.*, p. 45.
387. Allen, *Opus Epistolarum des Erasmii*, VII, 338.
388. *Ibid.*, VIII, 113; and cf. also Horst, *op. cit.*, p. 10.
389. Allen, *Opus Epistolarum des Erasmii*, X, 258; XI, 22, 35, 77, 149 f, 200-203, 251.
390. Dolan's "Review" of Horst, *MQR* (October 1969), p. 343.
391. Primarily the *Enchiridion*, 1503; the *Paraphrases*, 1517-1524 (especially Matthew, Romans, and Acts); *Querela Pacis*, 1519; Inquisitio de Fide, 1523-24; the *Diatribe seu collatio de libero arbitrio*, 1524; *De Immensa Misericordia Dei*, 1524.
392. Erasmus, *Handbook*, ed. Dolan, pp. 16, 120 (for a résumé of contrary opinions see *ibid.*, pp. 12-20; and Spitz, *op. cit.*, pp. 343-344 [notes 119, 121-122]).
393. Erasmus, *Handbook*, ed. Dolan, pp. 26, 35, 38, 50, 120-124.
394. Bender, *Conrad Grebel*, p. 68.
395. K. H. Oelrich, *Der späte Erasmus und die Reformation* (Münster, 1961), Chapter iii; cf. also Dolan (ed.), *The Handbook*, pp. 112, 114, which says, "Unless I see the fruits of the Spirit, I shall not believe that you are in the Spirit" (p. 114).
396. D. Erasmus, *Discourse on Free Will*, ed. and trans. C. F. Winters (New York: Fredrick Ungar Co., 1961), p. 63.
397. *Ibid.*, p. 22.
398. *Ibid.*, pp. 22-23.
399. *Ibid.*, p. 24.
400. *Ibid.*, pp. 20, 53, 93 (also *TA:HS*, p. 400).
401. *Ibid.*, p. 23.
402. *Ibid.*, p. 21, 25-30; for example, "The goodness of God does not refuse to any mortals this second grace . . ." but "God invites, but does not compel, to betterment . . . it is within our powers to turn our will toward or away from grace" (p. 29). "No one perishes except through his own fault" (p. 30).
403. *Ibid.*, p. 30.
404. Cf. Hubmaier and Denck's writings on free will; also Sattler's, "The Satisfaction of Christ."
405. Erasmus, *Discourse on Free Will*, pp. 29-30.
406. *Ibid.*, pp. 90-93.
407. *Ibid.*, pp. 85-86.
408. R. H. Bainton, "The Paraphrases of Erasmus," *ARG* (1967), p. 72; also C. R. Thompson (ed.), *Inquisitio de Fide, 1524* (New Haven: Yale University Press, 1950), p. 59; and C. A. L. Jarrot, "Erasmus' Biblical Humanism," *Studies in the Renaissance* (New York, 1970), XVII, 125-135.
409. *Ibid.*, pp. 59, 65. Also *D. Erasmi Roterdami Opera Omnia*, ed. J. Clericus (Leiden: 1703-1706), VII, 407-408.
410. Erasmus, *Discourse on Free Will*, p. 29.
411. *Ibid.*, pp. 70-71.
412. *Ibid.*, p. 77.
413. Erasmus, *Handbook*, ed. Dolan, pp. 92-94.
414. Bainton, "Paraphrases," pp. 67 (footnote 4), 70.
415. Erasmus, *Handbook*, ed. Dolan, p. 91; also *ibid.*, pp. 87, 95; and Erasmus *Discourse on Free Will*, pp. 83-84, which asserts that faith is only "the beginning of salvation and not its sum total," and that "faith and love . . . nurture each other mutually."
416. Cf. Beachy, *op. cit.*, p. 131.
417. Erasmus, *Handbook*, ed. Dolan, p. 9.

346 Anabaptism and Asceticism

418. *Ibid.*, pp. 42, 99-100, 123.
419. *Ibid.*, p. 143.
420. Erasmus, *Discourse on Free Will*, pp. 93, 64.
421. *Ibid.*, p. 90.
422. Erasmus, *Handbook*, ed. Dolan, pp. 22, 45-46; also P. Mesnard, *Essai sur le Libre Arbitre* (Paris, 1959), p. 60, which asserts that "the theology of Erasmus rests in fact on the central idea of divine perfection."
423. Erasmus, *Handbook*, ed. Dolan, p. 121.
424. *Ibid.*, p. 117.
425. *Ibid.*, pp. 121, 32, 99, 109, 143, 158.
426. Hillerbrand, "Origins of Anabaptism," pp. 58-60. (cf. also "Evangelium Matthaei Paraphrasis" in Erasmus, *Opera Omnia*, VII, 33).
427. Erasmus, *Handbook*, ed. Dolan, pp. 94-95.
428. *Ibid.*, pp. 95, 105, 124, 143.
429. Erasmus, *Inquisitio*, ed. Thompson, p. 67; Erasmus, *Handbook*, ed. Dolan, pp. 91, 78, 103-104, 110.
430. *Ibid.*, p. 77.
431. *Ibid.*, p. 68.
432. *Ibid.*, pp. 91-92, 78, 70-71.
433. *Ibid.*, pp. 69, 138.
434. *Ibid.*, pp. 70, 117.
435. *Ibid.*, pp. 94-95.
436. *Ibid.*, p. 78.
437. *Ibid.*, pp. 68-69, 117-118, 137-138.
438. Erasmus, *Inquisitio*, ed. Thompson, pp. 69, 71; also Bainton, "Paraphrases," p. 72.
439. Erasmus, *Discourse on Free Will*, p. 32.
440. Erasmus, *Handbook*, ed. Dolan, p. 68.
441. *Ibid.*
442. *Ibid.*, p. 95.
443. *Ibid.*, pp. 93-96.
444. Yoder, "The Turning Point," pp. 138-140.
445. Friedmann, "Doctrine of Two Worlds," in Hershberger, *op. cit.*, pp. 105-118.
446. Hillerbrand, "Origins of Anabaptism," pp. 159-160. (Cf. also Erasmus, *Opera Omnia*, V, 39; VII, 34.)
447. Erasmus, *Inquisitio*, ed. Thompson, p. 69.
448. Erasmus, *Handbook*, ed. Dolan, pp. 95-96.
449. *Ibid.*, pp. 114, 119.
450. *Ibid.*, p. 26.
451. Erasmus, *Inquisitio*, ed. Thompson, p. 69.
452. *Ibid.*, p. 71.
453. Fast, "Dependence of Anabaptists," pp. 110-111.
454. Cf. D. Erasmus, "The Complaint of Peace," in J. P. Dolan (ed. and trans.); *The Essential Erasmus* (New York: New American Library, 1964), p. 186; and Erasmus, *Handbook*, ed. Dolan, pp. 33-34.
455. Fast, "Dependence of Anabaptists," p. 110 (footnote 32).
456. Compare Erasmus, "The Complaint of Peace," p. 195 and *Handbook*, pp. 132-133.
457. Cf. J. M. Stayer, *"Anabaptists and the Sword"* (Lawrence, Kansas: Coronado Press, 1972).
458. Erasmus, *Inquisitio*, ed. Thompson, pp. 15-16; also Bainton, "Paraphrases." p. 74.

459. Hillerbrand, "Origins of Anabaptism," p. 158; Erasmus, *Handbook*, ed. Dolan, pp. 99, 132-133; Erasmus, *Discourse on Free Will*, pp. 6, 8.
460. Erasmus, *Handbook*, ed. Dolan, pp. 30, 133.
461. *Ibid.*, p. 129.
462. *Ibid.*, p. 121.
463. *Ibid.*, p. 108.
464. *Ibid.*, pp. 134-135.
465. Bainton, "Paraphrases," p. 72 (cf. *Opera Omnia*, VII, 192E, 93A-D, 647).
466. Erasmus, *Inquisitio*, ed. Thompson, p. 21.
467. Bainton, "Paraphrases," p. 74 (cf. *Opera Omnia*, VII, 99-102).
468. Bainton, "Paraphrases," p. 75.
469. Erasmus, *Handbook*, ed. Dolan, pp. 95, 121.
470. *Ibid.*, pp. 105-110 (Rule 5). Erasmus wrote: "If you believe in what takes place at the altar, bur fail to enter into the spiritual meaning of it, God will despise your flabby display of religion" (p. 109).
471. Hillerbrand, "Origins of Anabaptism," p. 160.
472. Spitz, *op. cit.*, p. 227.
473. Hillerbrand, "Origins of Anabaptism," p. 160.
474. Erasmus, *Discourse on Free Will*, p. 80.
475. Erasmus, *Handbook*, ed. Dolan, p. 63.
476. *Ibid.*, p. 96 (cf. also Erasmus' use of the term "initiate," in Bainton, "Paraphrases," p. 73 [*Opera Omnia*. VII, 3 verso, preface to Matthew]).
477. Erasmus, *Inquisitio*, ed. Thompson, pp. 65, 71; also Erasmus, *Handbook*, pp. 108-109.
478. Bainton, "Paraphrases," p. 73 (*Opera Omnia*, VII, 3 verso, preface to Matthew). Erasmus maintains that this rite really is not a second baptism any more than is the daily sprinkling of holy water. Though, this assertion may be interpreted that he meant only a completion of baptism (confirmation), yet the reuse of water is clearly implied.
479. *TA:HS*, p. 249.
480. Hillerbrand, "Origins of Anabaptism," p. 160.
481. Erasmus, *Handbook*, ed. Dolan, p. 108.
482. *Ibid.*
483. Erasmus, "The Complaint of Peace," ed. Dolan, p. 185.
484. Spitz, *op. cit.*, p. 341 (footnote 105).
485. J. Etienne, *Spiritualisme Erasmien et Theologien Louvanisten* (Louvain, 1956), p. 14 (cf. also Erasmus, *Handbook*, ed. Dolan, p. 21).
486. Erasmus, *Handbook*, ed., Dolan, p. 21.
487. Erasmus, *Opera Omnia*, VII, 133E.
488. Bainton, "Paraphrases," p. 73 (cf. *Opera Omnia*, VII, 551B-D).
489. Erasmus, *Handbook*, ed. Dolan, p. 111.
490. Erasmus, *Discourse on Free Will*, p. 15.
491. Erasmus, *Handbook*, ed. Dolan, p. 40.
492. Erasmus, *Discourse on Free Will*, pp. 8, 10, 20.
493. *Ibid.*, pp. 6, 8.
494. Erasmus, *Handbook*, ed. Dolan, pp. 41-42; cf. also Jarrot, *op. cit.*, p. 124.
495. *Ibid.*, p. 73; also, for case examples, see Bainton, "Paraphrases," pp. 68-69.
496. Erasmus, *Handbook*, ed. Dolan, pp. 24, 40, 45; Allen, *Opus Epistolarum des Erasmii*, IV, 113; Bainton, "Paraphrases," pp. 69-70.
497. Eramsus, *Discourse on Free Will*, pp. 16-18.
498. Erasmus, *Handbook*, ed. Dolan, pp. 105-107.
499. Erasmus, "The Complaint of Peace," ed. Dolan, p. 183.
500. Erasmus, *Handbook*, ed. Dolan, p. 38.

501. Fast, "Dependence of Anabaptists," p. 109 (from Leo Jud's translation of the *Enchiridion* [Basel, 1521]).
502. Erasmus, *Discourse on Free Will*, p. 6.
503. *Ibid.*, pp. 16-20.

BIBLIOGRAPHY

PRIMARY SOURCES

Acta des Gesprächs Zwüschenn predicantenn uund Tauffbrüederen Ergangen Inn der Statt Bern, 1538. Vol. LXXX of Unnütze Papiere, in Staatsarchiv des Kantons Bern. (Typescript copy in the Mennonite Historical Library, Goshen College.)
Die älteste Chronik der Hutterischen Brüder: Hrg. von A. J. F. Zieglschmid. Ithaca, New York: The Cayuga Press, 1943.
Anshelm, Valerius. Bernischen Chronik. Vol. V. Bern, 1896.
Augustinus, A. (St.) The Rule of St. Augustine. Translated by T. Hand. Westminster, Maryland: Newman Press, 1956.
Ausbund, das ist: Etliche Schöne Christliche Lieder. Scottdale, Pennsylvania: Herald Press, 1962.
Benedictus (St.). The Rule of St. Benedict. Translated by O. Chadwick in Western Asceticism. Philadelphia, 1958.
Bergsten, Torsten. "Two Letters by Pilgram Marpeck," translated by Wm. Klassen, MQR, XXXII (July 1958), 192-210.
Bossert, G. (ed.). Herzogtum Württemberg. Quellen zur Geschichte der Täufer, Vol. I; Quellen und Forschungen zur Reformationsgeschichte, Vol. XIII, Leipzig, 1930.
Braght, T. J. van (ed.). The Bloody Theatre or Martyrs Mirror. Translated from the Dutch edition of 1660 by J. F. Sohm, Scottdale, Pennsylvania: Mennonite Publishing House, 1951.
Brandt, Otto H. Thomas Müntzer, Life and Works. Jena, 1933.
Bucer, Martin. Martin Bucer's Deutsche Schriften. Vol. I. Edited by R. Stupperich. Martini Buceri opera omnia, Series I. Gütersloh: Verlagshaus Gerd Mohn, 1960.
Bullinger, H. Reformationsgeschichte. Edited by J. Hottinger and H. Vögeli. 3 vols. Arouenfeld, 1833-40.
―――. Der Widertöufferenn ursprung, furgang, Secten, wäsen, fürnemen und gemaine irer lees Artikel. . . . Zurich, 1561.
Calvin, John. Brieve Instruction Pour Armer tous bons fidels contres les Erreurs le la secte des Anabaptistes. Corpus Reformatorum. Vol. XXXV. Geneve, 1544.
Chadwick, Owen (ed.). Western Asceticism. Vol. XII. The Library of Christian Classics. Philadelphia:Westminster Press, 1958.
Denck, Hans. Hans Denck: Schriften. Edited by G. Baring and W. Fellmann. Quellen zur Geschichte der Täufer, Vol. VI; Quellen und Forschungen zur Reformationsgeschichte, Vol. XXIV. Gütersloh, 1955-60.
Doebner, R. (ed.). Annalen und Akten der Brüder des gemeinsamen Lebens im Luchtenhofe zu Hildesheim. Leipzig, 1903.
Dürr, E. and Roth, P. (eds.). Aktensammlung zur Geschichte der Basler Reformation in den Jahren, 1519-1534. 6 Bde. Basel, 1921.
Egli, Emil. Actensammlung zur Geschichte der Züricher Reformation in den Jahren 1519-1533. 3 vols. Zürich: J. Schabilitz, 1879.
Epistolae Grebelianae (1517-1525). Translated into English and edited by Edward Yoder. Unpublished typescript manuscript at the Mennonite Historical Library, Goshen College.
Erasmus, D. Desiderii Erasmi Roterdami Opera Omnia. Edited by J. Clericus. Leiden,

350 Anabaptism and Asceticism

1703-1706.

———. *Opus Epistolerum Desiderii Erasmi Roterdami.* Edited by P. S. Allen London: Oxford Press, 1906-1958.

———. "The Complaint of Peace," *The Essential Erasmus.* Translated by J. P. Dolan. New York: The New American Library, 1964.

———. *Discourse on Free Will, 1524.* Edited and translated by E. F. Winters. New York: Frederick Ungar Co., 1961.

———. *Handbook of the Militant Christian, 1503.* Translated by J. P. Dolan. Notre Dame: Fides Publishers, Inc., 1962.

———. "Concerning the Immense Mercy of God," *The Essential Erasmus.* Edited and translated by J. P. Dolan. New York: New American Library, 1964.

———. *Inquisitio de Fide: A Colloquy, 1523-24.* Edited by C. R. Thompson. Vol. XV. Yale Studies in Religion. New Haven: Yale University Press, 1950.

———. *Ten Colloquies.* Translated by C. R. Thompson. New York: Bobs-Merrill, 1957.

Franz, G. (ed.). *Wiedertäuferakten, 1527-1626.* Vol. IV: *Urkundliche Quellen zur Hessischen Reformationsgeschichte.* Marburg: Veröffentl. der Hist. Komm. für Hessen und Waldeck, 1951.

Gansfort, W. *Opera M. Wesseli Gansfortii Groningensis.* 1614 ed. Albert Hardenberg. Nieuwkoop: B. de Graaf, 1966.

Handlung oder Acta der Disputation gehalten zu Zoffingen. Zürich: Froschouer, 1532.

Heer, F. (ed.). *Meister Eckchardt, Predigten und Schriften.* Frankfort, 1956.

Hegenwald, Erhart. "Hegenwald an Konrad Grebel, Jan. 1, 1525." Stadtbibliothek St. Gallen, ms. 311222, 8 Seiten (typescript copy at the Mennonite Historical Library Goshen College).

Hubmaier, Balthaser. *Balthasar Hubmaier: Schriften.* Edited by G. Westin and T. Bergsten. *Quellen zur Geschichte der Täufer,* Vol. IX; *Quellen und Forschungen zur Reformationsgeschichte,* Vol. XXIX. Gütersloh: Gerd Mohn, 1962.

———. "The Writings of Balthasar Hubmaier." Translated by G. D. Davidson. Unpublished typescript of William Jewell College, Liberty, Mo., 1939. (Microfilm at Andover-Harvard Theological Library.)

Jackson, S. M. (ed.). *The Latin Works of Huldreich Zwingli.* 4 vols. New York: Putnam's Sons, 1912.

———. *Selected Works of Huldreich Zwingli.* Philadelphia: University of Pennsylvania, 1901.

Kempis, Thomas a. *The Imitation of Christ.* Edited by H. C. Gardiner. New York: Doubleday & Co., 1955.

Kessler, Johannes. *Sabbata, 1523-39.* Herausg. von E. Egli and R. Schoch. St. Gallen, 1902 (reprint).

Krebs, M. (ed). *Baden und Pfalz,* Vol. V. *Quellen zur Geschichte de Täufer;* Vol. XXII: *Quellen und Forschungen zur Reformationsgeschichte.* Gütersloh, 1951.

——— and Rott, H. G. (eds.). *Elsass, I, Stadt Strassburg 1522-32.* Vol. VII, *QGT*; Vol. XXVI, *QFR.* Gütersloh: Gerd Mohn, 1959.

——— and Rott, H. G. (eds.). *Elsass, II, Stadt Strassburg, 1533-35.* Vol. VIII, *QGT*; Vol. XXVII, *QFR.* Gütersloh: Gerd Mohn, 1959.

Das Kunstbuch. Collected and edited by George Maler, 1561. Unpublished sixteenth-century ms. collection of Anabaptist tracts and letters at the Bürgerbibliothek in Bern, Switzerland. (Typescript copy at the Mennonite Historical Library, Goshen College.)

Langenmantel, Eitelhans. "An Exposition of the Lord's Prayer." Translated by J. C. Wenger, *MQR*, XXII (1940), 40-42.

Luther, Martin. *Luther's Works.* 55 vols. Edited by J. Pelikan and H. Lehman. St. Louis: Concordia Publishing Co., 1955.

———. *Lectures on Galatians.* Vol. XXVII. *Luther's Works.* Philadelphia: Fortress Press, 1964.

———. *The Sermon on the Mount.* Vol. XXI. *Luther's Works.* Edited by J. Pelikan. St. Louis:Concordia Publishing Co., 1956.

———. *Table Talk.* Vol. LIV. *Luther's Works.* Philadelphia:Fortress Press, 1967.

Marpeck, Pilgram. "Confession of Faith." Translated by J. C. Wenger, *MQR*, XII (July 1938), 167-202.

———. *Testamentserläuterung durch Auszug aus heiliger biblischer Schrift* [n.p., n.d.]. (Microfilm copy at Andover-Harvard Theological Library.)

———. *Vermanung; auch gantz klarer/gründtlicher und unwidersprechlicher bericht.* Reprinted by Christian Neff in *Gedenkschrift zum 400 jährigen Jubiläum der Mennoniten oder Taufgesinnten: 1525-1925*, 1925.

Miller, E. W. and Scudder, J. W. *Wessel Gansfort, Life and Writings.* 2 vols. New York, 1917.

Müller, Lydia (ed.). *Glaubenszeugnisse Oberdeutscher Taufgesinnter*, I. Vol. III, *QGT*; Vol. XX, *QRG*. Leipzig, 1934.

Muralt, L. von and Schmid, W. (eds.). *Quellen zur Geschichte der Täufer in der Schweiz, I: Zürich.* Zürich: S. Herzel Verlag, 1932.

Oecolampadius, Johannes. *Briefe und Akten zum Leben Oekolampads*, I. Edited by E. Staehelin. Vol. X: *Quellen und Forschungen zur Reformationsgeschichte.* Leipzig: Nachfolger, Eger and Sievess, 1927.

Ott, J. H. *Annales Anabaptistici.* Basel, 1672.

Petry, R. C. (ed.). "Theologica Germanica," *Late Medieval Mysticism.* Vol. XIII. *Library of Christian Classics.* Philadelphia:Westminster Press, 1957.

Philip, D. *Handbook.* Translated by A. B. Kolb. Lagrange, Indiana: Pathway Publishing Corp., 1966.

Reublin, Wilhelm. "A Letter from Wilhelm Reublin to Pilgram Marpeck," 1531. Translated and edited by J. C. Wenger, *MQR*, XXIII (1949), 67-75.

Rideman, Peter. *Account of Our Religion, Doctrine and Faith* (1545). Translated by Kathleen Hasenberg. London: Hodder and Stoughton, 1950.

Sammelband. Published in the late sixteenth century or early seventeenth century. Copy in the Mennonite Historical Library, Goshen College (contains most of the Anabaptist tracts assigned to "M.S.").

Schornbaum, K. (ed.). *Markgraftum Brandenburg, Bayern*, I. Vol. II, *QGT*; Vol. XVI, *QFR*, Leipzig, 1934.

———. *Bayern, II.* Vol. V, *QGT*; Vol. XXIII, *QFR*. Gütersloh, 1951.

Steck, R. and Tobler, G. (eds.). *Aktensammlung Geschichte der Berner Reformation*, 1521-32. Bern, 1923.

Simons, Menno. *The Complete Writings of Menno Simons.* Edited by J. C. Wenger. Translated by L. Verduin. Scottdale, Pennsylvania: Herald Press, 1956.

Die Vadiantsche Briefsammlung der Stadtbibliothek St. Gallen. Vols. XXVII-XXIX: *Mit-*

teilungen zur vaterländischen Geschichte. St. Gallen, 1897-1908.
Vadian, Joachim. *Diarum, Deutsche Historische Schriften*, III. Herausg. von E. Goetzinger. St. Gallen, 1879.
Vadians Deutsche Historische Schriften. 3 vols. Edited by E. Goetzinger. St. Gallen, 1875-79.
Waddel, H. *The Desert Fathers.* Ann Arbor: The University of Michigan Press, 1957.
Walpot, Peter. *True Surrender and Christian Community of Goods.* Translated by K. Hasenberg. Bromdon, England: Plough Publishing House, 1957.
Wenger, J. C. (ed. and trans.). "Concerning Divorce," *MQR*, XXI (1947), 114-119.
———. (ed. and trans.). "Concerning the Satisfaction of Christ," *MQR*, XX (1946), 243-254.
———. (ed. and trans.). "An Early Anabaptist Tract on Hermeneutics ['How Scripture Is to Be Rightly Divided and Explained']," *MQR*, (1968), 26-44.
———. (ed. and trans.). "Martin Weninger's Vindication of Anabaptism, 1535," *MQR*, XXII (1948), 180-187.
———. (ed. and trans.). "The Schleitheim Confession of Faith," *MQR*, XIX (1945), 243-253.
———. (ed. and trans.). "Three Swiss Brethren Tracts," *MQR*, XXI (1947), 274-281.
———. (ed. and trans.). "Two Early Anabaptist Tracts," *MQR*, XXII (1948), 34-42.
———. (ed. and trans.). "Two Kinds of Obedience: An Anabaptist Tract on Christian Freedom," *MQR*, XXI (1947), 18-22.
Williams, G. H. and Mergal, A. M. *Spiritual and Anabaptist Writers.* Vol. XXV: *The Library of Christian Classics.* Philadelphia: Westminster Press, 1957.
Zwingli, Ulrich, *Huldreich Zwinglis samtliche Werke.* Edited by Emil Egli *et al.* Vols. 88-93, 95-101: *Corpus Reformatorum.* Leipzig: Verlag von M. Heinsius Nachfolger, 1905 ff.

SECONDARY SOURCES: MONOGRAPHS

Acquoy, J. G. R. *Het klooster to Windesheim.* 3 vols. Utrecht, 1875-1880.
Armour, R. S. *Anabaptist Baptism.* Scottdale, Pennsylvania: Herald Press, 1966.
Arnold, Gottfried. *Unparteyische Kirchen und Ketzer-Historie.* 3rd ed. Schaffhausen, 1740-42.
Augsburger, M. S. "Michael Sattler, Theologian of the Swiss Brethren Movement." Unpublished DTh dissertation,Union Theological Seminary,Richmond,Virginia,1964.
Bainton, R. *The Reformation of the 16th Century.* Boston: Beacon Press, 1956.
———. *Studies in the Reformation.* London: Hodder & Stoughton, 1963.
Baum, Johann Wilhelm. *Capito und Butzer, Strassburger Reformatoren.* Elberfeld: R. L. Friderichs, 1860.
Beachy, A. "The Concept of Grace in the Radical Reformation." Unpublished DTh thesis, Harvard Divinity School, 1960.
Bender, H. S. *Conrad Grebel.* Scottdale, Pennsylvania: Herald Press, 1950; reprinted 1971.
———. (ed.). *Hutterite Studies by Robert Friedmann.* Goshen, Ind.: Mennonite Historical Society, 1961.
Bergsten, Torsten. *Balthasar Hubmaier, Seine Stellung zu Reformation und Täufertum.* Kassel: J. G. Oncken, 1961.
Blanke, F. *Brothers in Christ.* Translated by N. Nordenhaug. Scottdale, Pennsylvania:

Herald Press, 1961 (in German, 1955).
Boas, George. *Essays on Primitivism and Related Ideas in the Middle Ages*. Baltimore: John Hopkins Press, 1948.
Bouyer, Louis. *Dictionaire Théologique*. Desclée et Co., 1963.
―――――. *The Meaning of the Monastic Life*. Translated by K. Pond. London: Burns & Oates, 1955.
Butler, E. C. *Benedictine Monachism*. Cambridge: Speculum Historiale, 1961 (reprint).
Capella, G. C. *Le Voeu d' obéissance des origines au XIIe siècle*. Paris: Librarie general ... de jurisprudence, 1957.
Catalogue of Books Printed in the XVth Century Now in the British Museum. Part VIII, 1949.
A Catholic Dictionary of Theology. New York: T. Nelson & Sons, 1962.
The Catholic Encyclopedia. New York: Appleton Co., 1907.
Chadwick, Nora. *The Age of the Saints in the Early Celtic Church*. London: Oxford University Press, 1961.
Chadwick, Owen. *John Cassian: A Study in Primitive Monasticism*. Cambridge University Press, 1950.
Cornelius, C. A. *Geschichte des Münsterischen Aufruhrs*. Leipzig, 1855-60.
Coulton, G. G. *Five Centuries of Religion*. Vol. IV. Cambridge: The University Press, 1950.
Courvoisier, Jacques. *Zwingli: A Reformed Theologian*. Richmond, Virginia: John Knox Press, 1963.
Cousin, Patrice. *Précis d' histoire monastique*. Belgium: Blaud & Gay, 1951.
Coutts, Alfred. *Hans Denck, 1495-1527, Humanist and Heretic*. Edinburgh: Macniven & Wallace, 1927.
Dacheux, Leo. *Un Réformateur Catholique à la fin du XVe siècle*, Jean Geiler de Kaysersberg. Paris: C. Delagrave, 1876.
Daniel-Rops, H. *The Protestant Reformation*. 2 vols. New York: Image Books, 1963.
Debongnie, P. *Jean Mombaer de Bruxelles*. Louvain, 1928.
Dolan, J. P. *History of the Reformation*. New York: Desclee Co., 1965.
Duckett, E. S. *The Gateway to the Middle Ages: Monasticism*. Ann Arbor: University of Michigan Press, 1961 (1938).
Egli, E. *St. Galler Täufer*. Zurich, 1887.
Emery, R. W. *The Friars in Medieval France*. Columbia University Press, 1962.
Fast, H. von Heinhold. *Der Linke Flügel der Reformation*. Bremen: Carl Shünemann Verlag, 1962.
Ferguson, John. *Pelagius: A Historical and Theological Study*. Cambridge: Heffer, 1956.
Fisher, G. P. *History of Christian Doctrine*. New York: C. Scribner's Sons, 1906.
Forell, George W. *Faith Active in Love: Principles underlying Luther's Social Ethics*. Minneapolis: Augsburg Publishing House, 1954.
Friedmann, Robert. *Mennonite Piety Through the Centuries*. Goshen College, 1949.
Garrigou-Lagrange, R. *Christian Perfection and Contemplation*. Translated by M. T. Doyle. St. Louis: B. Herder Co., 1951.
Gasquet, F. A. *Monastic Life in the Middle Ages*. London: G. Bell and Sons, 1922.
Geiser, S. *Die Taufgesinnten-Gemeinden*. Karlsruhe, 1931; enlarged ed., 1971.
Gemelli, A. *The Franciscan Message to the World*. Translated by H. L. Hughes. London: Burns Oates & Washbourne, 1934.
Gilmore, M. *The World of Humanism*. New York: Harper & Bros., 1952.

354 Anabaptism and Asceticism

Goeters, J. F. Gerhard. *Ludwig Hätzer, 1500-1529, Spiritualist und Antitrinitarier.* Gütersloh: Carl Bertelsmann Verlag, 1957.

Gratz, Delbert. *Bernese Anabaptists and their American Descendants,* Scottdale, Pennsylvania: Herald Press, 1953.

Guibert, Joseph de. *The Theology of the Spiritual Life.* Translated by Paul Barrett. New York: Sheed and Ward, 1953.

Hannay, J. O. *The Spirit and Origin of Christian Monasticism.* London: Mathuen & Co., 1903.

Harbison, E. *The Christian Scholar in the Age of the Reformation.* New York: Scribner's Sons, 1956.

Hardman, Oscar. *The Ideals of Asceticism.* New York: Macmillan Co., 1924.

Hay, Denys. *Europe in the 14th and 15th Centuries.* New York: Holt, Rinehart, 1966.

Henkel, Julia. "An Historical Study of the Educational Contributions of the Brethren of the Common Life." Unpublished PhD dissertation, University of Pittsburgh, 1962.

Hershberger, Guy F. (ed.). *The Recovery of the Anabaptist Vision: A Sixteenth Anniversary Tribute to Harold S. Bender.* Scottdale, Pennsylvania: Herald Press, 1957.

Hexter, J. H. *More's Utopia: The Biography of an Idea.* New Jersey: Princeton University Press, 1952.

Hillerbrand, H. J. *Bibliography of Anabaptism (1520-1630).* Elkhart, Indiana: Institute of Mennonite Studies, 1962.

Horsch, John. *The Mennonites in Europe.* Scottdale, Pennsylvania: Mennonite Press, 1942.

Horst, I. B. *Erasmus, the Anabaptists and the Problem of Religious Liberty.* Haarlem: H. D. Tjeenk Willink en zoon, 1967.

Huizinga, J. *Erasmus and the Age of the Reformation.* New York: Harper & Bros.: Harper Torch Edition, 1957 (original 1924).

Hulshof, Abraham. *Geschiedenis der Doopsgenzinden te Straatsburg von 1525 tot 1557.* Amsterdam: J. Clausen, 1905.

Hyma, A. *The Brethren of the Common Life.* Grand Rapids: Eerdmans, 1950.

―――――. *The Christian Renaissance.* 2nd ed. Hamden: Archon Books, 1965.

―――――. *The Youth of Erasmus.* Ann Arbor, 1930.

Imbart de la Tour, Pierre. *Les Origines de la Réforme.* 3 vols. Paris, 1905-1914.

Jenny, Beatrice. *Das Schleitheimer Täuferbekenntnis 1527.* Schaffhauser Beiträge zur vaterländischen Geschichte. Heft 28. Thoyngen: Karl Augustin Verlag, 1951.

Kawerau, Peter. *Melchior Hofmann als religiöser Denker,* Haarlem, 1954.

Keeney, W. E. *The Development of Dutch Anabaptist Thought and Practice from 1539-1564.* Nieuwkoop. B. de Graaf, 1968.

Keller, Ludwig. *Ein Apostel der Wiedertäufer.* Leipzig: G. Hirzell, 1882.

―――――. *Die Reformation und die älteren Reformparteien.* Leipzig, 1885.

―――――. *Von Staupitz und Anfänge der Reformation.* Leipzig, 1888.

Kiwiet, J. J. "Hans Denck and His Teachings." Unpublished BD thesis, Baptist Theological Seminary, Rüschlikon, Zürich, 1954.

―――――. *Pilgram Marpeck.* Kassel: J. G. Oncken Verlag, 1957.

Klassen, P. J. *The Economics of Anabaptism (1525-1560).* London: Mouton & Co., 1964.

Knowles, David. *Christian Monasticism.* New York: McGraw-Hill, 1969.

―――――. *The Religious Orders in England.* 3 vols. Cambridge, 1948-59.

Koehler, Walter. *Brüderlich Vereinigung etzlicher kinder Gottes sieben Artikel betreffend.* Leipzig, 1908.

Bibliography   355

Kohls, E. *Die Theologie des Erasmus.* Basel, 1966.
Krahn, Cornelius. *Menno Simons (1496-1561).* Karlsruhe: Heinrich Schneider, 1936.
Krajewski, Ekkehard. *Felix Manz.* Kassel: J. G. Oncken Verlag, 1957.
Kühler, W. J. *Geschiedenis du Nederlandsche Doopsgezinden in de Zestiende Eeuw.* Haarlem, 1932.
Landeen, W. M. "The Devotio Moderna in Germany in the 15th Century." Unpublished PhD thesis, University of Michigan, 1939.
Lindowsky, J. *The Psychology of Asceticism.* Translated by E. Heiring. Baltimore: Carroll Press, 1950.
Littell, F. H. *The Anabaptist View of the Church.* 2nd ed. Boston: Beacon Press, 1958. (Also titled *"The Origins of Sectarian Protestantism.* New York: Macmillan, 1952.)
Lüdemann, H. *Reformation und Täufertum in ihren Verhältnis zum Christlichen Prinzep,* 1896.
Luther, M. *The Bondage of the Will.* Translated and introduced by J. Packer and O. Johnston. Westwood, New Jersey: Fleming & Revell Co., 1957.
Malone, E. E. *The Monk and the Martyr.* Washington: Catholic University of America Press, 1950.
Mayer, Julius. *Geschichte der Benedictinerabtei St. Peter auf dem Schwarzwald.* Freiburg im Breisgau:: Herder, 1893.
McDonnell, E. W. *The Beguines and Beghards in Medieval Culture.* New Jersey: Rutger's University Press, 1954.
Meissinger, K. *Erasmus von Rotterdam.* Berlin, 1948.
The Mennonite Encyclopedia. 4 vols. Scottdale, Pennsylvania: The Mennonite Publishing House, 1955-59.
Mesnard, P. *Essai sur le Libre Arbitre.* Paris, 1959.
Mestwerdt, Paul. *Die Anfänge des Erasmus; Humanismus und "Devotio Moderna."* Herausgeben von Hans von Schubert. Leipzig: Rudolph Haupt, 1917.
Moore, John Allen. *Der Starke Jörg.* Kassel: J. G. Oncken, 1955.
Moorman, John. *A History of the Franciscan Order to 1517.* Oxford University Press, 1968.
Morison, E. F. *St. Basil and His Rule.* London: H. Frowde, 1912.
Muralt, L. von. *Glaube und Lehre der Schweizerischen Wiedertäufer in der Reformationszeit.* Zürich, 1938.
The New Schaff-Herzog Encyclopedia of Religious Knowledge. Grand Rapids: Baker Book House, 1950.
Oberman, H.A. *Forerunners of the Reformation.* New York: Holt, Rinehart & Winston, 1966.
———. *The Harvest of Medieval Theology.* Cambridge, Massachusetts: Harvard University Press, 1963.
Oelrich, K. H. *Der Späte Erasmus und die Reformation.* Münster, 1961.
Oyer, J. S. *Lutheran Reformers Against Anabaptists.* The Hague: Martinus Nijhoff, 1964.
Ozment, S. E. *Mysticism and Dissent.* New Haven: Yale University Press, 1973.
Peachey, Paul. *Die soziale Herkunft der Schweizer Täufer in der Reformationszeit: Eine religionssoziologische Untersuchung.* Karlsruhe, 1954.
Phelan, John Leddy. *The Millennial Kingdom of the Franciscans in the New World.* Berkeley: University of California Press, 1956.
Poschmann, Bernhard. *Penance and the Anointing of the Sick.* Translated by F. Courtney. New York: Herder & Herder, 1964.

356 Anabaptism and Asceticism

Post, R. R. *The Modern Devotion*. Leiden: E. J. Brill, 1968.
Pourrat, Pierre. *Christian Spirituality*. 4 vols. Westminster, Maryland: Newman Press, 1953.
Reinmann, G. J. *The Third Order Secular of St. Francis*. Washington: Catholic University of America, 1928.
Renaudet, A. *Préréforme et Humanisme à Paris, 1494-1517*. 2nd ed. Paris, 1953.
———. *Erasme, sa Pensée Religieuse*. Paris, 1926.
Ritschl, Albrecht. *Geschichte der Pietismus*, I. Bonn: Adolp Marcus, 1880.
Smith, P. *Erasmus*. New York: Harper & Bros., 1923.
Spitz, Lewis. *The Religious Renaissance of the German Humanists*. Cambridge: Harvard University Press, 1963.
Spoelhof, William. "Concepts of Religious Non-Conformity and Religious Toleration, as Developed by the Brethren of the Common Life (1374-1498)." Unpublished PhD dissertation, University of Michigan, 1946.
Spykman, Gordon J. *Attrition and Contrition at the Council of Trent*. Kampen: J. H. Kok, 1955.
Staehelin, D. E. *Das Buch der Basler Reformation*. Basel: Helbing & Lichtenhaln, 1929.
Stayer, J. M. *Anabaptists and the Sword*. Lawrence, Kansas: Coronado Press, 1972.
Strand, K. (ed.). *The Dawn of Modern Civilization*. Ann Arbor Publishers, 1962.
Stupperich, R. *Der Unbekannte Melanchthon*. Stuttgart: W. Kohlhammer, 1961.
Tavard, George H. *Holy Writ or Holy Church: The Crisis of the Protestant Reformation*. London: Burns and Oates, 1959.
Telle, E. V. *Erasme de Rotterdam et le Septième Sacrament*. Geneva, 1954.
Troeltsch, Ernst. *The Social Teachings of the Christian Churches*. 2 vols. New York: Harper Torch, 1960 (German edition, 1911).
Vedder, H. C. *Balthaser Hubmaier*. New York: G. P. Putnam's Sons, 1905.
Verduin, L. *The Reformers and their Stepchildren*. Grand Rapids: Eerdmans, 1964.
Verheyden, A. L. *Anabaptism in Flanders, 1530-1650*. Scottdale, Pennsylvania: Herald Press, 1961.
Viller, M. (ed.). *Dictionaire de Spiritualité ascétique et Mystique, Doctrine et Histoire*. Paris: G. Beauchesne et fils, 1937.
Walton, R. *Zwingli's Theocracy*. University of Toronto Press, 1967.
Weis, Frederick Lewis. *The Life and Teachings of Ludwig Hetzer*. Dorchester, Massachusetts: Underhill Press, 1930.
Wenger, J. C. *Even Unto Death*. Richmond, Virginia: John Knox Press, 1961. (German edition, *Die dritte Reformation*, 1963.)
Williams, G. H. *The Radical Reformation*. Philadelphia: Westminster Press, 1962.
Wiswedel, W. *Bilder und Führergestalten aus dem Täufertum*. Kassel: J. G. Oncken Verlag, 1952.
Wolkon, R. *Die Lieder der Wiedertäufer*. Berlin: 1903.
Wolter, Maurus. *The Principles of Monasticism*. Translated by B. S. Sause. St. Louis: B. Herder Co., 1962.
Workman, H. B. *The Evolution of the Monastic Ideal*. London: Epworth Press, 1927.
Yoder, John H. *Täufertum und Reformation*, Karlsruhe, I, 1962; II, 1968.
Zeman, J. K. *The Anabaptists and the Czeck Brethren in Moravia 1526-1628: A Study of Origins and Contacts*. The Hague: Mouton, 1969.
Zijl, T. P. von. *G. Groote, Ascetic and Reformer, 1340-1384*. Washington: Catholic University Press, 1965.

Bibliography 357

Zwingliana, Beiträge zur Geschichte Zwinglis, der Reformation und des Protestantismus in der Schweiz. Hg. von Zwingliverica. Zürich, 1897 ff.

ARTICLES

Albert, Peter. "Die Reformatorische Bewegung zu Freiburg bis zum Jahre, 1525," *Freiburger Diocezan Archiv* (1919), 1-80, 520-521.

Augsburger, Myron S. "Conversion in Anabaptist Thought," *MQR*, XXXVI (July 1962), 243-255.

Bacht, H. "L'importance de l'idéal monastique chez saint Pachôme pour l'histoire du monachisme chretiens," *Revue d'Ascétique et de Mystique* (1950), 308-326.

Bainton, Roland. "The Paraphrases of Erasmus," *ARG*, LVIII (1967), 67-75.

Beachy, A. J. "The Theology and Practice of Anabaptist Worship," *MQR*, XL (July 1966), 163-178.

Bender, H. S. "The Anabaptist Theology of Discipleship," *MQR*, XXIV (1950), 25-32.

──────. " 'Walking in the Resurrection,' the Anabaptist Doctrine of Regeneration and Discipleship," *MQR*, XXXV (April 1961), 96-110.

──────. "The Zwickau Prophets, Thomas Müntzer, and the Anabaptists," *MQR*, XXVII (1953), 3-16.

Bergsten, T. "Two Letters by Pilgram Marpeck," translated by Wm. Klassen, *MQR*, XXXII (July 1958), 192-210.

Bossert, G. (Jr.). "Michael Sattler's Trial and Martyrdom in 1527," translated by E. Bender, *MQR*, XV (1951), 201-218.

Clasen, C-P. "Medieval Heresies in the Reformation," *CH*, XXXII (December 1963), 392-414.

──────. "Sociology of Swabian Anabaptism," *CH*, XXXII (June 1963), 150-180.

Colombas, G. M. "The Ancient Concept of the Monastic Life," *Monastic Studies* (Epiphany, 1964), 65-118.

Duerksen, R. R. "Doctrinal Implications in 16th-Century Anabaptist Hymnody," *MQR*, XXXV (January 1961), 38-49.

Durnbaugh, D. F. "Theories of Free Church Origins," *MQR*, XLI (April 1968), 83-95.

Ebersole, M. "The Anabaptist View of the Church and the Therapeutic Community," *MQR*, XXXV (1961), 218-237.

Fast, Heinold. "The Dependence of the First Anabaptists on Luther, Erasmus, and Zwingli," *MQR*, XXX (April 1956), 104-119.

──────. "On the Beginnings of Bernese Anabaptism," *MQR*, XXXI (October 1957), 292, 293.

Foster, C. R. "Hans Denck and Johannas Buenderlin: A Comparative Study," *MQR*, XXXIX (1965), 115-124.

Friedmann, R. "Anabaptism and Protestantism," *MQR*, XXIV (January 1950), 12-24.

──────. "Concerning the True Soldier of Jesus Christ, A Hutterite Tract," *MQR*, V (1931), 87-99.

──────. "The Doctrine of Original Sin as Held by the Anabaptists of the Sixteenth Century," *MQR*, XXXV (July 1959), 206-214.

──────. "Ecumenical Dialogue Between Anabaptists and Catholics," *MQR*, XL (October 1966), 260-265.

──────. "The Essence of the Anabaptist Faith: An Essay in Interpretation," *MQR*, XLI (1967), 5-24.

———. "Hutterite Worship and Preaching," *MQR*, XL (1966), 5-26.

———. "Leonard Schiemer and Hnas Schlaffer, two Tyrolean Anabaptist Martyr-Apostles of 1528," *MQR*, XXXIII (January 1959), 31-41.

———. "On Mennonite Historiography and on Individualism and Brotherhood," *MQR*, XVIII (1944), 117-122.

———. "The Oldest Church Discipline of the Anabaptists," *MQR*, XXIX (April 1955), 162-166.

———. "Peter Ridemann on Original Sin and the Way to Redemption," *MQR*, XXVI (July 1952), 210-215.

———. "The Schleitheim Confession (1527) and Other Doctrinal Writings. . ." *MQR*, XVI (1942), 82-98.

———. "Thomas Müntzer's Relation to Anabaptism," *MQR*, XXXI (April 1957), 75-87.

Gingerich, M. "Change and Uniformity in Mennonite Attire," *MQR*, XL (1966), 243-259.

Goeters, Gerhard. "Ludwig Haetzer, a Marginal Anabaptist," *MQR*, XXIX (October 1955), 251-262.

Gratz, Delbert. "Bernese Anabaptists in the 16th Century," *MQR*, XXV (July 1951), 147-172.

Gritsch, E. W. "Thomas Muentzer and the Origins of Protestant Spiritualism," *MQR*, XXXVII (1963), 172-194.

Hall, Thor. "Possibilities of Erasmian Influence on Denck and Hubmaier in Their Views on the Freedom of the Will," *MQR*, XXXV (April 1961), 149-170.

Hillerbrand, H. J. "Anabaptism and the Reformation: Another Look," *CH*, XXIX (December 1960), 404-423.

———. "The Origins of Anabaptism: Another Look," *ARG*, LIII (1962), 152-180.

———. "Remarkable Interdependencies Between Certain Anabaptist Doctrinal Writings," *MQR*, XXXIII (January 1959), 73-76.

Horsch, John. "The Faith of the Swiss Brethren," *MQR*, IV (1930-31), 241-266; V: 7-27, 128-147, 245-259.

Hyma, A. "Erasmus and the Sacrament of Marriage," *ARG*, XLVIII (1957), 145-164.

———. "The Theology and Anthropology of the Brethren of the Common Life and the Anabaptists." Unpublished address delivered at the Goshen Biblical Seminary (Fall, 1965)'

Kiwiet, J. J. "The Theology of Hans Denck," *MQR*, XXXII (January 1958), 3-27.

Klaassen, Walter. "The Bern Debate of 1538," *MQR*, XL (1966), 148-156.

———. "Hans Hut and Thomas Müntzer," *The Baptist Quarterly*, XIX (1962), 209-227.

———. "Some Anabaptist Views on the Doctrine of the Holy Spirit," *MQR*, XXXV (April 1961), 130-139.

———. "Speaking in Simplicity: Balthasar Hubmaier," *MQR*, XL (April 1966), 139-147.

Klassen, Herbert. "The Life and Teachings of Hans Hut," *MQR*, XXXIII (1959), 171-205, 267-304.

Klassen, William. "Anabaptist Hermeneutics: The Letter and the Spirit," *MQR*, XL (1966) 83-96.

———. "Was Hans Denck a Universalist?," *MQR*, XXXIX (1965), 152-154.

Krajewski, Ekkhard. "The Theology of Felix Manz," *MQR*, XXXVI (January 1962). 76-87

Kreider, R. S. "Anabaptism and Humanism: An Inquiry into the Relationships of Human-

ism to the Evangelical Anabaptists," *MQR*, XXVI (1952), 123-141.
LeBras, Gabriel. "Place de l'ascétisme dans la sociologie des religions," *Archives de Socologie des Religions*, XVIII (Juillet, 1964), 21-27.
Littell, F. H. "The Discipline of Discipleship in the Free Church Tradition," *MQR*, XXXV (1961), 111-119.
——————. "Spiritualizers, Anabaptists, and the Church," *MQR*, XXIX, 34-43.
——————. "What Butzer Debated with the Anabaptists at Marburg, 1538," MQR, XXXVI (1962), 256-276.
Matthijssen, J. P. "The Bernese Disputation of 1538," *MQR*, XXII (1948), 19-33.
Miller, P. M. "Worship Among the Early Anabaptists," *MQR*, XXX (October 1956), 235-246.
Novak, M. "The Free Churches and the Roman Church," *Journal of Ecumenical Studies*, II (1965), 426-447.
Oberman, H. A. "Gabriel Biel and Late Medieval Mysticism," *CH*, XXX (September 1961), 259-287.
——————. " 'Institutia Christi and Institutia Dei'," *Harvard Theological Review*, LIX (January 1966), 1-26.
Oyer, J. S. "Anabaptism in Central Germany," *MQR*, Part I: XXXIV (1960), 214-248; Part II: XXXV (1961), 5-37.
——————. "The Writings of Luther Against the Anabaptists," *MQR*, XXVII (April 1953), 100-110.
——————. "The Writings of Melanchthon Against the Anabaptists," *MQR*, XXVI (October 1952), 259-276.
Pauck, Wilhelm. "Historiography of the German Reformation During the Past Twenty Years," *CH* (1940).
Peachy, P. "Anabaptism and Church Organization," *MQR*, XXX (July 1956), 213-228.
——————. "Social Background and Social Philosophy of the Swiss Anabaptists, 1525-1540," *MQR*, XXVIII (April 1954), 102-127.
Philoon, T. E. "Hans Greiffenberger and the Reformation in Nuernberg," *MQR*, XXXVI (1962), 61-75.
Post, G. Review of *The Last Day of Medieval Monachism* (Vol. IV of 5 *Centuries of Religion* by G. G. Coulton), *Speculum*, XXVII (January 1952), 96-99.
Rice, E. F. "Erasmus and the Religious Tradition 1495-1499," *Journal of History of Ideas*, XI (October 1950), 387-411.
Ritschl, Albrecht. "Wiedertäufer und Franziskaner," *Zeitschrift für Kirchengeschichte*, VI (October 1883), 499-502.
Rupp, E. Gordon. "Patterns of Salvation in the First Age of the Reformation," *ARG*, LVII (1966), 52-65.
Séguy, Jean. "L'ascèse dans les sectes d'origine protestante," *Archives de Sociologie des Religions*, XVIII (Juillet, 1964), 55-70.
——————. "Problémes Historiques et sociologiques actuals de l'anabaptisme," *Archives de Sociologie des Religions*, VII (January 1959), 105-116.
Smith, L. B. "The Reformation and the Decay of Medieval Ideals," *CH*, XXIV (September 1955), 212-220.
Stauffer, Ethelbert. "Anabaptist Theology of Martyrdom," *MQR*, XIX (1945), 179-214.
Stoesz, W. M. "The New Creature: Menno Simons' Understanding of the Christian Faith," *MQR*, XXXIX (January 1965), 5-25.
Swartzentruber, A. O. "The Piety and Theology of the Anabaptist Martyrs in von

Braght's *Martyrs Mirror,*" *MQR*, XXVIII (1954), 5-26.

Trinkhaus, C. "The Problem of Free Will in the Renaissance and Reformation," *Journal of History of Ideas*, X (January 1949), 51-62.

Trinter, Leonard J. "The Origins of Puritanism," *CH*, XX (1951), 33-57.

Vasella, Oskar. "Anfänge der Täuferbewegung in Graubünden," *Zeitschrift für Schweizerische Geschichte*, XIX, Heft II (1939), 165-184.

Verduin, L. "The Chambers of Rhetoric and Anabaptist Origins in the Low Countries," *MQR*, XXXIV (1960), 192-196.

Viller, R. P. "Martyre et Ascèse," *Révue d'Ascètique et de Mystique* (1925), 105-142.

Walton, R. "Was there a Turning Point of the Zwinglian Reformation?" *MQR*, LII (1968), 45-52.

Wamble, H. "Landmarkism," *Church History* (December 1964), 429-457.

Watson, P. "Wesley and Luther on Christian Perfection," *Ecumenical Review*, XV (April 1963), 291-302.

Weingart, R. E. "The Meaning of Sin in the Theology of Menno Simons," *MQR*, XLI (1967), 25-39.

Wenger, J. C. "The Theology of Pilgram Marpeck," *MQR*, XII (1938), 205-256.

———. "Grace and Discipleship in Anabaptism," *MQR*, XXXV (1961), 50-69.

Williams, G. "Sanctification in the Testimony of Several So-Called Schwärmer," *MQR*, XLII (1968), 5-25.

Wiswedel, W. "The Inner and the Outer Word, a Study in the Anabaptist Doctrine of Scripture," *MQR*, XXVI (October 1952), 297.

Wray, F. J. "The Anabaptist Doctrine of the Restitution of the Church," *MQR*, XXVIII (July 1954), 186-196.

Yoder, J. H. "Balthasar Hubmaier and the Beginnings of Swiss Anabaptism," *MQR*, XXXIII (1959), 5-17.

———. "The Turning Point in the Zwinglian Reformation," *MQR*, XXXII (April 1958), 128-140.

Zuck, L. H. "Anabaptism: Abortive Counter-Revolt Within the Reformation," *CH*, XXVI (September 1957), 211-226. Reply: C. Krahn, XXVII (March 1958), 92.

INDEX

Aberli, Heinrich 68, 105, 108
Adam (1st Man, or Old Adam) 75, 94, 119, 122, 137, 140, 141, 144, 146, 174, 175
Adelphi, Johann 101
Agricola 62
Agrippa, Henri 265
Albert V of Austria 57
Alexandria 44
Altenbach, Hans 99, 109, 110, 111, 112
Althamer, Andreas 20
Amersfoert 245
Amman 67
Amsterdam 272
Anthony (St.) 41, 43, 45
Appenzell 110
Aquinas, Thomas 132, 168, 189, 255, 262
Arrau 112
Athanasius (St.) 45
Augsburg 221, 222, 231, 242, 243, 245, 246
Augustine, Bp. of Hippo 45, 46, 47, 220, 297
Aurelius, Cornelius 268

Badius 274
Basel 55, 57, 58, 68, 96, 101, 109, 111, 118, 260, 273, 274, 275, 276, 277, 285
Basil (St.) 45, 46, 47
Bauer, Ludwig 273
Benedict (St.) 48, 49
Benedict XII (Pope) 55, 57
Bernard (St.) 245
Bernardino of Siena (St.) 60, 61
Berne (Bern) 28, 112, 118, 162, 166, 204, 209, 215
Berthold of Regensburg 235, 243
Biel, Gabriel 56, 57, 169, 254, 255, 262
Blaurock, George 75, 92, 93, 94, 95, 96, 97, 98, 112, 115, 117, 119, 120, 141, 180, 186, 201, 235

Bonaventura (St.) 236, 242, 246
Boscoop, Werembold De 245
Bosshard, Marx 94, 119
Bourges 59
Breisgau 113, 114, 276, 277
Breit, Peter 112
Briconnet, Bishop 265
Brixen 61
Brotli, Johann 81, 92, 95, 98, 112
Bruggback, Hans 94
Brugman, John 245
Bucer, Martin 115, 116, 124, 126, 136, 161, 257
Bude 263, 274
Buder, Johann 20
Buenderlin 223
Bullinger, Heinrich 20, 29, 74, 212, 229, 238, 242
Burgauer, Benedict 73
Bursfeld 55, 58
Busch, Johann 55, 56

Cajacob, Luzi 92
Calvin, John 19, 20, 124, 127, 277, 297
Capistrano, John (St.) 60, 61
Capito, Wolfgang 32, 113, 115, 116, 122, 126, 136, 144, 176, 265
Carlstadt, Andreas 27, 76, 81, 272, 292
Cassian 45, 46, 47
Cassiodorus 48
Castel (Kastel) 55, 57
Castelburger, Andreas 68, 92, 276
Celtis, Conrad 62
Charles VIII 59
Chezal-Benoit 59
Chrysostom, John 47
Chur 93, 108, 111
Cirey, Jean De 58
Clement (of Alexandria) 41, 167
Clichtove 263
Cluny 49, 58
Cochlaeus, Johann 277
Colet, John 269

362   Anabaptism and Asceticism

Collette (St.) 58, 59
Cologne 62, 263
Constance 33, 55, 57, 60, 63, 85, 115, 234
Constantine (Emperor) 41
Cop, Nicholas 263

David of Augsburg 242, 245, 246
Denck, Hans 34, 66, 67, 99, 113, 115, 145, 146, 147, 157, 170, 214, 221, 222, 223, 224, 225, 226, 227, 228, 229, 230, 231, 263, 270, 271, 277, 288, 290, 296
Deventer 56, 57, 245, 263, 268
Dieburg, Peter 250, 254, 257, 258
Dionysius 220
Doesburg 251

Eck, John 101, 104
Eckhart 224
Engelbrecht, Peter 113
Engelhart, 67
Erasmus, Desiderus 27, 30, 34, 62, 65, 67, 101, 102, 108, 113, 128, 145, 195, 201, 207, 215, 219, 223, 224, 225, 226, 235, 238, 245, 249, 257, 260, 265, 266, 267, 268, 269, 270, 271, 272, 273, 274, 276, 277, 278, 279, 280, 281, 282, 283, 284, 285, 286, 287, 288, 290, 291, 292, 297
Esslingen 25

Faber, John 128
Fabri, Jacques 265
Fabricius, Erasmus 84
Farel, Guillaume 263
Ferdinand I 114, 239
Ferrer, (St.) Vincent 61, 241
Ficino 269
Finsterbach, Arbogast 82
France 59, 60, 239, 240, 241, 254, 260, 263, 267
Francis of Assisi 29, 33, 34, 49, 51, 130, 134, 144, 233, 234, 235, 236, 245, 278, 293, 297
Francis of Paulo 60, 63
Franck, Sebastian 221, 223
Freiburg 65, 96, 100, 101, 113, 276, 277

Gansfort, Wessel 246, 249, 254, 255, 256, 257, 258, 259
Germany 58, 61, 114, 191, 219, 239, 240, 241, 250, 254, 256, 260
Gerson, Jean 63, 245
Glarean, Henri (Glareanus) 101, 265, 273, 274
Gottingen 58
Grebel, Conrad 26, 31, 34, 67, 68, 69, 70, 71, 72, 73, 74, 75, 76 77, 78, 79, 80, 81, 82, 83, 85, 87, 88, 89, 91 92, 93, 94, 95, 96, 97, 98, 100, 103, 104, 105, 107, 108, 109, 110, 111, 112, 113, 115, 117, 120, 121, 124, 125, 136, 139, 140, 150, 157, 162, 164, 166, 172, 173, 176, 177, 178, 180, 183, 185, 191, 194, 199, 200, 201, 202, 204, 205, 208, 209, 216, 220, 239, 240, 243, 263, 266, 270, 271, 272, 273, 274, 275, 276, 284, 285, 291, 296
Gregory I (Pope) 48
Groote, Gerhard 50, 51, 56, 219, 233, 245, 246, 250, 251, 252, 254, 257, 258, 259, 297
Gross, Jacob 108, 221
Grüningen 82, 108, 115, 120, 205, 215
Gulden, Nicolaus 112

Haetzer, Ludwig, 99, 222
Hallau 95
Haller, Bernhold 118
Hegenwald, Erhard 76, 78, 79, 80, 81, 89, 125
Hegius, Alexander 265, 268
Herp, Henry 241, 242
Hildesheim 254, 257
Hochrüttiner, Lorenz 111
Hoen, Cornelius 257, 258
Hoffman, Melchior 147, 209, 254, 261
Hofmeister, Sebastian 103, 104, 112
Höngy 70
Honorius III (Pope) 236, 237
Horb 116, 122, 144, 188, 213
Hottinger, Claus 68, 136
Hottinger, Heinrich 189, 202
Hottinger, Jacob 82
Hotz, Hans 162, 190

Hubmaier, Balthasar 34, 80, 96, 99, 100, 101, 102, 103, 104, 105, 106, 107, 108, 109, 110, 112, 117, 121, 122, 123, 126, 128, 135, 143, 144, 145, 146, 147, 148, 149, 150, 151, 152, 153, 154, 155, 156, 157, 158, 159, 160, 162, 164, 165, 166, 167, 170, 171, 172, 173, 174, 175, 176, 177, 178, 179, 181, 182, 183, 184, 185, 186, 188, 190, 191, 198, 200, 201, 205, 207, 208, 209, 211, 215, 216, 221, 224, 227, 228, 231, 240, 243, 255, 262, 263, 271, 277, 279, 285, 288, 289, 290, 296
Hut, Hans 34, 120, 121, 221, 227, 228, 229, 230, 231, 232, 239, 243

Ingolstadt 100
Innocent III (Pope) 236

James of the March 60
Jerome 45, 46, 47
Joachim of Fiore 238
John the Baptist 74, 106, 119, 154, 203, 204
John of Capistrano 238, 240, 241, 242
John of the Cross (St.) 132
John of Parma 238
Jouenneaux, Guy 59
Jud, Leo 68, 276

Kempis, Thomas à 52, 56, 249, 253, 255
Kenzington 114
Kessler, Johannes 11, 126
Geiler von Keysersberg, Johann 61, 119
Klingau 110
Krüsi, Johann (Hans Kern) 99, 109, 110, 111
Kuchenbacher, Hans 122, 210

Langenmantel, Eitelhans 121
Lefevre, D'Étaples 219, 235, 263, 264, 265, 266, 267, 274
Leinhardt, Jorg 122
Leipzig 93
Leo X (Pope) 101, 237
Lille 59
Lucerne (Luzern) 109, 110
Lull, Raymond 63

Luther, Martin 19, 20, 22, 24, 27, 29, 38, 64, 65, 66, 76, 100, 101, 102, 103, 104, 106, 108, 113, 125, 127, 128, 130, 132, 145, 146, 148, 149, 150, 155, 156, 158, 163, 164, 169, 172, 178, 181, 182, 187, 190, 191, 192, 193, 201, 215, 216, 217, 222, 223, 224, 226, 227, 233, 234, 235, 238, 241, 243, 251, 252, 254, 255, 258, 263, 265, 271, 272, 275, 276, 277, 278, 281, 292, 294, 295, 297
Luti, Hans 162, 204

Magdeburg 251
Maillard, Oliver 61
Maler, Gregor 221
Mande, H 249, 256
Manz, Felix 68, 69, 70, 71, 74, 75, 76, 81, 91, 92, 93, 95, 96, 97, 98, 100, 104, 106, 107, 108, 115, 117, 121, 125, 145, 165, 172, 181, 182, 192, 194, 202, 203, 204, 263, 276, 296
Marburg 122, 124, 162, 206
Marpeck, Pilgrim 147, 150, 180, 216, 270
Marquart, Hans 171
Martin of Tours 45
Maximilian (Emperor) 61
Mayence-Bramberg 57
Meaux 261, 263
Melanchthon, Philip 20, 229
Melk 55, 58
Mendieta, Geronimo 239
Menot, Michel 64
Mombaer, Jean (Mombaier) 59, 263, 267
Montanus 45
Moravia 25, 96, 111, 117
Münster 20, 25, 202, 232, 241, 277, 297
Müntzer, Thomas 25, 27, 28, 66, 76, 77, 80, 81, 87, 94, 95, 97, 103, 105, 120, 180, 185, 194, 213, 220, 221, 222, 223, 227, 229, 230, 231, 232, 239, 272, 291, 292
Mutian 62
Myconius, Oswald 67, 273, 275

Netherlands (Holland) 117, 124, 241
Neuenberg 114
Nicholas V (Pope) 114

364   Anabaptism and Asceticism

Nicholas of Cusa 58, 61, 263
Nicholas of Lyra 235
Nicolsburg 80
Nordheim 58
Nuremberg (Nürnberg) 65, 66, 114, 221, 222
Oberwinterthur 82
Occam, Wm. of 262
Oecolampadius 101, 103, 104, 105, 144, 152, 257
Olivi, Petrus 243
Origen 41
Othmar, Silvan 222
Otter, Jacob 113, 114

Pachomius 41, 42, 43, 47
Paris 59, 60, 261, 263, 266, 268, 273, 274, 275
Pelagius 45
Pellikan 101
Peters, G. 249
Petershausen 57, 58
Philips, Dirk 163, 216, 243, 277
Prague 28
Pupper, John 255
Pur, Bartime 68

Quarten 95

Radewijns 245, 246, 250, 254, 258
Raymond of Capua 60
Regensburg 100, 101, 235, 243
Reublin, Wilhelm 68, 74, 81, 95, 96, 97, 98, 99, 103, 105, 107, 108, 112, 114, 115, 177, 180, 263, 276, 296
Rhegius, Urban 20, 113
Rhenanus, Beatus 101, 265, 273
Riedmann, Peter (Rideman) 34, 150, 181, 212
Ritschl, Albrecht 26, 29, 30, 31, 32, 127, 219, 232, 233, 234, 235, 236, 237, 238, 239, 240, 242, 243, 244, 246, 247
Rode, Hemin 257, 258
Rolewinck, Werner 62
Rothman, Bernhard 277
Rottenburg 96
Ruggensberger, Sebastian, 110, 111, 112

Ruysbroek 63
Rychard, Wolfgang 101

St. Gall 57, 72, 73, 78, 109, 110, 111, 112, 126, 221, 274
St. Georgen 109, 110
St. Germain-De-Pres 263
St. Lebwin's 268
St. Leonard 260
St. Lucius 111
St. Luzi 93, 108
St. Martins 109
St. Nicholas 108
St. Omar 267
St. Peter's 113, 218
St. Sulpice 59
St. Victor 59
Salminger, Sigmund 243
Sattler, Michael 34, 99, 112, 113, 114, 115, 116, 117, 118, 122, 123, 125, 126, 129, 135, 136, 137, 138, 140, 141, 144, 146, 157, 158, 161, 162, 166, 172, 173, 176, 177, 179, 180, 181, 183, 184, 185, 188, 190, 194, 200, 202, 213, 215, 216, 219, 240, 243, 285, 296
Sceta 44
Schad, Jörg 120, 204
Schaffhausen 95, 108, 112, 114, 117, 118
Schiemer, Leonard 150, 212, 228, 243
Schlaffer, Hans 34, 228
Schlatt 114
Schlegel 108, 109
Schnabel, Jörg 122, 124, 125
Schumacher, Fridli 96
Schumacher, Hans 95
Schwenkfeld, Kaspar 30, 221, 223
Scotus, Duns 168, 169, 262
Sens 59
Simons, Menno 22, 34, 141, 150, 154, 155, 163, 173, 177, 216, 253, 254, 255, 261, 270, 277, 297
Solothurn 118
Spanheim 58
Spengler, Peter 114
Standonck, Jean 59, 254, 263
Staufen 113
Staupitz 221, 222

Index 365

Steyn 266
Storch, Nicholas 229, 230
Strassburg 114, 115, 116, 118, 122, 126, 187
Stumpf, Simon 68, 69, 70, 113, 125, 276

Tauler 63, 214, 221, 222, 223, 226, 227, 228, 229, 230
Tertullian 72
Tesch, Peter 162
Teufen 110
Thomann, Ruedi 94
Tours 59
Trent 297
Trins 93
Trithemius 58
Tübingen 96, 262

Ulimann, Wolfgang 92, 99, 110, 111, 112
Ulm 101
Utinger 67
Utrecht 245, 258

Vadian (Vadianus-Joachim von Watt) 72, 73, 78, 80, 81, 274, 275, 276
Vatable 263
Vienna 274
Vitrier, John 267

Waldshut 80, 95, 100, 101, 105, 107, 108, 109, 110, 114
Walpot, Peter 229
Weninger, Martin 34, 99, 117, 118, 119, 122, 136, 137, 157, 162, 173, 181, 187, 191, 193, 195, 202

Widemann, Jacob 221
Wilhelmi, Henricus 245
Windesheim 51, 52, 55, 56, 58, 59, 244, 246, 260, 261, 263, 266, 268
Winkler, Conrad 115
Wittenberg 28, 76, 78
Worms 222
Wurzburg 58
Wytikon 80, 97

Zasius 65, 113
Zerbolt 63, 245, 246, 248, 251, 261
Znaim 96
Zofingen 118, 157, 162, 166, 171
Zollikon 81, 94, 95, 96, 97, 115, 119, 189, 240
Zurich 23, 28, 31, 67, 68, 70, 74, 78, 80, 81, 82, 84, 88, 90, 93, 95, 96, 97, 98, 99, 100, 103, 104, 106, 107, 108, 109, 111, 114, 115, 117, 118, 119, 125, 136, 189, 202, 220, 229, 260, 261, 275, 276, 277, 285, 291
Zwickau 28, 229, 230, 239
Zwingli, Huldreich 19, 20, 26, 27, 29, 32, 66, 67, 68, 69, 70, 71, 72, 76, 79, 80, 81, 82, 83, 84, 85, 86, 87, 88, 89, 90, 91, 92, 93, 94, 95, 96, 97, 98, 99, 103, 104, 105, 107, 108, 112, 120, 125, 126, 128, 130, 141, 145, 156, 161, 187, 192, 201, 202, 203, 204, 207, 209, 210, 211, 214, 229, 257, 271, 272, 275, 276, 277, 278, 284, 292, 294, 295
Zwolle 51

Kenneth R. Davis was born in the province of Manitoba, Canada, in 1929 [in Swan River, June 30, 1929] and educated at the University of Toronto (BA), Wheaton College Graduate School of Theology (MA), and the University of Michigan (PhD in history, 1971).

He is presently an associate professor at the University of Waterloo, Canada, teaching Fifteenth and Sixteenth Century European Intellectual History with research emphasis on the Anabaptists and Christian humanism. He is a teaching member of the Guelph-Waterloo Inter-University Graduate Consortium in Reformation Studies.

Dr. Davis is also an ordained minister in the Fellowship of Evangelical Baptists in Canada; chairman of his denomination's Committee on Education, for which he coauthored *A Brief on Education for Evangelical Baptists*; and a member of the Canadian and American Societies of Church History and the American Society for Reformation Research.

www.ingramcontent.com/pod-product-compliance
Ingram Content Group UK Ltd.
Pitfield, Milton Keynes, MK11 3LW, UK
UKHW021249180426
11946UKWH00003B/45